# How to Fly the
# B-29
# Superfortress

# How to Fly the
# B-29
# Superfortress

## The Official Manual for the Plane that Bombed Hiroshima and Nagasaki

### New Introduction by Jeffrey L. Ethell

Greenhill Books
London

Stackpole Books
Pennsylvania

Greenhill Books

This edition of *How To Fly The B-29 Superfortress*
first published 1995 by Greenhill Books, Lionel Leventhal Limited
Park House, 1 Russell Gardens, London NW11 9NN
and
Stackpole Books, 5067 Ritter Road, Mechanicsburg, PA 17055, U.S.A.

*British Library Cataloguing in Publication Data available*

ISBN 1–85367–194–0

*Library of Congress Cataloging-in-Publication Data available*

Publishing History
*How To Fly The B-29 Superfortress* presents in facsimile
*Combat Crew Manual* produced by XXI Bomber Command, A.P.O. 234,
May 1945, and is reproduced now exactly as the original edition,
complete and unabridged. For this 1995 edition a new Introduction
by Jeffrey L. Ethell has been added.
In reprinting in facsimile from the original, any imperfections
are inevitably reproduced and the quality may fall
short of modern printing standards.

Printed and bound in Great Britain by
Butler & Tanner Ltd, Frome and London

# INTRODUCTION

When Curtis E. LeMay took the B-29 Super-fortress into combat over Japan in 1944 he was frustrated – very frustrated. The miracle weapon in which he and U.S. Army Air Forces Chief Hap Arnold believed so much was not living up to expectations. The ultimate example of strategic bombing capability, though formidable, was not getting bombs on target with the results LeMay wanted.

Superfortress crews had been thoroughly trained in the USA, using a plethora of hand-books, training films and individual instruc-tion, but somehow this was not translating to results. The end product of LeMay's frustration was the *XXI Bomber Command Combat Crew Manual* now reprinted as *How To Fly The B-29 Superfortress*. The type of aircraft did not need to be mentioned in the original manual since the Command flew but a single type.

Far more than just a pilot's handbook (which had been issued long before), this book was created and printed in the Pacific theater by those who had learned the B-29's strong and weak points at first hand. As a result, it is unique, like nothing else ever produced by the USAAF: this is going to war in the B-29 from the perspective of each crew member. By the time you finish reading this, you will have gained much more first-hand knowledge than has ever been previously available.

The B-29, Boeing's 'Hemisphere Defence Weapon', was contracted by the Army Air Corps on 4 February 1940; the description reflected the isolationist mentality of the time. By the Spring of 1944 four groups of the 58th Bomb Wing were deployed to India. The first combat mission was flown against Bangkok, using staging bases in China, on 5 June 1944.

The next mission, on 15 June, was flown against targets in Japan but this extremely drawn-out method of reaching the enemy did not work very well.

With the capture of several islands in the Marianas chain, five B-29 fields were immedi-ately built and combat operations were under way by November 1944, with a milestone hit on Tokyo on the 24th. Though high altitude missions increased in early 1945, accuracy did not. As the section on training in this book says, 'in by far the majority of cases, more aircraft than were necessary to accomplish the job have bombed targets. ... Nearly every pre-cision target has required repeat missions, and even then some were not knocked out.' The bottom line was that the B-29s were not hitting their targets from high altitude in daylight.

LeMay then made a very unpopular (at least to the crews) decision: on 9 March 1945 he sent his Superfortresses in at low altitude, at night, with incendiary bombs. It was a hellish night-mare, but firebombing, from that point on, literally scoured the cities off the surface of Japan. The B-29 missions against Hiroshima and Nagasaki with atomic bombs, bringing World War Two to an end, were the ultimate result of the bomber's effectiveness.

The B-29's major problem was engine fires, due to a number of technical faults in mating the Curtiss-Wright R-3350 to the aircraft. There never seemed to be enough cooling available for the cylinders, particularly those in the rear. The excruciatingly detailed engine handling procedures for the pilots leap out at the reader across time. It was a nightmare of complicated management where a single simple mistake could result in losing an engine.

This book contains, in the 'Airplane Commander' section, the most complete official description of flying the B-29 ever published. From beginning to end the airplane commander is not really a pilot (flying is taken for granted) but the manager of a very complex machine and the men in it. The guide to taking-off will raise anyone's hackles. Everything had to work or the temperamental engines would overheat and self-destruct. Losing an engine on take-off usually meant disaster at full gross weight: 'In some cases there is little else to do but chop your throttles and land straight ahead. Whatever the circumstances are it's un-doubtedly a gamble and it calls for split second decisions.'

The switchology for the radar operator on this first generation radar equipment is mind numbing, just to get it up and running. Cali-brating range and altitude delay was a highly involved process, and the radar operator was very much in the loop as the essential computer. His trouble-shooting section alone is enough to make its own book. Scope interpretation was an art in itself, both in navigation and in radar bombing, and both were the heart of the bomber. The radar operator could not allow his interaction with the navigator and bombardier to be muddled by miscommunication or lack of skill.

'Combat Navigation' is a complete dis-course on how to use every aid available out-side radio to get a bomber, or a long bomber stream, to the target and back home again. The procedures outlined here were state-of-the-art at the time, which may cause surprise since they are based on the same principles of celestial sighting and weather interpretation used by sailors for thousands of years. Fortunately the navigator had slaved fluxgate compasses and other instruments to help. It was also possible to navigate by LORAN, a radio system that has only just come back into favor for flying over the last few years. Reading the procedures for interpreting each radio trans-mission axis for a position is fascinating since today's LORAN sets do this automatically.

'Combat Bombing' gives an exhaustive look at how a bombardier used the war's most sophisticated equipment to put a bomb on target. This was an inexact science even though the USAAF PR officers would have the public believe a bomber crew really could drop a bomb in the proverbial pickle barrel from 20,000 feet. As LeMay found out, even the B-29 could not perform this feat on a regular basis. Reading the complex procedures here shows why: they were, quite simply, subject to far too many variables such as airspeed, tem-perature, different wind drift speeds at differ-ent altitudes, angle of bank, autopilot function – read it for yourself. This book will genuinely put you behind the crosshairs.

Radio procedure is not taken for granted. The radio operator is the lifeline to the outside world, and, for the first time since the war, we are told how to use every radio aboard: com-mand set, liaison set and radio compass. There is a thorough run-through of everything from radio navigation to proper radio procedure in coordinating fighters to correct radio tele-phone (R/T) pronunciation and phraseology (did you ever wonder what 'roger' and 'wilco' really meant?). Every ground radio station available in the Pacific at the time is described, opening up an entirely new understanding of combat flying in the theater. Since the radio operator was the key element in air–sea rescue operations there is an extensive rundown of all the radio, air and ship aids available for downed airmen.

Though the defensive fire power of the B-29 is no mystery, 'Combat Gunnery' goes into exhaustive detail on the effective use of the CFC (Central Fire Control system). Though a very accurate system for its day, the CFC had to be maintained like a fine watch – this book tells you how. Every gunner's station is de-scribed, with a checklist for bringing each one up to operational status. Then comes the long and detailed description of how to sight and fire the guns, which contains some revelations, in-cluding the surprising advice, 'Fire before the enemy does. Begin firing at 1000 yards range except in nose attacks when you should fire as soon as you see the target.' In other theaters this would have been called a waste of ammunition, but the B-29 was big – so big it could hold inordinate amounts of ammunition. Since the remote turrets were interconnected between different gunners, technique and coordination were paramount.

'Intelligence' provides a fascinating insight into USAAF assessment of the Japanese threat, particularly from the fighter planes. By and large, the USAAF had an excellent grasp of what B-29 crews were encountering, from time and duration of attack to preferred method of interception. Anti-aircraft fire is described in detail, from the initial relative ineffectiveness to the increasing accuracy and intensity, particularly over the Japanese mainland. There is also a large amount of information devoted to collecting intelligence from the Superfortress using visual sightings and radar observation, something that was not a factor for the B-17 and B-24; every B-29 had look-down radar.

A complete list and description of everything taken aboard a B-29 for combat flying, from parachutes to sun glasses, is given in the section on flying equipment. Even adjusting and testing the oxygen mask and system before flight was nothing as simple as turning on the valve and breathing – too much could go wrong. Use of clothing at altitude receives a lot of attention since it was easy inadvertently to make clothing lose its heat-trapping qualities. First-aid kits are also a subject of focus: they were used and used often.

Though the book deals with emergencies throughout, there is also a complete, separate section on emergency procedures, which goes into the intricacies of high altitude bailout, crash landing (with detailed positions for each crew member), ditching (a *long* section), fire and air–sea rescue. You really didn't want to go down in the Pacific.

This contemporary document concludes with 'Medical Aspects', containing some sobering advice for 'wounds inflicted by enemy fire', including sucking chest wounds, belly wounds, head wounds and burns. The B-29 was hated by the Japanese and they did all they could to bring it down. Lack of oxygen in the event of cabin depressurization at various altitudes was also a serious threat: at 35,000 feet oxygen failure would bring unconsciousness in forty-five seconds and death in fifteen minutes.

With every aspect of flying the Superfortress described in detail, this is an unique opportunity to feel what combat bombing in World War Two was like. So climb aboard and fly as a crewmember on the B-29!

Jeff Ethell, 1995

XXI BOMBER COMMAND.

# COMBAT CREW
# MANUAL.

A.P.O. 234.

MAY 1945.

# T A B L E   O F   C O N T E N T S

# T A B L E  O F  C O N T E N T S

## ( c o n t i n u e d )

# T A B L E   O F   C O N T E N T S

## ( c o n t i n u e d )

# T A B L E   O F   C O N T E N T S

## ( c o n t i n u e d )

-------------------------

# F O R E W O R D

TO: The Combat Crews -

The success of the development of the B-29 is an outstanding example of the technical leadership and resourcefulness which is the American way of doing things. It typifies the energies of a nation that is willing to work and work hard, to learn, and to improve. The industry and resources of a great nation went into the developement of the B-29. Without the foresight, experimentation, and study of many people the present operation of the B-29 would not have been possible.

You are charged with the responsibility of operating the B-29 in combat and of perfecting its employment to the highest degree. It is imperative that you be alert, conscientious, and learn by intensive training all you can about the operating of your airplane in the Pacific Areas.

This manual was prepared from many sources for your use and is the result of three years combat experience. Study it. The material has been gathered to help improve the combat efficiency of both new and old crews, to serve as a reference, and to orient you not only in your job but in the job of others who work to help you put more bombs on the target. Nowhere in the conduct of warfare does study yield such direct and large returns as it does in aerial warfare; yet, nowhere is the standard so exacting as that of high altitude precision bombing. It is felt this training manual will contribute toward the goal of "MORE BOMBS ON THE TARGET" with a minimum of loss to our forces.

CURTIS E. LE MAY
Major General, U. S. A.
Commanding

Headquarters
XXI Bomber Command
APO 234

# I TRAINING

The object of a strategic air force is to disrupt the enemy's war economy.  This object can be accomplished most effectively by destroying
his facilities for producing war goods with special emphasis on those
plants engaged in remedying deficits in equipment which are hardest to
replace.  Such plants are, in general, small targets, from a bombing
viewpoint, and to knock them out invariably requires accurate bombing
by one to several formations of aircraft.  The principle value of a
strategic air force depends upon how many strategic enemy targets it
can destroy in a given period of time.  Many factors effect the rate
of destruction accomplished; the number of aircraft arriving over the
target, the bomb load they carry, and the accuracy with which the bombs
are dropped.  All of these factors are directly influenced by, and, in
fact, are determined by your functioning as a B-29 combat crew.  You,
and you alone, operating as a smooth-functioning team, determine whether
your aircraft gets to the target, and whether the bombs are accurately
dropped so that they "pay off".  The most important factor upon which
bomb load is based is the ability you display and the skill with which
you operate your B-29 airplane as a team.  You have had placed into
your hands the best airplane and the best equipment that aeronautical
science has developed.  It is your job, now, to utilize that airplane
and equipment to the fullest in accomplishing the most important task
confronting all of us -- PUTTING BOMBS ON THE TARGET.

Experience has demonstrated that in, by far, the majority of cases,
more aircraft than were necessary to accomplsih the job have bombed
targets destined for destruction by the XXI Bomber Command.  Nearly
every precision target has required repeat missions, and even then
some were not knocked out.  Although quantity of bombs dropped must
be sufficient to accomplish the job, quality of bombing is the factor
that tells the story.  The quality of bombing depends upon the combined efforts of each and every individual on your crew and the weld-
ing of those efforts into efficient teamwork.  It takes practice to
be able to do your job well enough to be on a B-29 team -- lots of
practice.  There are a thousand and one things that each individual
must not only know but be one hundred percent proficient in carrying
out.  One error and your team may have lost the game where stakes
are the highest.  Errors can be eliminated through proper training and
maintenance of a high standard of proficiency.  **They** are being eliminated every day.  Each month the rate on "targets scratched" increases.
We are becoming a more and more potent fighting machine and this is due
largely to the combined results of training and experience which you
have gained.  Training and experience go hand in hand; one cannot be
gained without the other.

Whether you go on a mission, or whether you go on a training flight
or step into a classroom or trainer, you are receiving additional
training and gaining experience.  Stop and analyze your situation for

awhile. Wherein are you weak? What are your deficiencies? What can you do to eliminate them? Take full advantage of all training offered you and request additional training in those subjects in which you don't feel qualified. Training in the XXI Bomber Command is established on a proficiency basis and each crew member should feel responsible for improving himself to the point of highest proficiency for his job. You will not be required to spend long hours in classrooms if you are proficient in those subjects of ground and air training outlined in the XXI Bomber Command 50 series regulations. However, you must demonstrate that you are proficient before those long hours cease, and you will be required at frequent intervals to prove that your proficiency has not waned. Certain standards of proficiency will be required on a number of checks which you will be required to accomplish. You will already be proficient in many requirements. Others, you will find, are probably new and strange to you, a product of lessons learned and experience gained in this theatre. Training is a necessary item in any combat theatre. The process of forgetting is relentless: the problem of learning and relearning endless. A procedure not practiced is a procedure which, day by day, is being forgotten. Flight training, ground school or trainer time is not time wasted. For the airplane commander and pilot it spells increased knowledge of efficient coordination as a team- and with other similar teams. For the navigator it spells increased ability to get his airplane and his crew safely from one place to another fulfilling specific provisions. For the bombardier it means better CE. For the radar operator it means a sure and a correct course on the bombing run. For the flight engineer it spells more bombs, less fuel consumption and greater operational safety. For the radio operator it spells life to the crew or to some other crew in the event of an emergency. For the gunners it spells safety and protection to a large number of crews and doom to many Japanese fighters. For all it spells - BOMBS ON THE TARGET - and shortening of the war.

The charts on pages I-3 and I-4 present a picture of the combat and training time flown per assigned B-29 since the beginning of operations by this command.

Before the beginning of increased tempo of operations which began the middle of March, weekly training time flown had a general tendency to increase gradually with increased combat time, but only to a certain point. Above approximately 15 hours of combat per week per aircraft decrease in training time was almost inversely proportional to increase in combat time. Nevertheless, during January training time occupied 20.4 percent as much time as did combat operations. From this point it increased to 28.2 percent during February and to 30.5 percent during the first half of March. Beginning with the large scale incendiary strikes in mid-March, combat time showed an increase of approximately 200 percent over any past equivalent period and has remained at or near

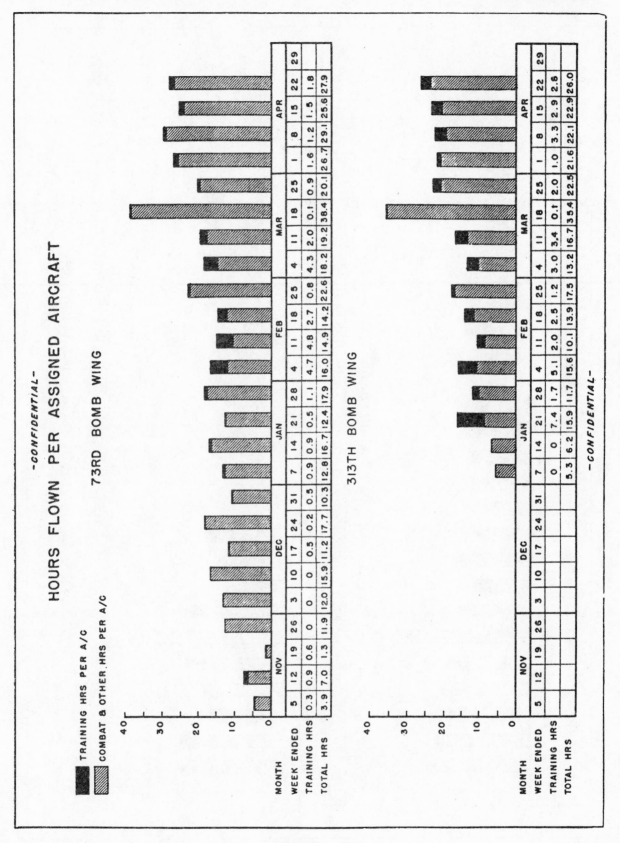

-CONFIDENTIAL-

## HOURS FLOWN PER ASSIGNED AIRCRAFT

### 73RD BOMB WING

■ TRAINING HRS PER A/C

▨ COMBAT & OTHER HRS PER A/C

| MONTH | NOV | | | DEC | | | | JAN | | | | FEB | | | | MAR | | | | APR | | | |
|---|---|---|---|---|---|---|---|---|---|---|---|---|---|---|---|---|---|---|---|---|---|---|---|
| WEEK ENDED | 5 | 12 | 19 | 26 | 3 | 10 | 17 | 24 | 31 | 7 | 14 | 21 | 28 | 4 | 11 | 18 | 25 | 4 | 11 | 18 | 25 | 1 | 8 | 15 | 22 | 29 |
| TRAINING HRS | 0.3 | 0.9 | 0.6 | 0 | 0 | 0 | 0.5 | 0.2 | 0.5 | 0.9 | 0.9 | 0.5 | 1.1 | 4.7 | 4.8 | 2.7 | 0.8 | 4.3 | 2.0 | 0.1 | 0.9 | 1.6 | 1.2 | 1.5 | 1.8 | |
| TOTAL HRS | 3.9 | 7.0 | 1.3 | 11.9 | 12.0 | 15.9 | 11.2 | 17.7 | 10.3 | 12.8 | 16.7 | 12.4 | 17.9 | 16.0 | 14.9 | 14.2 | 22.6 | 18.2 | 19.2 | 38.4 | 20.1 | 26.7 | 29.1 | 25.6 | 27.9 | |

### 313TH BOMB WING

| MONTH | NOV | | | DEC | | | | JAN | | | | FEB | | | | MAR | | | | APR | | | |
|---|---|---|---|---|---|---|---|---|---|---|---|---|---|---|---|---|---|---|---|---|---|---|---|
| WEEK ENDED | 5 | 12 | 19 | 26 | 3 | 10 | 17 | 24 | 31 | 7 | 14 | 21 | 28 | 4 | 11 | 18 | 25 | 4 | 11 | 18 | 25 | 1 | 8 | 15 | 22 | 29 |
| TRAINING HRS | | | | | | | | | | 0 | 0 | 7.4 | 1.7 | 5.1 | 2.0 | 2.5 | 1.2 | 3.0 | 3.4 | 0.1 | 2.0 | 1.0 | 3.3 | 2.9 | 2.8 | |
| TOTAL HRS | | | | | | | | | | 5.3 | 6.2 | 15.9 | 11.7 | 15.6 | 10.1 | 13.9 | 17.5 | 13.2 | 16.7 | 35.4 | 22.5 | 21.6 | 22.1 | 22.9 | 26.0 | |

-CONFIDENTIAL-

FIGURE   I

I - 3

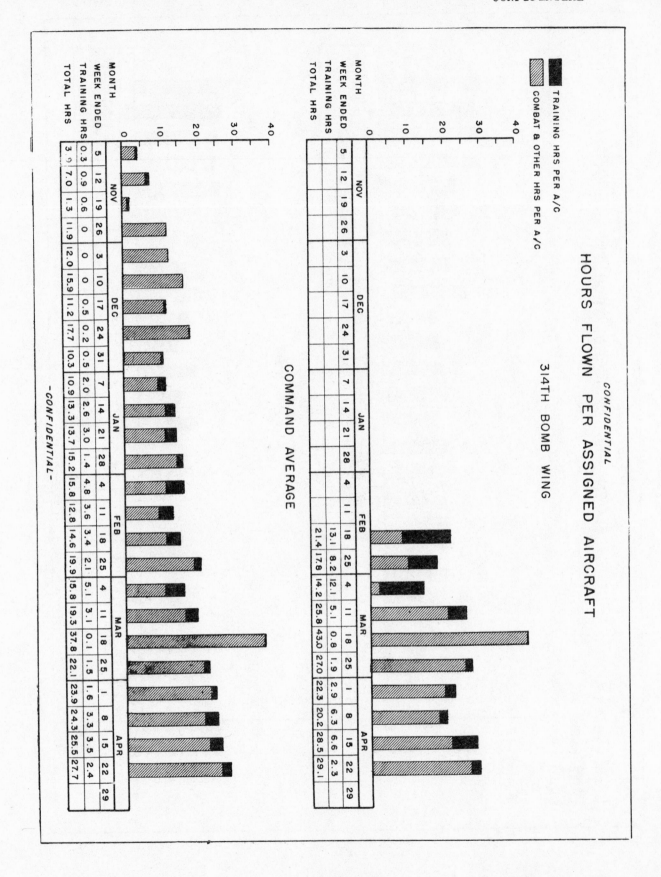

*CONFIDENTIAL*

# HOURS FLOWN PER ASSIGNED AIRCRAFT

## 314TH BOMB WING

■ TRAINING HRS PER A/C
▨ COMBAT & OTHER HRS PER A/C

### COMMAND AVERAGE

| MONTH | NOV | | | DEC | | | | | JAN | | | | FEB | | | | MAR | | | | APR | | | |
|---|---|---|---|---|---|---|---|---|---|---|---|---|---|---|---|---|---|---|---|---|---|---|---|---|
| WEEK ENDED | 5 | 12 | 19 | 26 | 3 | 10 | 17 | 24 | 31 | 7 | 14 | 21 | 28 | 4 | 11 | 18 | 25 | 4 | 11 | 18 | 25 | 1 | 8 | 15 | 22 | 29 |
| TRAINING HRS | | | | | | | | | | | | | | | 13.1 | 8.2 | 12.1 | 5.1 | 0.8 | 1.9 | 2.9 | 6.3 | 6.6 | 2.3 | |
| COMBAT HRS | | | | | | | | | | | | | | 21.4 | 17.8 | 14.2 | 25.8 | 43.0 | 27.0 | 22.3 | 20.2 | 28.5 | 29.1 | | |

### COMMAND AVERAGE

| MONTH | NOV | | | DEC | | | | | JAN | | | | FEB | | | | MAR | | | | APR | | | |
|---|---|---|---|---|---|---|---|---|---|---|---|---|---|---|---|---|---|---|---|---|---|---|---|---|
| WEEK ENDED | 5 | 12 | 19 | 26 | 3 | 10 | 17 | 24 | 31 | 7 | 14 | 21 | 28 | 4 | 11 | 18 | 25 | 4 | 11 | 18 | 25 | 1 | 8 | 15 | 22 | 29 |
| TRAINING HRS | 0.3 | 0.9 | 0.6 | 0 | 0 | 0.5 | 0.2 | 0.5 | 0.5 | 2.0 | 2.6 | 3.0 | 1.4 | 4.8 | 3.6 | 3.4 | 2.1 | 5.1 | 3.1 | 0.1 | 1.5 | 1.6 | 3.3 | 3.5 | 2.4 | |
| TRAINING HRS | 3.9 | 7.0 | 1.3 | 11.9 | 12.0 | 15.9 | 11.2 | 17.7 | 10.3 | 10.9 | 13.3 | 13.7 | 15.2 | 15.8 | 12.8 | 14.6 | 19.9 | 15.8 | 19.3 | 37.8 | 22.1 | 23.9 | 24.3 | 25.5 | 27.7 | |
| TOTAL HRS | | | | | | | | | | | | | | | | | | | | | | | | | | |

-CONFIDENTIAL-

FIGURE II

I - 4

that figure since. During the latter half of March training time fell
to 2.7 percent of the combat time. However, throughout the month of
April training time increased to 10% of the time spent in combat operations. Actually there has been very little decrease in the actual
number of training hours flown per month per aircraft; from 13.9 hours
in February and 8.2 hours during the first two weeks of March to 9.2
hours per aircraft during the first three weeks of April. As adjustment is made to the increased tempo of operations, training time will
probably continue to increase. Every effort is being made to push the
enemy now, as hard as possible. Your time available for flying training has unquestionably suffered slightly, but only slightly. It is
therefore more important than ever before that you efficiently utilize
every moment spent in training to increase to the maximum our overall
ability to deal the enemy a crushing defeat.

CONFIDENTIAL

# II. PLANNING THE MISSION

## A WHO DOES THE PLANNING?

The planning for every tactical mission originates in XXI Bomber Command
Headquarters. The Command Field Orders coordinate the effort, designate
the force required, bomb load to be carried, routes, flight and bombing
altitudes, times of take-off and support by outside agencies. These
plans are reviewed and approved by the 20th Air Force.

The actual selection of VLR targets was made in Washington prior to the
Command's departure from its training bases in the Zone of the Interior.
This directive has since been modified in the light of studies made by
the Joint Target Group, and a changing tactical situation.

The sequence desired for attacks on those targets was inferred by the
priority rating assigned each target by the original directive.

## B THE SEQUENCE OF THE PLANNING.

The XXI Bomber Command Staff Personnel study the weather trends, enemy
order of battle and capabilities, possible routes out and back, flight
plans and capabilities of other units for offering support (directly or
by diversion) and provisions for air-sea rescue.

Drawing up the details into written Field Orders is done by a Project
Officer in coordination with the pertinent staff sections and outside
agencies. When a draft has been prepared, it is submitted to the Commanding General; and, with his changes or additions, the plan is approved
and a field order is published on approximately D-3. Meanwhile, advance
information required by the Wings is transmitted by telecon to them, and
if a written field order cannot be made available by D-2 necessary frag-
mentary instructions are furnished by telecon.

## C FACTORS INVOLVED IN THE PLANNING.

The route is chosen so as to utilize all available aids to navigation
such as check points, celestial and loran. Attention is paid to avoiding enemy defenses and early warning equipment.

Special attention is devoted to selecting a landfall point which may
readily be identified by either visual or radar means. Route to the
target from landfall is planned to present an 8 to 10 minute bomb run,
generally upwind or downwind. Heavily defended areas are avoided when
possible, and the routes out of the target area are planned to confuse
the enemy defenses. Returning planes are routed by Iwo Jima which
serves as an emergency base and check point half way along the route.
Waves of attack against the primary target are spaced as closely as possible to permit the greatest saturation of enemy fighter and flak defenses.

Due to the fact that great distances, and therefore variable weather conditions, are involved in VLR operations, routes out, Initial Points, and axes of attack are chosen primarily from a radar standpoint, but must also furnish a good approach to the target from a visual bombing and bomb pattern standpoint while minimizing the exposure of our formations to enemy flak and fighter defenses.

The bombing altitude is chosen after considering and weighing the different factors, such as bombing accuracy, flak defense and fuel consumption at high altitudes.

Weather, of primary importance in all bombing operations, is the major factor in selecting the final date for a mission. Often it is necessary to change the date forward or backward at the last minute, or even change primary targets due to a forecast of a long period of bad weather in the original target area.

## D  CONCLUSION.

The above covers the fundamentals involved in planning a XXI Bomber Command tactical mission. Many types of specialist participate in the planning and their opinions receive careful consideration. The result is the plan which will most likely succeed in placing the maximum number of bombs on the target with the minimum loss to our forces.

AIRPLANE
COMMANDER

# III   THE AIRPLANE COMMANDER

## A.   THE AIRPLANE COMMANDER AND THE COMBAT CREW

### 1. Responsibility.

The airplane commander must be an outstanding personality, a skilled pilot, and a well-disciplined officer. He must possess an adequate knowledge of the duties of all crew members and of their responsibilities before he can successfully direct their efforts into smooth functioning teamwork.

Too many pilots consider themselves pilots alone and forget that they are responsible for a very intricate and expensive piece of machinery run by eleven men as a team. The failure of any one of the crew members to perform his assigned duty correctly might easily prove disastrous. The way in which you, as airplane commander execute your power of command to weld a highly trained group of men into a closely knit team will be reflected in the efficiency and capabilities of your crew. The Airplane Commander must truly be a versatile person. Among other things he must:

    a. Be both a pilot and a commander.

    b. Analyze each crew member and guide relations with him accordingly.

    c. Analyze himself and his relations with each crew member and act accordingly.

    d. Be a specialist on six different subjects pertaining to successful operation of a heavy bomber. These include piloting, bombing, navigation, engineering, gunnery and radar.

    e. Set the example in order to command the respect of all crew members.

    f. Promote a team feeling among his crew members.

    g. Not show favoritism.

    h. Stand up for his crew, individually and collectively.

    i. Compliment when compliments are due.

    j. Reprimand and discipline when necessary.

    k. Delegate routine duties to insure smooth operation and no slip-ups.

    l. Insist upon constant training for all crew members.

    m. Consult his crew as a commander consults his staff.

The Airplane Commander must bear in mind that the member of his crew are working, not *for* him, but with him in a concerted effort to accomplish their mission. Every crew member must have the confidence in, and the trust of, every other crew member. It is the Airplane Commander's responsibility to foster and develop that confidence and trust. Finally, the Airplane Commander must develop and expand the confidence of his crew in such a manner as to include the ground crew as an integral part of the team.

## 2. Air Discipline.

Air Discipline is based on the complete interdependence of the combat crew members. In the operation of the B-29 no one man is self-sufficient. Each and every man depends on the ten other men of the crew for the successful completion of his job under any circumstances. One small insignificant act, detrimental or helpful as the case may be, may mean loss of airplane and crew or successful completion of the mission. Missions may fail and airplanes and crews be lost because a pilot fails to fly the navigator's course, a flight engineer fails to figure the fuel reserve correctly, a bombardier misses a target and thereby necessitates another trip to the same target, a navigator sleeps through an opportunity to take a celestial shot, a gunner shoots before he recognizes.

Air Discipline starts on the ground, for you will find that a man not disciplined on the ground, cannot be disciplined in the air. The correct type of discipline is evidenced when a man has a duty to perform and he performs it to the best of his ability under any circumstances. If a man is unreliable on the ground, he will be unreliable in the air under combat or any other conditions.

To attain air discipline, first ascertain that your crew members are capable of doing the job assigned, then make sure that they perform their duties and perform them in the correct manner. Let each individual crew member know exactly what you expect of him. To accomplish this, daily "bull sessions" should be held with the entire crew present. Encourage crew members to create emergency situations in which the airplane and crew might find itself--then decide what the plan of action will be when that situation arises. Never give an order to a crew member unless you are positive you want that order carried out. Then check to see whether it has been carried out. Don't let a crew member get by if he fails to carry out an order. All orders given should be strictly of a business nature. There are different methods of giving orders in such a manner that they are welcomed. Say, "Let's do this" or "Will you do this" or "I'll do this and you do that." The Airplane Commander must allot himself just a few more routine duties than anyone else is given.

As we undertake larger formations in our operations, air discipline is of paramount importance. If eleven men cannot work as a team, elements cannot be expected to work together and larger units will not possess the coordination necessary for successful bombing and adequate defense.

Fire control gunnery, bombing procedure, ditching procedure, unceasing
vigilance and formation flying are examples of air discipline applied.
The XXI Bomber Command Tactical Doctrine and Standard Operating Procedures must be strictly adhered to by everyone operating in this command.
This will require thorough study and application of the principles involved. Remember, in combat, breach of air discipline usually results
in loss of life or damage to someone's airplane. See that your crew
maintains good air discipline!

3. <u>Training</u>.

Each Wing is responsible for conducting the prescribed training program.
The longer we remain in this theatre of operations the more training aids
and tactical operational knowledge will become available. It is your
responsibility, as airplane commander, to see that your men attend
scheduled classes, and in addition, get instruction covering any weakness-
es not covered by the current ground school. However, shaping your crew
into a coordinated team will not come from any ground school program.
It is your duty first to see that your crew members get the maximum amount
of training and understand all of their duties for any circumstances.
Organize your crew and practice working as a team. In the air put into
practical application and continued training those lessons learned on
the ground. Train your crew in such things as fire control, interphone
procedure, ditching procedure and abandoning ship in order that clock-
like precision can be reached and maintained.


## B.  OPERATING PROCEDURES

### 1. <u>Starting Procedure</u>.

Many engine failures on take-off and during flight have been traced directly to faulty starting procedure. You should be positive that the
flight engineer completes his check list and uses the proper procedure
in starting the engines. To prevent overheating the engines during
the ground run, the following procedure is recommended:

a.  Start the engines as quickly as possible. Three minutes should
be sufficient time to start all four engines.

b.  Keep cowl flaps open full (27°) during all ground operation.

c.  When possible complete the engine run-up immediately after
starting.

d.  Avoid holding rated power for long periods on the run-up.

e.  Taxi with 700 to 800 RPM where possible.

f. If cylinder temperatures rise above the maximum allowable shut down the engines, but don't hold up a formation by blocking the taxiway.

g. When possible turn the airplane into the wind for the run-up.

h. Do not attempt to take-off with the cylinder head temperature over the maximum allowable.

i. Follow the recommended engine run-up procedure. A few points to remember are:

(1) Advance and retard throttles with a smooth, steady movement. Damage to the engine may occur by too rapid movement of the throttles.

(2) Check magnetos at 2000 RPM by first moving switch to "left" and back to "both", then to "right" and back to "both. Remember holding the switch on one magneto too long will burn up the plugs.

(3) Check each engine individually prior to take-off if doubt as to proper operation exists. Otherwise check engines during first third of take-off roll.

(4) Moisture condensation on spark plug points may be cleared out by running up engine at full power for a few seconds, and then re-checking the magneto.

(5) Do not attempt to take-off unless the engines are functioning normally. Remember, you are operating at extremely heavy gross weights. Your most critical period will be immediately after leaving the ground, and before the wheels and flaps are retracted. You will contribute nothing toward accomplishing the mission by crashing at the end of the runway.

2. Taxiing.

Be sure to check your hydraulic pressure, both the main and the emergency, before attempting to taxi. Considerable power will be necessary to begin taxiing if you are heavily loaded, and for the same reason, considerable braking action will be necessary to stop. Keep a safe distance behind other aircraft, and don't taxi as if you were on a race track. Excessive use of the brakes will cause them to overheat, and lose their effectiveness, or even to completely fail. This usually happens just when the brakes are needed to avoid an accident. Use a combination of engine power and brakes in taxiing, and taxi at slow speeds. All turns should be made smoothly with the wheel on the inside of the turn kept in motion. A sudden sharp turn may easily throw off a tire, or at heavy gross weights it could cause a structural failure of the landing gear.

While taxiing, the entire crew should be kept alert and on the lookout for obstacles. The B-29 has a large wing-spread of 141 feet and it is difficult to judge the distance objects are from the wing tips. When taxiing between obstacles, have a man at each wing tip to guide you through. This is particularly important at night. A taxiing accident is usually one of the most humiliating you will ever experience, and unless you are alert it can easily happen to you.

3. <u>Before Taking-Off</u>.

Before taking-off be positive that the cylinder head temperatures are within limits. Be sure you have <u>completed the check list</u>. Everyone is fallible. The check-list is provided to prevent your forgetting something essential -- USE IT! Notify the crew to stand by to take-off, taxi out and line up with the center of the runway, using all of the available runway. The hundred feet behind you might make the difference necessary to clear an obstacle at the other end.

4. <u>Taking-off</u>.

The take-off under heavy gross weights is the most critical time you will encounter in your whole flight. The B-29 has proved its ability to perform this task. However, it is mandatory that the airplane be functioning properly in all respects before the take-off is attempted. So many little things can happen to affect the safety of the take-off that it is of the utmost importance for you to perfect your technique and to have worked out with your crew a thorough system to take care of all emergencies.

Some pilots prefer to hold the brakes at the end of the runway and get a power check before beginning the roll, and others prefer to make running take-offs. Care must be used not to overshoot the turn onto the runway when using the latter method as this might throw a tire. No matter which method you use, the important thing is to control the direction of the airplane by use of the rudder as soon as possible. If you use the brakes excessively for control you cause excessive wear on the brakes and are slowing down your speed thus requiring more runway. If you juggle the throttles excessively you reduce the available horsepower thereby also slowing down your speed. <u>Get control with that rudder</u>.

You will notice that a speed of 100 MPH is reached very quickly, but from there on up the speed accelerates comparatively slowly. When a speed of from 110 to 120 MPH has been reached, raise the nose wheel from 2 to 6 inches above the ground and hold the plane in this position until you have attained 130 to 140 MPH, at which time you will find that you have exceptionally good control. As soon as you have broken from the ground the landing gear should be retracted. Because of the aerodynamic cleaness of the airplane, the landing gear drag is relatively very great. Raising the gear is equivalent to adding more power. Power should not be reduced until the gear is fully up.

Flaps should be retracted when the indicated air speed is 40 MPH higher than the take-off speed. The power-off stalling speed with the flaps up is 15 to 20 MPH IAS higher than the lowest take-off speed with 25° flaps at any weight, therefore, a margin of 20 to 25 MPH IAS above flaps-up stalling speed must be held when retracting the flaps. As soon as terrain conditions permit, the air speed should be allowed to increase to 200 to 205 MPH before continuing the climb. This will increase the cooling effect on the engines.

At the beginning of the take-off roll, cowl flaps must be closed to 7½ to 9 degrees. If they are left in the wide open position, the airplane will never leave the ground. As the speed is increased the engines will be cooled by the increased flow of air. Remember that the maximum cylinder head temperature is 260°. Higher head temperatures result in reduction of power. The inter-cooler shutters will be in wide open position (15°) for take-off, ½ open after gear and flaps are retracted, and then cut down as required. When turbos are used for take-off a very high carburetor air temperature results with a consequent large reduction in power if the inter-cooler shutters are closed.

The use of flaps during take-off increases the drag during the run, but the flaps also increase the wing-lift and therefore take load off of the wheels, which in turn decreases the wheel rolling drag. The resulting net drag is not changed much, but the take-off speed is reduced with the use of 25° flaps. The use of more than 25° flaps increases the drag disproportionately to the amount of lift gained.

One common fault of many pilots is to get the nose wheel too high for take-off. This results in stalling the plane off and creates a definite critical point in case of engine failure. It is true that an engine failure is critical during any part of the take-off run, but there is no use to aggravate the situation.

At heavy gross weight take-offs, when the outside air temperature is 100°F or above, a take-off manifold pressure of 50 inches of mercury is permissible. However, continuously increasing the manifold pressure does not necessarily increase the horsepower output. A point is soon reached, due to engine pumping losses, when an additional increase in manifold pressure results in a decrease in horsepower delivered to the propeller shaft. Fifty inches manifold pressure will be exceeded only when an engine is lost on take-off and then only as long as it is possible to keep the engines out of the detonation range.

5. Climbing.

Normal climbs are performed at 200 MPH with a power setting of 43½" Hg and 2400 RPM. This setting will result in a maximum rate of climb while maintaining cylinder head temperature with the desired limits and yet using a minimum amount of cowl flaps. You must work very closely with the flight engineer during climbs. Check with him repeatedly on the position of the cowl flaps and the temperatures of the cylinder heads. Make him keep the heads at the allowable 248° temperatures. Remember, your primary object is to get to your predetermined altitude as quickly as possible. Any unneeded opening of the cowl flaps will only decrease your rate of climb thereby increasing the overall time high power settings must be used, which in turn decreases the life of your engines.

Ordinarily the climb to high altitudes will not be started until after several hours operation at low altitudes. As the fuel consumption is highest at altitude it is important that minimum altitudes be maintained as long as possible. This should be the primary consideration in the operation of the aircraft prior to starting the climb.

Before leveling off, you should climb to 500 feet above the designated altitude and then maintain rated power until the airspeed has increased to 220 or 230 MPH. Decrease your power to predetermined settings leaving the cowl flaps in the same position until cylinder head temperatures have started to decrease. Close cowl flaps as much as possible, maintaining 230° on your heads, and play with your altitude until you get the airplane "on the step" and the airspeed and cylinder head temperatures stabilize on cruise settings.

6. Cruise Control.

On all flights, other than local training missions, you as airplane commander, will be charged with operating the B-29 at maximum range. On combat missions it is up to you to drop the maximum number of bombs on the target. Proper use of the "Form F" in determining the center of gravity and gross weight goes hand in hand with closely following your cruise control charts. These charts are made from actual test figures and have proved themselves time and time again. You should consider them Bibles of operation, and govern your flight accordingly. Personal experimentation will get you nowhere.

Learn how to compute the "Form F" and know your cruise control charts and then check your engineer on them. Some strong points of cruise control are:

    a. Remain at minimum safe altitude as long as possible at heavy gross weights.

    b. Get into automatic lean as soon as possible.

    c. Beware of the back side of the power curve.

    d. Keep a close watch on your cylinder head temperatures and cowl flap settings.

e.  Be sure that you are flying "on the step" at all times.

f.  Be on the lookout for the "vicious circle" of cowl flaps and indicated airspeed.

g.  Fly the indicated airspeed for specific gross weights.

h.  Take advantage of your descent from altitude.  One of the factors governing the economy of fuel used is the descent from altitude.  Get together with your flight engineer and navigator and determine the point to start your descent.  By letting down at a slow rate of 200 feet per minute, required air speeds may be maintained at greatly reduced power settings.

Remember, power curves and standard operating procedures have proved themselves.  Use them and get the most out of your B-29.

7.  Landing.

Just a word of caution.  When it becomes necessary for you to make a landing at weights in excess of 130,000 pounds, be sure all of your drift is killed and that you don't drop it in.  At those weights excessive strain will easily cause your gear to fold.  Other factors concerning emergency landings will be covered in the emergency procedure section.

## C.  FORMATION FLYING

1.  Assembly.

As each mission will be a maximum range problem, assembly of the formation must be accomplished as quickly as possible.  In all cases the assembly will be accomplished as briefed prior to take-off.  The following observations may be of assistance in affecting the assembly.

a.  Normal Assembly.

(1)  Obtain sufficient flying speed before maneuvering.
(2)  Fly a collision course with the leader rather than use excessive power.
(3)  As the assembly plan will follow a predetermined series of headings, keep track of the time intervals and anticipate the turns of the aircraft ahead of you.
(4)  Anticipate the relative speed of the airplane ahead of you to avoid overrunning as much as possible.

b.  Assembly during the hours of darkness.

(1)  Assembly of a large formation during darkness is difficult even in good weather.  An aldis lamp shining from the tail of each ship will facilitate assembly.

(2) It is extremely difficult to judge distance at night, the approach to position in formation should be made with caution.

(3) The formation should be flown loosely until daylight.

c. **Assembly above an overcast.**

(1) Assembly above an overcast will be done in accordance with the existing tactical doctrine, and as briefed before take-off.

(2) Predesignated headings, air speed, and rate of climb must be strictly adhered to while climbing through an overcast.

(3) The flight will usually be assembled at a predesignated altitude above the overcast and over a radio range or homing beacon. Stick to the proper altitude to avoid assembly with the wrong flight.

2. **Climb.**

During the climb to bombing altitude you will find it easier to avoid straggling by staying in close formation. Straggling leads to use of excessive power settings, this overtaxes the engines and is the cause of a great percentage of abortives.

3. **Formation Enroute.**

The basic combat unit in our operations is the eleven (11) aircraft flight. The flight is composed of one (1) three (3) aircraft element and two (2) four (4) aircraft elements. The quality of the formation depends first on the ability of the flight leader and secondly upon the ability of the element leaders. The element leaders must maintain their position with a minimum of throttle changes and maneuvering. The leaders should have their navigators inform them in advance of any anticipated turns, climbs, or let downs so as to be ready for them. This is an excellent aid to the smooth execution of these maneuvers.

Leaders must be careful never to place their formation in the prop wash, or to maintain such high or low airspeeds that the rest of the formation will have difficulty in maintaining proper position. The leader should always bear in mind that he has other aircraft following him. The effort that the leaders put into their work will be reflected through the quality of the formation.

The element leaders and wingmen determine the depth of the formation and the number of turrets that may be brought to bear on enemy fighter attacks. A depth of thirty to fifty feet between aircraft gives the best results by allowing all turrets to be uncovered. All aircraft commanders should fly their positions with a minimum of movement and change in order not to force other aircraft out of position. Each movement of the aircraft in the lead of the formation is accentuated as it travels to the rear. Furthermore, abrupt changes in throttle settings invite supercharger and engine failures. The trim of the aircraft will change with each change in power setting, and it is fatiguing to fight the controls with each throttle change.

A tight formation is easier to fly than a loose one and will usually make an enemy fighter think twice before he attacks. When a close formation is flown it is easier to detect changes in relative postions and corrective measures will not have to be excessive. Straggling elements and single aircraft are always targets for concentrated attack by enemy fighters, so DON'T STRAGGLE.

The response of the B-29 to changes in power varies considerably with different loadings and different altitudes. As an example: A formation of B-29's averaging 105,000 lbs. weight is cruising at 25,000 feet, and after a maneuver, one airplane finds itself 100 yards behind its assigned position. In order to catch up, the pilot applies rated power. The total time required for him to regain his assigned position will be 35 seconds. Besides exposing himself to possible enemy aircraft, the pilot has exceeded his cruise control curve, and each application of rated power will cut down his fuel reserve. When the formation is flying open or spread out, changes in altitude are effective in gaining or losing speed in order to maintain a relative position. Also, small maneuvers of wingmen will aid in maintaining position without changing power settings.

As our missions are of long duration, the physical strain of flying formation is considerable and the co-pilot must necessarily be another first pilot. In addition, in certain positions of the formation, the co-pilot is the only one who has adequate vision to maintain formation. Therefore, the co-pilot must possess as much ability at formation flying as the pilot. Whoever is not piloting will be the fire control officer and will also keep watch on the RPM and MP guages.

Cabin supercharging is a tremendous aid in reducing fatigue at high altitudes. In formation flying, to prevent abrupt changes in cabin pressure, due to large changes in throttle settings, a good practice is to maintain the inboard throttles in a constant position, and to regulate the air speed with the outboard throttles.

4. Let Down.

When a let down is started it is possible to maintain your cruising speed with a large reduction in power, resulting in economy of fuel. The let down should be performed at standard rates, and must be started at the proper time in order to obtain maximum range. Excessive power settings and rates of descent will quickly use your fuel reserve. During the let down, the formation should be maintained and the crew kept on alert status to prevent surprise attacks by enemy fighters. Be prepared for an attack at all times when within range of enemy fighters.

## 5. Landing.

Landing the flight in favorable weather conditions is a comparatively simple process. However, when bad weather prevails, the landing of an airplane can become complicated. Although the B-29 is a large airplane, proper use of the flaps in the traffic pattern will enable you to make a slow pattern and a short approach.

If each aircraft tends to make a longer approach than the preceding one, the third or fourth aircraft will not be able to see the runway when they start the approach. Consequently, they miss the runway and have to "go-around". "Go-arounds" not only disrupt the traffic pattern, but are bad practice in the B-29 due to the probable shortage of fuel, and the excessive drag produced by the flaps and landing gear. Do not lower the landing gear until the landing is a "sure thing" and then allow one minute for the gear to be extended.

The correct landing approach will make the landing simple. Final approach should be 30 MPH, IAS, above the power off stalling speed with the flaps all the way down. Boost should be full on, and the RPM set to 2400. It is important not to reduce the power rapidly during any part of the approach. Never allow the speed to fall below the power off stalling speed even when landing. Although the airplane will stand inadvertent three-point landings on the main wheels and the nose wheel, it is not a good practice. Neither should the tail skid be allowed to touch first unless making a short field landing. The best method is to land on the main wheels and then allow the nose wheel to settle as the airspeed drops off. If the nose wheel is held off too long, it will drop with considerable force when the airspeed falls off and may result in structural damage.

## D. THE COMBAT MISSION

Since our primary objective is aimed at the heart of the Japanese Empire the majority of our missions will be run from the Forward Bases. In the past we have run both individual night and daylight formation strikes. Since the night strikes present few problems other than those normally encountered this section will deal, for the most part, with daylight formation strikes.

## 1. Initial Point and the Bombing Run.

The procedures to follow at the initial point and during the bombing run are covered by "Formation Assault" in the Tactical Doctrine. From the initial point in to the target, and on the first leg away from the target will be your most dangerous period. Here you can expect, and will get, the greatest concentration of enemy fighter attacks and anti-aircraft fire. The formation should be tight to offer concentrated defense against enemy fighter attacks. A tight formation will also present a smaller target for AA.

You have flown a long distance with the purpose of dropping bombs on the target, so don't spoil the effectiveness of the effort in the last few minutes. The leader must use the AFCE to obtain the maximum bombing results. The wing men must drop immediately on the leader. It is here that proper crew coordination becomes important. Here your combat crew will prove whether they are a close-knit team or just eleven individuals out for a ride. If you keep cool and calm, even in an emergency, the rest of the crew will follow your example.

When you are under attack there is a possibility of losing your cabin pressure as a result of gun fire. Require your crew members to have their oxygen masks on with tubes connected and ready for instant use.

Use of the radio in the target area is recommended when it is needed to aid in maintaining formation. Needless chattering over the air, however, may prevent an important message from getting through.

2. <u>Return from the Target Area</u>.

On the break away after photographs have been taken the leader must remember that the formation is following him. Additional airspeed must be gained by losing altitude and not by increasing power. If any aircraft is crippled, the formation must be slowed down to pick him up, providing the safety of the entire formation is not jeapordized. If your aircraft is crippled, employ every expediency to remain in formation. Observe other aircraft that have been shot down or that may leave the formation later. Note the position, altitude, heading and how many parachutes have been seen to open.

If you have an engine knocked out you will be able to maintain formation by using higher power settings on the remaining three engines until you are out of the danger area. Immediately after leaving the target make an interphone check with the crew members to determine battle damage and casualties. It will be necessary to know this in order to properly plan your return flight.

Send in the required radio messages after leaving the target, and upon entering the control zone. If you fail to turn on your IFF, units in the friendly area will be alerted. This will lead to much confusion and disrupted plans, particularly at night.

During the flight out and back, make note of any unusual activities observed or installations not previously reported. Reliable information of enemy dispositions and facilities in occupied territory and in Japan proper is difficult to obtain from other sources. Anything unusual that you observe may be valuable information to the Intelligence Section.

3. <u>Landing.</u>

On reaching the field carry out the normal formation landing procedure, unless you have sustained battle damage, or have wounded crew members aboard.  Remember that there is a relatively short period of time to land all the ships of your Group and all of them will be short of gas. If you have sustained structural damage to your airplane and there is the slightest doubt that you will be able to clear the strip after landing, circle the field until all other ships have landed, or if you are low on gas use the crash landing strip when one is available.  Before entering the traffic pattern be sure to go over your check list completely.  Check the operation of your flaps, watch the brake pressure, and have your gunners check for flat tires.  With wounded aboard, aircraft will make approach blinking red identification lights.  When rolling down the runway flash a series of red dots from the nose with the Aldis Lamp.  If the situation warrants, aircraft will call the tower for a straight in approach using above mentioned signals while landing.  Aircraft will then proceed to hardstand or area marked by red cross where medical assistance is waiting.

### E.  MAINTENANCE

In the past we have had many abortions due to lack of knowledge and skill on the part of the combat crew in flying the airplane, and on the part of the mechanics performing maintenance.  This lack of skill was understandable due to our short training period with the B-29.  As our experience has increased, the percentage of abortions has decreased.  The key to the success of a mission is good, precise maintenance.  Insured maintenance will insure missions completed.

In our operations, a large share of the maintenance falls upon the members of the combat crew.  Close coordination between the airplane commander, the flight engineer, the crew chief, and the engineering officer is necessary.  The airplane commander must maintain constant supervision over the maintenance being performed on his airplane.  It has been clearly shown that the airplane with a commander who supervises the maintenance will participate in the largest number of missions, and will have fewer aborts.  You must know your airplane thoroughly, the maintenance needed, the best and most efficient means of getting the work done, parts needed and how to get them, and when the airplane will be ready to fly again.

Preventive maintenance before the airplane takes off will help insure its completing the mission.  When you have had a successful flight, give a "pat-on-the-back" to the ground crew.  Let them know you are aware of their part in the mission.  If the flight is not a successful one, give the crew chief all of the helpful information possible.  If you do not know exactly what the trouble was, find out, and see that it is properly remedied. Never be afraid to get your own hands or clothes greasy in working on the airplane. It is to your advantage to increase constantly your practical knowledge in maintaining the airplane.

Another factor that causes abortions is carelessness. The human element is always present, and you must constantly be on guard against it. Follow the standard procedures in pre-flight inspections and insist that your ground crew and combat crew do the same. Too many airplanes have aborted due to loose fuel and oil tank caps coming off during flight. The B-29 is too large for one person to be responsible for the entire pre-flight inspection. Certain duties must be assigned to separate individuals. This will prevent the often heard remark, "I thought the other fellow was going to check that".

1. Before the Mission.

When the airplane returns from a mission work should immediately be started on preparing it for the next one. A complete and thorough pre-mission shakedown inspection is necessary. Each group will have its standard procedure for accomplishing this inspection.

Following the inspection a pre-mission engineering flight is necessary. This flight should be for the purpose of thoroughly testing the engines and equipment of the airplane. During the flight you should have each crew member check each item of his equipment for efficient operation.

Personal equipment for the flight should be inspected and placed in the airplane prior to reporting for the flight. While each individual is responsible for his personal equipment, you, as airplane commander, are responsible that everyone is completely equipped and ready to conduct the mission.

2. Before Station Time.

It is essential that a thorough inspection be made of the exterior of the airplane. This will often prevent starting engines or taking off when some part of the equipment is out of place, or is malfunctioning. Consult your flight engineer and crew chief on defects noted in the Form 1A.

Many airplanes have failed to release bombs at the proper time due to improper bomb loading. Don't let this happen to you. Insure yourself that the bombing equipment is functioning properly, and that bombs are correctly loaded. Your primary object is to release bombs on the target, and not to jettison them in the Sea.

3. After Landing.

After you have landed and performed the crew inspection, go over the airplane with your crew chief. Tell him what was wrong during the flight and explain the symptoms. If the defects are properly written up in the

Form 1A and explained to your crew chief, he will have less difficulty in performing the needed maintenance.

The Form 1A should be filled out in the air. As defects are discovered by members of the crew, they should call in this information to the flight engineer who will then record it in the Form 1A. Nothing should be omitted. The pilot who fails to write up defects to spare crew chief's feelings is doing everyone concerned an injustice. Your crew chief should take pride in correcting every defect that is noted.

## F.  EMERGENCY OPERATIONS

### 1.  Loss of an Engine on Take-off.

The loss of an engine just prior to or immediately after take-off is the most crucial emergency you will encounter in the B-29. Once you are committed to take-off there is little you can do but continue, and for that reason it is essential for you to have a definite procedure established with your crew for such an emergency. There are so many points where the loss of an engine can influence your decision that it is difficult to put down any set rule; however, if you are just airborne the first requisite is to reduce drag as quickly as you can. Bring up the gear and flaps as soon as possible. In raising the flaps milk them up to 15 degrees at 140 MPH and raise the rest of the way at 165 MPH when operating at gross loads of 135,000 pounds. Feather the bad engine and increase power on all others, and have your engineer close the cowl flaps as much as possible. This must be instantaneous. As soon as a safe flying speed and sufficient altitude have been reached, salvo as much of the load as possible and move crew members around to secure the most favorable C.G. Reduce power and continue around pattern with normal three engine operation.

With the increased power settings and closed cowl flaps, cylinder head temperatures will rise quickly to the detonation point and, therefore, must be watched closely. Don't use excessive power longer than you absolutely have to. In some cases there is little else to do but chop your throttles and land straight ahead. Whatever the circumstances are it's undoubtedly a gamble and it calls for split second decisions. Train your crew for such emergencies.

### 2.  Three Engine Operation.

The B-29 has flying characteristics very similar to the B-24 under three engine operating conditions. Providing the propeller can be feathered, trim tabs may be used in a way so that no unusual flying conditions are encountered.

The primary concern of three engine operation is the increased fuel consumption in case an engine is lost at extreme ranges from the home base. Experience has shown that if you can descend to an altitude where automatic lean may be used (fly from 10 to 15 MPH below the airspeed required by power curves if necessary to get into auto-lean) you should have no difficulty in reaching the home base.

## 3. Two Engine Operation.

Two engines out on the same side presents the difficulty of maintaining direction; however, it can and has been done. Altitudes may be maintained if at light enough weights. Extending your range sufficiently to reach home base under these conditions is highly improbable; however, it may mean the difference of reaching friendly territory or not. Do not hesitate to lighten the load any way possible under these conditions.

## 4. Emergency Landings.

Whereas the B-29 is proving itself capable of taking belly landings equally well as the B-17, experience has shown that if only one wheel fails to extend better results are accomplished if a landing is made on any combination of two wheels extended. However, if two wheels fail to extend it is recommended that the operative wheel be retracted and a belly landing be made.

If either of the main gears fail to extend make a normal landing as slow as possible keeping the wing up with ailerons as long as possible. Cut all switches as soon as you are definitely on the ground. To date there have been no resulting fires from this type of landing, and in one instance the plane was back in commission in a period of two weeks.

In case the nose wheel fails to lock in the down position make a normal landing, holding the nose in the air as long as possible, but do not hold it up so long that the nose will tend to slam down on the runway. Be sure to get the C.G. as far aft as possible with safety.

## G. CONCLUSION

We are cognizant of the fact that further operation of the B-29 will continue to change the outlook on some of the information in this manual. This manual was not written as a directive, but rather as a guide.

Remember - there is nothing that will take the place of experience and training. Keep your mind open, continue to learn, and you and your crew will stand an excellent chance of successfully completing your combat tour.

## IV   THE FLIGHT ENGINEER

You, as flight engineer, should begin planning at the first notice of an impending mission.  First, determine the general condition of the airplane; second, find out what kind of load and weight is to be carried; and third, actually plan the flight.

Due to the rapicity of the development of flight engineering, and the variety of information that directly effects the successful completion of the flight engineer's assignment, it has been deemed necessary to publish this section under separate cover as the Flight Engineer's Information File.  Publication of the file under separate cover, and distribution to flight engineers alone, provides a more flexible vehicle for the dissemination of information than does continual extensive revision of the Combat Crew Manual.

Although the file is distributed to flight engineers only, it is still to be considered a section of the Combat Crew Manual.  Airplane commanders and pilots will be responsible for the thorough knowledge of its contents at all times.

The file and its revisions are issued to the wings for distribution as follows:

     2 ea Wing Headquarters

     2 ea Group Headquarters

     2 ea Squadron Headquarters

     1 ea Flight Engineer

RADAR OPERATOR

# V  RADAR

## Introduction

Airborn Radar is a relatively new weapon and many different methods have been used in its employment in combat. When it is used extensively, as is the case with any weapon, considerations of coordination within crews and between crews necessitates the adoption of a Standard Operating Procedure. This does not mean that progress in the science of making best use of the Radar weapon has been retarded. Rather, the employment of a method in a substantial number of cases makes possible scientific statistical conclusions as to the worth of the method. It is the policy of this command to make changes in the Standard Operating Procedures used by the crews when it is indicated that a change will improve the percentage of bombs which strike our assigned targets. It is known that better procedures than the ones being used will be developed. When these better procedures are isolated from the many other suggestions by tests in combat, changes will be made in the Standard Procedure, resulting in a gain in efficiency. However, the indiscreet use by crew members or crews of some method which <u>might</u> yield better results if every crew knew it and expected it to be used, will contribute materially to confusion and lack of coordination between crew members and crews. The Radar procedures now in effect are those developed in more than a year and a half of combat use of Radar in four theatres of war. If you use these procedures and use them correctly you will make improvement of them possible; you will also be rewarded with the high efficiency which results only from coordinated efforts.

It is not intended to tell you that a procedure alone will guarantee good results. Prerequisite to the intelligent use of any weapon, whether it is Radar or merely a Radar Procedure, is a good understanding of the problems to be solved and the methods used to solve them. For example, all members of the Radar bombing team, (Pilot, Navigator, Bombardier, and Radar Operator) should have a good understanding of the bombing problem and a good knowledge of the conditions for bombing over the Japanese Empire. Further, all members of the bombing team should understand the current method of solving the bombing problem in conditions found over our targets. Without this understanding and knowledge, the crew cannot make effective use of any Standard Operating Procedure, however good it may be.

You will already be familiar with many of the details to be found in this Manual. It is necessary now that you learn them all; the other members of your crew and other crews will depend upon it. For convenience of presentation the subject has been divided into five parts; Set Operation and Maintenance, Radar Scope Interpretation, Radar Navigation, Radar Bombing and Radar Procedures. No one of these parts is independent of the other four, and it is necessary that each crew member who uses Radar or Radar information memorizes the last; Radar Procedures, and has a thorough understanding of the first four.

## A   SET OPERATION

1. Procedure for placing the set in operation:

    a. Place all switches in the OFF position.

    b. Turn INTENSITY control on both scopes fully CCW.

    c. Press the POWER ON button, adjust intensity, focus and centering.

    d. At high altitudes and cold temperatures allow the set to warm up 15 minutes before proceeding.

    e. Adjust the AC voltage to 118 V with the potentiometer in the large junction box to the right of the operator's knees.

    f. Place manual TUNING knob in its center position.

    g. Turn meter selector switch to XTAL and adjust AFC VOLTAGE for maximum XTAL current.

    h. Turn meter selector switch to AFC V and check that the voltage is between 140 V and 180 V. If the AFC voltage is not in this range, repeat steps f. and g. for a different XTAL current peak.

    i. Press TRANS ON button.

    j. Adjust gain and tilt control for maximum target return and then adjust tuning control for maximum target return.

    k. Turn on AFC and check by observing target return.

    l. If no targets are available, tune the set using the water return.

2. Procedure for Turning on AZIMUTH STABILIZATION:

    a. Allow sweep to rotate several revolutions before turning azimuth stabilization ON.

    b. Stop antennae rotation before turning Azimuth Stabilization OFF.

    c. Do not start antennae rotating again for at least one minute after azimuth stabilization is turned OFF.

3. Range Calibration:

    a.  Turn the calibrate switch to Range.

    b.  Turn the Cal. Zero-Normal Switch to Cal. Zero.

    c.  Turn on the bombing circle switch.

    d.  Turn on 1-mile range marks and switch to 4-mile range.

    e.  Turn computer drum to 1-mile slant range.

    f.  Adjust range zero control on the synchronizer until the neon bulb is a minimum brightness and the bombing circle is near the 15-mile range mark.

    g.  Turn computer drum to 15-mile slant range, and turn range selector to 20-mile range.

    h.  Adjust range slope control on the synchronizer until the neon bulb is a minimum brightness and the bombing circle is near the 15-mile range mark.

    i.  Repeat steps e. and f.

    j.  Check for neon bulb dimming when the computer drum is at each exact mile.

    k.  If step j. cannot be accomplished check the count divider calibration as follows:

        (1)  Flip the COUNT TEST-NORMAL switch on the range unit to COUNT TEST.
        (2)  Turn to 20-mile range.
        (3)  Turn receiver gain control fully CCW.
        (4)  Set the COUNT CONTROL adjustment so that 9 circles appear between each of the brighter circles on the scope.

    l.  Repeat the steps a-k above and if calibration still cannot be accomplished so that the neon bulb dims when the computer drum is set on each exact mile, set the range accurately at dropping slant range. Advise the bombardier that radar synchronization is not possible.

    m.  When the airplane is at an adequate altitude, read the altitude with the bombing circle. Compare this with the correct altitude wherein it will be possible to check whether or not the set is calibrated for the correct dimming points.

4. Altitude Delay Calibration:

    a. Before calibration check the position of the computer chart with relation to the 3, 4, and 5-mile markers on the altitude scale and calibrate according to the computer chart.

    b. Turn calibrate switch to altitude.

    c. Place Cal. Zero-Normal Switch in normal position.

    d. Place the altitude hair on the computer drum to 3-mile position. Adjust Altitude zero for minimum brightness of the neon bulb.

    e. Place the altitude hair on the computer drum to 5-mile position and adjust altitude slope for minimum brightness of the neon bulb.

    f. Repeat step c. and d. until dimmings are on the exact mile.

5. Procedure for turning set OFF:

    a. Turn all switches to the OFF position. Turn off Azimuth Stabilization.

    b. Turn scope intensity controls CCW.

    c. Press the TRANS OFF button.

    D. Press the POWER OFF button.

6. Trouble Shooting:

Air maintenances describes those maintenance procedures which the radar operator can perform during flight. It is necessarily limited by the accessability of equipment, the tools at hand, and the availability of replacement parts. The following is intended to guide the radar operator in the determination of troubles and their correction.

    a. <u>General Maintenance Notes</u>.

        (1) PRELIMINARY CABLE CHECK: Tighten all cable connections before turning on power.

        (2) WARM-UP PERIOD: IMPORTANT, When possible, allow a fifteen (15) minute WARM-UP before making any corrective adjustments or tests.

        (3) POWER CHECK: Feel dust covers for warmth or look for lighted tubes.

(4) TUBE CHECK: Look for lighted filaments or feel shell for warmth. In case of doubt replace the tube. All tubes in the Operators Electronic Kit should have been checked in a bench MOCK-UP as well as a mutual conductance tube checker.

(5) CABLE CHECK: Turn power off before disconnecting any cables. If tightening cable doesn't relieve the trouble, disconnect and examine contacts. Clean any that are dirty or corroded and reassemble. NEVER squeeze, spread, or otherwise distort contacts.

(6) CHECK WITH HEADSET: Use a low impedence headset such as is furnished with the aircraft interphone system. Check cables and jacks carrying audio frequency wave forms (sweep and trigger pulses) by touching the tip of the headset jack to the center conductor and the shank of the headset jack to the outer conductor. A piece of bare wire secured to the shank of the headset jack will facilitate making the double connection.

(7) WARNING: Dangerous potentials exist in many components of this equipment. **TURN OFF ALL POWER BEFORE REMOVING ANY CABLES, COVERS, OR FUSES.**

b. Specific Maintenance Procedures.

(1) The arrangement of this section is in accordance with the procedure for placing the equipment in operation. If malfunctions are noted at any step in the starting procedure, clear the difficulty before continuing.

(2) If the symptom of malfunction can be identified with one described in this manual, make the checks in order, until trouble is located. Some troubles cannot be checked or corrected in the air. In these cases, no action is prescribed. DO NOT TINKER WITH THE EQUIPMENT.

(3) No equipment other than that normally carried in the plane is necessary for performing these checks.

(a) INVERTER.

1. INVERTER WILL NOT START.

a. Check door switch on J-40.

b. Check D-C lead connections to Inverter.

    c. Check 10 and 30 amp fuse in Inverter.

    d. Secure cable #44 to Inverter.

    e. Secure cable #2 to Control Box.

    f. Start by closing control relay.

    g. Wedge control relay in closed position.

2. INVERTER STARTS BUT CUTS OUT WHEN POWER ON BUTTON IS RELEASED.

    a. Wedge control relay in closed position.

3. INVERTER STARTS BUT CUTS OUT BEFORE REACHING NORMAL SPEED.

    a. Insert paper between contacts of cuter relay on Inverter until normal speed is reached.

4. A-C METER SHOWS NO VOLTAGE.

    a. Check position of meter switch.

    b. Check 20 amp fuse in Inverter.

    c. Check meter connections in J-40.

5. A-C METER NOT READING 115 VOLTS.

    a. Adjust R1105 in J-40.

6. INVERTER FAN INOPERATIVE.

    a. Check 5 amp fuse in Suit Heater Fuse Box.

    b. Check wiring to Fan.

    c. Leave floor boards up for better circulation.

7. INVERTER STILL NOT OPERATING CORRECTLY.

    a. Use other Inverter.

(b) INDICATORS.

1. NO SPOT ON EITHER INDICATOR (WARNING: DO NOT TURN ON TRANSMITTER UNTIL THE TROUBLE HAS BEEN CLEARED).

    **a.** Turn up intensity controls.

    **b.** Check fuse F1105 in J-40 (AC to RA-90).

    **c.** Secure H.V. cables from Rectifier RA-90 to Indicators (cables #22, #23, and #26.)

    **d.** Secure cable #7 from J-40 to RA-90 (AC to RA-90).

    **e.** Check fuse F1102 in J-40 (AC to Indicators).

    **f.** Secure cables #5 and #6 to Indicators.

**2.** NO SPOT ON ONE INDICATOR.

    **a.** Turn up intensity control.

    **b.** Secure HV cable #22 or #23.

    **c.** Secure cable #5 or #6.

    **d.** Remove rear cover of Indicator and check for lighted heater. If not lighted, trouble lies in CRT or cabling to CRT.

**3.** SPOT INTENSITY ON BOTH TUBES CANNOT BE CHANGED. NO READING ON AFC VOLTS.

    **a.** Check RA-88.

        **(1)** Feel for warmth.

        **(2)** Check fuse F1108 in J-40.

        **(3)** Secure cable #4 to Rectifier.

        **(4)** Check tubes V801, V802, V804, V805 and V806.

**4.** SPOT INTENSITY ON ONE TUBE CAN'T BE CHANGED.

    **a.** Secure cable #5 or #6.

**5.** NO SWEEP ON EITHER INDICATOR.

    **a.** Check and secure #34 from Range Unit to Synchronizer.

<u>b</u>.  Check Range Unit.

    (<u>1</u>)  Check unit for power.

        (<u>a</u>)  See if neon lamp is lighted.

        (<u>b</u>)  Feel dust cover for warmth.

        (<u>c</u>)  Check panel fuse.

        (<u>d</u>)  Check fuse F1109 in J-40.

        (<u>e</u>)  Secure cable #33 from Range Unit to J-39.

    (<u>2</u>)  Check sweep output tone at J1602 with a low impedence headset, or (2a.) Set calibrate switch on ALTITUDE position, set CAL-ZERO-NORM switch on Computer to NORM, and rotate altitude knob on Computer to pass 3 and 4 mile settings.  Look for dimming of neon lamp.

        If tone is heard in headset or if neon lamp dims, the Range Unit sweep trigger is all right.

    (<u>3</u>)  Check divider circuit output at J1604 with a low impedence headset, or turn on Transmitter and check for TX current.

        If tone is heard in earphones or TX current is obtained, and there is no sweep output by previous test, check tubes V1612, V1613, and V1614.

    (<u>4</u>)  If no tone is heard in earphones and TX current is not obtained check tubes V1606, V1610, and V1611.

<u>c</u>.  Check Synchronizer.

    (<u>1</u>)  Check power.

        (<u>a</u>)  Feel dust cover for warmth.

        (<u>b</u>)  Check fuse F1108 in J-40.

(c) Secure cable #12.

(2) Check sweep output at J406 or J408 with a low impedance headset.

(3) Ajust intensity for a dim spot on cathode ray tube. Turn GAIN fully CCW and switch on range marks. If spot intensity does not change, check tubes V409, V410, and V411. (If V408 is defective, sweep can still be obtained but the length will be too great.)

(6) NO SWEEP ON OPERATOR'S INDICATOR.

(a) Secure cables #19 and #27.

(b) Check for sweep output tone at J405 with a low impedance headset.

(c) Check tube V415 in Synchronizer.

(7) NO SWEEP ON AUXILIARY INDICATOR.

(a) Secure cables #21 and #28.

(b) Check for sweep output tone at J407 with a low impedance headset.

(c) Check tube V416 in Synchronizer.

(8) SWEEP TRANCE TOO SHORT.

(a) Adjust SWEEP AMPLITUDE on Synchronizer.

(9) SWEEP TRANCE TOO LONG AND IRREGULAR.

(a) Adjust Sweep Amplitude in Synchronizer.

(b) Check tube V408 in Synchronizer.

(10) UNSTEADY OR RIPPLING TRACE, OR RANGE MARKS APPEARING AS A RIPPLING CIRCLE.

(a) Check AC voltage as read on meter attached to set. If it is varying, a slight voltage increase by screw-driver adjustment on R1105 on J-40 may help cure this (Do not change by more than 5 volts).

(b) If variation is too bad, change to 718 Inverter.

(11) FINE SUNBEAMING OF TRACES ON SCOPE.

(a) Fine sunbeaming with AFC ON may be cured by operation with AFC OFF.

(12) BROAD SUNBEAMING OF TRACES ON SCOPE.

(a) Check gain control tube V404 by turning down gain as far as possible and still have noise. If trouble persists, replace V404.

(b) Replace tube V419.

(c) Replace tubes V551, V552, V553, V554, and V555 in that order.

(13) NO RANGE MARKS.

(a) If noise or bomb release circle can be obtained on both scopes, check tubes V406 and V407 in Synchronizer.

(b) If none of the above signals appear, check the video channel, tubes V401, V402, and V403 in Synchronizer and V601 in the Indicator. Note: Change V601 in Indicator only when signals appear on the other Indicator.

(14) NO BOMB RELEASE PIP.

(a) If noise, or range markers cannot be obtained on either scope, check the video tubes V401, V402, and V403 in the Synchronizer, also V601 in the Indicator.

(b) If above signals can be obtained, proceed as follows:

1. Be sure switch on Computer is on.

2. Secure cable #35 between Range Unit and Synchronizer.

3. Check bomb release mark output tone at J1601 on Range Unit with a low impedance headset.

Turn switch on Range Unit to RANGE. Rotating drum of Computer should cause neon lamp to dim at every mile. If no dimming occurs, trouble is in Range

Delay Channel. (Note: If sweep is OK, but lamp doesn't dim on either ALT or RANGE, trouble is probably in V1612, indicator amp.) If no tone or dimming is obtained, check tubes V1601, V1602, and V1603 in Range Unit.

<u>4</u>. Check Synchronizer end of cable #35 with a low impedance headset.

(15) NO SWEEP WHEN RANGE DELAYS ARE SWITCHED IN.

   (a) Check that calibrate switch on Range Unit is set on Normal.

   (b) Check tubes V1610, V1605, V1609 and V1608 in Range Unit.

c. <u>Transmitter</u>.

(1) TRANSMITTER CANNOT BE TURNED ON: NO RELAY CLICKS IN J-40 WHEN TX <u>ON OFF</u> BUTTONS ARE PUSHED.

   (a) Check interlock switch on Modulator.

   (b) Check fuses F1110 and F1111 in J-40.

(2) NO TRANSMITTER CURRENT, RELAY IN J-40 CLICKS WHEN TX <u>ON OFF</u> BUTTONS ARE PUSHED.

   (a) Check F1106 in J-40.

   (b) Use low impedance headphones to check Modulator Trigger pulse tone at Jack J1604 on Range Unit and at Modulator end of cable #16. Sweep on Indicator scopes is evidence that trigger from Range Unit is present.

   (c) Secure cable #17 from Modulator.

   (d) Increase Transtat setting.

(3) TRANSMITTER KICKS OFF.

   (a) With set on 50 mile range, turn Transtat up until transmitter kicks off repeatedly. Then back off Transtat control until transmitter stays on when switching from 50 to 20 mile range and back. (Optimum setting of transtat should be approximately 8 milliamperes.)

d. <u>Beat Oscillators</u>.

(1) NO OSCILLATOR XTAL CURRENT.

    (a) Check position of meter switch.

    (b) Adjust Receiver tuning control.

    (c) Check for repeller voltage (AFC Volts.)

    (d) Check for other XTAL current.

(2) NO RADAR OR BEAC XTAL CURRENT, AFC VOLTS ARE PRESENT.

    (a) Operate Power ON-OFF button several times in case crystal gate relay is stuck.

    (b) Check fuses F1110 and F1111 in J-40 (Crystal Gate Relay).

    (c) Check fuse F1106 in J-40. (AC to RF Unit)

(3) NO AFC VOLTS (ALSO NO XTAL CURRENT).

    (a) Secure cable #1 to Control Box.

    (b) Check Rectifier RA-88.

        <u>1</u>. Rectifier RA-88 not working.

           <u>a</u>. Check for AC power in Rectifier by feeling front panel for warmth or looking for lighted filaments.

           <u>b</u>. Secure cable #4 to Rectifier.

           <u>c</u>. Check fuse F1108 in J-40 (AC to RA-88).

           <u>d</u>. Remove dust cover and check tubes V803, V809, and V810. If tubes are cold, replace them.

(4) NO METER READINGS ON CONTROL BOX.

    (a) Tap meter lightly.

    (b) Meter may be defective, operate without meter.

(5) BEACON XTAL CURRENT BUT NO RADAR XTAL CURRENT.

    (a) AFC-BEAC switch may be defective, try to operate anywa;

    (b) If beacon osc. is set to radar osc. frequency, use BEAC ON.

  (6) XTAL CURRENT TOO HIGH (OVER 1.5 MILS).

    (a) Change oscillator node.

      1. Set RCVR Tune to Mid-Point.

      2. With meter switched to read crystal current, readjust AFC Voltage in counter-clockwise direction until new current maximum is reached. This should e lower than other.

  (7) CRYSTAL CURRENT TOO LOW.

    (a) Check AFC Volts, should be between 140 and 210.

    (b) Turn Power OFF and ON in case crystal gate is not opening completely.

  (8) REPELLER VOLTAGE OVER 210 OR UNDER 140.

    (a) Readjust AFC voltage as in (6) (a) 2 unless this makes XTAL current too high.

e. Signal Channel.

  (1) NO ECHOS ON EITHER SCOPE.

    (a) Check for XTAL current.

    (b) Try AFC ON.

    (c) Try AFC OFF and adjust RCVR TUNE (use 10 mile range).

    (d) If little grass can be obtained (with receiver gain 3/4 CW and rotating RCVR TUNE control slowly):

      1. Check cable #15 to Synchronizer.

      2. Check all IF tubes in Signal Channel. V419, V551, V552, V553, V554, and V555.

  (2) GAIN CONTROL HAS NO EFFECT.

    (a) Check tube V404 in Synchronizer.

(3) NO SIGNALS ON ONE INDICATOR.

    (a) Check cable #18 to Operator's Indicator or cable #20 to Auxiliary Indicator. Use headset.

    (b) Check tube V419 to Indicator.

(4) VERY "NOISY" SCOPE.

    (a) Requires tube change, probably V419, Auxiliary I.F. Amp. in Synchronizer.

(5) TARGETS DISAPPEAR WHEN AFC TURNED ON.

    (a) Check AFC system as follows:

        <u>1</u>. <u>a</u>. Set meter switch on AFC Volts.

            <u>b</u>. Turn RCVR TUNE fully CCW.

            <u>c</u>. Switch AFC ON.

            <u>d</u>. Rotate REC TUN from fully CCW to fully CW and back. AFC Volts should lock in at correct setting and remain locked in through center two thirds of RCVR TUNE control rotation.

            <u>e</u>. If AFC Volts does not lock in, secure cable #41 to Synchronizer.

            <u>f</u>. Check tubes V501, V502, and V503 in Synchronizer.

        <u>2</u>. If AFC Volts change when AFC switch is changed from OFF (with maximum echoes on scope) to ON, changing the setting of the AFC VOLTAGE control, keeping it so that RCVR TUNE control will still tune through a crystal current maximum may restore AFC operation. (WARNING: Do not exceed 210 AFC Volts.)

    (b) Operate with AFC OFF and tune manually.

f. <u>Antenna Rotation and Tilt.</u>

(1) SWEEP DOES NOT ROTATE ON EITHER INDICATOR.

    (a) Check for changes in echo pattern along sweep as indication that Antenna is or is not rotating. If Antenna is not rotating, check as follows:

<u>1</u>. Check 30 amp fuse in Inverter.

<u>2</u>. Check fuse F1113 in J-40.

<u>3</u>. Check CW relay K1105 and CCW K1104 in J-40. Free relays if stuck.

<u>4</u>. Secure cable #2 to Control Box.

(b) Check selsyn system as follows:

<u>1</u>. Check fuse F1102 in J-40.

<u>2</u>. Secure cables #40, #45, #31, #39, #30, #38, #42, and #43 or in other words all cables to Selsyn Phasing Unit, and Torque Amplifier, and cable #31 to Azimuth Control Box.

<u>3</u>. Disconnect cable #39 from Selsyn Phasing Unit, insert special shorting plus, and operate without Torque Amplifier and Selsyn Phasing Unit, (Note: Azimuth Stabilization can't be obtained when the shorting plug is used.)

(2) SWEEP ROTATES ON ONE INDICATOR BUT NOT THE OTHER.

(a) Secure cable #5 or #6 to that Indicator.

(b) Turn power off, remove top cover casting and inspect gears.

<u>1</u>. If idler gear is missing or damaged, the Indicator cannot be used.

<u>2</u>. If selsyn is frozen the Indicator can not be used.

<u>3</u>. If selsyn and gears turn easily proceed as follows:

<u>a</u>. Replace cover, turn on power and rotate Antenna (AZIM STAB OFF) until sweep coils on other Indicator are lined up with the Antenna.

<u>b</u>. Stop the Antenna where the lubber line appears.

<u>c</u>. Turn off the power and connect a jumper wire between terminals 1734 and 1736 in J-39 to short out the phasing switches.

<u>d</u>. Remove the cover casting from the defective Indicator, and without removing the idler gear,

rotate the large gear until mark on fiber cam is aligned with Micro-switch roller. Replace cover casting before turning on power.

   **e.** Since phasing switches are now inoperative, do not turn off power while antenna is rotating, otherwise the Indicators can become out of phase with the Antenna by multiples of 36°.

(3) SWEEP ROTATES BUT CATCHES IN LOWER PORTION OF SCOPE AND LUBBER LINE IS OFF.

   (a) Autosyn Inverter not turned on. (Switch on Flight Engineers panel.)

   (b) Check fuse F1112 in J-40.

   (c) Fluxgate Compass or Azimuth Stabilization Equipment is out. By-pass the azimuth stabilization equipment by disconnecting cable #39 from Selsyn Phasing Unit and attacking by-pass plug to the end of the cable. If no plug is available, disconnect cable #39 and install jumpers in J-39 between terminals 1737 and 1741, 1738 and 1842, 1739 and 1743.

   (d) Indicators and Antenna not properly aligned. Proceed as in (c) above and turn Azimuth Stabilization on. Note the reading of the lubber line and correct all readings by this amount. Operate in the above manner until mechanic can re-align the selsyn system.

(4) PHASING SWITCHES OUT OF ORDER, SWEEPS ON SCOPES OUT OF PHASE BY MULTIPLES OF 36 DEGREES. PROCEED AS FOLLOWS:

   (a) Turn off all power and connect a jumper wire between terminals 1734 and 1736 in J-39 to short out phasing switches.

   (b) Turn on power.

   (c) Stop antenna where lubber line appears. Note the degrees between the sweep and top of the Scope.

   (d) Disconnect cable #39 from Selsyn Phasing Unit.

   (e) Push Power OFF button and remove front cover casting from the Indicator or Indicators in which the sweep does not appear at the top.

(f)   Rotate the large ring gear 4/9ths of a tooth per degree required to place sweep at zero position.

(g)   Replace Indicator cover.

(h)   Reconnect cable #39 to Selsyn Phasing Unit and turn on power.

(i)   Since phasing switches are now inoperative, do not turn off power while Antenna is rotating, otherwise steps (c) through (h) will have to be repeated.

(5)   NO SECTOR SCAN.

(a)   Check fuse F1112 in J-40.

(b)   If click of relay can be heard in Azimuth Control Box check operation of relays K1105 and K11-5 in J-40. Turn off power and free relays if stuck.

(6)   NO LUBBER LINE.

(a)   Turn off "Continuous" and turn on Sector Scan. If Sector Scan is not obtained, check fuse F1112 in J-40.

(b)   If sweep blanks out entirely on Sector Scan, blanking relay in Synchronizer should be checked. It may be possible to listen for its clicking without removing dust cover. Otherwise turn off power, remove cover, and free relay if stuck.

(7)   LUBBER LINE NOT 0°.

(a)   This adjustment can be made only on ground. Take error into account when reading bearings.

(8)   AZIMUTH STABILIZATION INOPERATIVE.

(a)   Check that flux gate compass inverter is turned on (Flight Engineers position).

(b)   If Torque Amplifier case isn't warm, check fuse F1112 in J-40.

(c)   Secure all cables to Torque Amplifier, Selsyn Phasing Unit, Junction Box J-38/APQ-13, and Azimuth Control Box.

(d)   Operate without azimuth stabilization by screwing shorting plug on end of cable #39.

(9) TILT METER DOES NOT MOVE WHEN SET IS TURNED ON.

    (a) If antenna won't rotate, check fuse F1113 in J-40.

    (b) If scope pattern changes when tilt switch is raised or lowered, operate without defective meter.

(10) TILT METER JUMPS WHEN SET IS TURNED ON, BUT SHOWS NO INDICATION OF TILT MOVEMENT.

(11) RANGE INDICATOR LIGHTS.

    (a) If Indicator lights do not work, check fuses F1110 and F1111 in J-40.

## B   SCOPE INTERPRETATION

Scope interpretation is one of the most important jobs of the Radar Observer and Navigator. Regardless of how well the Radar Operator can operate his set, or how well he knows the Bombing Procedure, if he and the Navigator cannot orient themselves with what they see on the Scope, the mission will be futile.

In order to make a mission successful, many hours of intensive study must be made of charts, maps, target folders, and PPI Scope Pictures of the route to the target and the target area.

1. Factors affecting a Scope Picture.

There are many factors which affect a scope picture. Some of those are terrain features and others are characteristics of the Radar Set.

    a. Terrain and Man-made Features.

        First, what are some of the factors of terrain that affect returns on the Scope? Lakes, harbors, rivers, or other water features will show dark on the scope with shore lines clearly outlined. Air ports or level areas free of structures within cities will show dark or medium dark on high gain, and black on low gain settings. Railroad terminals, marshalling yards, with busy tracks and standand cars, round houses, shops, etc., will cause very bright return from nearly any approach. Large factories, industrial concentrations, airport hangers, and buildings will cause bright returns and be especially reliable if they are isolated, i.e. situated in poorly built-up areas or residential suburbs.

b. Clouds and Islands.

Clouds and Islands can give similiar returns, but by use of tilt
and studying outline of return, they can be distinguished.
Clouds usually have fine, misty, soft edges, while Island edges
are more pronounced. By raising the tilt setting, Islands will
disappear while clouds will remain. Another good way to avoid
false identification is to know location of aircraft at all times.

c. Operational Characteristics.

Now, what affect does the Radar Set have on Scope Pictures? Every
Radar set is slightly different, and what works on one may not
work on another, but certain general characteristics are true
of all Radar Sets. These characteristics affect: Tilt setting,
gain adjustment, brilliance adjustment and focus of trace line.
Tilt, gain, and brilliance vary with different ranges. The closer
the target becomes to the aircraft's position, the lower the tilt
setting, and the less the gain. Particularly is this true on the
bombing run. With Sector Scan on and the target blown up with the
20-mile variable sweep knob, better tilt and gain adjustments can
be made.

Targets within an industrial area can be brought out very distinct-
ly if proper orientation is maintained and gain reduced as the target is expanded in size.

d. Inherent Characteristics.

There are some inherent characteristics of the Radar Sets. These
are azimuth, fussiness, and range fussiness due to the radar beam
width and radar pulse length respectively.

e. Radar Beam Width.

The effective beam width of the Radar Set is between $2^o$ and $3^o$,
measured in the slant plane. Consequently a point is spread into an arc on the Scope. The arcs representing adjacent targets
smear into one another if they are too close together, and two
targets appear to be one. For example: At a slant range of
40,000 feet, two reflecting details must be 1,700 feet apart in
azimuth direction if they are to be resolved.

f. Radar Pulse Length.

As the image of a point reflector is spread in Azimuth by the
width of the beam, so is it spread in range by the length of
time that the transmitter stays on in sending out the pulse.

At the beginning of the cycle, the transmitter is turned on and radiation begins going out, some of which travels towards the point reflector shown. Meanwhile the electron beam starts traveling across the scope. At a time, depending upon the range of the reflector, the first radiation sent out by the transmitter reaches the spinner. It intensifies the electron beam, which paints a bright spot on the scope at a distance from the center corresponding to the range to the reflector. Since the electron beam continues traveling out on the scope, the spot stays bright due to the reception of reflections of later portions of the transmitted radiation. The lines representing radically adjacent targets smear into one another if they are too close together and the two targets appear to be one. The transmitted pulse has a duration of about 0.5 microseconds. In this length of time, a radio wave travels 500 feet and since a round trip is involved for the radio wave, two points targets will be smeared together radically on the scope if their slant range differs by less than 250 ft. due to Radar Pulse Length alone. If the sighting angle is 30°, the points must be 500 feet apart along the ground if the Radar is to be capable of resolving them.

g. Size of Spot on Scope.

There is also another characteristic of the Scope Picture which is Fussiness due to the size of spot on the scope. Even if the Radar Beam were infinitely narrow and the pulse infinitely short, a point target would not have a point image on the scope. This is due to the fact that the electron beam which paints the picture is not infinitely small in diameter. Actually, the effective spot is about 1/30 inch in diameter. Thus, two points separated by less than 1/30 inch on the face of the scope would merge into one image due to scope spot size alone.

2. General Conclusion.

Thus, with these inherent errors in the Radar Set, the importance of proper set tuning, use of brilliance, tilt and gain, as well as constant scope and target study cannot be overemphasized. Remember to always have the trace line on the scope as thin and fine as possible for better target responses.

Contact Radar Intelligence frequently for material on Scope Photographs, Targets, Target Areas, and different approaches to the target areas. Actually plot the position of the airplane on a chart from these Scope Photographs and identify all important returns. Invaluable knowledge can be gained through this plotting and study for future missions. KNOW YOUR TARGET WELL!

## C   RADAR NAVIGATION

From a navigation viewpoint, the APQ-13 Radar Set is essentially a fixing device.  Its worth in the solution of navigation problems is exactly as good as the accuracy of the fixes which the Radar Observer obtains
with it.  This is true whether the Radar Observer is using Radar to determine the wind, to stay on course, or to make good a briefed axis of
attack.  Then the inaccuracies in obtaining fixes are effectually eliminated, the Radar Observer's results in Radar navigation are as go 1
as his ability to use his computers and plotting equipment.  A knowledge of the technique of measuring range and bearing with the Radar
equipment is accordingly required of every Radar Observer.

1.  Bearings.

Measuring bearings of returns on the Radar Scope seems at first so simple
that it requires no discussion.  It is, however, the largest source of
error in taking Radar fixes.  First of all, since the track line used in
measuring bearings is placed on a glass nearly $\frac{1}{4}$ inch in front of the
face of the screen upon which the return lies, the line of the observers
sight must be perpendicular to the plane of the scope glass through the
return the bearing of which is being measured.  The use of an unbent and
untwisted scope visor will usually prevent any error to a poor line of
sight.  To measure accurate bearings, the trace must be centered on the
scope.  Good centering controls are provided and should be used.  Errors
due to poor centering are at a minimum in measuring bearings of returns
nearest the outer edge of the scope.  When it is possible, and it usually
is with the 20-mile variable range, the return used in obtaining a fix
should be placed near the edge of the scope as soon as orientation is
accomplished.  The errors due to an uncentered sweep are shown below for
a case in which the return is near the center of the scope and a case
in which the same return has been moved to the outer edge of the scope.

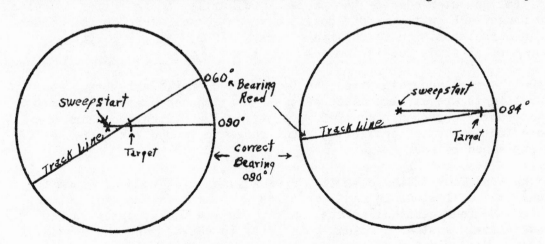

READING BEARINGS ON SCOPE RETURN

FIGURE   I

Each return presented on the Radar Scope has a minimum arc width of three degrees due to the three degree width of the transmitted Radar Beam. The center of a small return may be used in measuring its bearing, but care should be used in measuring the bearings of the ends of returns, i.e. a peninsula, end of a bridge, such a return is elongated 1½ degrees on each end and the bearing line should be placed on the return 1½ degrees away from the end.

It is important that the navigator knows at all times whether the Set is being operated with Azimuth stabilization on or Azimuth stabilization off. The heading line should be checked for Zero with stabilization off, and compared with the Master Indicator of the fluxgate compass with stabilization on. If stabilization is off and bearings are taken, remember that true bearing equals relative bearing as read on azimuth ring plus true heading.

2. Distances.

Compared with taking bearings, the measurement of distances with Radar is at once more complex and more accurate. Except in one special case, quadruple drift which is discussed later in the bombing section, the inscribed lines on the scope glass are never to be used in measuring distances. One mile and five mile range marks are available in addition to the bombing circle and sweep delay.

When the range is in excess of fifteen miles, the limit of the bombing circle measurements without the use of sweep delay, it is usually more practical to use the range marks for measuring distances. In counting range marks to a target. count from the center out, being careful not to miss any marks lost in the ground return. The use of the 20-mile variable control and the possibility of an error in the range adjustment setting on other ranges, makes it impractical to count range marks in from the outer edge of the scope. Ordinarily, it is better to switch the range mark switch to off position when the Cal. Zero-Normal Switch is in normal position as the range marks are then in error by the amount of altitude set in the computer box.

Since the most accurate fixes can be obtained on a nearby point and most flights are at high altitudes, it is often necessary to convert slant range to ground range before plotting the fix on the chart. A convenient method of converting slant range to ground range on the E6B is explained below:

On the wind face of the computer, draw a line down from the Grommet equal to the altitude in nautical miles x 10 with the heading set on one of the four cardinal points (NSEW). Rotate the computer 90 degrees wherein another cardinal point will be shown under the heading marker. Read slant range x 10 on the ground speed scale. Read ground speed x 10 range at the Grommet, and sighting angle as 90 minus the drift angle shown.

3. Radar Winds.

The system of Air Plot is probably the most accurate method of determining a wind. Using Air Plot, the data is obtained over a longer period of time and a small error in time will not enter a large error in ground speed. However, because of the short time between the time the first fix is obtained from the Japanese Mainland and the time the wind must be known for the bomb run, it is well to be able to use a shorter method. The best of the shorter methods involves the measurement of a bearing and distance on one point as it crosses each of several range marks. It is described and illustrated in the Radar Navigation Procedures Section.

4. Allowance for Turn.

   a. Allowance for turn is the distance measured perpendicular to the axis of attack at which turn must be begun to place the airplane on the axis of attack when the turn has been completed. It is to be remembered that allowance for turn used properly enables the Radar Observer to start the bomb run on the correct axis of attack, but it does not insure that the plane will pass over the I.P. Since the policy is to pass over the IP on course to the target, the turn must be begun to the left of the IP for right turns and to the right of the IP for left turns. The amount to the left or right of the IP will be computed for each mission with a margin for error; this is a separate problem. The following discussion deals with allowance for turn.

   b. The allowance for turn will usually be computed by the staff navigator before the mission. As long as the wind is approximately as briefed and the approach to the IP is made as planned, the computed allowance for turn should be used. A convenient method of fixing the point to begin turn by radar once the allowance is known is given in steps as follows:

      (1) Radar Operator should select a range which will include the target and/or IP when the plane is at least ten miles back from the IP.

      (2) With azimuth stabilization off, place the center drift line off zero in the direction of turn a number of degrees equal to the difference between the axis of attack and the true heading of the airplane as it approaches the turn.

      (3) Draw a line with a grease pencil above and parallel to the center grid line so that the perpendicular distance between the center grid line and the grease mark is equal to the

allowance for turn. The range of the scope sets the scale for this distance, and the range used while drawing the line should appear under the center drift line when the turn has been completed.

c.  It is practical to compute the allowance for turn on the E6B. The steps of this computation are as follows:

(1)  Find circumference of turn by multiplying T.A.S. by time in turn. (For $\frac{1}{4}$ needlewidth turns the time is 8 minutes, i.e. T.A.S. = 280. Turn, $\frac{1}{4}$ needlewidth, or 8 minutes. Circumference of turn is 37.3.)

(2)  Find radius of turn by dividing circumference of turn by 2 π, (6.28). Place 6.28 on the inner scale under cir-cumference of turn on outer scale of E6B. Read radius of turn on the outer scale opposite (10) on the inner scale, i.e. 37.3 ÷ 6.28 = 6 N.M.

(3)  For a 90° turn into an upwind or downwind run, the allow-ance for turn is exactly equal to the radius of turn. For a 60° turn, the allowance is equal to $\frac{1}{2}$ the radius, from which it can be seen that the allowance is not proportion-al to the number of degrees. Actually the relationship for turns less than 90° is: Allowance = radius - radius x cos Θ. For turns greater than 90°, relationship is: radius plus radius x cos (180 - turn angle). This can be approximately solved conveniently on the E6B computer as follows: Place the grommet down the square grid, radius of turn distance and mark the top center of the grid. Turn the azimuth ring to the number of degrees of turn and read turn allowance down from the top of the grid. As long as the axis of attack is downwind or upwind this is a satisfactory answer.

(4)  Allowance for turn may also be worked on E6B computer for a $7\frac{1}{2}$° or 10° bank.

5.  Limitations of Radar Navigation.

Radar is a good aid to navigation; it supplements, but does not replace any other means of navigation. The theoretical limits of the ranges are set by their respective pulse recurrence frequencies and the Radar Horizon. Experience in this theatre with the APQ-13 has indicated that the navigator cannot rely on a Radar sighting of the islands, includ-ing that of his home base, at a range any greater than forty miles even though there have been many instances in which that range was exceeded.

Radar resolution of land areas is considerably limited and the well known need for good dead reckoning in visual pilotage is even more apparent in Radar pilotage. Radar fixes should be logged and classified; it may be that the point from which the fix was taken was not correctly located on the chart, and a fix marked as doubtful will be more quickly disregarded if it is in error.

6. Radar "WIND RUN" Procedures.

    a. As soon as landfall is made, the radar observer will:

        (1) Request pilot to hold steady course for wind run.
        (2) Select some sharp point on radar scope as early as possible.
        (3) Turn on range marks.
        (4) Measure exact time it first touches range marker, start stop watch and measure relative bearing.
        (5) Repeat time, bearing, and range reading every couple of minutes as point touches successive range markers.
        (6) After 5 to 10 minutes run, at time point touches range marker take reading and stop the stop watch.
        (7) Plot all positions on chart and lay average track thru them.
        (8) Lay off T.H. on chart.
        (9) Measure distance travelled between first and last positions.
      (10) Using elapsed time from stop watch, compute G.S. on E6B.
      (11) Divide T.A.S. and measured G.S. by 3 and plot wind vector on E6B.
      (12) Extend track line by D.R. and use wind on E6B to determine turns and heading to control point and IP.

    b. Explanatory "WIND RUN" Problem:

        (1) Approaching point on Japanese coast:
            Indicated Air Speed...................................195 m.p.h.
            Pressure Altitude....................................25,000 ft.
            Temp. Reading (-22°) Corrected Temp. ...............-30°C
            True Heading.........................................335°
            T.A.S. (Using G-1 Computer).........................257 Knots.

        (2) Following ranges and bearings were measured using range markers:

| TIME | REL BRG. | + | T.H. = | TRUE BRG. | SLANT DISTANCE |
|------|----------|---|--------|-----------|----------------|
| 1300 | 018° | | 335° | 353° | 45' |
| 1302 | 016° | | 335° | 351° | 35' |
| 1304 | 012° | | 335° | 347° | 25' |
| 1305½ | 010° | | 335° | 345° | 20' |

(3) Plot the ranges and bearings for positions on Navigation
Chart:
Read Track on Chart....................................359°
Measure distance travelled on Chart.................25½ N.M.
Stop Watch Time.....................................5' 28"
Ground Speed on E6B (25.5 n.m. in 5' 25")..........278 Knots.

(4) Get wind on E6B by dividing vectors by 3:
TAS/3     - 256/3..................................85.7
GS/3      - 278/3..................................92.7
Drift.............................................24° R.
True Heading......................................335°
Wind Direction....................................246°
Wind Vector.......................................38
Wind Vector x 3 to get wind velocity..............114 Knots.
Wind..............................................246/114 Knots.

c. Allowance for Turn Procedures.

(1) Course should be set to a point well to the left of the IP
for a right turn onto the target and to the right of the
IP for a left turn onto the target.

(2) Azimuth stabilization should be off as the IP turn is ap-
proached.

(3) The track line should be set off zero in the direction of
a turn, a number od degrees equal to the difference between the axis of attack and the true heading of the airplane.

(4) Draw a line above and parallel to the track line so that
the perpendicular distance between the line drawn and the
track line is equal to the allowance for turn.

(5) Begin the turn when the IP and/or target is under the
line drawn following the instructions above. The number
of degrees of turn is equal to the difference between
true heading and the true heading on the bomb run measured
in the direction of turn.

(6) While turn is being made, move the track line to the predicted drift setting. If allowance for turn has been correctly made, the target will be under the track line when
the airplane rolls out of the turn.

## D   RADAR BOMBING

The importance of Radar as an aid to visual bombing, and the usefulness
of the bombsight rate mechanism in solving for the correct release point
in Radar Bombing has caused the development of a combined Radar-Bombsight method which is now standard throughout the USAAF. A year's use
of the method has shown valuable versatility and good bombing results.
Since it has been found advisable to make all approaches so that this
method may be used, the terms "Radar-Bombsight Method" and "H2X Syn-
chronous Bombing" have been replaced by the term "Standard Bombing Procedure". .

### 1.   Course.

The first step in bombing is to set up a collision course to the target.
If the predetermined wind is correct and the allowance for turn has been
correctly made, the airplane will roll out of the turn onto the bombing
run on a collision course to the target. This will rarely be the case,
although the more accurately the turn is made and the wind computed, the
more easily collision course is established and the smaller the difference between actual and briefed axis of attack. Until actual drift on
the run can be determined it is advisable to fly a heading which allows
for the predicted drift. Therefore, the first step after the turn is
to correct the heading of the airplane until the target lies under the
track line set on predicted drift. If the preset drift is correct, the
target will remain under the track line. However, the preset drift is
seldom exactly correct and steps must be taken to correct the drift
setting and the airplane heading. A method has been found which has
materially lessened the deflection errors in Combat Radar Bombing.
This method is known as the quadruple drift method and is based on the
off-course correction method, the principle of which is as follows:
To make good a course to a target, the course correction needed is equal
to the change in bearing of the target divided by the fraction of the
total distance to the target traveled while measuring the change in bearing. For example, if the fraction of the distance traveled is $\frac{1}{4}$ the
total original distance and the change in bearing is 2°, the correction
is 2 divided by $\frac{1}{4}$ or 8°. The airplane is considered to have traveled
$\frac{1}{4}$ the distance to the target when the target has moved from a position
under the fourth inscribed line on the scope glass to a position under
the third inscribed line. Altitude hole must be IN (Cal. Zero-Normal
Switch in Cal. Zero Position) for this measurement. Use of the inscribed lines permits measurement of the change in bearing to begin at any
time the target can be placed under the fourth circle using the various
ranges, or the 20-mile variable range. For convenience, the target is
usually placed just outside the fourth circle and its bearing accurately
measured as it comes under the fourth and third circles. The airplane's
heading is corrected in the direction of the change in bearing an amount
equal to four times the change in bearing plus one degree for each five
degrees of the product. This last addition to the correction is made

to compensate for the time lost in correcting the heading. A constant heading must be held during the time the target is moving from the fourth circle to the third circle.

Small corrections in the Plane's heading should be made to keep the target under the track line or to place a more exactly located aiming point under the track line. Always correct in the direction the target lies from the track line. If the Bombardier takes over the run visually, he will so advise the crew in order that the Radar Observer will not continue to give the pilot course corrections. The Radar Observer will follow the target with his track line and be prepared to take back the run at any time. Good course corrections can be made without reference to the range of the target. The guiding principle in this method is that the heading must be changed more than the number of degrees the target has moved off the track line. This will make it necessary to move the track line in the direction opposite to that of the correction given. If the track line is placed on the target immediately after each correction and corrections are made as soon as it is noticed that collision course is not established, accurate collision course can be set up quickly.

2.  Rate and displacement.

When collision course to the target has been established, there remains the problem of determining the exact time the airplane is at the correct point of release. If altitude is known, the exact location of the airplane at any instant on the collision course can be defined by stating the angle between the true vertical and the line of sight to the target or by stating the distance along the line of sight to the target. This angle is the sighting angle and the distance is termed slant range. If one is known the other can readily be found by the equation:

$$\text{Cosine of sighting angle} = \frac{\text{Altitude}}{\text{Slant Range}}$$

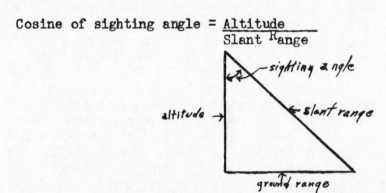

TRIGONOMETRIC RELATIONSHIP OF BOMBING FUNCTIONS

FIGURE II

The dropping angle is simply the sighting angle to the target measured from the correct point of release. Dropping slant range is simply the slant range measured from the correct point of release to the target. The point of correct release along the collision course depends upon wind ground speed, altitude, and type of bomb. If ground speed is known, the dropping slant range to be set in the Radar Set and the dropping angle to be set in the bombsight can be precomputed. If the bombsight is inoperative on a combat mission, the bombs can then be dropped on the dropping slant range. While altitude and type of bomb are accurately known before the run, ground speed usually is not. It is possible for the bombsight to determine the ground speed on the run by synchronization. The bombsight is designed in such a way that when data determined from the altitude, true airspeed and type of bomb is set into the sight, synchronization automatically sets up the correct value of dropping angle. Synchronization amounts to adjusting the speed of drive of the bombsight telescope so that the line of sight continually remains on the target, once the line of sight is displaced there. If the bombsight has been synchronized and the line of sight once placed on the target, the telescope indicator will read the correct sighting angle to the target for all positions on the collision course when the airplane reaches these positions on the collision course. The bombs are automatically released when the sighting angle reaches the dropping angle.

If the Radar Bombing circle is set at a slant range equivalent to a sighting angle and the telescope is set at that angle when the target is on the bombing circle, the cross hairs of the bombsight will be on the target at the instant of setting. If the telescope is being driven at the correct rate, it will remain pointed at the target, and will, therefore, always be at a sighting angle equivalent to the slant range to the target. After once setting the sighting angle, the rate of drive of the telescope can be checked by comparing the slant range to the target and the sighting angle shown on the telescope indicator. For convenience setting points of 70° and 68° and checking points at each five degrees (65, 60, etc.) thereafter, have been established. It is necessary at each checking point to re-aim the telescope by placing it exactly on the sighting angle indicated by the slant range. Each check point then, is also a setting point. Resetting the angle must be done at the instant the target is at the slant range equaivalent to the sighting angle set, as it is only at that instant that the sighting angle is correctly known. Errors in the rate are indicated by the difference between the sighting angle announced from slant range measurement and the sighting angle read on the telescope before re-setting. The Bombardier should correct the rate immediately after setting the telescope on the correct sighting angle. The Rate Knob is always turned in the same direction the displacement knob was turned to move the telescope from it erroneous position to the correct sighting angle.

It has been found convenient to place lines for each of several sighting angles on the computer chart. This enables the Radar Operator to set the bombing circle for the slant range to correspond to those sighting angles by simply setting the altitude bar to the correct altitude of the plane above the target and turning the computer drum until the sighting angle line desired is under the cross hairs. The altitude bar setting should be made by reference to the chart itself, not by reference to the altitude delay scale on the computer. The altitude bar serves only as aid in reading the graph. Since the relationship between slant range and sighting angle depends upon the altitude, the Radar Operator must know the true altitude above the target at all times if the sighting angles given the bombardier are to be correct.

3. Set Operation on Bomb Run.

The radar set should be very carefully handled during the bombing run. Correct settings for gain, tilt, and expansion, are much more easily made if sector scan is used. This allows the operator to check any adjustments he makes due to the increased number of times per minute the picture is painted on the screen. Settings for identifying parts of cities are different from those which clearly indicate parts of coastlines. It is usually best to keep tilt as high as possible to differentiate built-up areas. The operator must be careful not to lose the target at a critical point in the bombing procedure. The target should be kept well away from the center of the scope using the 20-mile variable control. To make smaller ranges more usable the altitude hole should be switched out just before rate synchronization is begun.

4. Verstility.

The method of setting sighting angles by slant range is extremely versatile. If the bombardier can see the ground anywhere short of the target, he can synchronize for rate visually and displace his telescope to the target by setting it at a sighting angle called by the Radar Observer. This would cause the bombs to be dropped on a visual rate and a Radar displacement setting. The bombardier may read drift in a case such as this, but he should not attempt to set course to the target unless he can see the target or reference points which will indicate the location of the target. Normally the rate can be adjusted at each sighting angle called after the first clutch-in, but if the rate seems to be abnormally in error the bombardier can make a displacement correction only until another sighting angle is called when he will be able to again check the rate. If the Radar observer relocates the aiming point at any time after clutch-in, he should tell the bombardier to make a displacement correction only in order that the bombardier will not think the difference between the sighting angle he reads and the sighting angle is due to an error in rate.

E   RADAR OPERATORS STANDARD BOMBING PROCEDURE

1.  High Altitude Procedure:

    a.  The following things must be accomplished before the turn at the
        IP:

        (1)  Wind computed and the results given the bombardier.

        (2)  Drift and ground speed on bomb run computed and results
             check with the navigator and/or bombardier.

        (3)  Allowance for turn computed and drawn on scope.

        (4)  Track line offset from zero in the direction of turn a num-
             ber of degrees equal to the difference between the axis of
             attack and true heading of the aircraft as it approaches the
             turn.

        (5)  Pilot advised of number of degrees of turn.

        (6)  I.P. and/or target identified on scope.

        (7).  Following set adjustments made:

            (a)  Bombing circle switch "ON".

            (b)  Range marks "OFF".

            (c)  Range selected which will include the target.

            (d)  Altitude given by bombardier set in.

            (e)  Scope checked for centering.

            (f)  Sector scan checked, correctly positioned, and the
                 switched off.

            (g)  Altitude hole "IN".

            (h)  Heading line checked for "ZERO".

            (i)  Computer drum turned until clutch-in sighting angle
                 line is under center of altitude bar.

        (8)  Duties on bomb run reviewed.

b.  Steps on the bomb run:

(1)  While still in turn over IP, set track line on anticipated drift.

(2)  If, when pilot gives "on course", target is not on track line set on predicted drift, give pilot the correction necessary to place it so.  (This correction, as is the case for all turn corrections is in the direction the target lies from the track line.)

(3)  Set track line exactly on target and turn on sector scan.

(4)  Keep target under track line by overcorrecting for any amount it drifts off and placing track line back on target after each correction.  Make corrections as soon as it is apparent that they are needed.

(5)  An alternate method of making most of the corrections needed is the off course correction or quadruple drift solution. It can be employed as follows:

(a)  Using the various ranges or the 20-mile variable knob, place the target just beyond the fourth circle on the scope glass.  Read the bearing of the target as it comes under the fourth and third circles of the scope glass.  Make no course corrections or changes in range during the time the target is between the two circles. Correct the airplanes heading, in the direction of the change in bearing, an amount equal to four times the change in bearing plus one degree for each five degrees of turn.  This correction may be made using the forty and thirty mile range marks instead of the prescribed lines.

(6)  When the target nears the bombing circle, warn the bombardier that "clutch in" point is approaching.

(7)  When bombing circle (70° sighting angle) is coincident with target, call:  "Ready" .... "Mark".

(8)  Immediately after "Mark" turn the computer drum until the next sighting angle line is under the center of the altitude bar and announce the sighting angle by saying:  "Coming up on 68 degrees".

(9)  Again call:  "Ready" ...."Mark", when target is coincident with bombing circle.

(10) If aiming point is relocated during synchronization, advise bombardier that his next adjustment is to be for displacement only.

(11) Make small corrections in course if necessary during synchronization.

2. Low Altitude:

The method of employing radar at altitudes between 5,000 and 10,000 feet varies with each target and approach. Several of the methods used or considered by units of this command are given for your study. Their principles should be understood in order that the method given at briefing can be used correctly

  a. Methods.

    (1) Direct. The direct methods, which can be used only when the target can be identified on the scope, are the most simple and the most accurate. Types are as follows:

      (a) Synchronous. This method is exactly similiar to the standard bombing procedure except that a slant range - sighting angle table must be used. As soon as the bombing altitude is determined, slant ranges for the sighting angles to be used should be written down for ready reference during the bombing run. Dropping slant range should also be written in the event of failure of synchronization.

      (b) Non-synchronous, using the bombsight. This method uses the same procedure as (a) above except that no attempt is made by the bombardier to refine rate. The bombardier should be careful to set the sighting angle accurately near the dropping angle.

      (c) Direct without the bombsight. In this method, bombs are dropped on dropping slant range converted from the bombardiers dropping angle. This is a practical easy method. The error in rate, which this method does not attempt to eliminate, is of no great consequence in bombing from a low altitude.

    (2) Off-set.

      (a) Timing along a heading from a OAP. A certain heading is taken up 3 miles before reaching the offset aiming point. The turn at this point must be small. The IP, OAP, and target are usually on a common line to minimize the deflection error. In this method, any error in ground speed computation operated throughout the timing period and the actual time of fall of the bombs will not materially effect the range error if the timing period is not too great.

(b) Back slant range to the OAP. This method limits the time that ground speed computation errors are effective to the actual time of fall of the bombs.

(c) Use of Off-Set to identify a target return. By flying a definite heading toward the target and knowing the slant range distance from an OAP, it is usually possible to identify target returns by their location on the scope in relation to the OAP radar return. If the target return is not identified, the release can be made at correct back slant range.

COMBAT NAVIGATION

## VI COMBAT NAVIGATION

### A INTRODUCTION TO COMBAT NAVIGATION

The requirement for first class navigation is extremely important in a Very Long Range bomber. The fundamental problem of getting to the target and back to base as prescribed in the field order is a long ardous, and difficult one in VLR airplanes and it is further complicated in Pacific operations by difficult weather conditions, long over water flights, and few aids to navigation. The most important phase of navigation develops from tactical operations, and you can't afford to be satisfied with mediocre results or efforts. You have to be right the first time. The necessary combat and flying odds against a successful mission are sufficient without adding further uncertainty from equipment trouble and lack of knowledge, technique, and cooperation.

1. Crew Coordination.

Navigation to the target and back will require the cooperation of all your crew members. The degree of cooperation you obtain will have a direct result on the quality of your navigation.

a. Navigator - Pilot. Navigator-pilot cooperation is absolutely essential. Decisions should be mutual and completely in accord with the pilot's and your estimation of a situation. A pilot should have unquestioned confidence in his navigator's decisions and you should, through competence and diligence, deserve this confidence. You should teach your pilot how hard it is to take a shot in an unsteady airplane, how important it is to fly a good course, and how important it is to fly climbs and let-downs according to plan and on the C-1 autopilot.

b. Navigator - Bombardier. You can expect pilotage information, drift checks, ground speed, and wind direction and velocity from the bombardier. You can provide the bombardier with ground speed, wind direction and velocity, and aid him in target identification. You will attend target study classes with your bombardier and you both should memorize the details of the enemy coast line and target areas.

c. Navigator - Radio Operator. From the radio operator you can obtain QTE's, QTF's, QUJ's; and from the radio compass you can get relative and true bearings. The radio operator picks up sundry information by listening. You will give the radio operator times at which necessary reports must be made.

d. Navigator - Radar Operator. The radar operator can give you ground speed, wind direction and velocity, coastline landfalls, drift checks and fixes according to azimuth and ground range. It will be your responsibility to inform the radar operator of possible targets and their general bearing and distance from your course.

e. Navigator - Flight Engineer. You and the flight engineer are the two people who intregrate the two important factors of: "How much gas have we?" and "How far do we have to go?" A fuel consumption expert remarked on B-29 navigators, "Analysis of flight logs to date shows that increased navigation proficiency will do much to reduce the variation in fuel consumption among airplanes on the same mission. This is a very lucrative source for improvement in overall efficiency and every possible means should be used to impress the navigator with the effect his errors have on the fuel consumed."

In the first raids on Japan some of the navigators were very impressed with the effect their errors had on the fuel consumed: They will not forget how close they came to not getting back! Work with your flight engineer and learn the gas problem.

f. Navigator - Gunners. You will find that your gunners will be interested to learn more about navigation. They can give you a great deal of help sighting islands along the route and reporting intelligence information necessary for interrogation reports. It will be your job to alert them in areas of possible fighter contact and times for test firing guns.

2. Standard Navigation Procedures.

The procedures set forth here apply to lead and wing navigators alike. Distinction between lead and wing navigators is essentially one of responsibility. The lead navigator is responsible for getting the formation to the target and back as directed in the field order. Wing navigators, though handicapped by the difficulties encountered while navigating on a wing, accomplish the same navigation that the lead navigator accomplishes. The only difference in navigation is one of method. Wing navigators do DR based on follow-the-pilot procedures, but they must be always ready to assume leadership of the formation.

a. Flight Plan and Mission Preparation. It is absolutely necessary to have at hand before a mission as many answers as possible concerning the proposed flight. When first hand information is limited, a flight plan properly followed provides a good general basis on which to make decisions. You are required to make a flight plan for each mission.

The first consideration of the navigator, after the field order for a mission has been published, is to analyze the order and ascertain what types of navigation and which of his navigation facilities he is able to use to best advantage under the particular conditions set forth in the field order. In most cases this planning will be done by the group navigator, but in order to put it into effect each navigator must understand it thoroughly. He must know the route to the target and all the check points enroute. He must be prepared to use the sun to best advantage during a day mission. He must therefore know when good speed or course lines are available to him and when the sun will be at meridianal altitude. He must study the coast line or territory surrounding his target so that he can orient himself immediately. At night his knowledge of the stars should enable him to shoot three star fixes without hesitation; and he should be able to coordinate at all times his Loran, radio and radar facilities with his other information to give him the best possible knowledge of his position.

The navigator's mission folder contains all the data for the mission: the flight plan, charts, weather data, radar bombing data, emergency procedures, position reporting procedure, maps showing Japanese held and unfortified islands, and all pertinent communication data. After this data has been thoroughly checked and assembled so that it is available instantly when needed, the next step is to prepare the charts, plot courses, radio aids, emergency landing fields, and important intelligence data, especially rescue data, on the master chart.

b. Log book. Since the log is the principle record of the airplane's movements on any particular mission, it is absolutely essential that it be a complete and readable record which can be interpreted at a glance by anyone qualified to navigate an airplane. If such a log is kept, any person on board the airplane who has more than a smattering of Dead Reckoning can carry on the navigation and have a reasonable chance to save the crew and plane in case the navigator is injured.

A standardized log procedure has been adopted which will be the SOP for the entire Bomber Command. It calls for an entry in the log every fifteen minutes of the flight, plus an entry of all important check points, turning points, control points, and the bombing run. Every hour, the entry will be complete from Position to ETA, including Air Position and wind. These will also be plotted on the chart. Every half-hour the entry will be complete from Position through to ETA. Every quarter-hour the following items will be entered: Compass heading, calibrated air speed, altitude and temperature. With practice a navigator should be able to record an average compass heading and air speed reading every fifteen minutes by constant watchfulness even though there are slight variations on these instruments between entries.

Another function of the log is to provide the information required by the interrogation officer. Therefore, every important happening during the entire mission must be entered on the log. This includes take-off time, landing time, time and position of assembly, time and position at rendezvous or control points, time and position at I.P., aircraft, or surface craft, record of enemy formations, types of attack, damage sustained and a record of the I.F.F. on and off.

3. Weather Study.

Your knowledge of weather conditions, reactions and trends influences every navigational decision you make. Be sure you know and understand navigation weather so you can evaluate and use the various methods of navigation accurately. The "metro" section usually provides good winds aloft and enroute weather, but you must realize that this is a difficult process because of the great distance involved and because of limited reporting facilities. There has been a great deal of instrument flying on missions in the Pacific and unpredicted wind shifts have caused trouble. Learn the weather of this area as well as you can because, as always, weather is the greatest factor affecting all sorts of navigation.

4. Navigator's Check List.

Before going on a mission, it is necessary for you to check carefully all your equipment and materials. The following navigator's check list is standard in this command:

1. Pre-flight.

   a. Mission data.

      (1) Complete flight plan with latest wind in log book or on special sheet provided by Group. Run over this with the crew.

          (a) ETA at target.
          (b) ETA at base.
          (c) Rendezvous.
          (d) ETA in enemy territory in and out plus ETA at important enemy areas.
          (e) Escape areas.

      (2) Charts prepared and checked.
      (3) Celestial procedure for mission organized.
      (4) Inspect and check communication and intelligence flimsies. Plot all radio aids, emergency landing fields, and important intelligence data on master chart.

   b. Navigation Kit. Complete set of navigation equipment for celestial and dead-reckoning navigation anywhere in the intended operational area. This equipment will include:

(1) E6B computer, C-2 and G-1.
(2) Weems plotter.
(3) Dividers, triangles, parallel rule (optional).
(4) A-13 chronometer.
(5) A-11 hack watch.
(6) A-3 stop watch.
(7) Current Air Almanac.
(8) Necessary H.O. 218 tables.
(9) Ageton or Dreisonstok and forms.
(10) Rude Star Finder.
(11) Supplementary blank forms, TD's, and H.O.

c. <u>Charts</u>.

(1) Complete set of AAF Aeronautical Charts, scale, 1:500,000 for pilotage anywhere in the general target area.
(2) Necessary AAF Long Range Air Navigation Charts, scale, 1:3,000,000 or similar charts covering the entire operational area.
(3) Sufficient 1:3,000,000 mercator plotting charts or V-P plotting charts.
(4) Loran Charts either VL or special.

d. <u>Sextant and accessories</u>.

(1) Check sextant for correction using either a stationary curve or a collimeter.
(2) Check sextant batteries and light bulbs.
(3) Check bubble for operation.
(4) Check averaging device.

e. <u>Weather</u>.

(1) Terminal forecasts.
(2) Route forecasts.
(3) Winds aloft.

f. <u>Correct time</u> (time tick frequency).

(1) Obtain time tick.
(2) List of frequencies from which to obtain time ticks.
(3) Chronometer rate.

g. <u>Astro compass</u> aligned properly.

h. <u>All calibration cards</u>. Date zeroed on deviation cards with dates of calibration displayed on master indicator and remote indicators for gyro-fluxgate compass.

2. Before Take-Off.

    a. Check personal effects including clothing, parachute, life vest, flak suit, helmet, sheck CO2 capsules, escape kit, and flashlight.

    b. Synchronize all aircraft clocks and watches of crew members.

    c. Check oxygen systems.

    d. Set altimeter 29.92 to read pressure altitude.

    e. Gyro-fluxgate compass. Check to see:

        (1) Uncages on (on) at all times.
        (2) System is functioning.
        (3) Compass sensitivity set properly.
        (4) Spare fuses available.

    f. API functioning and set properly.

3. During Flight.

    a. Continually check and cross check all navigation instruments.

        (1) Check T.H. with astro compass. Check GFG compass against the magnetic compass to see that GFG is operating correctly. See that GFG variation knob is at desired position.
        (2) Continually set proper data into CFC Gun Computer Handset.
        (3) See that IFF is on and off at the proper times.

    b. Enroute to target.

        (1) Rendezvous control points must be made good in time, place, and altitude.
        (2) Inform crew when they may test-fire guns.
        (3) Constantly brief crew with respect to enemy territory and installations.

    c. Navigation in the Target Area.

        (1) Record as much as you can of enemy aircraft, anti-aircraft, observed damage, and formations.
        (2) Get a pinpoint before leaving the target area.

    d. Navigation to Home Base. This is the navigation that is by far the most difficult. You have to find your base in the middle of a large ocean without much help from terrain or radio aids. You must never relax until you are on your field. You must constantly be prepared to fly directly to an emergency field. Be sure you are

squared away on the help you can get from your radio operator.
Be prepared to give accurate position report and carry out standard ditching procedure.

4. **After landing.**

    a.  Check all switches and stow equipment.

    b.  Interrogation.

    c.  Turn in your charts, flimsies, and log sheets.

## B  NAVIGATION INSTRUMENTS

Precision navigation is possible only to the limits of accuracy of instrument calibration and adjustment.  Each navigator must satisfy himself that each of his instruments is properly checked and calibrated before each mission.  Any navigator who does not know how to care for his
instruments or lacks the drive necessary to get the job done is jeopar-
dizing the safety and the opportunities of his crew.  There will be times
when you will be obliged to fly another crew's aircraft but it will be
your responsibility to ensure the reliability of the instruments you use.

1. **Astro Compass Alignment.**

The astro compass mechanically solves the celestial triangle for true
bearing of a celestial body using hour angle, declination and latitude;
the same arguments used in solving LOP's.  This part of the astro compass solves for azimuth or true bearing of the object, but the other part
of the instrument must be aligned with the fore and aft axis of the aircraft in order that true heading of the plane can be read when the relative bearing of the object is mechanically subtracted from the true bearing.  The primary point is that the astro-compass requires alignment with
the fore and aft axis of the airplane if it is to be used accurately.
The component parts of the instrument are:

    a.  The astrocompass.

    b.  The base mount.

    c.  The mounting bracket.

    d.  The four mounting stations in the astrodome.

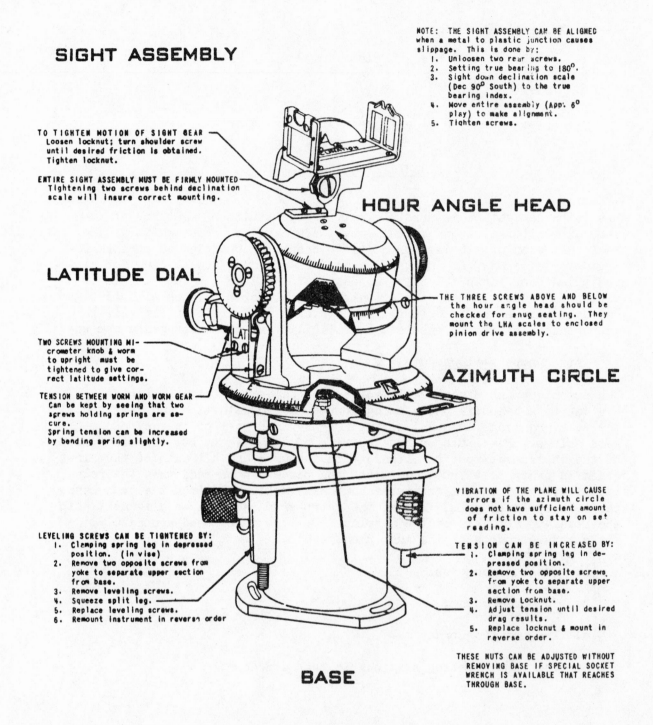

## SIGHT ASSEMBLY

NOTE: THE SIGHT ASSEMBLY CAN BE ALIGNED when a metal to plastic junction causes slippage. This is done by:
1. Unloosen two rear screws.
2. Setting true bearing to 180°.
3. Sight down declination scale (Dec 90° South) to the true bearing index.
4. Move entire assembly (App. 6° play) to make alignment.
5. Tighten screws.

TO TIGHTEN MOTION OF SIGHT GEAR
Loosen locknut; turn shoulder screw until desired friction is obtained. Tighten locknut.

ENTIRE SIGHT ASSEMBLY MUST BE FIRMLY MOUNTED Tightening two screws behind declination scale will insure correct mounting.

## HOUR ANGLE HEAD

## LATITUDE DIAL

THE THREE SCREWS ABOVE AND BELOW the hour angle head should be checked for snug seating. They mount the LHA scales to enclosed pinion drive assembly.

TWO SCREWS MOUNTING Micrometer knob & worm to upright must be tightened to give correct latitude settings.

TENSION BETWEEN WORM AND WORM GEAR Can be kept by seeing that two screws holding springs are secure. Spring tension can be increased by bending spring slightly.

## AZIMUTH CIRCLE

VIBRATION OF THE PLANE WILL CAUSE errors if the azimuth circle does not have sufficient amount of friction to stay on set reading.

LEVELING SCREWS CAN BE TIGHTENED BY:
1. Clamping spring leg in depressed position. (in vise)
2. Remove two opposite screws from yoke to separate upper section from base.
3. Remove leveling screws.
4. Squeeze split leg.
5. Replace leveling screws.
6. Remount instrument in reverse order

TENSION CAN BE INCREASED BY:
1. Clamping spring leg in depressed position.
2. Remove two opposite screws from yoke to separate upper section from base.
3. Remove Locknut.
4. Adjust tension until desired drag results.
5. Replace locknut & mount in reverse order.

THESE NUTS CAN BE ADJUSTED WITHOUT REMOVING BASE IF SPECIAL SOCKET WRENCH IS AVAILABLE THAT REACHES THROUGH BASE.

## BASE

ADJUSTMENT OF THE ASTROCOMPASS

FIGURE I

VI - 8

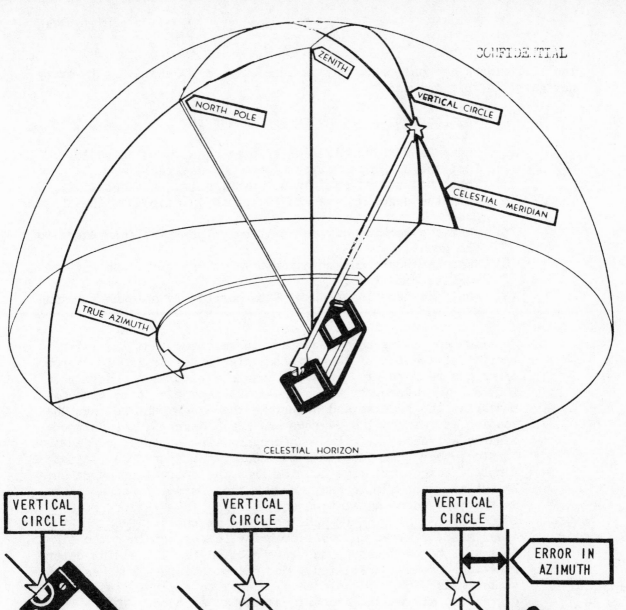

NORTH POLE

ZENITH

VERTICAL CIRCLE

CELESTIAL MERIDIAN

TRUE AZIMUTH

CELESTIAL HORIZON

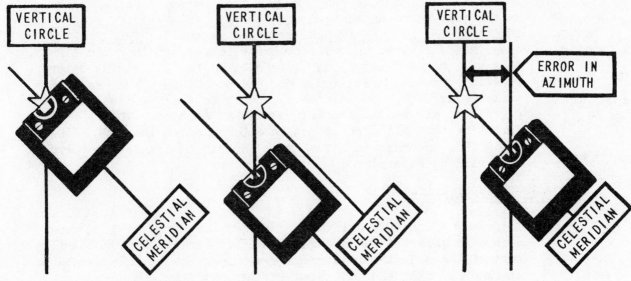

VERTICAL CIRCLE

VERTICAL CIRCLE

VERTICAL CIRCLE

ERROR IN AZIMUTH

CELESTIAL MERIDIAN

CELESTIAL MERIDIAN

CELESTIAL MERIDIAN

CORRECT POSITION

CORRECT SIGHTING

INCORRECT SIGHTING

8-44

CORRECT METHOD OF SIGHTING

FIGURE II

VI - 9

The following alignment procedure is laid out for standard use by every navigator in this command:

a.  Visually inspect the astrocompass to assure:

    (1)  There is tension and lack of play on all moving parts.
    (2)  That the sight is neither loose nor damaged.
    (3)  That the bubbles are clean, normal size, and sensitive.
    (4)  That the sighting assembly is properly aligned.  (See Figure One)
    (5)  That the locking device positively locks the instrument to the mount.
    (6)  That the mount and mounting bracket are solid and in good working condition.
    (7)  That the mounting bracket fits positively at each mounting station.

b.  In alignment it is only necessary to remember that the relative bearing of the top of the vertical stabilizer is 180 1/3° from the right rear mount. This bearing is of course the same on all B-29's. Therefore, by using the astrocompass as a pelorus and measuring the bearing and adjusting the base mount so that the reading is between 180 degrees and 180 $\frac{1}{3}$ degrees, the astrocompass is aligned. It will be necessary also to enter corrections for the other three mounting stations. The procedure is just as simple. Take a relative bearing from the correct mount on some object at least a mile away, remove the astrocompass and place in the next mounting station and, LEAVING THE RELATIVE BEARING SCALE SET THE SAME AS IT WAS, note the amount the TRUE BEARING index must be moved in order to bring the object into the sights. This will be the correction to be applied to all heading determinations from that station. For example if the True Heading scale reads 356°, it would be necessary to apply a plus four degrees to all readings obtained at that station. NOTE: It is important that all corrections be determined on the TRUE HEAD-ING SCALE, in order to insure that the right sign of the corrections will be determined.

2.  Driftmeter Alignment.

a.  Alignment of the B-5 driftmeter follows the same standard procedure in general use throughout the Air Forces. Prior to align-ment of the B-5, the pentograph system and the reticle should be checked for alignment as shown in Figures Three and Four.

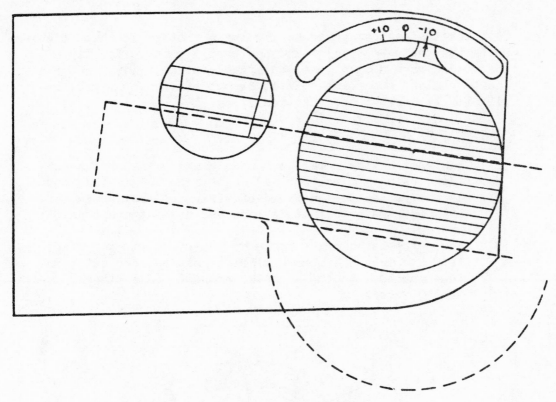

ALIGNMENT OF RETICLE

FIGURE III

b. Lay a straight edge or plotter on the ground glass face parallel to the black lines. It should then be parallel to the reticle lines. If it does not parallel them, the instrument is out of alignment.

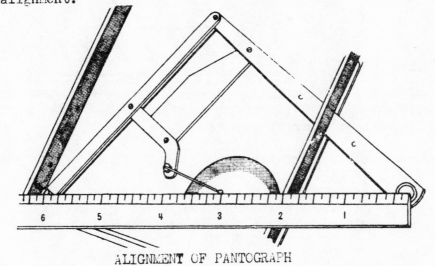

ALIGNMENT OF PANTOGRAPH

FIGURE IV

c. To check the pantograph mechanism lay a plotter so that it connects the pantograph joint and the pencil point. The tip of the needle should then just touch the plotter, midway between the pencil and the joint. If it is out of line it may be bent slightly to correct its position.

d. Alignment with fore and aft axis:

    (1) Construct a line parallel to the center line of the airplane, using a plumb bob and chalk line. This line must be constructed in the field of vision of the driftmeter.

    (2) Align driftmeter with this line and note apparent drift reading.

    (3) Loosen screws on drift scale at top of drift recording plate and make the apparent drift reading zero with the lines parallel to those on the ground. (See Figure Five)

    (4) Tighten screws.

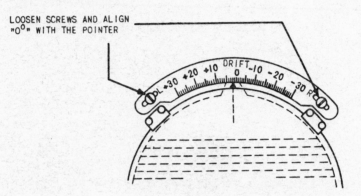

DRIFTMETER ALIGNMENT

FIGURE V

3. <u>Airspeed Meter Calibration</u>.

The procedure for calibrating the Airspeed Meter can be accomplished in two ways. The preferable one is by timing between two landmarks whose distance apart is accurately known.

The alternate method is as follows:

a. Fly directly up-wind at 190 Ind. A.S. and with the drift scale set at <u>zero</u>, get a ground speed vector by timing. Three or more timings should be made on each run.

b. Turn 180° by gyro and repeat above procedure.

c. Record pressure altitude and temperature on each run.

d.  Repeat for 200 and 210 m.p.h.

e.  Average up-wind and down-wind speeds to obtain T. A. S.

f.  Using temperature and pressure altitude, figure Ca. A. S. for each run.

g.  Plot indicated against calibrated and draw up a curve.

It is essential that the second method of calibration be flown up-wind and down-wind, since any deviation from the procedure will introduce excessive errors in the computation of T. A. S.

4.  Fluxgate Compass.

The brains of the fluxgate compass is a small, triangular coil located in the transmitter which is situated in the left wing tip. This delta coil is held in a horizontal position by a gyro similiar to that in the B-3 Driftmeter. The gyro keeps the coil level in order that it can utilize only the horizontal component of the earth's magnetic field and also provide the navigator with a constant heading even though the air is extremely rough. Unlike the gyro in the dirftmeter, this gyro will permit a bank of 65 degrees before it will tumble. It has a self-erection unit which will erect the gyro at a rate of about one degree per two minutes, and will maintain the coil in a position within eight minutes of the perfect horizontal.

Each leg of the coil picks up a separate voltage from the earth's magnetic field, the strength of each one depending upon the direction of the earth's field with respect to that leg. These voltages are led through the amplifier to the Master Indicator where they are translated into direction. The Master Indicator corrects this direction for deviation and variation and then sends this corrected or TRUE HEADING to its needle or pointer and to the repeaters located in other parts of the airplane.

The fluxgate system also incorporates a caging device which is used ONLY for erection purposes. When the system is first turned on, it requires about ten minutes for the gyro to reach its full speed and when it has neared its top speed, the self-erection mechanism starts to erect the gyro. It can be readily understood that at its slow rate of erection, it would require one-half hour or longer for the gyro to become erect if this were the sole means. Because of this, the electrical caging unit has been added and by running through the cage-uncage cycle when the gyro has enough speed to maintain its rigidity, the gyro can be erected in a matter of about one minute. However, this cage-uncage cycle will always leave the gyro in the same attitude as the airplane. Thus, in a climb, the gyro would be left in a tilted angle and it would still require several minutes before the self-erection system could complete the erection.  This is the reason why ten or fifteen minutes should elapse between the cage-uncage cycle and the start of any compass swing.  If the gyro lacks one degree of being erect, it can produce an error of two or more degrees in the heading.

The caging device consists of two parts -- a small D.C. motor located in the wing five to ten feet from the transmitter and a caging switch or button located near the navigator.  The older models have a toggle switch with a "Cage" and "Uncage" position and the newer models have a push-button.  If properly synchronized when installed, it is impossible to leave the gyro in the caged position with the newer models.  The navigator who finds he has the toggle switch type should remember to leave the switch in the "Uncage" position at all times except when going through the cage-uncage cycle.  More gyros have been damaged through neglect of this than by all other troubles put together.

NEW PUSHBUTTON CAGING SWITCH

FIGURE  VI

| CAGING | CAGED | UNCAGING | UNCAGED |

TOGGLE TYPE CAGING SWITCH

FIGURE VII

The last unit of the fluxgate compass is the Amplifier. The amplifier
serves many purposes. It not only amplifies the time induced voltages
to a size where they can be utilized; but it also serves as a junction
box for the fluxgate system, provides power for the gyro, supplies the
repeater system with its current, and acts as an auto-transformer. On
the Amplifier there is a gain control which permits operation of the
compass in very high magnetic latitudes. In order to obtain the best
operation from this compass, the gain control should always be set <u>one</u>
position lower than the setting which produces oscillation of the needle
or pointer of the Master Indicator. The Amplifier acts as the safety
device for the whole system by incorporating a fuse which will break
the circuit from the inverter should a short circuit develop. It is a
one-Ampere fuse and under no circumstances should a larger fuse be used.
<u>Spare fuses should always be carried</u>, but the navigator should report
any burned out fuses to the maintenance personnel immediately, because
that is a positive indication of mal-function of some part of the system.

The operating procedure for the fluxgate compass is quite simple and
requires only the following steps:

a. Turn on the inverter and then check to see that the green light
   in the Amplifier is glowing.

b. Allow at least five minutes for the gyro to gain speed and then
   run through the cage-uncage cycle.

c. Set in the Local Variation on the Master Indicator.

d. Set the Gain Control on the Amplifier to the position just under
   that which produces fluctuation of the pointer.

e. Adjust the Variation setting as changes are encountered in flight.

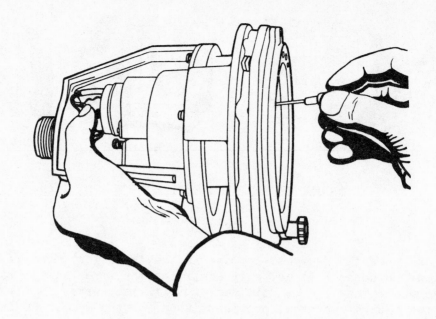

COMPENSATING MASTER INDICATOR

FIGURE· VIII

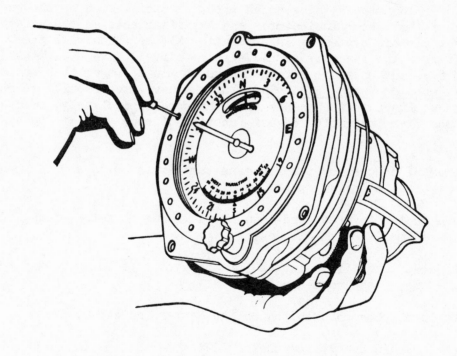

COMPENSATING MASTER INDICATOR

FIGURE IX

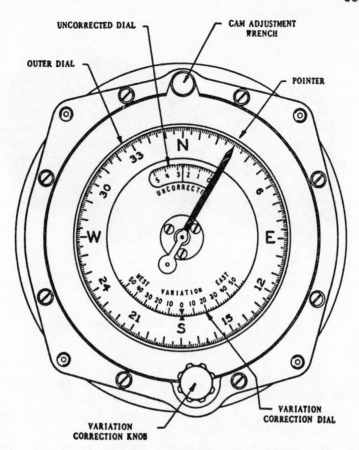

MASTER INDICATOR

FIGURE X

The compensation procedure for the fluxgate compass is a bit more involved than that of other types of compasses, but it has the unique advantage that all the deviations can be removed and a perfect Magnetic or True Heading will be shown on the Master Indicator at all times.

Obviously, the first step is the compass swing. While an air swing is always preferable, this compass can be swung on the ground with reliable results. Of prime importance on either type of compass swing is the knowledge that the sensitive element in the wing is perfectly horizontal. This can be accomplished by permitting the set to run for about fifteen minutes after the gyro has been run through the cage-uncage cycle and then starting the swing. When performing the swing it is necessary to read the "Uncorrected Dial" only. These uncorrected readings are actually the compass headings and should then be plotted on a graph against magnetic headings and a smooth curve drawn up. It should be remembered when drawing this curve that the sensitive element is located far from strong magnetic disturbances and that as a result, the final curve will probably reflect the effect of "soft" iron or induced magnetism more than that of "hard" iron. The result may be a curve that crosses the zero axis more than once. The curve should always be analyzed before compensation is begun.

MASTER INDICATOR (REAR VIEW)

FIGURE XI

Compensation is quite simple and accurate if two precautions are observed. First among these is the preservation of the life of the Master Indicator. Unless the navigator has the latest type instrument, it will be necessary to remove the cover of the Master Indicator. If, during this operation, dust or moisture are allowed to get into the instrument, it will materially decrease its length of operation and may cause the set to become inoperative at a very crucial moment.

The second precaution is that against placing too much stress on the compensating cam. This should seldom be encountered in the B-29 Aircraft because the transmitter is so well situated that only a few degrees of deviation should exist. Should there be more than four degrees, the navigator must be extremely careful when compensating to see that he does not break the cam. In such cases it is a good idea to make a three degree adjustment, go to the next heading and put in three and then come back and complete the first one.

The compensation procedure is listed as follows:

    a. Remove the Master Indicator from its bracket.

    b. Unscrew the three small screws on the back of the instrument and remove the cover.

    c. Unscrew the thumbscrew at the top of the face of the indicator. This is a small Allen Wrench.

    d. Remove the bezel ring and insert the Allen wrench into the hole nearest the zero degree mark.

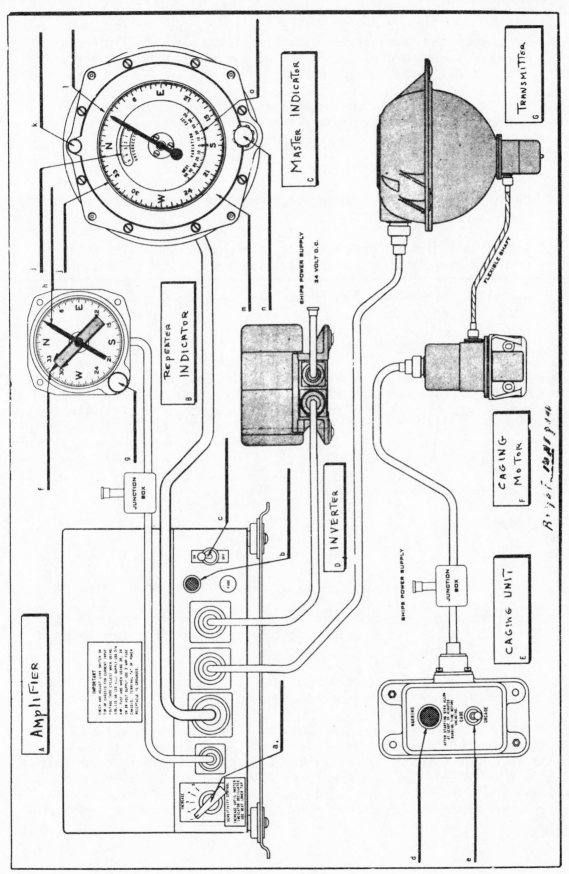

FLUXGATE COMPASS SYSTEM

FIGURE XII

e. By turning the rotor of the induction motor with the fingers, the uncompensated dial can be set on the desired reading taken from the deviation curve.

f. Turn the compensating screw until the pointer reads Magnetic Heading while the dial shows the compass heading.

NOTE: THE VARIATION KNOB MUST BE SET EXACTLY ON ZERO DURING THE ENTIRE COMPENSATION PROCEDURE.

g. Go through the entire 360 degrees, removing the deviation on each 15 degree heading.

h. After completion of the above, go through the procedure again, removing any additional small deviations which may be present.

i. Replace the cover and then replace the instrument and electrical plug.

5. Air Position Indicator.

The Air Position Indicator is a system comprising four or five unit parts. It provides an accurate air plot of true Heading and true Airspeed for the navigator. The Air Position Indicator is made up of the following unit parts:

a. Air mileage pump.

b. Pressure Control unit.

c. Computer unit.

d. Amplifier.

e. Remote reading compass which is either the fluxgate or magnesyn.

The primary purpose of installing the API in B-29's is to provide an aid to dead reckoning while airplane is executing evasive action or undergoing attack in a combat area.

All the navigator has to do to plot a DR position is to lay the wind off down-wind from the coordinates indicated on the API.

The API will usually keep a no-wind position to within 3% of the distance flown, and after the navigator has used the equipment for some time, he will find that he can calibrate it down to even greater accuracy than this. Navigators who have not flown with the API sufficiently to understand its capabilities and intricacies must beware of the tendency to rely blindly upon the instrument for all DR navigation. The navigator who makes this mistake may sometime find that a cam has become stuck and he is hopelessly lost. This point cannot be over-emphasized. The use of the API to accomplish the DR for the navigator in straight and level flying is purely a secondary adaptation of the equipment, and even though the API is used, the complete log procedure should be followed.

AIR POSITION INDICATOR

FIGURE XIII

The fluxgate compass is tied in with the API in the B-29 airplanes to feed in true heading into the computer of the API. There is a course indicator on the face of the computer unit, and the computer actually uses the heading indicated on this course indicator as true heading of the airplane. It is, of course, known by all navigators that true heading is magnetic heading corrected for variation. Navigators must understand that

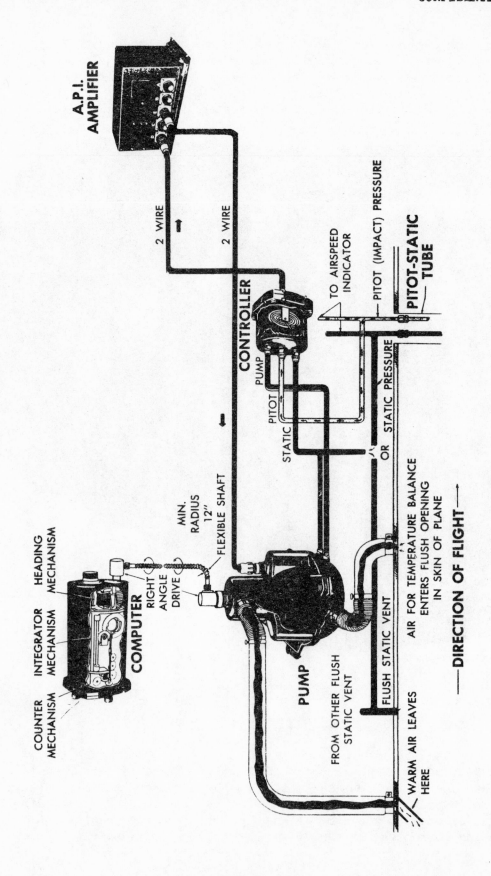

A.F.I. SYSTEM

FIGURE XIV

when variation is set into the fluxgate compass, that true heading is indicated on the pointer of the master indicator, and is transmitted via the repeater system to the API, with a possible plus or minus 2° error. There is a variation setting knob on the face of the computer unit of the API which was placed there for the usage with the Magnesyn compass in order to supply true heading. It is only reasonable that if variation is set in the fluxgate compass, the variation setting device on the API will be left at zero. It is, of course wrong to set variation both on the fluxgate and on the API computer.

The desired practice is to set the variation in on the fluxgate, as it can be set more accurately. There is, however, another use which can be made of this variation knob on the API. A navigator can use this knob to make the API pointer read exactly what the Master Indicator shows. This is done by adjusting the API variation knob just enough to make the pointer read true heading. Since the computer has already been compensated, this correction will seldom be over two degrees. A note of caution must be added, however: Remember, when using this method to zero the API, that the procedure must be accomplished every time the aircraft turns to a new heading. By very careful following of this procedure, it is possible to incorporate an accuracy into the API coordinates that can not be equalled by any other Dead Reckoning means.

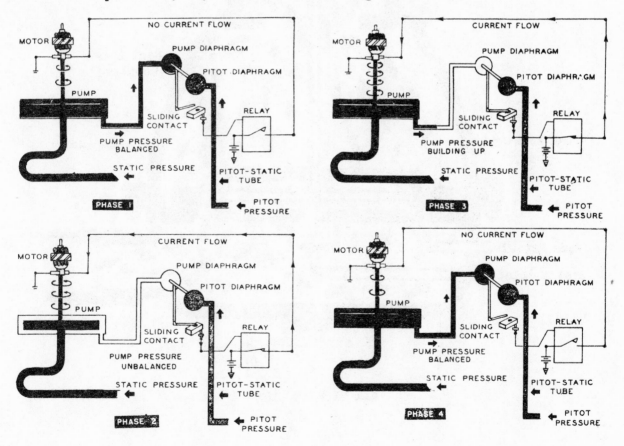

AIR MILEAGE PUMP

FIGURE XV

The general location of the component parts of the API will be of value to the navigator using this equipment. The air mileage unit or pump is usually located under the navigator's table, near the skin of the airplane so that its cooling tubes will be as short as possible. In order for the mileage pump to rotate at a speed proportional to the true air speed of the airplane, the air inside the pump must be kept at the temperature of the outside air, in which the airplane is flying. This pump functions as illustrated on the preceding page in Figure XV.

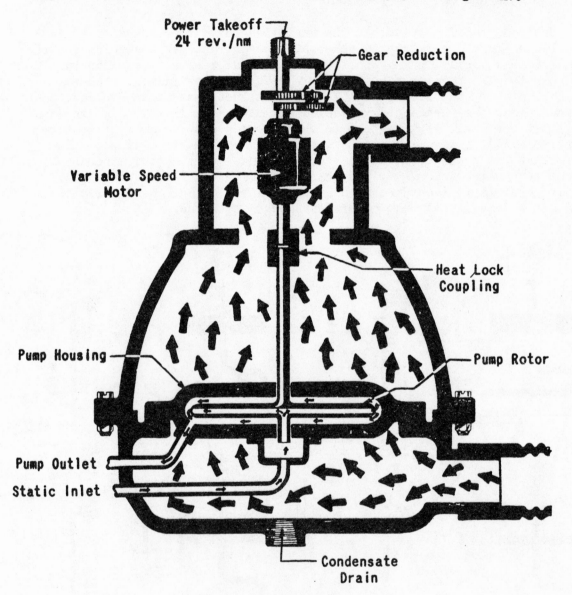

Power Takeoff
24 rev./nm

Gear Reduction

Variable Speed
Motor

Heat Lock
Coupling

Pump Housing

Pump Rotor

Pump Outlet

Static Inlet

Condensate
Drain

AIR MILEAGE UNIT

FIGURE XVI

VI - 24

The control unit of the API is only a clearing house for pitot pressure, pump pressure, and static pressure, and actuates an electrical circuit which runs the pump, and makes it rotate at the speed proportional to the true air speed of the airplane. As the pump runs. there is a flexible shaft connected at the top of the unit, which feeds rotation into the computer unit, such that every 24 revolutions equals one nautical mile of true air speed. As the fluxgate compass is feeding true heading into the computer unit, the intergrators have only to combine the two and integrate from an initial position setting, giving on the counters in the face of the computer unit, Latitude and Longitude of the plane's no wind position at all times. This computer unit is located on the navigator's table.

The operation for the API is as follows:

a.  Set Latitudinal and Longitudinal coordinates on computer. making certain the flip levers are properly set.

b.  Turn set on immediately before take-off.

c.  Record beginning figures in air mileage counter, and record time.

d.  Reset coordinates whenever actual position is known. (Note: If computer is reset after celestial or radio fix, the navigator should DR ahead to the time of reset, and should not record the coordinates of the fix, since he has already passed those coordinates.)

e.  Record all air mileage and reset data in the lob book.

f.  Reset computer when the Landfall is established and, if possible, before all climbs and descents.

g.  Check periodically to see that the API coordinate corresponds with the Air Plot position to insure that the set is operating correctly.

## C  DEAD RECKONING

Dead reckoning is the recognized basic form of navigation. All other methods are contributing factors to successful dead reckoning. You will have all the latest radar and celestial aids to assist you, but their value will be directly proportional to the quality of your dead reckoning. Dead reckoning is at best a form of navigation subject to error. Your slightest error will become cumulative and can easily result in a 5 percent error. Your work will require constant and detailed attention. and all air speeds, temperatures, and compass headings must be averaged. Nothing can be left to chance.

Before considering the special dead reckoning problem of a mission to Japan, let us consider some of the basic causes of error and special techniques which will be of help to you.

Use of G-1 and C-2 computers. In a small survey conducted in one of the squadrons on the first few Empire missions, it was found that ETAs were running a consistent 20-35 minutes early. These problems are still arising and are due largely to a misuse of data and instruments in the computation of TAS. Planes have not been, and are not being properly calibrated. Also some navigators are still persisting in the use of the E6B computer in figuring TAS. Yet TAS and a good ETA on the Japanese coast and the target I.P. are of immeasurable help in the completion of a successful bombing mission. Further the correct wind determination in daylight is all but impossible without correct TAS.

The E6B is accurate at low altitudes, but the scale of the E6B is small when high altitudes of over 20,000 feet are figured on it. This fact alone causes inaccuracies. Further, TAS is the result of a constant relationship between IAS, pressure altitude of density, and temperature. At high altitudes, the E6B simply cannot figure TAS to anywhere near the limits of navigational accuracy.

The computer which will be used by navigators of this command for figuring TAS will be the G-1 computer. Most navigators have cast aside the G-1 as another piece of unnecessary equipment which can easily be dispensed with. That one action has caused the navigators involved an error of 5% in his ETA to the Japanese coast, when flying at higher altitudes.

For accurate results the indicated free air temperature should be corrected for heat of compression and friction. The correction is always subtracted and varies with the true airspeed.

| TRUE AIRSPEED IN KNOTS | TEMPERATURE CORRECTION IN DEGREES C |
|:---:|:---:|
| 160 | - 2.7 |
| 180 | - 3.4 |
| 200 | - 4.2 |
| 225 | - 5.4 |
| 250 | - 6.6 |
| 275 | - 8.0 |
| 300 | - 9.5 |

A typical problem:

Pressure altitude - 30,000 feet.
Temperature - 30°
C.A.S. - 170 Knots.
The G-1 computer T.A.S. is 282 K.
The E6B computer T.A.S. is 287 K.
By applying compression error of (-8) on the G-1 computer our correct TAS is 277 K.

In the compution of altitude the E6B computer must again be discarded. If the SCR-718 is available, the chances are that the navigator will use it in determining altitudes for ground speed by timing. On the other hand, occasions may arise when the SCR-718 may be inoperative. At such times a more accurate true altitude and absolute altitude may be obtained by the use of the C-2 rather than the E6B computer.

Of course the C-2 method of altitude computation is subject to limitations. There are many variable factors, pressure altitudes, and temperature of the point at flight level. Forecast barometric pressures are obviously not always accurate. The use of the C-2 altitude computer is then a substitute for the SCR-718.

Having covered the TAS and altitude problem, the wind problem must now be considered. Nowhere in the world's fighting areas are such high winds encountered as on the run to the Japanese Empire. Velocities of 120 knots to 150 knots are common and winds of 210-220 knots have been recorded. Such winds require a special technique in their handling and interpretation.

The basic vector diagram gives the clue to the handling of high wind velocities. It will be remembered that the vector diagram consists of three sides representing the components of:

    a.  Wind direction and force.
    b.  T.A.S. and true heading.
    c.  Track and ground speed.

If any basic vector diagram is taken and the velocities of each of the three components increased, or decreased, by equal amounts, it will be seen that the angles of the resulting similiar triangles are the same.

Sample problem:

T.A.S. - 300 K. = Ground speed - 435 K.
Wind - 240° 150 K. = Drift - 10° left.
T.H. - 90°

As this problem cannot be plotted on the E6B, a third of the airspeed and wind will be plotted. The resulting ground speed will then have to be multiplied by three. As angles of both triangles are the same, the drift is the same.

If the B-5 is used, the actual computation is easily performed on the computer which is a part of the driftmeter itself. At high altitudes, ground speed by timing offers difficulties on a light sea, but with patience it can be done.

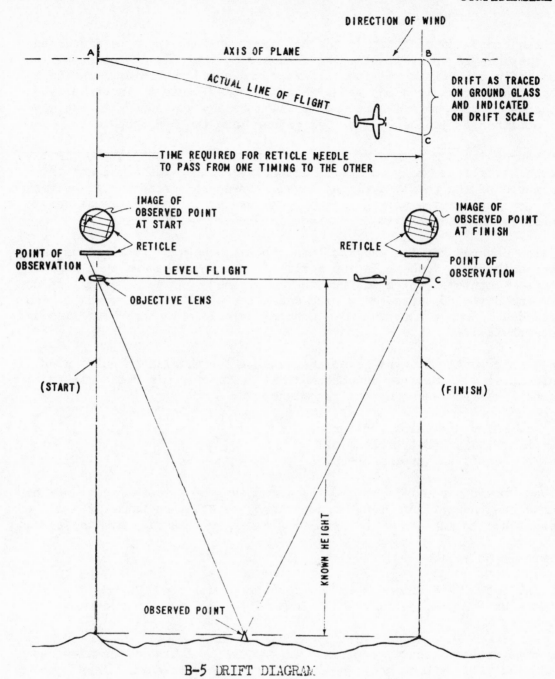

B-5 DRIFT DIAGRAM

FIGURE XVII

The B-3 driftmeter can be used like the B-5, measuring the time between front and rear grid lines. This is called the zero angle method. A constant factor of .177 is used. The equation is:

$$\text{G.S. in knots} = \frac{H \text{ (alt) x .177}}{T \text{ (time)}}$$

This factor, .177, is accurate for most B-3 driftmeters. However the factor for a particular driftmeter can easily be checked. (Reference paragraph 151-D in TM 205) The use of the zero angle method, so called because the driftmeter is set at 0 trail, is just as easily done as with the B-5. The formula can be set up on the E6B and since the factor is constant the E6B becomes a computer as easily operated as the computer on the B-5 driftmeter. The zero angle method may be used when smooth seas prevent tracking a white-cap for a long period of time as required in the Trail Angle Method.

Trail Angle Method for B-3:

The procedure for ground speed by timing using the trail angle of the B-3 is as follows:

a. Set the driftmeter to read the correct drift.

b. Using the trail angle, sight somewhat ahead of the plane to pick up a conspicuous object.

c. Turn the trail angle back until the zero detent is felt.

d. Wait at that position until the object passes into view. When the object crosses one of the timing lines, start timing.

e. Turn the trail angle back until the fifth degree detent is felt.

f. When the object reaches the same timing line that was used to begin the timing, mark the end of the time period.

g. Determine the absolute altitude of the plane.

h. The following equation is used:

$$\frac{GS}{FACTOR} = \frac{ABS.\ ALT\ (ft)}{TIME\ (sec)}$$

Sample Mission:

The first phase of your flight may well be at 1,000 feet. Check the fluxgate compass as soon as a level-off position is made and check the heading with the astro-compass and pilot's compass as soon as you are on course. A radio compass, radar, and visual check may be made at Iwo Jima.

During the first phase of your flight, you will be approximately 6 hours at low altitudes but even in daylight your navigational aids are abundant.

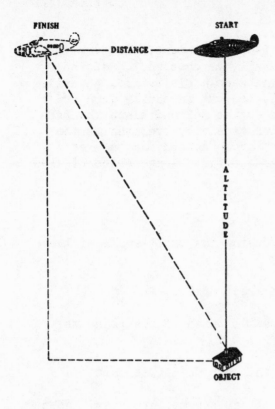

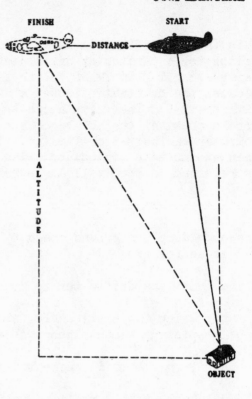

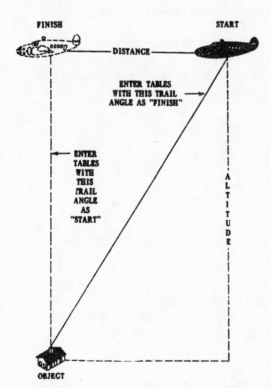

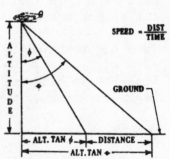

$$SPEED = \frac{DIST}{TIME}$$

$$\underline{\text{GROUND SPEED}} = \underline{\text{ALTITUDE}}$$
$$\quad\ \text{FACTOR} \qquad\quad \text{TIME}$$

GROUND SPEED - KNOTS
ALTITUDE - ABSOLUTE ALT. (FEET)
TIME - TIME IN SECONDS
FACTOR - .592 (tan $\theta$ - tan $\phi$ )
  $\theta$ - STOPPING ANGLE
  $\phi$ - STARTING ANGLE
.592 - CONSTANT TO CONVERT
       FEET/SECOND TO KNOTS

B-3 TRAIL ANGLE DIAGRAM
FIGURE XVIII

Drift reading on water, ground speed by timing, ground speed by sunlines, combining ground speed with drift readings to obtain a wind, are all sources of information. These aids in themselves should be sufficient but in addition, the track and ground speed method will give you winds from Loran fixes: and radio lines of position. obtained from homing and range beacons, crossed with sunlines may be used. Another aid is wind pilotage, on estimation of wind direction and velocity from the water surface.

| VELOCITY In Knots | SURFACE CONDITION |
|---|---|
| 0 | Smooth slick sea. |
| 0-2 | Small occasional ripples. |
| 3-4 | Small ripples all over - no calm areas. |
| 5-6 | Well defined waves - smooth with no breaking |
| 7-9 | Occasional white caps. |
| 10-11 | Pronounced waves, frequent whitecaps carrying a short distance. |
| 12-13 | White-caps close together, carrying over a distance equal to the wave height. Slight traces of wind streaks. |
| 14-16 | Clearly defined wind streaks whose lengths are equal to about ten wave lengths. Light flurry patches. |
| 17-19 | Long, well defined streaks: waves and streaks coming from the same direction. |
| 20-22 | Streaks are long and straight; white-caps on every crest; wind picks up and carries mist along; large waves. |
| 23-26 | Large seas with waves forming on them: wind picks up and carries occasional wave crests. |
| 27-30 | Heavy seas, pronounced white streaks, wind picks up frequent wave crests and carries along; breaking, rolling waves are forming. |
| 31-37 | Continual rolling waves; wind carries along all wave crests for a distance equal to $\frac{1}{2}$ wave length. |
| 38-43 | Well defined waves form on the heavy seas; waves and seas breaking and rolling. Sud or form streaks. |

NOTE:   a.  When streaks are long and straight the wind is steady in force and direction for that locality.

   b.  When streaks are curved, be alert for a change in wind direction.

   c.  When a distant line on the surface appears similiar to a rip tide, be alert for a reversal of wind direction.

   d.  Until proficiency in observation is obtained, winds are usually of stronger velocity than the observer estimates.

Don't relax because you know your position. You'll find a wind shift of 180° from base to the point of climb and a right correction at the start will usually be left correction somewhere north of the Bonins.

Your point of climb is one of the crucial points in the flight. A climb too late or early may be disastrous to the entire mission. This is where your cooperation with the flight engineer is essential. He has planned the mission to give you a reserve for return to base. But the combination of an early climb at excessive gross weights and the increased head winds at high altitude will burn up your fuel reserve.

If you arrive at altitude too late, the results may be even more disastrous. The Jap fighter operates much better at a lower altitude and likes nothing better than a sitting duck in a climb. Then, too, you should plan to level off 50 miles before the enemy coast to obtain a good radar wind.

The climb phase will require your top navigation. This is the zone where most of the bad weather is located. Many times you'll find drift reading impossible because of cloud cover, and yet the sudden changes in wind will result in a rapid change in drift.

When drift reading is impossible, it will be necessary to use metro winds. This requires very careful averaging and in cases where the wind shift is great, separate computations must be worked out.

When there are no whitecaps, you'll find drift reading at high altitude extremely difficult with the B-5; but with practice you will find your reading sufficiently accurate.

You will be giving your pilot frequent changes in course during this period, and you must check your compass regularly to determine that he is maintaining the correct headings.

The primary consideration here is to make each correction as soon as it occurs. A correction made on the basis of a point 15 minutes past is of little use because of the high speed of the plane. In such a case, over-correction is the only answer. The principle is simple - a correction is made to parallel course and an additional one to put the ship back on track after a set period of time. If such an over-correction is made, the navigator must remember to further correct when the ship has returned to the track.

While in formation, of course, sudden large corrections are impossible. Small corrections are not difficult to apply, but large corrections will have to be broken down into a series of smaller ones or else a single correcting turn of approximately $\frac{1}{4}$ needle width may be made.

During this climb phase, you will be tempted to use your API rather than average your air speeds, compass readings, temperature, and altitudes. But remember its accuracy is within a 3% limitation, and must be frequently reset to stay within that range of error. Use your API as a check rather than a substitute.

The finding of the wind is the navigator's reason for being on the crew. Not only does he fly a successful navigation mission thereby but the bombardier's success in large measure hangs by the same wind.

Missions are planned to reach altitude fifty or sixty miles off the enemy coast, so that you can obtain a radar wind for your bomb run. The navigator must be prepared to give the bombardier the best available data. The success of a bombing run at high altitudes depends in large measure on the accuracy of the data which the bombardier has preset in his sight. Therefore, the navigator must give the bombardier, before the radar wind is made, the best available wind direction and velocity, true air speed for the target run, and ground speed and heading for the target run. This data is then used by the bombardier and the sight is set upon that basis.

If the radar wind run is then impossible or unsuccessful, the bombardier still has the best available data in the sight. If the radar wind run is successful and shows an appreciable change in the data set up, the sight settings may then be modified on that basis. The setting in of the best available data prevents a last minute rush where errors might easily enter in.

When you make landfall, it will be even more necessary to do precision dead reckoning. Visual land marks are not an adequate guide for a proper turn. It requires considerable space and time to turn a large formation more than 30° right or left. Especially does it require time to turn from I.P. to target. The more accurate the landfall, the better the turn from I.P. can be executed. In making for the I.P. the lead navigator must not only figure his true heading from I.P. to target, but he must consider the turning radius of his information in order that the formation may roll out on the prescribed track and heading. This fact cannot be emphasized too much. Numerous bomb runs have been ruined because this turning radius was not calculated and used. The resulting turns, because they could not be made tight enough in formation have thrown the lead bombardiers so far right or left of the prescribed target run as to make accuracy impossible.

You should have the heading of your turn off the target planned in advance, and cooperate with the bombardier in avoiding flak areas. Your trip home should be planned to utilize the most favorable winds and altitude levels.

You'll have a tendency to relax on the trip to base but the mission is only one half over for you. You must have an accurate position available within a matter of seconds. In case of ditching or the reporting of another aircraft, air sea rescue must be able to narrow its search to the smallest possible area.

If the DR work has been properly kept up this will not be impossible. If the navigator has been lazy and allowed his DR to slide, a good position will take many minutes to obtain - thus endangering his life and the lives of his comrades. He must be alert to record or figure the positions of other planes in distress and all aborts should be duly noted with the time and coordinates of the abort.

Every shred of information available to the navigator must be weighed and used in its proper place. In cases of poor visibility, navigators have often become confused and excited when they failed to sight the base on completion of their ETA, and abandoned all DR procedure while making an aimless search for base. This is the time when you should make use of all your radio, radar, and celestial aids, but if none of these are available a navigator directed search procedure will get you to base. You can always work back from your last sure position, make a practical estimation of error, and plan your search accordingly.

## D  RADIO FACILITIES AND AIDS TO NAVIGATION

### 1.  Facilities Available for Use by XXI Bomber Command B-29's.

The following is a list and brief description of the equipment comprising the radio facilities and aids to navigation available to this command.

    a.  **Liaison Radio:** With this equipment, your radio operator can, when necessary or desirable:

        (1)  Contact the ground stations.
        (2)  Request and receive HF D/F bearings up to 700 miles radius.
        (3)  Send urgent and distress signals.

    b.  **VHF Command Set:** The pilot has the controls for this "Voice" set and can make voice contact with:

        (1)  Other B-29's in your formation.
        (2)  Rescue Facilities.
        (3)  VHF/DF ground station for bearings up to 100 miles radius.

    c.  **Radio Compass:** This equipment can be employed for the following:

        (1)  Homing on Homing Beacons, ranges, or long dashes from Rescue Facilities.

(2) Bearings and Homing on OWI and other high power broadcast stations.

(3) A good emergency receiver over frequency range of 100-1730 Kcs.

d. IFF: This equipment:

(1) Can be used by your base to give you a bearing up to 100 miles radius.

(2) Enables submarines to shoot range and bearing on you to determine your position.

(3) Tells naval and ground radar equipment that you are in trouble when in emergency position.

e. Radar Set: This equipment:

(1) Enables you to pick up rescue submarines and rescue airplanes beyond visual range.

(2) Enables you to position yourself with respect to Islands and coastlines, determine wind and direct the bombing.

(3) Permits homing on or near rescue facilities or Islands.

(4) Permits you to fix position accurately from radar beacon up to 150 miles radius.

2. Distress Procedure - For any Plane any Time.

If you are about to ditch, the following steps must be taken in order given:

a. Radar Operator turns IFF to EMERGENCY position.

b. Navigator must know Loran Line, Latitude, Longitude, nautical miles from nearest reference point and true bearing from reference point and the correct name of that reference point. (The navigator gives this information to both the pilot and the radio operator).

c. Pilot immediately calls on Channel "B" and states "This is Happy 21 in distress switching to Channel "C". Pilot then switches to Channel "C" and advises Dumbo or Lifeguard on Channel "C" that he is ditching.

Example: "Hello Smelly Nelly, this is Happy 21, 15 Smelly Nelly 180, over". (Radio Operator will furnish Pilot with CSP 1270 Direct Authentication or "Shackle" if required).

Pilot will instruct tail gunner to throw Radio Ransmitter Buoy (AN/CRN-1) out rear escape hatch when pilot gives him the signal.

d. Radio Operator will immediately contact his Wing Air-Ground station on his assigned strike frequency and give the following information, encoded on CSP 1270: "Am about to ditch, Loran Line, Latitude, Longitude, Course, Speed, and Altitude."
Example: ØØV535 V 21V537 - O - BT QUB 23ØØ
1Ø22N 142 31 E 32Ø 195 8ØØØ K
(Encoded in CSP 1270)

The radio operator will get a receipt for this message from the Wind Air-Ground Station. While this Wing Air-Ground Station is decoding this message, the radio operator will switch to 4475 Kcs (Voice) and send the message that his pilot had previously transmitted to Dumbo and Lifeguard and then switch to 4475 Kcs (CW) and send the same message.
Example: SMELLY NELLY V HAPPY 21 BT 15 SMELLY NELLY 180 K.

If the radio operator does not receive an acknowledgment of this message from Dumbo and Lifeguard, he will immeditely switch back to his assigned strike frequency and, if his Ground Station is not trying to contact him by this time, he will call the Ground Station and ask for a bearing.
Example: ØØV535 V 21V537 INT QUJ K

The Ground Station will call him back and ask him to send his call sign followed by a 20 second dash.
Example: 21V537 V ØØV535 QTN K

The aircraft will then send call sign and 20 second dash.
Example: 21V537_____21V537
(20 Second Dash)

The ground station will then call the aircraft and give him his bearing (True course to steer to reach the ground station).
Example: 21V537 V ØØV535 QUJ 153 K

If the aircraft receives the bearing, he will receipt in the following manner:
Example: ØØV535 V 21V537 R QUJ 153 AR

3. Radio Compass and HF-DF Bearings.

These radio facilities are very important aids to navigation in this theatre. It is essential that navigators be fully aware of them to assure their proper use.

a. The first and most common type of bearing available is the ordinary radio compass bearing on a Range Station or Homing Beacon. This bearing will be taken by the Radio Operator except in the later modified airplanes which are coming out with the Radio Compass Controls installed at the Navigator's station. A quick way for a Navigator to take and plot a bearing is to:

(1) Tune to the station frequency.
(2) Set T.H. from fluxgate on Variation Index of Radio Compass.
(3) Read blunt end of needle for T.B. from station.
(4) Plot T.B. and time of bearing.

Bearings may be obtained on the radio broadcast station at Saipan and Guam. A 50,000 watt OWI station operates intermittently, broadcasting material for Japanese consumption. The radio compass bearings on this powerful station will become increasingly important as it extends operations.

While radio compass bearings have been taken as far as 450-500 miles out, reliability is close to 150 miles. It is difficult to generalize on this point due to changing weather conditions.

Often a bearing can be obtained by an Aural Null when it can not be obtained by compass. With the antenna set in "Loop" position, rotate the Left-Right switch on the receiver panel until a "Null" or "No-sound" position is obtained. With the variation knob of the radio compass on "O", the resulting bearing is the relative bearing of the station from the plane. The Aural Null is extremely valuable in this theatre where thunder storms may affect the automatic compass. Ranges for an effective Aural Null are possibly 50 miles greater than for the Automatic Compass.

Note should be made of the fact that the Radio Compass Receiver can be used as an emergency receiver on 100-1750 Kcs.

b. The next type of Radio Bearing is the VHF/DF (Voice) bearing. The procedure is to request the Pilot to call for a bearing on VHF. Fighter Control will come back with a QUJ which is a true course to base. This method of receiving a bearing is usually effective within 100 miles. The variable factor here is the ability of the planes VHF transmitter to reach the Ground Station.

DF Bearings may be requested by the Radio Operator on the Liaison Set. These bearings may be received at greater distances, reliable up to 500 miles and often greater. In actual practice such a bearing is used in emergencies and usually at a distance of 150-200 miles. It takes approximately one minute to get an HF-DF bearing under ideal conditions.

## E  CELESTIAL TACTICAL PROCEDURE

Celestial tactical procedure in this theatre is very little different than is found in other theatres but in importance ranks the highest. Celestial is the highest expression of the navigator's art. It requires a high degree of proficiency, yet with that proficiency the navigator is able to establish his position accurately and with facility. A good three star fix will be one of your most accurate positioning aids.

It is essential that each navigator be able to combine his celestial with every navigation aid in the airplane without the slightest hesitation or uncertainty. He must be able to plot a sunline, cross it with a radio bearing, a Loran line, a moon line, or even a coast line if he is near the mainland.

It is your personal responsibility to be familiar with all the information available to you. If you've forgotten how to plot sunrise and sunset you will find an explanation in the back of your air almanac. Many times you'll find it important to know the local zone time of sunrise or sunset at base or the duration of darkness on a night weather strike mission.

You will find the planet position diagram on the AM side of your air almanac very helpful, and it should be remembered that the diagram also illustrates the declination of the bodies as well as the SHA.

The accuracy necessary in this theatre will require that you apply all corrections to your sextant observations. The sextant correction should always be known by the navigator and should be checked prior to take-off. In determining the sextant error, the navigator should check it through altitudes from $0^\circ$ to $90^\circ$, since some few sextants will have errors that will vary with altitude.

The dome refraction should be tabulated on the inside rim of the astro-dome. If it is not there, the navigator should determine these errors by a series of observations through the dome when the airplane is on the ground. It must be remembered that in order to determine the dome refraction, the navigator must be proficient enough with his sextant to shoot on the ground with no error.

Atmospheric refraction is a correction which must be applied on occasion. The tables in H.O. 218 are corrected for any refraction which would be present when the aircraft is at an altitude of 5,000 feet. The proper correction can be found by entering the refraction table (Table VI) in the back of the volumes.

Parallax is a correction that is necessary only with observations on the moon. It will vary in size with seasons and with altitude of the body. This correction is always added to the sextant observation. The values for the parallax correction will be found on the right hand side of the AM page of the Air Almanac.

But the final accuracy of all celestial procedures is dependent upon complete coordination of the pilot and navigator. You will notice that one of the greatest sources of your course errors will be during the climb phase and the long slow descent to base. It will be absolutely necessary to take celestial shots during these periods, and it will be your responsibility to insure that descent and climb rates are sufficiently constant to allow reasonable accuracy. Bubble acceleration can be excessive if care is not taken while shooting. For instance, a course deviation of two degrees during the period of observation will cause an error of approximately _nine_ miles. An airspeed change of _one_ mile per minute will introduce an error of approximately _two_ miles in the observation. Best results are obtained with the airplane flying the C-1 and with the use of the two minute averaging sextant. The navigator should _always_ notify the pilot before he begins to shoot. It is also wise to let the pilot know when you are through shooting so that he will know he is free to make any course, altitude, or power setting changes he has been postponing during the period of the observations. The use of the sextant support is a _must_ at all times and especially if there is turbulence.

Once in flight on the way to the Empire, the heading of the aircraft should be constantly checked by the astro-compass. It is the one completely accurate way of checking heading. Checking on heading with the astro-compass does not mean that the compass deviation on a heading is found once and then forgotten. Resort to the astro-compass should be made at frequent intervals.

The accuracy of sunlines, their usefulness enroute and in making a successful landfall on the Japanese coast depends upon the navigators. ability to interpret the single line of position. A large part of this interpretation can be done on the ground before the flight. The navigator should check azimuth for estimated positions during the flight and plan to use them accordingly. You don't want to waste time taking useless shots.

When used as ground speed checks, sunlines can be combined with drift to obtain a fix. A noon fix can frequently be obtained, though a fix of this sort gives only an indication. When the sun is at its zenith, the latitude can easily be obtained. The navigator should determine and mark on his chart before he ever leaves the ground, the approximate position on his course at which the sun will transit his meridian. If the moon and sun are both in the sky, an accurate fix may be obtained.

Since it is valuable on almost every mission flown from this theatre, it is well to review and practice the Noon Fix, meridianal altitude LOP, and the co-altitude fix.

Noon Fix.

A noon fix is a combination of a meridianal altitude shot and two other observations, one before and another after that of the meridianal transit. These two shots must cut each other at a good angle, over 45°.

It is obvious, therefore, that the speed at which the sun's azimuth is changing will determine just how much before transit the observer takes his shot. Since the nearer the sub-point, the more quickly the azimuth changes, it applies that the nearer the observer is to the sun's sub-point the shorter can be the elapsed time between shots in order to get a good cut - and the farther away the longer the elapsed time.

These few figures will help in figuring time for the "Before and After" shots:

| Difference between observer's latitude and declination of sun at time of transit: | Time to take shots before and after meridian transit: |
|---|---|
| 15° | 40 min. |
| 10° | 30 min. |
| 5° | 20 min. |
| 3° | 15 min. |

Using these figures will result in at least a 45° cut between the first and third shots. EXAMPLE: If one's latitude was 14°N the sun's declination was 4°N and the time of meridian transit was 2040 GCT, the observer would shoot at 2010 GCT, get a meridian transit shot at 2040, and then get the third shot at 2120 GCT, and would move the shots that were more closely course lines to the line that was more nearly a speed line.

Meridian Altitude Diagram and Explanation.

Start shooting the sun about five minutes before GHA of sun equals observers DR longitude and continue taking shots until five minutes after the sun crosses DR longitude. Record the time for the highest shot. This is the Meridian Transit shot.

Draw a diagram of the plane of the great circle passing through the poles, draw the equator and locate the sun by its declination at the time of observation. The latitude then can be found by applying the appropriate equation. NOTE: An approximate fix can also be obtained by using the GHA of the time of highest observation as longitude.

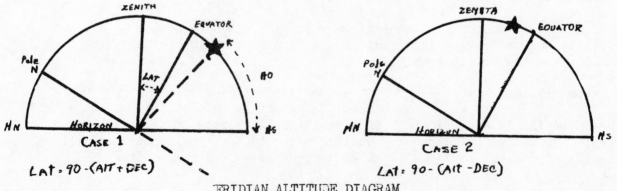

MERIDIAN ALTITUDE DIAGRAM

FIGURE XIX

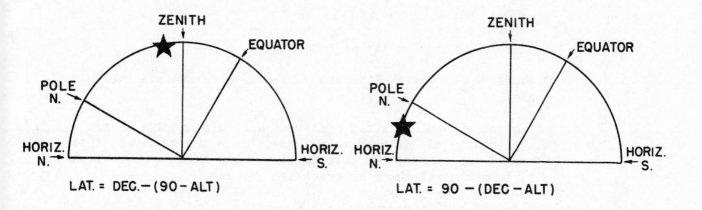

MERIDIAN ALTITUDE DIAGRAM

FIGURE XX

Co-Altitude Method.

Many times the observer is so near the sun's sub-point that the HO will be higher than 80°, at which times HO 218 is no longer workable. A co-altitude method may be used in these cases.

These facts are involved:

a.  Co-altitude is, by definition, the difference between 90° and the HO, or:   90 - HO.

b.  At the sub-point of any body an observer will get an HO of 90°.

c.  Therefore, co-altitude in minutes will be the distance in nautical miles from the sub-point to the observer's position.

To use this method the body's sub-point must be found and plotted. Declincation and GHA become latitude and longitude; example - for a given day and time the Air Almanac gives the sun's declination as 16° 13' N and its GHA as 148° 12'.  This would make the position of the sub-point 16°13' N latitude and 148° 12' W longitude.

Given:

HO 1 .......... 84°18'
HO 2 .......... 87°42'
HO 3 .......... 84°25'

Required:  To obtain a Fix -

    a.   Plot the sun's sub-points.

    b.   Find co-altitude (90-94°18' = 342 n.m.)

    c.   Measure 342 n.m. with dividers, using an accurate mid-latitude scale.

    d.   Using the sub-point as the center of a circle, strike an arc with a radius of 342 n.m. to intersect your track.  If it intersects at two places, the bearing of the sun from your position will determine at which intersection you are.

    e.   Follow the same procedure for the next two, using radii of 138 n.m. and 335 n.m. respectively.

    f.   To obtain a fix, move the sub-points of the shots which, by inspection, show them to be more nearly course lines, using the DR course and G.S.  Plot arcs from these new sub-points to intersect the speed line.

On the return trip the last $3\frac{1}{2}$ to 4 hours may be made in darkness.  Clouds are the only bar to successful celestial work.  It should not be necessary to tell navigators how to choose stars properly, yet some persist in shooting stars whose azimuth cannot possibly result in good fixes.  In these latitudes, navigational stars are plentiful, but the ability to identify them quickly and without resort to the waste of time incurred in the use of the Air Almanac or the Rude Star Finder is very important.  Polaris will usually be available, and you should be able to apply the correction in the Air Almanac immediately.

Even if the sextant is out of adjustment, ground speed checks can be made with it by measuring from LOP to LOP using an LOP as a reference point.  These ground speed checks can then be combined with a radio or Loran bearing and a fix obtained.

While descending on course you will almost be forced to fly fix to fix because of varying winds, yet even here you should not ignore any definite off course trends.  Gas reserves are too small to stray from course, in emergencies, a landfall may be flown off Polaris or a similar star, but here again the navigator dare not be too far off because of gas.  It is best practice to DR in as closely as possible and make the turn in to base on a radio bearing.  The DR navigation should not be discontinued until the airplane is on the ground.

If the plane has been flying under instrument conditions for sometime and then breaks out where shots can be obtained, the navigators DR position should still be roughly correct.  In case you sometime become lost, a lost plane procedure, with the pilot holding the correct DR heading should

be instituted.  A fix can then be taken, a course correction made, and
a second fix and wind obtained.  From this point on straight celestial
procedure applies.


## F  RADAR NAVIGATION AND BOMBING


### 1.  Radar Navigation.

As need for security decreases, the islands enroute to the mainland will
be used more frequently as navigational aids.  It will be your responsibility to make proper use of APQ-13 in conjunction with your other navigation procedure, you should inform the radar operator of possible island
return, and make wind run whenever possible as a check on your dead reckoning.

Experience has shown that radar returns from the Japanese mainland can
normally be received up to 50-60 miles.  The coastline features of Japan
are such that it is highly improbable that any navigator will fail to
recognize the coastal features where landfall will be made if he has
studied the terrain feature to be expected.

If the crew does not have a radar navigator at the set, it will be necessary for the navigator at the auxiliary scope to make the radar approach
and the radar bombing run.  The standard radar-bomb sight procedure de-
mands close cooperation on the part of the navigator, the bombardier,
and the radar operator.  Each of these three men must know implicitly
what can be expected of the other two; each must know his procedure and
the crew must discuss and practice these procedures constantly.

The standard radar bombing procedure is simple and direct; however, it
requires well organized work to assure that details are accomplished in
the proper sequence.  The wind run must be made as soon as the landfall
has been made and the airplane is flying straight and level at bombing
altitude.  This must be done early to permit the navigator sufficient
time for a precision turn onto the axis of attack prior to passing over
the I.P.  A sub-section follows, which allows for wind run procedure,
allowance for turn, and detailed bombing procedure.  Prior to the turn,
the navigator must have:

. Computed the latest wind and advised the bombardier of the wind,
   ground speed and drift on the axis of attack.

b. Noted the T.H. necessary to make good the axis of attack.  Advise pilot in advance of this T.H. and the number of degrees of
   turn at I.P.

c. Set the track line on the radar scope to the axis of attack and
   mark with a grease pencil the allowance for radius of turn.

d.  Check radar for the position of the set controls. If stabilization is on, correct the lubber line on your scope with the variation setting knob on the fluxgate.

The navigator should attempt to locate the target return on the scope prior to the turn. If this is not practicable, a reference check point should be located close to the target to facilitate target recognition at the earliest possible time.

If the turn has been correctly computed and flown so as to place the airplane on the axis of attack at the I.P., you should find the target under, or very nearly under the track line. If the target is not within a degree of the track line, you should correct the pilot until it is, then ask for sector scan. You are now ready to refine your drift and course in sequence. This is a strict precision step but not particularly difficult and can best be kept in mind with reference to the interphone procedure on the bombing run. This bomb run procedure is covered in detail in a following sub-section.

2.  Check List for the Standard Bomb Run Procedure.

Proceeding over the I.P., the navigator will:

a.  Check to locate the target under, or very nearly under the track line. Request bomb bay doors open and sector scan.

b.  Request necessary turn to be made to place target within one degree of track line.

c.  Place track line exactly on the target return.

d.  Request radar operator to move the target return exactly under the fourth circle on the scope using 20 mile variable range.

e.  Note bearing of the target being careful that your eyes are in place to avoid parallax.

f.  When the target has moved into the third circle on the scope glass, note the bearing and give the pilot a course correction equal to four times the change in bearing plus one degree for each five degrees of the product. For instance, if the target has moved off two degrees to the right: 4 x 2 = 8 plus 1 or 9 degrees right turn request.

g.  Upon receipt of on course signal from pilot, request radar to again place target under fourth circle on the scope glass.

h.  Keep repeating these quadruple, drift corrections, steps d. e. and f., as long as the 68° bombing circle is less than 2/3 the distance from the center of the scope to the target.

i. Alert the bombardier to begin rate determination when the target cuts the 68° bombing circle.

j. Call the bombardier ready - mark - when the target is on the 68° bombing circle.

k. Repeat step j. for successive bombing circles for rate refinement.

l. Make necessary course corrections during rate refinement without moving the track line.

m. Keep correcting by radar until bombardier takes over "visual" or until "bombs away".

3. Radar Wind Run Procedure.

As soon as landfall is made, the navigator will:

a. Request pilot to hold steady course for wind run.

b. Select some sharp point on radar scope as early as possible.

c. Request range markers from radar.

d. Measure exact time it first touches range marker, start stop watch and measure relative bearing.

e. Repeat time, bearing and range reading every couple of minutes as point touches successive range markers.

f. After 5 to 10 minutes run, at time point touches range marker, take reading and stop the stop watch.

g. Plot all positions on chart and lay average track thru them.

h. Lay off T.H. on chart.

i. Measure distance travelled between first and last positions.

j. Using elapsed time from stop watch, compute G.S. on E6B.

k. Divide T.A.S. and measured G.S. by 3 and plot wind vector on E6B.

l. Extend track line by DR and use wind on E6B to determine turns and heading to control point and I.P.

Explanatory "Wind Run" problem:

a. Approaching point on Japanese coast:

| | |
|---|---|
| Indicated Air Speed | 195 m.p.h. |
| Pressure Altitude | 25,000 ft. |
| Temp. Reading (-22°) Corrected Temp. | -30°C. |
| True Heading | 335° |
| T.A.S. (Using G-1 Computer) | 257 Knots. |

b. Following ranges and bearings were measured using range markers:

| Time | Rel Brg | + | T.H. | = | True Brg | Slant Distance |
|---|---|---|---|---|---|---|
| 1300 | 018° | | 335° | | 353° | 45' |
| 1302 | 016° | | 335° | | 351° | 35' |
| 1304 | 012° | | 335° | | 347° | 25' |
| 1305½ | 010° | | 335° | | 345° | 20' |

c. Plot the ranges and bearings for positions on Navigation Chart or use E6B:

| | |
|---|---|
| Read Track on Chart | 359° |
| Measure distance travelled on Chart | 25½ n.m. |
| Stop Watch time | 5' 28" |
| Ground Speed on E6B (25.5 n. in 5' 25") | 278 Knots |

d. Get wind on E6B by dividing vectors by 3:

| | |
|---|---|
| TAS/3 - 257/3 | 85.7 |
| GS/3 - 278/3 | 92.7 |
| Drift | 24° Right |
| True Heading | 335° |
| Wind Direction | 246° |
| Wind Vector | 38 |
| Wind Vector x 3 to get wind velocity | 114 Knots. |
| Wind | 246°/114 Knots |

4. Detailed Bombing Procedure "Interphone".

As soon as the airplane levels off at altitude, the navigator will remind the Aircraft Commander of his ETA to enemy coast and control points, proceeding in the following manner:

| | |
|---|---|
| Navigator: | "Pilot from Navigator, Over" |
| Pilot : | "Go ahead" |
| Navigator: | "Latest ETA to enemy coast - 1015" |
| Pilot : | "Roger" |
| Navigator: | "Radar Operator from Navigator, Over" |
| Radar Op.: | "Go ahead" |
| Navigator: | "Estimate distance to coast 75 miles. Set in maximum range." |
| Radar Op.: | (After compliance) "Maximum range set in." |

| | |
|---|---|
| Radar Op.: | (After obtaining return) "Land return at 65 miles, bearing 330°" |
| Navigator: | (After checking return) "Roger" |
| Radar Op.: | "Bombardier from Radar, Over" |
| Bombardier: | "Go ahead" |
| Radar Op.: | "What is bombing altitude?" |
| Bombardier: | "Bombing altitude 26,000 feet" |
| Radar Op.: | "Roger" (Sets in altitude) |
| Navigator: | "Pilot from Navigator, Over" |
| Pilot : | "Go ahead" |
| Navigator: | "Ready on wind run. Maintain heading, altitude, and airspeed." |
| Pilot : | "Wilco" (or reason for not taking run at this time) |
| Radar Op.: | "Ready on wind run" (Scope adjusted, range markers in) |
| Navigator: | (Taking a series of fixes, plotting same on chart, and computing wind) "Wind run completed. Corrected heading to I.P. is three four zero degrees" (Calculates allowance for turn on to axis of attack) "Heading on bomb run is nine four degrees, will call turn in approximately three minutes. You will turn 124° right" |
| Pilot : | "Roger" |
| Navigator: | "Begin turn now to nine four degrees" |
| Pilot : | "Wilco ... on course" |
| Navigator: | "Pilot two degrees right" |
| Pilot : | "On course" |
| Navigator: | (Quadruple drift correction) .. "Nine degrees right" |
| Pilot : | "..... On course" |
| Navigator: | "Radar switch to 20 mile range" |
| Radar Op.: | "Roger .... Ready on 70°" |
| Navigator: | ".... Ready .... Mark" |
| Radar Op.: | "Coming up on 68°" |
| Navigator: | ".... Ready .... Mark" |
| Radar Op.: | "Coming up on 65°" |
| Navigator: | ".... Ready .... Mark" |
| Radar Op.: | "Coming up on 60°" |
| Navigator: | ".... Ready .... Mark" |
| Radar Op.: | "Coming up on 55°" |
| Navigator: | "Displacement correction only .... Ready .... Mark" |
| Radar Op.: | "Coming up on 50°" |
| Navigator: | ".... Ready .... Mark" |

(Continues till bombs away)

## 5. Allowance for Turn.

Allowance for turn is the distance measured perpendicular to the axis of attack at which turn must be begun to place the airplane on the axis of attack when the turn has been completed. It is to be remembered that allowance for turn used properly enables the navigator to start the bomb run on the correct axis of attack, but it does not insure that the plane will pass over the I.P. Since the policy is to pass over the I.P. on course to the target, the turn must be begun to the left of the I.P. for right turns and to the right of the I.P. for left turns. The amount to the left or right of the I.P. will be computed for each mission with a margin for error: This is a separate problem. The following discussion deals with allowance for turn.

The allowance for turn will usually be computed by the staff navigator before the mission. As long as the wind is approximately as briefed and the approach to the I.P. is made as planned, the computed allowance for turn should be used. A convienient method fixing the point to begin turn by radar can be used and is given in steps as follows:

   a. Have the radar operator select a range which will include the target and/or I.P. when the plane is at least ten miles back from the I.P.

   b. With azimuth stabilization off, place the track line off zero in the direction of turn a number of degrees equal to the difference between the axis of attack and the true heading of the airplane as it approaches the turn.

   c. Draw a line with a grease pencil above and parallel to the track line so that the distance between the track line and the grease pencil mark is equal to the allowance for turn. The range of the scope sets the scale for this distance, and the range used while drawing the line should be used when making the turn.

   d. Begin the turn when the target and/or I.P. is under the grease mark. While the turn is being made, set the line or predicted drift for the bomb run; the target should appear under the center drift line when the turn has been completed.

For no wind, up-wind, and downwind runs:

Radius of turn is equal to: $\dfrac{\text{TAS} \times \text{Time for 360 turn}}{2\pi} = \dfrac{\text{TAS for 8 min.}}{2\pi}$

For turns less than 90 degrees:

Allowance for turn is equal to Radius - radius x Cos turn angle.

For turns more than 90 degrees:

Allowance for turn is equal to Radius plus Radius x Cos (180-Turn Angle)

For turns with a wind not parallel to the axis of attack:

Compute turn allowance with formulae above and apply the wind vector for the time of turn backwards, from the point thus determined on the chart. Connect the end of the wind vector with a perpendicular to the axis of attack. The length of this perpendicular is the allowance for turn.

Example:

a.  For TAS = 260 knots; axis of attack down-wind 90°
    Radius of turn = $\dfrac{260 \text{ knots for 8 min.}}{2 \pi}$ = $\dfrac{34.7 \text{ N.M.}}{6.28}$ (= 5.4 N.M.)

    Allowance for turn from true heading of 330° to axis of attack of 90° = turn for 120°
    = 5.4 N.M. plus 5.4 x Cos 60°
    = 5.4 plus 5.4 x 5
    = 8.1 N.M. back from I.P.

b.  For TAS 260 Knots W/V = 300°/100 K axis of attack 90°
    From 319° Heading to Heading for attack of 79° = 120°
    Allowance for turn (downwind) = 8.1 N.M.
    Approximately 3 minutes turn with 100 K wind = 5 N.M. of wind effect.

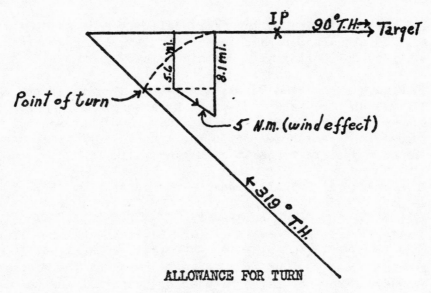

ALLOWANCE FOR TURN

FIGURE XXI

G  LORAN

The present loran equipment has been used to obtain lines of position and fixes 700 miles from base in the daylight and 1400 miles at night. Operation is independent of weather condition and when the set has been aligned properly, it is impossible to obtain false readings.

Navigators will often find this will be their only navigational aid and
should make it their personal responsibility to be familiar with simple
air maintenance and maximum utilization under extreme range conditions.

1.  Theory.

    a.  Transmission.  Each loran chain consists of a number of stations
        each two adjacent stations constituting a pair.  Because the
        radio waves used become attenuated rapidly over land, the two
        stations are separated only by water and are from 200 to 300
        miles apart.  Although a single station may be common to two
        pairs, for the purpose of this discussion a single pair will be
        considered.

        One station is considered the "Master", and emits signals on a
        certain frequency.  These signals are forty microseconds in dur-
        ation, a microsecond being 1/1,000,000 second.  One pair of the
        chain transmits a signal every 40,000 microseconds, (actually
        30,000 in this theatre) the second pair every 39,800 microseconds,
        etc.  For reasons of simplicity, the pair that transmits at
        intervals of 40,000 microseconds (25 pulses per second) will be
        considered.

        The second station of the pair, called the "Slave", will also
        emit 25 signals per second, not simultaneously with the master
        station, but following a certain delay.

        In Figure XXII, page VI-51, the Master Station is at "A", and the
        "Slave" station is at "B".  Let us assume that the stations are
        such a distance apart that it takes 1,000 microseconds for the
        pulses to travel from one to the other.  Further assume that the
        master and slave transmit simultaneously.

        An operator at "A" will receive the pulse from "A", 1,000 micro-
        seconds ahead of the pulse from "B".  The same reading will re-
        sult if he is anywhere along the base line extension from "A".
        Similarly, if the operator is at "B" or in the base line exten-
        sion from "B", the pulse from "B" will be received 1,000 micro-
        seconds ahead of that from "A".  If he is at the midpoint, or
        anywhere along the perpendicular bi-sector of the base line,
        both signals will be received simultaneously.

        At position "C", the signal from "B" will arrive before the sig-
        nal from "A", the time difference being the length of time nec-
        essary for the pulse to travel the difference indicated on line
        "AC".  At every position along the hyperbola (with foci at "A"
        and "B") running through "C", the time difference, is the LOP's
        obtained with loran equipment.

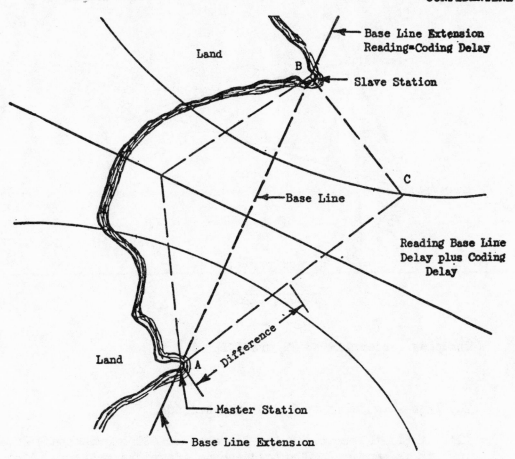

A PAIR OF LORAN STATIONS

FIGURE XXII

In order to eliminate the possibility of confusion arising from not knowing which pulse (master or slave) is received first, a base line delay is incorporated into the slave signal. This delay actually insures that the slave station will not be received first, regardless of the position of the observer. This can be explained further by reference to Figure XXII. A pulse emitted by master station "A" is received 100 microseconds later at slave station "B". If, at this later instant, "B" then emits its pulse, careful study of the figure shows that at no position would it be received first. The time difference would be 0 microseconds at "B" and 2,000 microseconds at "A". The base line delay is always such that it is exactly equal to the length of time it takes the master pulse to traverse the distance to the slave station.

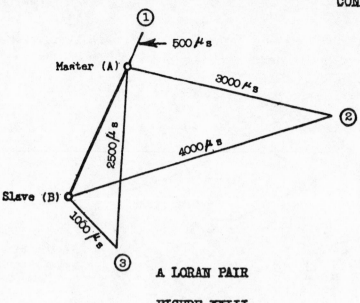

A LORAN PAIR

FIGURE XXIII

Examples (referring to Figure XXIII ):

The base line delay is 2,000 microseconds.

(1)  At (1) the master pulse is received 500 microseconds after
     it is sent.  2,000 microseconds after the master station
     pulses, the slave station pulses and it takes 2,500 micro-
     seconds for this pulse to reach (1).  The time difference
     at (1) is then 2,500 + 2,000 - 500 = 4,000 microseconds.
     Time difference equals base line delay plus distance (in
     microseconds) from slave station minus distance (in micro-
     seconds) from master station.

(2)  3,000 microseconds after the pulse leaves "A", it arrives
     at (2).  The "B" pulse leaves 2,000 microseconds after the
     "A" pulse and travels for 4,000 microseconds before arriv-
     ing at (2).  The time difference 4,000 + 2,000 - 3,000 =
     3,000 microseconds.

(3)  Time difference at (3) is 1,000 + 2,000 - 2,500 = 500
     microseconds.

A second delay called the coding delay, is also introduced at
the slave station.  This coding delay serves two purposes.  In
the previous examples, on the base line extension from the slave
station, time differences were 0 microseconds.  In practice this
would involve difficulty.  An additional coding delay of approximately 1,000 microseconds is incorporated so that the lowest
reading will be about 1,000.  The coding delay serves another

function in that it may be varied at regular intervals so as to preclude the use of Loran by the enemy. The formula given above must be amended to read:  Time difference equals base line delay plus coding delay plus distance from the slave station minus distance from the master station.

b.  Reception.  On the Loran indicator the navigator receives a pair of signals from a pair of stations, reads the time difference (in microseconds) between the pulses, makes an adjustment if the coding delay has been changed, and, referring to specially prepared charts, converts this reading into an LOP. Two or more LOP's constitute a fix.  LOP's are advanced in the same manner as celestial LOP's using track and ground speed.

Radio waves from the transmitting stations emanate in all directions.  The waves which travel along the earth's surface are known as ground waves.  In the daytime, the ground waves give reliable signals up to about 700 nautical miles.  At night, the effective range is reduced to about 400 nautical miles.

Sky waves, on the other hand, can be received effectively only at night.  Sky waves are those which are reflected to the receiving station from the ionosphere and, because of the extra distance which they travel, arrive later than the ground waves. When using the specially prepared tables or charts to convert readings to LOP's, a correction is given which must be applied if sky waves are used.  Sky waves have an effective range from 1200 to 1400 nautical miles.  How sky waves may be distinguished from ground waves will be discussed later.

2.  Operation.

a.  The receiver. The receiver illustrated in Figure XXIV is used to receive and amplify the incoming signals.  These signals are transmitted to the indicator which places them on a flourescent screen in such a manner that the reading may be taken. A channel selector switch for four positions unables the receiver to be tuned to the operating frequencies.  At present, in this theatre, only channel No. 3 is used.  Two other toggle switches are on the receiver face.  One is used to turn the source of power on or off; the other provides an additional filter circuit to cut out some of the interference.  When the use of this  switch does not materially aid reception, it should be turned off.

A double throw antenna switch is usually provided and connected so that in one position the trailing antenna is connected to the loran equipment and the fixed antenna is connected to effect liaison.  In the other position the antenna connection is reversed.

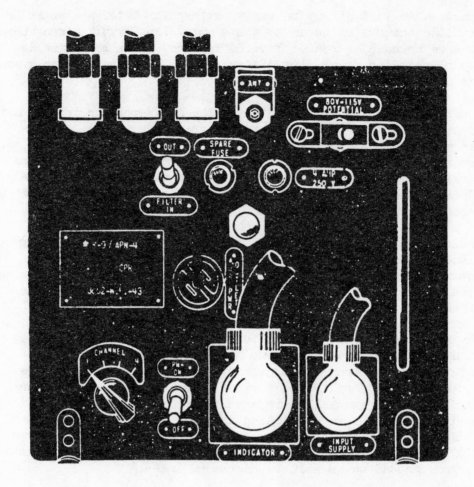

RECEIVER

FIGURE XXIV

b.  The indicator.  In the presence of much light it is advisable
to install the visor on the rim of the scope mounting so as to
see the traces and pulses more clearly.

Set "sweep speed" control to position 1.  Set both gain and
"amplitude" balance controls approximately at mid-scale.  Adjust focus control until traces are clear and stable (Figure
XXVI).Turn "intensity" control so the traces are visible and
readable, but keep this at the minimum necessary for clear
visibility.  It will be observed that vertical lines extend
upward from both traces.  These are the signals mentioned in
the previous section.  They are observed to be travelling horizontally to the right or left, or standing still, and to be
travelling in pairs.

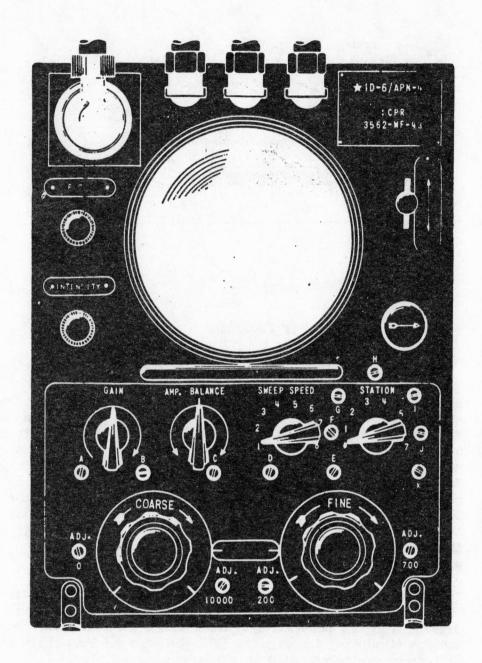

RECEIVER AND INDICATOR

FIGURE XXV

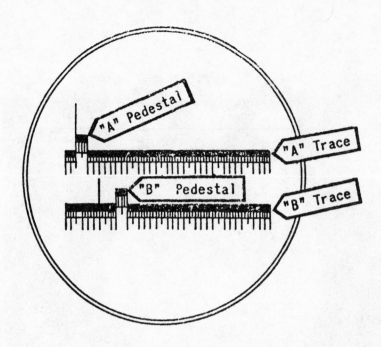

TRACES ON INDICATOR

FIGURE XXVI

By turning the switch labelled "station" to various positions, it
will be noticed that first one pair of signals and then another
will stop. Select the pair that it is desired to work with and
stop this pair on the traces. Now move them to the right or left
using the right-left switch so that one signal is placed on the
"A" or upper pedestal. If the other signal is on the "B" or lower
pedestal and to the right of the "A" signal, then the master pulse
is on the "A" pedestal as it should be. If not, continue to move
the signals until the master pulse is on the "A" pedestal, near
the left edge. If the signal has a tendency to drift, stop the
movement by the use of the "crystal phasing" control.

Turn the "coarse delay" dial until the "B" pedestal is under the
"B" signal. Turn the fine delay dial until the signal is on the
left side of the pedestal (Figure XXVII). The following steps will
consist of placing the signals in a position so that their time
difference can be measured in microseconds.

The first operation is to enlarge the pedestal tops so that the
pulses may be more properly matched. Turn the "sweep speed" control to position 2. Increase or decrease the "gain" control until the bottom signal is below the top signal. If the pulses

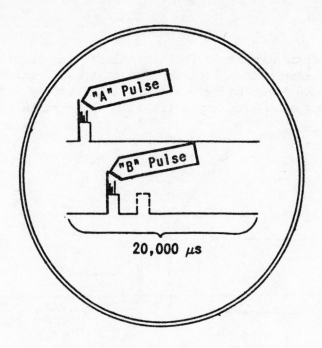

FINE DELAY ADJUSTMENT

FIGURE XXVII

have a tendency to drift, use the "crystal phasing" control. Use
the right-left switch until the signals are on the left side of the
traces.

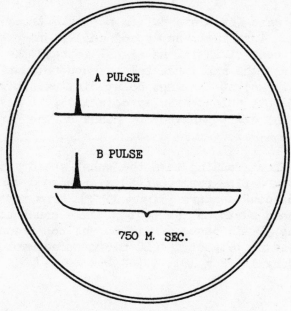

ENLARGEMENT OF PEDESTAL TOPS

FIGURE XXVIII

The next operation is to further enlarge the critical area to permit finer alignment.  Turn the "sweep speed" control to position 3.  Move the "fine delay" dial until the bottom signal is below the top signal.  Stop any drift with the "crystal phasing" control.

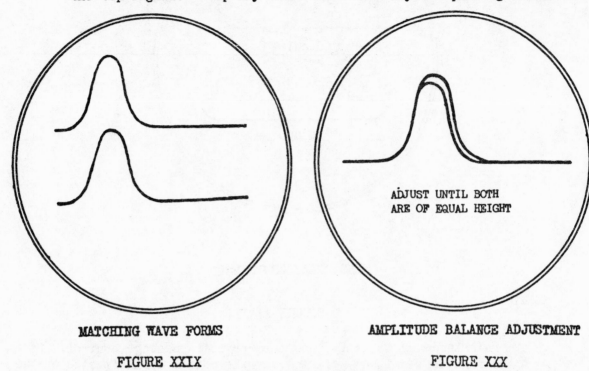

MATCHING WAVE FORMS

FIGURE XXIX

ADJUST UNTIL BOTH
ARE OF EQUAL HEIGHT

AMPLITUDE BALANCE ADJUSTMENT

FIGURE XXX

Now both wave forms are put on a single trace for purposes of matching.  Turn the sweep speed control to position 4.  Adjust the gain control until one signal is near the top of the screen.  Then adjust the amplitude balance control until both signals coincide.  Adjust the fine delay dial carefully so that the left sides of both pulses exactly coincide.  It may be necessary to correct any drift tendency by means of the "crystal phasing" control.

For the first reading turn the sweep speed control to position 5.  The downward pips represent 50 microsecond markers; the upward, 10 microsecond markers (Figure XXXI).  From any one of the long 50 microsecond marks on the bottom trace count to the right, to the next long 50 microsecond mark on the top trace.  Interpolate the final reading between the 10 microsecond markers.  In this example the reading is $(2 \times 10) + 5 = 25$.

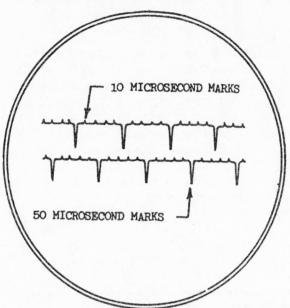

SWEEP SPEED CONTROL, POSITION 5

FIGURE XXXI

For the second reading turn the sweep speed control to position
6. The longer downward pips represent 500 microsecond markers;
the shorter downward pips, 50 microsecond markers (Figure XXXII).
From any one of the 500 microsecond markers on the bottom trace,
count to the right to the next 500 microsecond marker on the top
trace. It is not necessary to interpolate, as the odd part of
the 50 microsecond is the 25 microsecond previously measured. In
this example the reading is (4 x 50) or 200 microseconds. Add to
this the previously obtained 25 microseconds, the reading is 225.

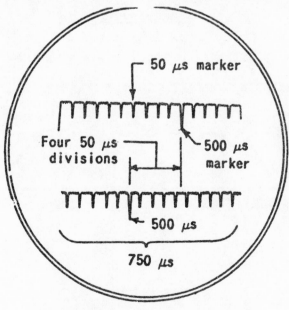

SWEEP SPEED CONTROL, POSITION 6

FIGURE XXXII

For the final reading turn the sweep speed control to position 7. The longer downward pips are 2500 microsecond markers; the shorter downward pips 500 microsecond markers. Count the number of 500 microsecond markers on the lower trace, from the left edge of the upper pedestal to the left edge of the lower pedestal. The reading in this case is (8 x 500) = 4000 microseconds. Therefore the total reading is 4000 plus 225 or 4225 microseconds. Counting the 500 microsecond markers will be simplified by remembering that there are 5 of them between each two 2500 microsecond markers.

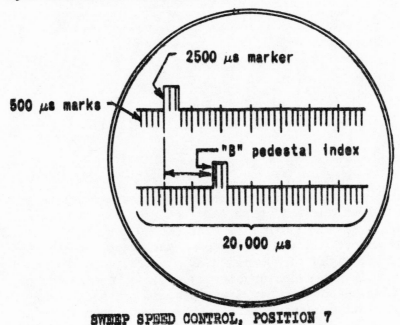

SWEEP SPEED CONTROL, POSITION 7

FIGURE XXXIII

Dangerous Splitting: First Component Fading.

NOTE: Cycle is from Left to Right and Return.

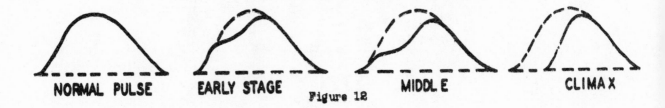

NORMAL PULSE   EARLY STAGE   Figure 12   MIDDLE   CLIMAX

FADING

FIGURE XXXIV

c.  Sky Waves. Sky waves will become noticeable at night and will
always appear to the right of the corresponding ground waves on
the trace. When the airplane is mo e than 600 nautical miles
from the station, the sky wave will be the only visible wave.
With the sweep speed at position 3 or 4, a sky wave may be recognized by its tendency to change position or "split" as shown
**in Figure XXXIV. Dangerous splitting results when the left or**
"leading edge" fades. Reading must not be taken when this oc-
**curs. Harmless splitting (Figure XXXV) results when the second**
component fades. It must be remembered that two ground waves
may be matched, or two sky waves, but NEVER a ground wave with
a sky wave. If sky waves are used, a correction is applied before converting to an LOP.

Harmless Splitting:  Second Component Fading.

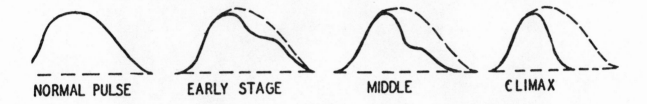

| NORMAL PULSE | EARLY STAGE | MIDDLE | CLIMAX |

SECOND COMPONENT FADING

FIGURE XXXV

d.  Converting Readings into LOP's. There are two methods for converting readings into LOP's. If no charts are available, Loran
tables are provided. However, a better system involves the use
of a specially prepared Mercator Chart which has LOP's already
plotted, each pair of stations being represented by a different
color. It is necessary to interpolate between LOP's. The chart
has the skywave correction printed directly thereon. Certain
charts also have slight inaccuracies in the printed LOP's and
corrections need be applied. The navigator should check with
intelligence whenever he draws a map to determine if it is correct.

The loran procedure appears at first glance to be long and complicated. Actually, once the procedure has been mastered, a
reading may be taken and the corresponding LOP plotted in one
minute. A fix, consisting of 2 or 3 LOP's may be obtained in
3 minutes. The accuracy of the system depends upon a number
of factors, but, in general, it may be said that the maximum
error encountered will be approximately one percent of the distance of the aircraft from the stations. LOP's will be more
accurate if the aircraft is near the center line of the pair
and the fixes will show greater accuracy if the LOP's have a
good cut.

## 3. Calibration.

The loran receiver and indicator, although comparatively simple from the
standpoint of operation, can, if not properly adjusted and aligned, result
in erroneous flight calculation.  It is the responsibility of the navigato
to make certain that the loran mechanics maintain perfect adjustment of
the equipment.  The navigator should thoroughly understand the procedure c
checking and maintaining calibration and alignment during the flight mission.  Occasionally a change of temperature or of altitude will affect the
adjustment of the sweep speed (counter circuit) and station selector calibration.  A check of these two adjustments should be made during flight
approximately every four hours of operation.  Because adjustment may be
necessary, it is necessary that a suitable screwdriver be available during
flight.

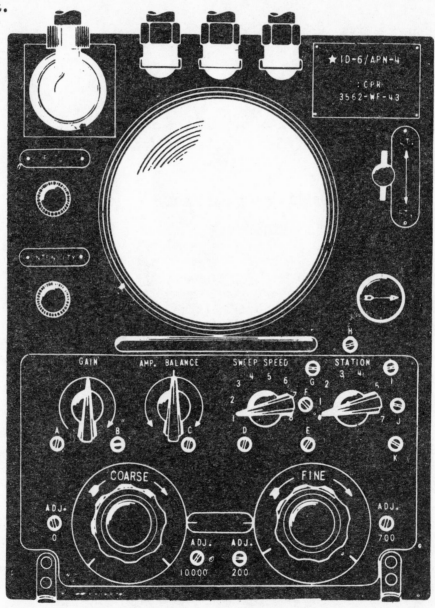

RECEIVER AND INDICATOR

FIGURE XXXVI

Accurate function of the indicator depends upon the various counter adjustments made through holes lettered A. B. C. and D.  The proper procedure for checking and making these adjustments is:

a. Sweepspeed Control Adjustments:

(1)  Turn the sweep speed switch to position 5.  As shown in Figure XXXVII, there should be four upward markers between any two sucessive downward markers.  This divides each 50 microsecond interval into 5 equal 10 microsecond intervals.  If such is not the case, adjust screw A to the mid-point of the region in which there are four upward makers between any two successive downward markers.

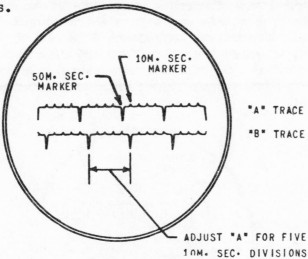

ADJUSTMENT, STEP 1
FIGURE XXXVII

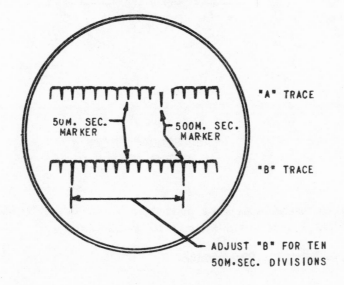

ADJUSTMENT, STEP 2
FIGURE XXXVIII

(2) Turn sweep speed to position 6, each trace shows a series of downward markers, two of which are longer than the rest. The shorter markers are 50 microseconds apart and the longer markers should be 500 microseconds apart. Screwdriver adjustment B is set at the mid-point of the region in which nine of the 50 microsecond markers appear between two 500 microsecond markers. This insures that there are exactly ten 50 microsecond spaces between two consecutive 500 microsecond markers.

(3) Turn sweep speed to position 7, the traces now show a series of long downward markers which are 500 microseconds apart, and heavier, more intense markers which should be 2500 microseconds apart. Screwdriver adjustment C is set to the mid-point of the region in which there are four 500 microsecond markers between the heavier 2500 microsecond markers. These 500 microsecond markers divide each 2500 microsecond interval into five equal spaces.

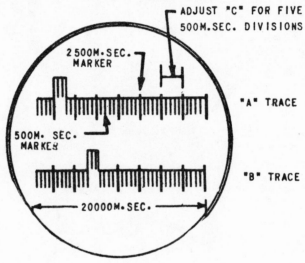

ADJUSTMENT, STEP 3
FIGURE XXXIX

(4) With sweep speed at position 7, adjust D until there are six 2500 microsecond spaces on each trace.

b. Station Selector Adjustments:

(1) Turn sweep speed switch to position 8 and station selector to 0. Ten horizontal rows of dots will appear on the screen.

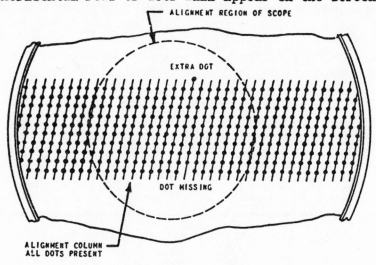

If this condition does not exist, readjust "A", "B", "C" & "D" to a greater degree of accuracy.

ADJUSTMENT, STEP 1

FIGURE XXXX

(2) Turn the station selector to position 1. If a dot does not dis-sappear, or if two dissappear, adjust E to the center of the range in which one dot dissappears.

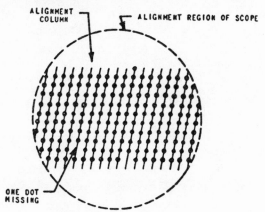

ADJUSTMENT, STEP 2

FIGURE XXXXI

(3) After making any necessary adjustments on position 1, turn the station selector to position 2. If the screwdrover adjustment F is set properly, the dot which is immediately above the vacant space created on position 1 will dissappear. Set F to the center of the range in which this occurs.

(4) Repeat this procedure on the remaining positions of the station
selector. An additional dot should dissappear for each position the switch is turned clockwise

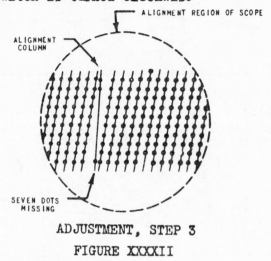

ALIGNMENT REGION OF SCOPE

ALIGNMENT
COLUMN

SEVEN DOTS
MISSING

ADJUSTMENT, STEP 3

FIGURE XXXXII

c. Coarse-Fine Delay Adjustments:

(1) Turn sweep speed switch to position 7. Turn the coarse and fine
controls counterclockwise until their right index marks are in
line with the panel index marks. Turn adj. 0 until the leading
edge of the B pedestal is slightly to the right (200 microseconds)
of the leading edge of the A pedestal. It will move to 500 microsecond jumps.

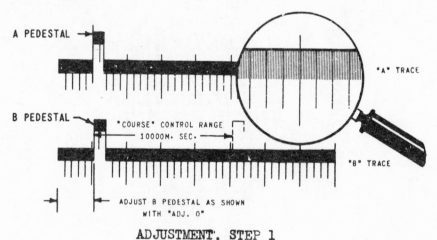

A PEDESTAL

"A" TRACE

B PEDESTAL

"COURSE" CONTROL RANGE
10000M. SEC.

"B" TRACE

ADJUST B PEDESTAL AS SHOWN
WITH "ADJ. 0"

ADJUSTMENT, STEP 1

FIGURE XXXXIII

Turn coarse control clockwise until the left dial mark is in line
with the panel index. Turn adj. 10000 until the B pedestal is
slightly to the right (200 microseconds) of the fifth 2500 microsecond marker. It will now be 10000 microseconds to the right of
the adj. 0 position.

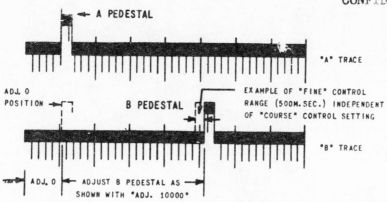

ADJUSTMENT, STEP 2

FIGURE XXXXIV

(2) Turn sweep speed switch to position 6. Move coarse control to
the center position. Turn fine control counterclockwise until
the right index mark is in line with the panel index mark. Turn
adj. 200 until four 50 microsecond spaces appear between the
500 microsecond marker on the B trace, and the first 500 microsecond marker to its right on the A trace.

Turn fine control clockwise until the left dial mark is in line
with the panel index. Turn adj. 700 until four 50 microsecond
divisions appear between the 500 microsecond marker on the B
trace and the 500 microsecond marker on its right on the A trace.
The indicator pattern is the same for adj. 200 and adj. 700.
Because of interlocking, make alternate readjustments of adj.
200 and adj. 700 to obtain correct results.

Proper functioning of the equipment will only be insured when it
is in proper adjustment. A qualified loran man should completely
check the alignment at least after every three days of operation
or before use if the equipment has been idle for three or more
days. More frequent checks are necessary on the counter circuit
and station selector. It is therefore imperative that the navigator be thoroughly familiar with these adjustments, however,
he may refer to the Handbook of Operating Instructions if there
is some doubt as to the procedure.

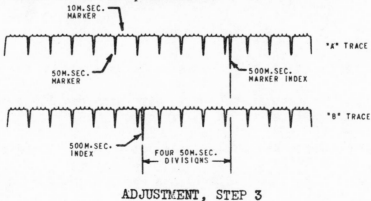

ADJUSTMENT, STEP 3
FIGURE XXXXV

**d.** Loran - (1D-6B/APN-4)

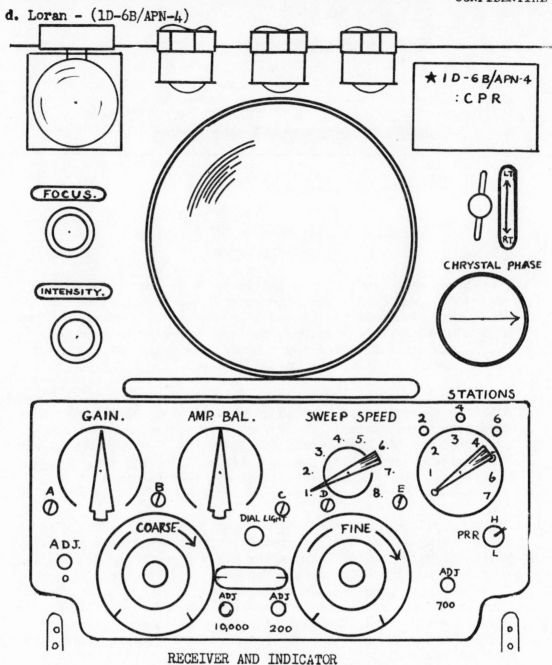

RECEIVER AND INDICATOR

FIGURE XXXXVI

1D-6B/APN-4. This set is the same as 1d-6/APN-4 with a few modifications:

(1) A switch has been installed to give high and low pulse rate repetition. Our net is set up    for high P.R.R.

(2) All adjustments are the same except on sweep speed eight.

(3) On sweep speed eight adjustments are made only on stations 2, 4, and 6.

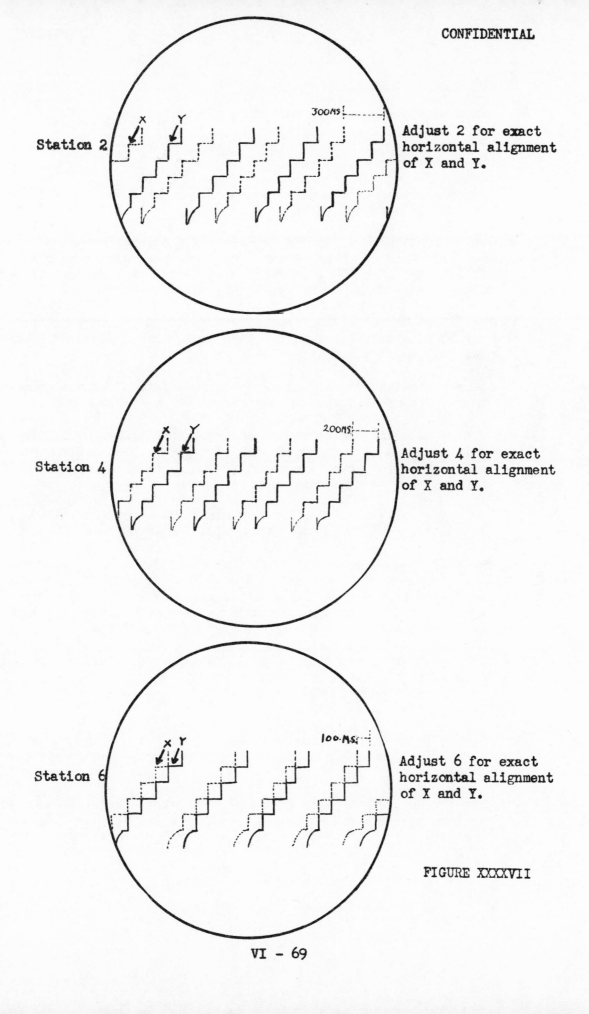

Station 2      300NS      Adjust 2 for exact horizontal alignment of X and Y.

Station 4      200NS      Adjust 4 for exact horizontal alignment of X and Y.

Station 6      100.MS      Adjust 6 for exact horizontal alignment of X and Y.

FIGURE XXXXVII

4. <u>Operating Procedure</u>.

   a. Turn receiver power off-on switch to ON position.

   b. Turn Gain Control to the extreme counter-clockwise position and Sweep Speed to position 7.

   c. Adjust focus and intensity to obtain sharp definition of the traces and vertical markers.

The equipment is then ready to use for measuring time differences. The Sweep Speed Switch is so arranged that the procedure for taking a reading begins with position 1 and proceeds in numerical sequence up to position 7, where the reading is completed. To take a reading:

   a. With Sweep Speed at position 1, set Amplitude Balance at the center of its range and turn the Gain Control clockwise until signal pulses are clearly seen.

   b. Select station pair by use of Station Selector. Pulses from station selected will appear to stand still on the scope.

   c. Drift pulses across screen by means of the left-right switch until one pulse is on the pedestal of the top trace and the other pulse is on the lower trace and to the right of the pulse on the top.

   d. Move the pedestal of the lower trace by means of the course delay until it is below the slave pulse (pulse on lower trace).

   e. Switch to sweep speed 2. Adjust crystal phasing to stop drifting of pulses if necessary. Adjust fine delay control to bring the pulse on the lower trace directly underneath that on the upper trace. Using the left-right switch, drift the pulses until they appear close to the left edge of the trace.

   f. Switch to sweep speed position 3. Readjust crystal phasing if necessary. Adjust gain until pulses are about on inch high. Amplitude Balance should be adjusted until pulses are of approximately equal amplitude.

   g. Switch to sweep speed position 4. Adjust fine delay and amplitude balance controls so that the two pulses are exactly superimposed.

   Both pulses are the same distance along their pedestals and the reading may be obtained by measurement of the distance between the pedestals . When matching, remember that particular attention is given to the leading (left) side of the pulses. When using the equipment at night, use ground waves if they are received. If it is not possible, then use the sky waves, but do not match ground wave against sky wave. Therefore, unless the ground wave from each station in a station pair is visible, use the first sky wave.

When using sky waves, it is well to observe each pulse separately before final matching of the pulses. This should be done with sweep speed at position 3 by adjusting the gain and amplitude balance to produce amplification of the pulses separately. If splitting is observed on the foremost position of the leading edge, special care must be exercised in matching, making sure that the pulses match at the leading edges. In most cases it is advisable to wait until the better waves forms are obtained. However, good results may be obtained by increasing the gain until the leading component can be readily distinguished.

If there is considerable interference on the traces, the filter on the receiver may be thrown to the IN position. If it does not cut down interference, it should be left in the OUT position.

h. Set Sweep speed to position 5. Read the number of microseconds that appear between any 50 microsecond marker on the lower trace and the first 50 microsecond marker to the right on the upper trace.

i. Set Sweep speed to position 6. Count the number of 50 microsecond markers between any 500 microsecond marker on the lower trace and the first 500 microsecond marker to its right on the upper trace. Multiply the number of intervals by 50 and add the resulting figure to that obtained in the previous step.

j. Set Sweep speed to position 7. Count the number of 500 microsecond markers between pedestals and multiply the number by 500, adding the number to that obtained previously. The resulting figure is the time difference between the pulses.

## H  DRIFT DETERMINATION BY RADIO ALTIMETER

Principles: Wind velocities can be estimated by measuring the horizontal rate of change of pressure over a given distance or in simple form, measuring the difference between your radio altimeter reading, and pressure altitude at 29.92.

The following system has been designed to provide the navigator with a reserve method of checking drift on course. A simple table has been provided so that no mathematical formulas are necessary.

a. The navigator can provide the bombardier with the mid-latitude of the observation, the distance flown between readings, and the TAS while the bombardier notes the difference between the radio altimeter reading and the pressure altimeter set at 29.92.

    i.e.  Radio altimeter altitude    10660
           Pressure altimeter altitude  10410
$$D = + 250$$

b. It should be noted that if the radio altimeter reading is greater than the pressure altimeter, D is plus. Conversly if the pressure altitude is greater than the radio altimeter, D is minus.

c. For reliable results, altitude should be read to the nearest ten feet. Reading should be read by the same person so that the same portion of the lobe is used for all readings. Such readings are reliable for determining drift since every constant error of the radio altimeter reading does not affect rhe value of D.

d. It again should be emphasized that the pressure altimeter must be read with a setting of 29.92 to the nearest 10 feet. The pressure altimeter must be tapped before reading to prevent sticking of the hands. The radio altimeter and pressure altimeter must be read at as nearly the same time as possible to obtain sufficiently accurate values of D.

e. Upon obtaining the values from the radio altimeter, and pressure altimeter, D is obtained by algebraically subtracting the value of the pressure altitude from the value of the radio altitude.

The first value obtained is called $D_1$. The second is $D_2$.

To go into the table it is now only necessary to subtract $D_1$ from $D_2$. The sign of the result should be noted for this will tell you the direction of your drift.

In the northern hemisphere:

Drift is the left if $D_2-D_1$ is positive.
Drift is to the right if $D_2-D_1$ is negative.

f. The first step in the table is to locate the intersection of your distance (i.e. 100) and latitude (i.e. 30). Distance is represented by the horizontal lines labeled on the outside of the table at the left and right with the lines for 25, 35, 46, and 150 nautical miles omitted.

Latitude is represented by the lines sloping from the lower left to the upper right and is labelled on the outside at the bottom and the top.

g. The second step is to move vertically up or down from the coincidence of your latitude and distance to the sloping line representing $D_2-D_1$ (i.e. 100). This line slopes from the lower right to the upper left, and islabelled on the inside at the bottom, top and left with the lines for 15, 25, 35, 150, 250 and 350 feet being omitted. It should be noted that in cases where the value of $D_2-D_1$ can not be found to coincide when moving down from the coincidence of distance and latitude, the lines can be used to represent 1/10 of the labelled values, i.e. as the line for 300 feet can be used to represent 30 feet.

h. You next move horizontally to the right from the $D_2-D_1$ line to the point of intersection with the TAS (i.e. 200) line which is represented by vertical lines in the right position labelled at the bottom, and with the lines for 150, 250, and 350 knots being omitted. This point of coincidence will lie on your drift angle (i.e. 12°) represented by the sloping lines in the right portion, labelled at the right and top. The solid lines are used when the labelled values of $D_2-D_1$ are used and the dashed lines are used when 1/10 the values of $D_2-D_1$ are used.

Your drift (direction; not correction, but <u>direction</u>) will be left since D2-D1 is positive.

Example:

```
Distance       =  85
Mid-latitude   =  30°
TAS            =  280
D₂-D₁          =  30 (note that 30 is used on 300 lines)
Drift          =  3°R (note that because 1/10 of labelled value is
                       used for D₂-D₁, the dotted value of drift is
                       used.)
```

Note: Altitude must not be changed between first and second reading. A change greater than 300 feet will make drift value inaccurate.

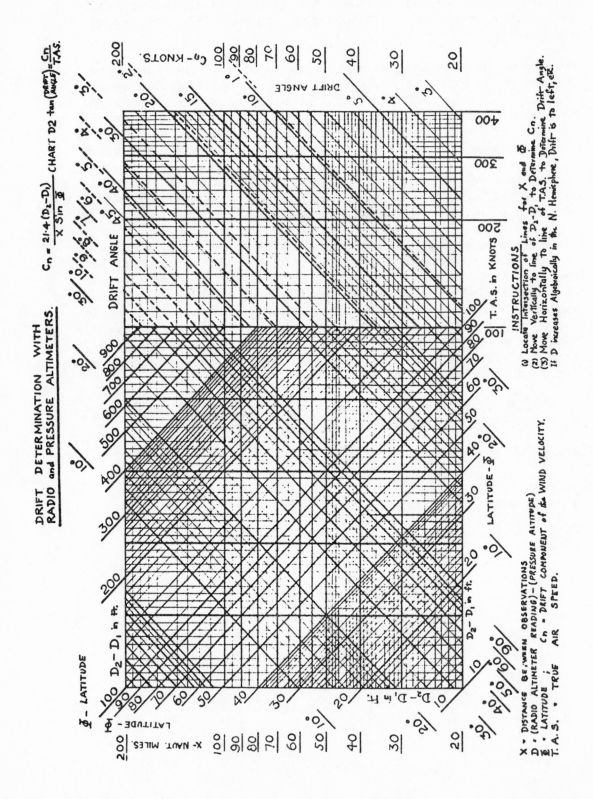

DRIFT DETERMINATION CHART

FIGURE XXXVII

COMBAT BOMBING

COMBAT BOMBING

PART I - BOMBING

A   INTRODUCTION

This section of the Combat Crew Manual is designed primarily as an information file for bombardiers of this command.  It is divided into two parts.

The first section contains information that will be helpful to you in actual air operations.  The second section is concerned with bombing computations and the equipment with which you work.  This manual, used in conjunction with the Lead Crew Manual and Tactical Doctrine, will serve not only as information for each individual bombardier, but also as a guide for lectures by instructors in the training program.  Information beneficial to you will be continuously published; this information will be marked for insertion in Combat Crew Manual and should be inserted in its proper place.  If the manual is kept up to date it will prove a direct aid to the air training and operational program of the command.

B   COMBAT BOMBING

The combat bombing run, from the Initial Point until bombs are away, will seldom last more than a few minutes, but the offensive effort of bombing and the purpose of the mission is achieved in that fractional part of an hour.  To be able to achieve that purpose, you, as bombardier, have spent many hours over the bombing ranges of the United States.  Now you will spend more practice hours flying over the Pacific Ocean Area.  You must continue to learn and to perfect your technique even to the day when you have completed this operational tour.

Much is expected of you as a bombardier.  If you are leading, you aim not only your bombs but those of the rest of the formation.  If you are flying a wing ship, your job is to release your bombs at the proper instant to supplement the pattern determined by the lead ship.  If your navigator is injured, you must be able to continue with the navigation accurately and confidently.  You will also man a gun sighting station; and you must be proficient in its use, care, and operation.  Learn all you can about your Central Fire Control equipment.  Your knowledge and skill in gunnery is sound insurance.  You will be the photographer of your crew and as such will be responsible for obtaining strike photographs of your bombs.  It will be necessary to make periodic checks to determine that the camera equipment is in proper working condition.

Thus, a heavy responsibility befalls the bombardier and it entails more than a few minute's work on the bombing run.  Every bombardier, after his training period is concluded, is capable in the mechanics of hitting any target within reason. Nevertheless, many more new techniques must be mastered and the old ones constantly practiced before accurate combat bombing is achieved.

## C  FLYING THE WING POSITION

There are two prime requisites in formation flying:

a.  A tight formation with every aircraft in its assigned position.

b.  Every aircraft releasing its bombs simultaneously on the lead aircraft.

The pattern achieved on the ground can be no better than the formation that dropped that pattern. It is a proved fact that the greater the concentration of G.P. bombs on a specified aiming point the greater overall damage sustained by the entire installation. Always assume the theory that it is impossible to achieve too great a concentration of bombs on any target.

Except for the actual sighting operation, there is not much difference between the job the lead bombardier must do and the job the men flying on his wings should do. At any time you may be called on to take over the lead. In some future mission you may be lead bombardier, and without the practice of actually checking data while flying on a wing, the chances of having a successful mission when you do lead the group, are greatly reduced. So - BE PREPARED AT ALL TIMES TO TAKE THE LEAD.

## D  BOMBARDIERS AS NAVIGATORS

Because of the excessive length of combat missions in this theatre, navigational fatigue is quite common. To alleviate this condition, all bombardiers must become proficient as navigators. There will be many times when you will be asked to spell the navigator, and conceivable a time when your knowledge of navigation will mean getting home or not. You are working for Uncle Sam up until the time that bombs are away, but from then on you are working on your own time.

## E. BOMBARDIER'S COMPLETE CHECK LIST

The bombardier should develop a standard procedure for checking and operating his equipment. The best method of doing this is to prepare a check list and use it. The following is a complete detailed check list. When the bombardier becomes thoroughly familiar with each pre-flight procedure, he can prepare a much shorter check list.

### CHECK LIST

### BEFORE TAKE OFF

Bombardier's kit should contain the following:

1. Target Folder.

    a. Aerial Photographs of target and approaches.

    b. Target chart.

    c. Bombardier flimsy and metro data.

    d. Sectional Map of Area.

2. Bombing Tables for Bombs carried.

3. E-6B, G-1 and C-2 Computers.

4. Stop Watch.

5. Tachometer (Check for malfunction).

6. Weems plotter.

7. AB Computer Scales (if available).

8. Screw Driver and Pliers.

### CHECK BOMBS, RACKS, & FUSES

1. Check to see that the release and arming arms of the shackles are properly engaged in the levers of the release.

2. Check racks for proper operation prior to bomb loading.

3. Check to see that the end of the shackle marked "Front" is towards the nose of the ship.

4. Check to see that shackles are properly engaged in the bomb rack carrying hooks.

5. Check all arming wires to insure that the arming wire loop is properly engaged in the shackles and the arming wire is properly engaged in the fuse with the Faunstock Clip in place. Check the arming wire for twists, kinks and proper length.

6. Check the bomb rack cannon plugs for tightness.

7. Check the bomb bay door safety switches to make certain they close when bomb bay doors are in vertical position.

8. Check Bomb Fuse Setting.

## CHECK ELECTRICAL FUSES FOR VARIOUS CIRCUITS

1. Check for burned out fuse both above bombardier's panel, and rear bomb bay solenoid shield.

2. Check all electrical fuses for security clips and looseness of glass.

3. See that there is spare fuse for each one in place.

## CHECK CAMERA EQUIPMENT

### INTERVALOMETER

1. Check electrical connections.

2. Press single exposure; check to see that counter works.

3. Check warning light while making camera test.

### CAMERA

1. Check electrical connections

2. Check vacuum connections.

3. Check position of vacuum switches.

4. Check camera doors, open them by the remote handle, and check to see that they operate properly and lock in the open position.

5. Check Trunion Locks and see that camera is rigid and there is no possibility of movement while in the air.

6. Check operation by having someone turn on **camera master switch** and listen to camera. If it is functioning properly, a clicking can be heard. As well, if it is functioning, it is possible to see the film spools rotating. Run two exposures through on the interval set by the ground photographic crew.

7. Press stop control after two exposures and check over interphone with the person listening to the camera, to see that operation has ceased.

8. Turn off camera master switch.

## CHECK THE INTERPHONE

### CHECK AND ARRANGE PERSONNAL EQUIPMENT BEFORE TAKE OFF

1. Parachute.

2. C-1 Emergency Vest.

3. Flak Suit and Helmet.

4. B-4 Life Preserver.

5. Oxygen Mask and Helmet.

6. C-2 Life Raft.

7. B-8 Goggles.

8. Summer Flying Gloves.

9. H-1 or H-2 Bailout Bottle.

10. One canteen full of water.

11. E-5 or E-17 Intelligence Kit.

### OXYGEN EQUIPMENT

1. Check the fit of the mask by holding thumb over the quick disconnect fitting and inhaling gently.

2. Be sure the gasket is on the male quick disconnect fitting. The fitting should fit snugly, requiring about a 10-pound pull to separate the two parts.

3. Be sure the knurled collar on the regulator is tight. Check to see that the diaphragm is intact. Check the emergency valve to see if oxygen flows; then close the valve firmly.

4. Breathe from the regulator normally with the Auto-mix "Off" to check the function of the flow indicator. Turn the Auto-mix to the "On" position.

5. Check the oxygen pressure. Pressure should be from 400 to 425 pounds per square inch, including that in the walk-around bottle.

## NOSE SIGHTING STATION

1. Make sure the optic head is clean.

2. Push in breaker switches and switch "On" AC power.

    a. Dynamotor starts.

    b. Reticle lamp lights (target size numerals, aiming dot, and range circle).

3. Turn rheostat from dim to bright and be sure that reticle responds.

4. Turn reticle lamp selector switch to check lamps second filament.

5. Turn target size adjusting screw to check change of numerals and change in diameter of circle of range dots.

6. Turn range adjusting handle to check change of diameter of circle of range dots. Make sure the reticle circle is clear.

7. Sight at some distant object, move your head, and make sure the dot still seems to be on the object, no matter where you hold your head.

8. Turn "On" computer switch on control box. This starts gyroscope and computer unit.

9. Turn the computer standby switch to "In". This cuts computing mechanism into your circuits.

10. Make sure the warning light which lights when computer is at standby, has gone off when action switch is closed.

11. Be sure the friction adjustments are just right for smooth tracking. If you wear gloves on the mission, test the adjustments with the gloves on.

12. Turn "Off" switches.

13. Move sight to forward horizontal position and lock.

14. Lock pantograph.

## INSTRUMENTS

1. Set bombardier's altimeter.

2. Be sure pilot's altimeter is on 29.92.

3. Check operation of SCR-718 absolute altimeter.

   a. Have radar operator turn on SCR-718 inverter.

   b. Turn on and allow time to warm up, note that pilot light comes on.

   c. When trace appears, adjust circle size control so that the circle trace is barely visible as a luminous ring at the outer edge of calibrated scale.

   d. Adjust gain so that lobe is approximately $\frac{1}{4}$ inch in height.

   e. During take-off, just as aircraft's wheels are on the verge of leaving ground, adjust zeroing knob until counter-clockwise edge of lobe is on zero.

## PRE-FLIGHT BOMBSIGHT

NOTE: The numbers following certain items refer to a more complete discussion given in the second section, Bombardier's Information File.

Preliminary Steps:

1. Make sure that there is power to the bombsight (26-28v); check cannon plugs for security and loose wires.

2. Turn "On" stabilizer switch.

3. Check for security of bombsight clutch connection arm and sight stem locking pin.

4. Be sure all glass parts are clean.

VII - 7

5. Check action of rate, displacement and search knobs through entire range. (14-16)

6. Check stabilizer mount for security.

## While Bombsight Warms Up:

1. Turn "On" servo, bombsight, and P. D. I. switches.

2. For night missions check bubble and cross-hair lights. (Gyro Caged) (34)

3. Check alignment of the dovetail, and also check for cross-trail tilt. (24)

4. Check for improper trail in the cross-trail mechanism. (23)

5. Turn "On" rate motor and check drive. (15, 17, 22)

6. Check Hi-Lo gear shift and Disc Speed drum through its entire range. (18)

7. Check for pre-set trail in the rate end. (19, 20)

8. Check ATF (ZERO Trail Setting) and at the same time, check for roller slippage and erratic disc speed. (18, 21)

## After Bombsight has Warmed Up:

1. Check servo action. (1, 2, 4)

2. Rotate turn knob through 30° R - 30° L, and rotate drift knob through 360°. (6, 8)

3. Check one to one ratio between sighthead and stabilized brush. (10)

4. Check stabilized brush and pilot's P. D. I. (30, 33)

5. Check action of leveling knobs. (25, 26)

6. Check precession of bombsight gyro. (28, 29)

7. Check precession of stabilizer gyro. (3)

8. Check action of directional, autopilot and drift clutches. (5, 6, 9, 13)

9. Cage gyro, disengage bombsight clutch, and turn off all switches.

### THE BOMBARDIER SHOULD ASSIST THE PILOT IN MAKING THE FOLLOWING GROUND CHECK OF THE C-1 AUTO PILOT

1. Disengage bombsight clutch.

2. Center PDI and engage secondary clutch.

3. Turn on master switch.

4. Set all adjusting knobs on PCB to 12 o'clock position.

5. Manually operate airplane controls through their full range and observe action of telltale lights. One light should remain on and not blink when off center position.

6. Turn on PDI servo switch.

7. Without centering engage aileron rudder and elevate switches.

8. Turn each centering knob slowly through its range.

    a. Observe controls for correct direction of movement.

    b. Controls should move in small even steps with pecking action, but not jerkily.

    c. Observe for uniform pecking action on both sides of electrical center, and one step each time light flashes.

    d. Check direction of control movement with each entering knob.

9. Disengage secondary clutch and move arm to extreme position.

    a. Check for binding of clutch arm on lever clamp of directional arm lock.

    b. Check for correct direction of control movement.

10. With secondary clutch arm to extreme position, rotate Bank Trimmer through its limits. Aileron control surface should move an appreciable amount.

11. Return PDI to center and engage secondary clutch, rotate Bank Trimmer through its limits. There should be no movement of aileron control surface.

12. Adjust dash-pot.

13. Rotate turn control for 30° bank.

    a. Check direction of control movement.

    b. Check directional arm lock for proper action.

14. Leave equipment in following condition:

    a. Bombsight clutch disengaged.

    b. Turn control in detent, control transfer at pilot's position.

    c. All pointers at 12 o'clock.

    d. All switches off.

## AFTER TAKE-OFF

1. Assist pilot in looking for other aircraft, especially in turns and making assembly.

2. Assist the navigator in his dead reckoning by taking drifts and determining ground speeds with the bombsight, when possible.

3. Pull pins. Pins to be pulled at an altitude over 5,000 feet.

4. Check guns.

5. Be on the alert at all times for aircraft, shipping and survivals.

6. Open camera vacuum valves prior to pressurization.

7. Determine the disc speed for the intended bombing altitude and for 1,000 feet above and below the intended bombing altitude. Set these values into the sight and mark on disc speed drum.

8. Study target area maps and photographs.

The following procedure is that used by the bombardier in the lead aircraft:

## MISSION NEARING ENEMY COAST

1. On day missions turn on camera master switch and direct radar operator to open camera doors. On night missions turn on camera master switch at IP and have camera doors opened.

2. Read free air temperature gauge, apply scale correction and correct for compression error. If this corrected value is appreciably different from the predicted metro value, re-compute bombing altitude and

A TYPICAL PRECISION TARGET
IN JAPAN PRIOR TO STRIKE

THE SAME PRECISION TARGET
DURING A STRIKE

CONFIDENTIAL

check against SCR-718 absolute altimeter.  Adjust the disc speed and
trail for new altitude.

3.  Give radar operator value of bombing altitude to be used.

4.  Set up $\underline{BA \times DS}$ opposite (10) on inner scale of E-6B and mark.
    7770

5.  When navigator gives wind, ground speed, and drift on axis of
attack, determine TAN DA from E-6B and set in sight, also give the value
of the dropping angle in degrees to radar operator.  Set wind and TAS in
AB computer and see that proper tangent scale is on computer (if equipment is available).

6.  Warm up rate motor by running for 10 minutes, then set telescope
index on 70° and clutch in with rate motor off.

7.  Set and turn on intervalometer.

8.  Do pilotage watching for check points that would help navigator
determine position and locate I. P.

9.  Try to pick up I. P. and study target folder.

10.  Aid in setting up C-1 autopilot, make several gentle turns with
course knobs to check operation of C-1 autopilot.

11.  Level stabilizer.  Check the level when aircraft is flying
straight and level.

## AFTER COMPLETING TURN AND PASSING OVER IP ON
## BRIEFED AXIS OF ATTACK

1.  Lead aircraft opens bomb bay doors six (6) minutes before release
point.  Other aircraft open doors three (3) minutes before.

2.  Observe action of C-1 autopilot.

3.  Study target area until target is picked up.  Use all check points
possible to help locate target.

4.  Turn on rack selector switches.

5.  Turn on nose arming switch.

6.  Check altimeter reading and make any necessary changes using marks
on disc speed drum.

### VISUAL BOMBING RUN

1.  Pre-set the latest drift from the Navigator and make normal bombing run.  The radar operator, and navigator, however, will follow through
with the standard radar bombing procedure.

## COMBINED RADAR-BOMBSIGHT RUN

1.  Pre-set latest drift from Navigator.

2.  When radar operator says, "Ready on seven zero degrees (70°)"-be prepared for "Ready, Mark". At the command "Mark", the bombardier turns on rate motor switch.

3.  Bombardier keeps hand on displacement knob and when radar operator says, "Ready on six eight degrees (68°)", be prepared for "Ready, Mark". At the command "Mark", the bombardier turns displacement knob to set telescope index on six eight degrees, (68°).

4.  When radar operator says, "Ready on six five degrees (65°)", be prepared for "Ready, Mark". At the command "Mark", bombardier first turns the displacement knob to put the telescope index on sixty five degrees (65°) and quickly rotates the rate knob a slight amount in the same direction as the displacement knob.

5.  This procedure is repeated at sighting angle intervals of five degrees (5°) until the value five degrees before the dropping angle is reached. At this point only a displacement correction is made.

6.  If at any time during the run the target can be seen visually, the bombardier will say, "I see it", and proceed with normal visual run. If the target is again obscured, the bombardier will say, "Radar, take over", and the radar synchronization will continue.

7.  If at any time during this rate determination run the radar operator changes his aiming point, he will notify the bombardier that the correction is for displacement only.

## AFTER RELEASE

1.  Start camera immediately after release, or as briefed.

2.  Lock racks, close bomb bay doors and inform pilot when bomb bay doors are closed.

3.  Turn off rack selector switches.

4.  Stop camera after bomb impact, or as briefed.

5.  After impact give strike report to radio operator.

6.  Turn off bombsight.

### F. REFERENCE POINT BOMBING

Reference Point (RP) Bombing is a technique of bombing necessary when the target is obscured by smoke or clouds, or in certain cases of camouflage. Knowledge and practice of this technique will be an insurance on missions which would otherwise be failures.

1. The simplest and probably the most accurate method of this type bombing (which will be employed by this command) is as follows:

The target is covered by a well-placed smoke screen and the exact position of the AP is in doubt. The bombardier from the target study (and by reference to his target chart) has picked a reference point in line with the AP and along the axis of attack.

a. Reference point #1 lying along axis of attack. Fore and aft cross-hair is placed on this point.

b. Target with AP obscured by smoke.

FIGURE I

The bombardier then kills course on this reference point and is ready to synchronize for rate. He will select a reference point (point #2) in the optics which he knows is perpendicular to his axis of attack at the AP and displace lateral cross-hair onto this point. This lateral aiming point must be chosen so that it is within the field of vision of the optics. Since the field of vision is approximately 18°, the point can not be out more than 9°. The allowable distance can be found by multiplying the altitude by the tangent of 9° or .158.

a. Course killed on this point.

b. Horizontal cross-hair placed on point #2.

c. By reference bombardier knows that AP is in this position.

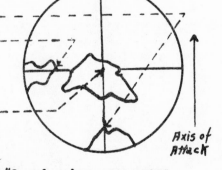

FIGURE II

Bombardier then refines rate on point #2 and makes any necessary corrections in course on point #1. When indices cross, bombs are dropped in normal manner.

2. The A-6 bomb trainer is most adaptable to the Reference Point method of bombing. The desired effect may be obtained by simulating smoke or clouds on the photo plates over the target area. The same effect may be obtained by placing a small piece of paper over the cross hairs in the bombsight and sighting in normal manner.

## G.  DR BOMBING

For the bombing of an obscured target through the overcast, where the distance between the target and a visible reference point is known, the bomb release point is obtained in the following manner:

1.  Add trail distance to the total distance between reference point and target.  Trail distance is obtained by multiplying the number of mils trail by the corresponding altitude in thousands of feet.

2.  To the total distance in (1) devide the ground speed of the airplane to obtain the total number of seconds that will elapse from the point of reference to the position of the plane at the time of impact.

3.  Subtract from (2) above, the ATF for the particular release altitude.  The result is the number of seconds that must elapse after passing over the last reference mark, before the bombs are released.

4.  After killing the drift on the reference point, move the telescope index to 0 degrees and the moment the cross-hairs intersect the reference point, start the stopwatch operating.

5.  Toggle bombs at expiration of number of seconds computed in step (3).

## PART II - BOMBARDIER'S INFORMATION FILE

### A. ALTITUDE COMPUTATIONS

1. **Radio Altimeter.**

If the radio altimeter, SCR-718 is installed and operative, use it in preference to computed altitude:

    a.  Before take-off check and adjust.

    b.  Keep the gain control adjusted so that the lobe is approximately $\frac{1}{4}$ inch in height.

    c.  Read altitude to nearest 25 feet at the counter-clockwise edge of reflection lobe. The proper 5,000 foot interval can be determined from the pressure altimeter.

2. **Altitude Computation using the C-2 Computer.**

    a.  **Altimeter:**  The altimeter will be set to indicate pressure altitude (Kollsman Scale set at 29.92). Necessary corrections must be applied to the altimeter and airspeed indicator readings for scale and installation error.

    b.  **Pressure Altitude Aloft:**  Pressure altitude aloft is pressure altitude as indicated on altimeter corrected for scale and installation errors.

    c.  **Mean Temperature·**  Mean temperature is found by adding one degree centigrade per thousand feet of pressure altitude above the target to corrected temperature at bombing altitude. The free air temperature gauge must be corrected for compression error. This error varies with the true airspeed as given below:

| True Air Speed | Compression Error |
|---|---|
| 210 - 236 | 4°C |
| 237 - 261 | 5°C |
| 262 - 284 | 6°C |
| 285 - 305 | 7°C |
| 306 - 325 | 8°C |
| 326 - 344 | 9°C |

This correction should always be applied so as to make the temperature colder.

    d.  <u>Pressure Altitude of Target</u>:  Use pressure altitude of target as forecast by weather.  To find pressure altitude of target when this information is not directly available from the weather data:  For every .01 inch the altimeter setting is over or below 29.92, correspondingly subtract or add 10 feet to target's known elevation.

    e.  <u>Pressure Altitude above the Target</u>:  Pressure altitude above the target is found by subtracting pressure altitude of the target (as given in weather forecast) from pressure altitude aloft.

    f.  <u>Solution by C-2 Computer</u>:

        (1)  Set black cursor to pressure altitude of target, as found in paragraph (d) above, and clamp.

        (2)  Position pressure altitude above the target as found in paragraph (e) above, on the indicated altitude scale, under the black cursor.

        (3)  Set red cursor at mean temperature, as found in paragraph (c) above.

        (4)  Read bombing altitude on true altitude scale.

3.  <u>Altitude Computation Using E-6B Computer</u>.

The method to be discussed here is a simple accurate method of obtaining a bombing altitude.  It is based on the equation:

$$\text{Bombing Altitude} = \frac{\text{ACTUAL MEAN ABSOLUTE TEMP.}}{\text{STANDARD MEAN ABSOLUTE TEMP.}} \times \frac{\text{HEIGHT OF AIR COL-}}{\text{TO BE CORRECTED.}}$$

The E-6B computer is used only as a circular slide rule to make the computation.  The above equation can be found in the TO on Altimeters and in various books on aircraft instruments, and it is the same equation upon which the C-2 computer is based.

Actual method of computation:

    a.  <u>Altimeter Setting</u>:  The bombardier will set his altimeter on the <u>predicted altimeter setting</u> for the target.

    b.  <u>Target Elevation</u>:  Surveyed Elevation of Target.

c. <u>True Air Speed</u>: True air speed will be determined using the G-1 computer. The free air temperature gauge reading, corrected for compression error, will be used on this computer.

d. <u>Compression Error</u>: See compression error under C-2 computer.

e. <u>Corrected Mean Temperature</u>: Corrected mean temperature will be determined as follows: The flight level free air temperature gauge reading will be corrected for compression error. Disregard the sign of the compression error and always apply it to make the temperature <u>colder</u>. Subtract target elevation from flight level altimeter reading to obtain height of air column. Add one degree for each thousand feet to the corrected flight level temperature to obtain the corrected mean temperature.

Example:

| | |
|---|---|
| Flight level free air temperature gauge reading: | -30°C |
| Compression Error: | 8°C |
| Corrected flight level temperature: | -38°C |
| | |
| Flight level altimeter reading: | 30,800 feet |
| Target Elevation: | 200 feet |
| Height of air column: | 30,600 feet |
| | |
| One degree for each thousand feet: | 30.6 or 31 |
| Corrected flight level temperature: | -38 |
| Corrected mean temperature: | -7°C |

This method of computing corrected mean temperature is based on the assumption that the temperature gets 2° warmer every thousand feet from flight level down. This is a fairly accurate assumption for high altitudes. The value obtained is the same as would be obtained if the flight level temperature were projected down to target elevation at the rate of 2° per 1000 feet and the flight level temperature and target temperature were averaged.

f. <u>Mean Altitude</u>: Add target elevation to one half of the height of air column to get <u>Mean</u> altitude, or add target elevation to flight level altimeter reading and divide by two. This factor represents mean standard temperature.

g. <u>Bombing Altitude</u>: Bombing altitude will be determined as follows: Subtract <u>target elevation</u> from flight level altimeter reading to get height of air column to be corrected. This value was previously found in determining the corrected mean temperature. In the altitude window on the back of the E-6B, set <u>mean</u> altitude opposite corrected mean temperature, read bombing altitude on the outer scale opposite height of air column on the inner scale.

Example:

Corrected Mean Temperature:                                         -7°C

Flight level altimeter reading:                              30,800 feet
Target elevation                                                200 feet
Height of air column                                         30,600 feet

Mean altitude $\frac{30,600}{2}$ plus 200 :                  15,500 feet

In the altitude window set 15,500 opposite -7°C.  On the outer scale read
the bombing altitude, 31,600 feet, opposite the height of air column,
30,600 feet, on the inner scale.

## B. DETERMINATION OF GROUND SPEED AND DRIFT USING THE BOMBSIGHT

It is assumed that every bombardier is familiar with the procedure in placing a wind vector on the E-6B using full scale values. The steps are prepeated here only for review:

    a. Set TAS under Grommet.

    b. Set Wind Direction under True Index.

    c. Draw in Wind Arrow directly under the Grommet an amount equal to the magnitude of the Wind Speed.

The winds encountered over Japan at high altitudes exceed the limits of the E-6B computer. It then becomes necessary to use a fractional part of both TAS and Wind Speed. As long as both of them are divided by the same value, the computer may be used for the solution. It must be remembered that using fractional values does not effect the drift solution. THE DRIFT VALUES ARE CORRECT AS READ FROM THE COMPUTER AND SHOULD NOT BE MULTIPLIED BY THE FRACTIONAL VALUE! The reason for this can be noted by reviewing the basic Wind Vector Triangle. We know that two triangles are similar when their respective sides are proportional. Also that corresponding angles of similar triangles are equal. Therefore, considering two wind triangles - one using actual values, the other using fractional values, the corresponding angles are equal.

Sample Problem using Vector Side of E-6B Computer:

Given: Wind 200 mph from 270 $^\circ$. TAS 320 mph
Find: Ground Speed.

Solution: Use fractional values equal to one fourth:

1. Set TAS of $\frac{320}{4}$ or 80 mph under the Grommet.

2. Set wind direction 270$^\circ$ under the True Index.
3. Draw in wind of $\frac{200}{4}$ or 50 mph.

4. Rotate Compass Rose until true heading of 70$^\circ$ is placed under True Index.
5. Read drift of 8$^\circ$ R and a Ground Speed of 128 x 4 or 512 mph.

Ground speed may also be obtained by timing the interval between two fixes or two check points of known distance apart.

Sample Problem:

Given:  Distance 6 miles.  Time 52 seconds.
Find:   Ground Speed.

Solution:  Set 52 on inner scale opposite 6 miles on outer scale.
           Opposite 36 on inner scale read Ground Speed on outer scale
           which will be 415 mph.

NOTE:  36 is used in this solution rather than 60 because time is ex-
       pressed in seconds rather than minutes.  In changing minutes to
       hours use 60.  Changing seconds to hours use 60x60 or 3,600.

At times the bombardier can be of aid to the navigator in obtaining drift
and ground speed by means of the bombsight.  The following method explained in detail will make use of the bombsight and E-6B to solve the
problem.  This method is flexible in as much as any disc speed may be
used including the disc speed at bombing altitude.  In setting up the
sight, the TRAIL ARM IS ALWAYS SET ON ZERO TRAIL.  Set in any convenient
disc speed with the tachometer.  Example:  200 rpm at 10,000 feet;  150
rpm at 20,000 feet;  110 rpm at 30,000 feet.  With the bombsight in operation, all switches on, uncage the vertical gyro and level the bubbles.
Then engage both the directional and secondary clutches, and by means of
the turn knob only, rotate sight head until correct drift is set up.
This method gives an accurate drift solution since there is complete
stabilization.

CAUTION:  Do not attempt to read drift in a turn.

Now set up proper rate by synchronizing on landmark or white caps.  When
correctly synchronized, read the tangent value of the rate indicator.
Since there was zero trail set up in the sight, this is the value of the
tangent of the whole range angle.  From theory of bombing, take this
basic formula:

WR = GS x ATF and solving for ground speed in mph.

$$GS = \frac{WR}{ATF} \times \frac{60}{88}$$

In order to solve this equation using information from the bombsight we
substitute for ATF:  $\frac{5300}{DS}$

Remembering that Tan WR = $\frac{WR}{BA}$ and solving for WR we get: WR = Tan WR x BA

Now substituting in our basic equation we get:

$$GS = \frac{Tan\ WR \times BA}{\frac{5300}{DS}} \times \frac{60}{88} \quad \text{or simplifying:} \quad GS = \frac{DS \times BA \times Tan\ WR}{7773}$$

For the proceeding equation, the DS and Tan WR are taken from the bomb-sight and the BA is obtained from the SCR-718 altimeter or from computations. From the equation it will be noted that $\frac{DS \times BA}{7773}$ will be constant for any given altitude, and can be set up on the E6B. Set 7773 on the inner scale opposite the D on the outer scale. Read value on outer scale above BA on inner scale opposite pencil mark and opposite Tan WR on inner scale read GS on outer scale.

NOTE: From observation it will be noted that if a DS of 150 is used at higher altitudes then the equation becomes:

$$GS = \frac{150 \times BA \times Tan\ WR}{7773} \text{ or } \frac{BA \times Tan\ WR}{52}$$

And if DS of 400 is used at lower altitudes, the equation then becomes:

$$GS = \frac{400 \times BA \times Tan\ WR}{7773} \text{ or } \frac{BA \times Tan\ WR}{19.4}$$

While this method is correct, it is felt that it is less flexible than the general method of using any DS. Using any DS we are able to use the DS for bombing altitude to solve for correct ground speed and as we shall discuss in a later lecture we are also able to use this same equation to solve for the correct tangent of dropping angle. In other words, by the use of just one equation, we are able to solve for both ground speed and tangent of dropping angle.

Sample Problem: Obtain GS from Bombsight.

Given: DS = 150 rpm; BA = 20,000 feet; Tan WR = .85
Find: Ground Speed

Solution: 1. Set 7773 on inner scale opposite 150 on outer scale.

2. Read value on the outer scale opposite 20,000 on the inner scale and make pencil mark.

3. Set 10 on the inner scale opposite mark and read GS on outer scale opposite .85 on inner scale, or 328 mph.

In computing a wind, the above procedure is used to solve for the Ground Speed, and the Drift is read from the bombsight. The TAS is obtained from the G-1 computer. The TH is placed under the True Index. The TAS is placed under the Grommet. The intersection of the drift line and Ground Speed line is the end of the wind arrow and the wind vector is drawn from this point to the Grommet. Rotate compass rose until wind vector falls directly below the Grommet. Read Wind direction and Speed.

Sample Problem:

Given:   BA = 25,000 feet;   Temp. = -24°C;   TH = 310°;   CIAS = 200 mph;
         Drift = 10°L;   DS=130 rpm;   Tan WR = .95

Find:    Wind Direction and Speed.

Solution:   1.   Using G-1 Computer TAS = 300 mph.

2.   Using E-6B and method previously explained, GS = 400 mph.

   NOTE:   From observation it will be noted that the wind
           is greater than 100 mph. The E-6B can only ac-
           comodate 60 mph, therefore, a fractional scale
           of ½ will be used.

3.   Place TAS $\frac{300}{2}$ or 150 under Grommet. TH of 310 under T.I.

4.   Locate intersection of GS $\frac{400}{2}$ or 200 and 10°L drift.

5.   Draw wind vector from this point to grommet.

6.   Rotate compass rose and read wind speed and direction or
     58 x 2 = 116 mph from 93°.

CONFIDENTIAL

## C. DETERMINATION OF DROPPING ANGLE

The following formula may be solved by E-6B computer to determine Tangent of WR when an accurate GS has been obtained:

$$GS = \frac{DS \times BA \times Tan\ WR}{7773}$$

Solution: Set 7773 on the inner scale opposite DS on the outer scale, read value on outer scale opposite bombing altitude on inner scale and make pencil mark at this value. Set 10 on inner scale opposite pencil mark and opposite ground speed on outer scale read Tan WR on inner scale.

Knowing the tangent of the WR, the tangent of the dropping angle may be solved by the following formula:

$$Tan\ DA = Tan\ WR - \frac{Trail}{1000}\ (in\ mils)$$

Sample Problem:

Given: Trail = 74 mils; DS = 144 rpm; BA = 20,000; GS = 380 mph.

Find: Tan DA

Solution:

1. Set 7773 on the inner scale opposite 144 on outer scale.

2. Read value on the outer scale opposite 20,000 (20) on the inner scale and make pencil mark.

3. Set 10 on inner scale opposite pencil mark and read Tan WR on the inner scale opposite GS of 380 on outer scale.

4. Tan WR = 1.02; Tan DA = 1.02 - $\frac{74}{1000}$ = .95

Answer: Tan DA = .95

## D. AB COMPUTER

(NOTE:  Scales now in use are calibrated for 160 I.A.S.)

1.  Set the trail and disc speed in the bombsight for the altitude being flown and the bomb to be dropped on that mission, using the correct tangent scale.

2.  Compute true airspeed from the G-1 computer and set on AB computer and tighten knurled nut.  If TAS exceeds 210 mph, set in half of the TAS value on ABC, using the double true air speed scale.

3.  Set the compass rose to the compass reading of the airplane and fasten (compass heading setting should be frequently checked because of tendency of directional gyro to precess in turns).

4.  Find drift by using bombsight as driftmeter.

5.  Synchronize for rate on a point whose elevation is approximately the same as the target's.

6.  Holding drift pointer on pre-determined drift set in desired tangent of the dropping angle on the tangent ground speed scale.  Lock with knurled nut.

7.  Fasten wind gear scale to compass rose.

8.  The drift, tangent of dropping angle, ground speed and wind velocity may be read off the AB computer for any heading.  However, as the TAS value was originally halved, the indicated ground speed and wind velocity value on the ABC must be doubled to obtain the correct ground speed and wind velocity. Drift remains the same.

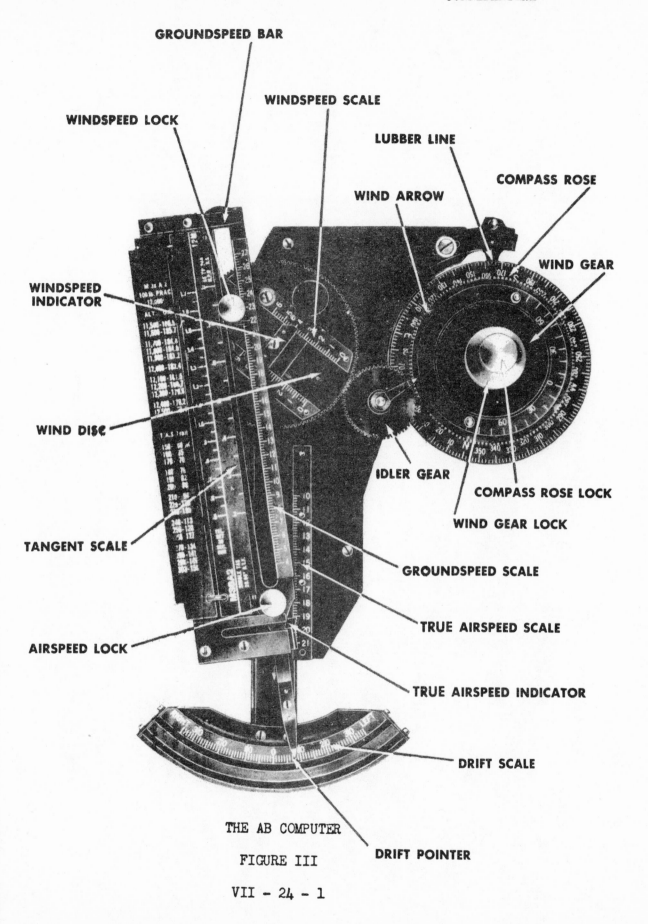

GROUNDSPEED BAR

WINDSPEED SCALE

WINDSPEED LOCK

LUBBER LINE

COMPASS ROSE

WIND ARROW

WIND GEAR

WINDSPEED
INDICATOR

WIND DISC

IDLER GEAR

COMPASS ROSE LOCK

WIND GEAR LOCK

TANGENT SCALE

GROUNDSPEED SCALE

TRUE AIRSPEED SCALE

AIRSPEED LOCK

TRUE AIRSPEED INDICATOR

DRIFT SCALE

THE AB COMPUTER

FIGURE III

DRIFT POINTER

VII - 24 - 1

## E.  BALLISTIC WIND AND DISC SPEED CHANGE

### 1.  INTRODUCTION.

The bombsight solves the bombing problem as though the wind were constant
from the flight level to ground.  With the winds encountered over Japan
at high altitudes, considerable error is thus introduced.  As an example,
take the following data:  500 lb GP bomb;  bombing altitude 25,000 feet;
True Airspeed 300 mph;  160 mph tailwind.  As the bombsight solves this
situation, the bomb is expected to be carried forward in a block of air
moving 160 mph.  However, as the bomb descends, the wind becomes less
and less, hence the bomb is not carried as far forward as expected and,
therefore, will fall short.  In this case about 530 feet short.  For a
headwind obviously the bomb would fall over.  The effect upon the bomb
depends upon the wind velocity of each layer and the length of time it
takes the bomb to pass through that layer;  since both of these vary, a
complicated problem arises.

### 2.  DEFINITIONS.

Ballistic Wind (BW) is an imaginary wind, constant in speed and direction from flight level to ground, which would cause the same point of
impact as occurs under actual conditions.  It amounts to a weighted
average wind and will always be smaller than the actual flight level
wind.

Differential Ballistic Wind (DBW) is the difference between the
actual flight level wind and the Ballistic Wind.

Range Wind (RW) is the component of flight level wind parallel to
the track.  It is approximately the difference between ground speed and
True Airspeed.  This approximation is good for drifts up to about $10^\circ$.
Above $10^\circ$ the range wind will have to be found by multiplying the wind
force by the cosine of the angle between the wind and the track.  Whenever there is a crosswind it is necessary to use range wind instead of
the actual flight level wind.

Range Ballistic Wind (RBW) is the component of the ballistic wind parallel to the track.

Range Differential Ballistic Wind (RDBW) is the component of the differential ballistic wind parallel to the track.

Effective True Airspeed (Eff. TAS) is a hypothetical True Airspeed which
will compensate for range differential ballistic wind error if trail and
disc speed are based on it.

3. <u>Mathematical Relationships</u>.

Ballistic Wind can be expressed as a certain fraction of the actual flight level wind. This fraction depends upon the manner in which the winds vary from flight level to ground. Mathematical analysis based on meteorological observations have shown this fraction to be approximately .7. Stated as an equation this is:

Ballistic Wind = .7 x Actual flight level wind.

Since differential ballistic wind is the difference between actual flight level wind and ballistic wind:

Differential Ballistic Wind = .3 x Actual flight level wind.

Range wind is the difference between ground speed and true airspeed, approximately.

Range Wind = Ground Speed - True Airspeed.

Therefore:  Range Ballistic Wind = .7 Range Wind, and
            Range Differential Ballistic Wind = .3 Range Wind.

The Effective True Airspeed has been found to be:

Effective True Airspeed = Actual True Airspeed plus .3 Range Wind
                                                    (Tailwind)

or:  Effective True Airspeed = Actual True Airspeed - .3 Range Wind
                                                    (Headwind)

One method of correcting for differential ballistic winds is to use the effective true airspeed as though it were the true airspeed, that is, enter the bombing tables and obtain trail and disc speed corresponding to the effective true airspeed and set these values into the bombsight. This method works well for a straight tail, or head, wind, however, for a cross wind, a cross trail error is introduced.

The deflection error due to differential ballistic wind is always <u>upwind</u>.

With a cross-headwind the trail was decreased to allow for range differential ballistic wind, since the effective TAS was less than the actual TAS. This makes the cross trail too small, causing a downwind error. The deflection error caused by the differential ballistic wind is upwind, therefore, the two errors tend to compensate.

With a cross-tailwind, the trail was increased to allow for range differential ballistic wind, since the effective TAS was larger than the
actual TAS. This makes the crosstrail too large, causing an upwind
error. The deflection error caused by the differential ballistic wind
is upwind, therefore the two errors are in the same direction and will
add.

Example:

Bomb: 500 lb. GP, M-64
Bombing Altitude: 25,000 feet
Actual True Airspeed: 300 mph
Wind: 260° at 170 mph
Axis of Attack: 260°

Find: The disc speed and trail to allow for differential ballistic
wind.

Since there is a direct headwind, the range wind and the wind are the
same, therefore:

Effective True Airspeed = 300 - .3 x 170
= 300 - 51
= 249 mph

Enter the bombing tables, using 249 mph as the true airspeed:

Trail = 68 mils; Disc Speed = 126.6 rpm

It is better to allow for the differential ballistic wind error by
changing the disc speed. To do this the amount of error in feet must
be found. This amount can be computed from the following equation:

$$\text{Range Ballistic Wind Error} = \frac{\text{ALT}}{1000}\left(\text{Trail}_{\text{Eff. TAS}} - \text{Trail}_{\text{Actual TAS}}\right) - \text{GS}\left(\text{ATF}_{\text{Eff. TAS}} - \text{ATF}_{\text{Actual TAS}}\right)$$

Where the trail is in mils and the ground speed is in ft/sec.

Once the amount of error is found, the necessary disc speed change to compensate for it may be computed as explained in subsequent paragraphs.

The differential ballistic wind deflection error caused by a crosswind may be found by multiplying the range error by the tangent of the angle between the track and the wind. The only way to allow for this is to aim downwind an amount equal to the error.

Tables are being prepared for certain clusters which will include a disc speed and tangent of dropping angle which will allow for the excess trail which cannot be set into the bombsight and also for the ballistic wind error. In these tables, the deflection errors tend to compensate on any crosswind run.

4. <u>Disc Speed Change</u>.

Some types of clusters have more trail than can be set into the bombsight. The amount of trail over 150 mils can be allowed for by increasing the disc speed a certain amount.

Also, the bomb impact can be offset in range from a given aiming point by changing the disc speed. Either of the two following equations can be used to make the required computation:

$$\text{Disc Speed Correction} = \frac{\text{Disc Speed Normal x Range Error}}{\text{Ground Speed x Normal ATF - Range error}}$$

$$\text{Correct Disc Speed} = \frac{5300 \text{ x Ground Speed}}{\text{Ground Speed x Normal ATF - Range Error}}$$

In both equations, Disc Speed is in rpm, ATF in seconds, Range Error is in <u>feet</u>, and Ground Speed is in <u>feet per second</u>. The term range error is the amount of trail in feet that can <u>not</u> be set into the bombsight or is the distance in feet that it is desired to offset the bomb from an aiming point. The algebraic sign before the range error is always minus for trail deficiency and for causing an impact over the aiming point. However, to cause an impact short of the aiming point, the sign is plus in both equations.

Example:

Bombing Altitude:     25,000 feet
Ground Speed:         420 mph
Disc Speed:           48.0 sec.
ATF:                  110.5 sec.
Trail:                276 mils

Find:  The disc speed to allow for excess trail with 150 mils set into
       the bombsight.

Ground Speed: $= 420 \times \dfrac{88}{60} = 616$ ft/sec

Range Error $= (276 - 150) \dfrac{25000}{1000} = 3150$ feet

Using the first equation:

Disc Speed Correction $= \dfrac{110.5 \times 3150}{616 \times 48 - 3150} = 13.2$

Correct Disc Speed = 13.2 plus 110.5 = 123.7 rpm

Using the second equation:

Correct Disc Speed $= \dfrac{5300 \times 616}{616 \times 48 - 3150} = 123.7$ rpm

The tangent of the dropping angle can be found in the usual way using
corrected Disc Speed and subtracting the amount of trail set in the
sight in thousands from the tangent of whole range angle:

GS $= \dfrac{BA \times DS \times Tan\ WR}{7773}$

Tan WR $= 1.055$
Tan DA $= 1.055 - \dfrac{150}{1000} = .905$ or $.91$

Example:

BA = 23,000 ft;  GS = 120 mph;  DS = 132.5 rpm;  ATF = 40 sec;  Trail =
80 mils

It is desired to cause an impact 1200 feet short of the aiming point.

Ground Speed $= 120 \times \dfrac{88}{60} = 176$ ft/sec.

Range Error $= 1200$ feet.

Using the second equation:

Corrected Disc Speed $= \dfrac{5300 \times 176}{176 \times 4 + 1200} = 113$ rpm

Tan WR = .359

Tan DA = .359 - .08 = .279 or .28

## F.  MISCELLANEOUS BOMBING FORMULAS

| | |
|---|---|
| **Whole Range**<br>WR | $= GS \text{ (Ft/sec)} \times ATF$ |
| **Actual Range**<br>AR<br>AR (Ft)<br>AR (Mils) | $= WR - T$<br>$= Alt \times Tan\ DA$<br>$= Tan \times 1000$ |
| **Disc Speed**<br>DS | $= 5300 / ATF$ |
| **Tan Drop Angle**<br>Tan D $\angle$ | $= \dfrac{GS \text{ (Ft/sec)} \times ATF - T}{Alt.}$ |
| **Ground Speed**<br>GS (mph) | $= \dfrac{DS \times Alt \times Tan\ WR}{7773}$ |
| **Cross Trail**<br>CT | $= T \times Sin\ Drift\ Angle$ |
| **App. Precession**<br>AP | $= 17.45\ cos\ Lat\ \text{(4 min. time)}$ |
| **RCCT** | $= Trail\ (1 - cos\ Drift\ Angle)$ |

To convert miles per hour to feet per second, multiply 1.467 x miles per hour.  This may be done on E-6B computer by placing 1.467 on inner scale opposite 10 on outer scale and reading feet per second on inner scale opposite miles per hour on outer scale.

# TRIGONOMETRIC FUNCTIONS

| Angle ° | Sin | Cos | Tan | Cot | |
|---|---|---|---|---|---|
| 0 | .000 | 1.000 | .000 | ..... | 90 |
| 1 | .017 | 1.000 | .017 | 57.29 | 89 |
| 2 | .035 | .999 | .035 | 28.64 | 88 |
| 3 | .052 | .999 | .052 | 19.08 | 87 |
| 4 | .070 | .998 | .070 | 14.30 | 86 |
| 5 | .087 | .996 | .087 | 11.42 | 85 |
| 6 | .105 | .995 | .105 | 9.514 | 84 |
| 7 | .122 | .993 | .123 | 8.144 | 83 |
| 8 | .139 | .990 | .141 | 7.115 | 82 |
| 9 | .156 | .988 | .158 | 6.314 | 81 |
| 10 | .174 | .985 | .176 | 5.671 | 80 |
| 11 | .191 | .982 | .194 | 5.145 | 79 |
| 12 | .208 | .978 | .213 | 4.705 | 78 |
| 13 | .225 | .974 | .231 | 4.331 | 77 |
| 14 | .242 | .970 | .249 | 4.011 | 76 |
| 15 | .259 | .966 | .268 | 3.732 | 75 |
| 16 | .276 | .961 | .287 | 3.487 | 74 |
| 17 | .292 | .956 | .306 | 3.271 | 73 |
| 18 | .309 | .951 | .325 | 3.078 | 72 |
| 19 | .326 | .946 | .344 | 2.904 | 71 |
| 20 | .342 | .940 | .364 | 2.747 | 70 |
| 21 | .358 | .934 | .384 | 2.605 | 69 |
| 22 | .375 | .927 | .404 | 2.475 | 68 |
| 23 | .391 | .921 | .424 | 2.356 | 67 |
| 24 | .407 | .914 | .445 | 2.246 | 66 |
| 25 | .423 | .906 | .466 | 2.145 | 65 |
| 26 | .438 | .899 | .488 | 2.050 | 64 |
| 27 | .454 | .891 | .510 | 1.963 | 63 |
| 28 | .469 | .883 | .532 | 1.881 | 62 |
| 29 | .485 | .875 | .554 | 1.804 | 61 |
| 30 | .500 | .866 | .577 | 1.732 | 60 |
| 31 | .515 | .857 | .601 | 1.664 | 59 |
| 32 | .530 | .848 | .625 | 1.600 | 58 |
| 33 | .545 | .839 | .649 | 1.540 | 57 |
| 34 | .559 | .829 | .675 | 1.483 | 56 |
| 35 | .574 | .819 | .700 | 1.428 | 55 |
| 36 | .588 | .809 | .727 | 1.376 | 54 |
| 37 | .602 | .799 | .754 | 1.327 | 53 |
| 38 | .616 | .788 | .781 | 1.280 | 52 |
| 39 | .629 | .777 | .810 | 1.235 | 51 |
| 40 | .643 | .766 | .839 | 1.192 | 50 |
| 41 | .656 | .755 | .869 | 1.150 | 49 |
| 42 | .669 | .743 | .900 | 1.111 | 48 |
| 43 | .682 | .731 | .933 | 1.072 | 47 |
| 44 | .695 | .719 | .966 | 1.036 | 46 |
| 45 | .707 | .707 | 1.000 | 1.000 | 45 |
| | Cos | Sin | Cot | Tan | Angle ° |

## G. BOMBING ERRORS IN SYNCHRONOUS BOMBING

1. Overs:

    a. Dropping angle set up too small.

    b. Disc speed too fast.

    c. Indicated altitude too high.

    d. Altimeter registering lower than it should.

    e. Too much trail set into the sight.

    f. Air speed too slow.

    g. Air Speed indicator registering higher than it should.

    h. Positive pre-set trail not allowed for.

    i. Synchronized slow.

    j. Free air temperature gauge registering lower than it should.

    k. Fore-and-aft bubble off to the rear.

    l. Mirror drive cable too short.

    m. Aircraft in a climb at the instant of release.

    n. Range component of cross trail.

    o. Excessive lag in the operation of the bomb racks.

2. Shorts:

    a. Dropping angle set up too large.

    b. Disc speed too slow.

    c. Indicated altitude too low.

    d. Altimeter registering higher than it should.

    e. Too little trail set into the sight.

    f. Air speed too fast.

    g. Air speed indicator registering lower than it should.

    h. Negative pre-set trail not allowed for.

i. Synchronized fast.

j. Free air temperature gauge registering higher than it should.

k. Fore-and-aft bubble off to the front.

l. Mirror drive cable too long.

m. Aircraft in a dive at the instant of release.

n. Roller slippage.

o. Extended vision rolled in and not removed. (Usually a short, although under certain conditions an over may result).

p. Bomb defects.

3. Analysis of Errors:

a. Incorrect vertical.

(1) Lateral bubble Off: Error opposite direction in which bubble is off, and amount of error is equal to approximately 36 mils for a complete bubble length off.

(2) Fore-and-aft bubble off: Error opposite direction in which bubble is off. The amount of error is equal to the difference of the tangent of the correct dropping angle and the tangent of the dropping angle that was used, multiplied by the altitude.

b. Incorrect Altitude: An error in altitude corresponds to an error in actual time of fall set into sight. Altitude too high, the bomb will fall over; if too low, the bomb will fall short. The amount of error over or short is equal to the difference in ATF of the computed altitude and the actual altitude flown times ground speed in feet per second.

c. Incorrect air speed: An error in air speed corresponds to an error in trail. If the airspeed is too fast the bomb will fall short. The distance short will be the difference in the trail of the airspeed that should have been flown and the airspeed that was actually flown.

d. Incorrect Trail: Trail setting too great, error over a distance indicated by error in trail setting.

e. Disc Speed Errors: Disc speed too fast, bomb will hit over. When the disc speed is rotating at too great a speed, the roller must be brought too far towards the center of the disc in order to synchronize. This decreases the actual range, which in turn decreases the dropping angle. The decreased dropping angle allows the plane to approach too near the target before the bomb is released, causing an error over. The amount of range error is solved by either formula given on Page VII - 31.

## H.   DETECTION OF COMMON MALFUNCTIONS
### TROUBLE SHOOTING

It is absolutely essential that the equipment for which the bombardier is reponsible be in the best possible operating condition, if accurate results are to be obtained.  So that he can be assured of a preflight inspection that will be thorough, the bombardier should follow a definite plan of inspection.  A hit-and-miss preflight is not good enough. It must be methodical and at the same time complete and thorough in order to detect any and all malfunctions.  An outline of the preflight inspection which has been designed to save time and yet not omit any necessary steps in the check list on Page VII - 5.  The following is a more complete explanation of how to check for, and how to recognize each malfunction.

1.  Complete failure of the stabilizer gyro:  With the stabilizer and servo switches on and the directional clutch engaged, the sight head will rotate in one direction until it hits the stop.  (With directional clutch disengaged, drum merely rotates.)

NOTE:  This action will not be observed if the stabilized brush is on the neutral sector.

2.  Slow running stabilizer gyro:  With the stabilizer and servo switches on and the directional clutch engaged, a torque applied to the sight head or movement of the turn knob will produce an oscillation of the sight head.

3.  Precessing stabilizer gyro:  With the stabilizer and servo switches on the secondary clutch engaged and PDI centered, the stabilized brush will move off zero continously in one direction.

With the directional clutch engaged under the same conditions, and zero indicated on the drift angle scale, the sight head will move off zero in the same direction.

NOTE:  If the gyro precesses more than 1° in an hour, it is considered excessive.

4.  Failure of the servo unit:  With the stabilizer and servo switches on and the directional clutch engaged, a steady torque applied to the sight head will be resisted for a short period and then the stabilizer gyro will be precessed to its stop and the sight head will move easily.

5.  Turn knob binding:  Rotate the turn knob through its entire limits (30°L to 30°R).  If it is difficult to rotate at any point, there is binding of the turn knob.

6. Burred drift gear: Rotate the drift knob until the drift gear has turned 360°. If there is binding at any point, a burr is probably present on drift gear.

7. Improper mesh between drift worm and drift gear (back lash): When the drift knob is rotated, there is movement of the knob before the stabilized brush is displaced.

8. Improper mesh between drift worm and drift gear (too tight): When attempts are made to rotate the drift knob, the force necessary to turn the knob is great or else the knob cannot be rotated at all.

9. Directional clutch too tight: With the stabilizer and servo switches on and the directional clutch engaged, a steadily increasing torque applied to the sight head will be resisted within the limits of the servo unit. When the servo unit is overcome, the gyro will be precessed to its stop and the sight head will move easily.

NOTE: Care should be taken in order to distinguish this from failure of the servo unit.

10. Drift clutch too loose: With switches on and directional clutch engaged and the secondary clutch disengaged, when the drift knob is rotated, the stabilized brush will not be displaced the proper amount.

NOTE: Check 1 to 1 ratio!!!

11. Drift clutch tighter than the directional clutch: With switches on and directional clutch engaged, move the secondary clutch against either stop. Then rotate the turn knob so as to keep the secondary clutch against the stop. The sight head should rotate; if it does not, the drift clutch is tighter than the directional clutch.

12. Drift clutch tighter than the secondary clutch: With switches on and secondary clutch engaged, rotating the drift knob will displace the secondary clutch if the drift clutch is tighter than the secondary clutch.

13. Secondary clutch binding: This would manifest itself in the same fashion as having the secondary clutch engaged. On a bombing run it would be impossible to set up course.

14. Binding in the rate knob: Movement of the rate knob would be difficult or impossible.

15. Sheared optic clutch pin: With the telescope motor on and the optic clutch engaged (disc speed clutch engaged) there would be no movement of the telescope indicator or of the lateral hair. If telescope motor is not running, this check can be made by engaging optic clutch and rotating the displacement knob manually.

16. Broken cable or cable off the sheaves: With the telescope motor on and the optic clutch engaged, (disc speed engaged) there would be movement of the telescope indicator, but the lateral hair would show no movement.

17. Failure of the rate motor: With bombsight and telescope motor switches on and the disc speed clutch engaged, the tachometer adapter will not rotate.

18. Erratic disc speed: With the bombsight and telescope motor switches on and any disc speed set in the sight, check with a tachometer. The readings obtained should be the same.

19. Negative preset trail: With rate index set at -.05, and trail arm locked at 50 mils, high disc speed set on D.S. drum (450 rpm), the telescope index set at a small tangent, turn on the telescope motor and engage the optic clutch. If there is negative preset trail present, the telescope index will drive toward 70°.

20. Positive preset trail: With the same settings as in #19 above, turn on the telescope motor and engage the optic clutch. If there is positive preset trail, the telescope index will drive toward 0°.

21. Roller slippage: Set the trail arm on zero. With the telescope motor on and disc speed clutch in high position, set in with a tachometer a disc speed of 265 rpm's. (This will give an ATF of 20 seconds.) Set the rate index at the tangent of the dropping angle if it is known; if not set at .7. Turn on the telescope motor and engage the optic clutch. Time the drive of the telescope index from coincidence point to zero with a stop watch. If the timing is greater than 20 seconds, there is roller slippage or negative preset trail present. (A check for preset trail will determine whether or not the malfunction is negative preset trail.) Make the timing check again for a smaller and a larger tangent. (Tan .3 and 1.4 are suggested.) If all the timings are within .2 of a second of the ATF, there is no appreciable roller slippage present. If timing is less than 20 seconds, there is positive preset trail in the rate end.

22. Dis placement knob brake springs weak: Turn on the telescope motor and engage the optic clutch. If the brake springs are weak, the telescope index will remain stationary and the displacement knob will rotate.

23. Incorrect trail in the cross trail mechanism: Lock trail arm at 0 mils, remove sight stem pin and rotate the bottom of sight stem. No movement of the fore and aft cross hair should be apparent. If there is movement of the hair, there is incorrect trail in the cross trail mechanism.

24. Misaligned dovetail: With the drift angle at 0°, move the trail arm through its limits. No movement of the fore and aft cross hair

should be apparent.  If there is movement, there is misalignment of the dovetail.

NOTE:   On sights with no trail arm stop, care should be taken to have rate index at a tangent of .5 or less, thereby preventing the roller carriage from being forced against the upper spindle bearing and the trail arm from being slipped around the shaft. (Negative preset trail would be induced in the rate end.)

25.   Leveling knob sticking:  With gyro uncaged, rotate the knob without pushing in.  If the gyro is precessed, the leveling knob is sticking.

26.   Leveling knob not making contact:  Uncage gyro.  Use leveling knob in the normal manner.  If this does not precess the gyro, the leveling knob is not making contact.

27.   Complete failure of the B.S. gyro:  Uncage gyro.  If the gyro is cold, it will tumble toward the bombardier.  If it is warm, it may not tumble;  but the application of the leveling knobs will show whether or not the gyro is running.

28.   Slow running B.S. gyro:  Excessive precession of the vertical gyro will be noted and the gyro will be extrememly sensitive to the action of the leveling knobs.

29   Excessive precession of the vertical gyro:  Watch the bubbles with the gyro uncaged.  If either bubble precesses, more than one-half bubble length in two minutes (on a gyro that has been running for 10 to 15 minutes), this is excessive.

30.   Burned out stabilized resistor coil (PDI):  With PDI switch on, secondary clutch disengaged, rotate drift knob.  A reading will be evidenced on the pilot's PDI only from the point where the coil is burned out to the nearest end of the coil.

31.   Improper wiring between B.S. and pilot's PDI:  When the bombardier displaces his PDI needle to the left, if the pilot's PDI needle moves to the left, the wires from the B. S. to the PDI instruments are reversed.

32.   Stabilizer brush not making proper contact with resistor coil PDI: Erractic reading of pilot's PDI - possibly no reading.

33.   Defective pilot's PDI:  Erratic reading on pilot's PDI - Possibly no reading.

34.   No cross hair illumination:  With a caged B.S. gyro, check to see that lamp is OK;  that coil is not burned out;  that rheostat brush is making contact with the coil.  If these are in order, readjust the mirror.

NOTE:  Be sure that B.S. switch is off before removing lamp housing.

## I.    C - 1 AUTOPILOT

The day before each mission the C-1 autopilot should be given the ground check listed below.  The ground check takes only about five minutes and will uncover many malfunctions that would not otherwise be discovered until it is too late to do anything about it.

Ground Check Procedure:

1.  Check can be made with put-put or engines running.
2.  Disengage bombsight clutch.
3.  Center PDI and engage autopilot clutch.
4.  Turn on master switch.
5.  Set all adjusting knobs on A.C.P. to 12 o'clock position.
6.  Manually operate airplane controls through their full range and observe action of telltale lights.  When controls are in center position, lights should be off.  At all other positions, one light or the other should remain on steadily.  If the lights flicker at off-center control positions, the corresponding servo "pot" requires cleaning.
7.  Turn on PDI-Servo switch.
8.  Without centering, engage aileron, rudder, and elevator switches. If one light is on when switch is engaged it will go out as controls reach center position.
9.  Turn each centering knob slowly through its full range, observe manual controls for correct direction of movement.  Only one control should move in response to each centering knob.  Controls should move in small even steps with pecking action, but not jerkily.  Observe that this pecking action is uniform on both sides of the electical center. Also one step each time light flashes.
    a.  Clockwise rotation of aileron centering knob should cause the control wheel to turn clockwise.  Also right aileron surface should move up.
    b.  Clockwise rotation of rudder centering knob should cause the right rudder pedal to move forward.  Also the rudder surface should turn to the right.
    c.  Clockwise rotation of the elevator centering knob should cause the control column to move back, and also the elevator surface to move up.
10.  Disengage autopilot clutch and move clutch arm to extreme left.  Be sure that it moves freely without bending.  The control wheel should move clockwise and the right rudder pedal forward.
11.  Move clutch arm to the extreme right.  The control wheel should move counter-clockwise and the left rudder pedal forward.
12.  With the clutch arm to the extreme right position, rotate the Bank Trimmer through its limits.  The aileron surface should move an appreciable amount.  This is the check on the action of the Bank Trimmer.
13.  Center PDI and engage autopilot clutch.  Rotate Bank Trimmer through its limits.  There should be NO aileron control movement.

14. Adjust dashpot. Remove cover from the directional panel. Unlock adjusting nut by turning lock ring counter-clockwise. Actuate rudder wiper by rotating course knobs on bombsight. For a slow uniform rotation of the course knobs the rudder wiper should move, but remain vertical without a "kick". With a rather fast rotation of the course knobs the rudder wiper should have an advanced movement or "kick". Rotate knurled adjusting nut up to decrease initial rudder "kick" or down to increase initial rudder "kick". When adjusted, lock adjusting nut with lock ring. If a further adjustment is needed in the air, it will not be more than ¼ turn.

15. Rotate the pilot's Turn Control knob for a 30° right turn. The control wheel should turn clockwise and the right rudder pedal should move forward. Observe whether the directional arm lock clamps the autopilot clutch arm and holds it so that it is almost impossible to move it.

16. Rotate the pilot's Turn Control knob for a 30° left bank and observe the direction of control movement.

17. Turn off all switches, check that turn control is in detent, and disengage bombsight clutch.

## SETTING UP C-1 AUTOPILOT

In setting up the autopilot there should be the closest cooperation between the airplane commander and the co-pilot. After the airplane commander manually trims the ship, the co-pilot should hold the altitude and keep the ship level, while the airplane commander sets up the autopilot.

Procedure for Setting up Autopilot:

1. Before take-off set all control knobs on the ACP to 12 o'clock. Check to see that all switches are off and the Turn Control in detent.
2. After take-off when it is desired to set up the Autopilot turn on the master switch and wait 5 to 10 minutes.
3. Turn on PDI-Servo switch.
4. Trim the ship manually for straight and level flight "hands off" at the airspeed that it is intended to fly. Check with instruments.
5. Allow ship to fly straight and level for a few minutes to allow the vertical flight gyro to erect itself to the vertical. Do not bank plane immediately before setting up C-1.
6. Disengage auto-pilot clutch and center PDI. Hold it centered with the directional arm lock.
7. Turn all three sensitivity knobs to maximum.
8. With wings level, adjust Aileron Centering knob until both telltale lights are out. Immediately throw on Aileron Engaging Switch.
9. Observe the gyro compass. If the plane is turning slightly it can be noticed on the gyro compass. Adjust the aileron centering knob until the turning is stopped.

10. With PDI centered and ship flying straight and level, adjust the rudder centering knob until both lights are out, then immediately engage the rudder engaging switch. Engage autopilot clutch.
11. Turn the aileron and rudder sensitivity pointers back to 12 o'clock.
12. With plane flying level and zero rate of climb, adjust elevator centering knob until both lights are out, then immediately engage elevator engaging switch. Turn the elevator sensitivity pointer back to 12 o'clock.

Final adjustment of the Autopilot:

If after engaging the aileron and rudder switches the PDI is off center a small amount, throw off the rudder switch. Turn the Bank Trimmer to minimum. Adjust the aileron centering knob until there is no turning as observed from the gyro compass. Turn up Bank Trimmer slowly - the plane will then bank into the PDI until it is centered. Now with lights out re-engage the rudder switch. Remember that after the aileron and rudder switches are engaged even a slight change made with aileron centering will necessitate a readjustment of rudder centering. The action with respect to these two axes is very closely linked together. Adjust the sensitivity for each of the three axes by turning up (clockwise) the sensitivity until the particular control chatters, then reduce the sensitivity just enough to eliminate the chatter.

Adjust the ratio for each of the three axes by turning up (clockwise) the ratio until a ship hunt develops. A good way of checking aileron and rudder ratio is to disengage the autopilot clutch, move the clutch arm slowly to its stop, then engage the autopilot clutch and observe the recovery. If the wings move past level position reduce aileron ratio until the overshooting is eliminated. If the PDI overshoots and oscillates from side to side, reduce rudder ratio. If this does not eliminate the rudder hunt or fishtailing, it will be necessary to adjust the dash pot. Screw the adjusting nut up to eliminate fishtailing or screw it down if the recovery is too slow.

The bombardier's turn must be coordinated, and can only be coordinated by a turn from the bombardier's compartment, that is coordinating a turn made with the turn control will not coordinate the bombardier's turn.

Procedure for Coordinating Bombardier's Turn:

1. After the C-1 is set up and all of the previously discussed adjustments made, disengage the autopilot clutch and move clutch arm slowly against stop and hold there.
2. Adjust Bank Trimmer to give an 18° bank or with limit stop in place a 12° bank.
3. Adjust skid trimmer until ball is centered.
4. Adjust up-elevator knob until altitude is maintained.
5. Engage autopilot clutch and allow plane to recover.

It must be thoroughly understood that unless the bombardier's turn is carefully coordinated the bombardier cannot do good bombing, for in a turn which is not coordinated there are forces set up due to accelerations which will precess the bombsight gyro. If the gyro is one degree out of the vertical at 30,000 feet it will cause an error of 1000-1500 feet, depending on ground speed.

## J.  THE A - 2  MECHANICAL RELEASE SYSTEM

1. <u>Group Selector Switches</u>: There are four of these switches. Two of them control the racks in the forward bomb bay and two of them control the racks in the rear bomb bay. Their purpose is to open or close the electrical circuit from the bombardier's compartment to the racks.

2. <u>Nose Fuse Arming Switch</u>: This switch operates a solenoid which retains the nose arming wire or allows it to fall with the bomb if the switch is not in the armed position.

3. <u>Camera Switch</u>: This makes power available for the camera circuit.

4. <u>Bomb Bay Door Selective Switches</u>: In some aircraft there are switches which give selectivity over which bomb bay doors will open. A standard modification is being installed with three switches to give selectivity. One switch is "single" or "Both"; another,"Forward" and the third "Rear". To open the rear bomb bay door only the first one is positioned at "Single" and the third one to "Open". These switches do not actually open the doors, they only set up the selectivity. The bomb bay door switch must be actuated to open the door, or doors.

5. <u>Bomb Bay Door Control Lever</u>: This lever actuates a switch which opens or closes the bomb bay doors.

6. <u>Bomb Release Lever</u>:  This lever has three positions:

    a.  <u>Lock</u>:  In this position the racks are mechanically locked against any release except by the emergency release handles and emergency release wheel. An electrical impulse will not fire the releases.

    b.  <u>Selective</u>:  In this position the racks are unlocked and the releases may be fired by an electrical impulse.

    c.  <u>Salvo</u>:  In this position all bombs are released mechanically almost simultaneously and tail fuse unarmed. The nose depends on the position of the nose arming switch. This lever is designed so that it can not be placed in salvo without first having placed the Bomb Bay Door Lever in "Open".

7. <u>Emergency Release Wheel</u>:  Turning this wheel two and one-half times forward will open the bomb bay doors and mechanically release everything in both bomb bays regardless of the position of any other switches or levers. To close bomb bay doors after using this wheel, it must be turned backwards as far as possible, then the Bomb Bay Door Control Lever placed in "Open" until the scres are fully extended, then placed in "Closed".

8. <u>Fuel Tank Safety Switches</u>: One of these switches is located in each bomb bay. Their purpose is to prevent electrical release in either bomb bay.

9. <u>Emergency Release Handles</u>: There are two of these handles - one by the pilot and the other aft of the pressure bulkhead. One pull of this handle will mechanically open the bomb bay doors and release everything in both bays. The doors are closed by the same procedure given under the paragraph on Emergency Release Wheel.

10. <u>Bomb Bay Door Safety Switches</u>: There are cams on the doors which operate these switches to prevent any electrical release until the doors are completely open.

11. <u>Emergency Operation</u>: There is an emergency motor provided to supply the necessary drive to the door screws. This motor is mounted on the forward edge of the center wing section, on the left-hand side next to the aileron servo motor of the C-1. It is fastened in place by means of four screws of the butterfly type.

The motor is operated from the ship's power supply. For use with the bomb bay doors there are two mounting positions provided, one in each bomb bay. These positions will be found approximately in the center, of the bomb bay, in the right hand catwalk. For its source of supply a cannon plug is provided directly forward of each station, and towards the outboard side of the plane.

To operate, the motor is mounted at the desired station by means of the four winged nuts. Its drive assembly, similar to that of the C-3 Motor Hoist, fits directly into the drive mechanism of the bomb bay doors; driving the screw to the extended position and thus opening the door. Only one pair of doors at a time can be thus opened.

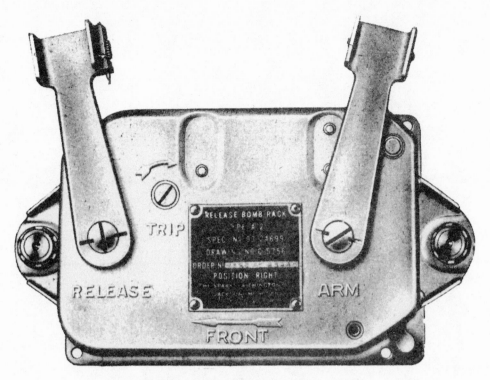

A-2 RELEASE SHOWING TRIPPING SCREW

FIGURE IV

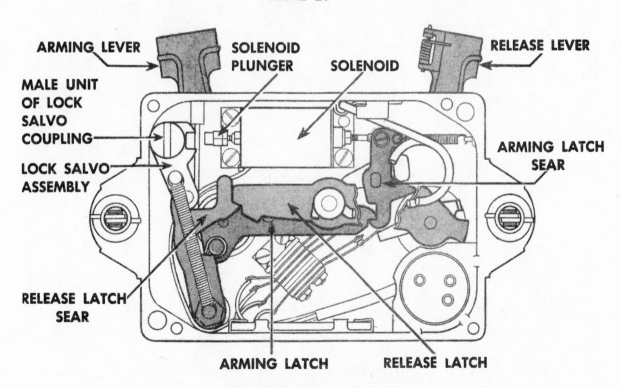

A-2 RELEASE MECHANISM

FIGURE V

## K.   A - 4   ALL ELECTRIC RELEASE SYSTEM

1. Operation of the Bomb Bay Doors:
   a. May be operated by either the pilot or the bombardier.
      (1) The Bombardier's Master Circuit Switch must be "ON" for the Bombardier's switch to energize the Bomb Bay Door Motors.
      (2) Should the pilot or co-pilot open or close the doors selectively, it is necessary that the bombardier shall have previously made the selectivity.
      (3) Make certain that the bomb bay door switch is held in the OPEN position a few seconds after the bomb bay door indicator light is illuminated.
   b. Probable malfunctions:
      (1) Fluttering of the doors, caused the Door Safety Switch to open and close intermittently.  Check the adjustment of the cam.
      (2) Bomb bay door motors not energized.
         (a) Circuit Breaker not closed, use the Pilot's switch.

2. Bombardier's Control Panel:
   a. Group selector switches:  To manually control the selectivity of the racks:
      (1) Close both switches for that bomb bay being used.
      (2) Probable malfunctions are either a broken lead or a bad switch.  Check by listening to the relays in the RS-2 when the switches are closed.
   b. Master bomb circuit switch and circuit breaker switch control all electrical power to the bombardier's control panel for normal release.
      (1) To operate the normal release system these switches must be CLOSED.
      (2) The probable malfunctions:  Circuit Breaker thrown to the OFF position.
   c. The nose arming control switch and indicating light.
      (1) Purpose:  to energize the type A-2 arming control solenoid.
      (2) Always move the switch to "ARM" position before opening the doors.  Do not leave the solenoids energized for excessive lengths of time.
      (3) Probable malfunctions:
         (a) Burned-out solenoids.
         (b) Bent bracket at the bomb rack.

3. Intervalometer:
   a. Purpose:  To control the number of, and the distance between, the bombs dropped.
   b. Position the counter knob to at least five more than the actual number of bombs to be dropped.  Set the interval control dial to the correct ground speed and the desired distance between bombs.

c.  To turn the unit off, the train-select switch must be set on **train** and the counter dial on zero. The unit should be turned on three minutes before it is to be used to allow the tubes to warm up.
  d.  Probable Malfunctions:
    (1)  Length of impulse not correctly adjusted.
    (2)  Counter mechanism not correctly adjusted.

4.  Rack Selector Relays, Type RS-2.
  a.  Their purpose:  To transmit impulses to the various racks in such manner that the dropping of bombs will not disturb the balance of the aircraft and to omit any group of bombs from the train without omitting a bomb from that train.
  b.  Actuated by the Group Selector Switches and the impulses from the "Intervalometer".
  c.  Probable Malfunctions - None.

5.  Bomb Indicator Light Panel.
  a.  Indicator light test switch and circuit breaker.
  Purpose:  To check the illumination of the indicator lamps.
    (1)  Hold the Mom. Test Switch in the "test" position.
    (2)  Probable Malfunctions:
      (a)  Circuit Breaker in "OFF" position.
      (b)  Lamps burned out.  Replace with spare lamps installed on Indicator Light Panel.
      (c)  Phillips Head, Flush screws to common ground at base of lamps may be loose.
  b.  Bomb Indicator switch.
    (1)  Purpose:  To indicate by the illumination of the lamps the station not tripped.
    (2)  To operate, hold the Mom. Indicator Light Switch on the C position.  Caution:  Do not hold this switch in the ON position while dropping bombs in select or train.
    (3)  Probable Malfunctions:
      (a)  Broken leads.
      (b)  Bad rotary switch.
      (c)  Bad A-4 release.

6.  Cannon Connectors to Bomb Racks.
  a.  Purpose:  To permit the omission of a rack from a group with the omission of a bomb from the normal train.
  b.  Switches located inside the cannon connector close, permitting the impulse to by-pass that particular cannon connector when the rack male bayonets are not installed.
  c.  Probable Malfunctions:
    (1)  Double release on two separate racks caused by the contacts not opening.
    (2)  One full rack of bombs returned should the contacts not close.
    (3)  Check to see the connectors are turned on full hand light and that the connectors not in use are thoroughly sealed with masking tape.

7. A-1 Release Recepticles:

    a. Purpose: To permit the omission of an A-4 release from the rack without omitting a bomb from the normal train.

    b. A switch located inside the release closes, permitting the impulse to by-pass that particular station, when release is not installed.

    c. Probable Malfunctions:

        (1) Double release on one rack, caused by contacts not opening.

        (2) A part of a rack returned because of the contacts not closing.

        (3) Check to see that the A-4 release is securely installed and that these A-1 Recepticles not in use are thoroughly sealed with masking tape.

8. A-4 Bomb Release Unit:

    a. Purpose: To permit the dropping of bombs either armed or safe, depending upon the discretion of the bombardier.

    b. This select operation is accomplised by the electrical control over the arming and release levers of the A-4 release.

    c. Probable Malfunctions:

        (1) Rotary Release Solenoid burned out.

        (2) Salvo plunger sticky.

        (3) Skip station contacts inoperative.

9. Salvo Operation.

    a. Accomplished by any one of three switches: bombardier's, pilot's or gunner's.

    b. Both Bomb Bay Doors are actuated by any one of the three salvo switches.

    c. The bomb salvo relay is energized by any one of the salvo switches and permits a flow of current to the time delay relays if the bomb bay doors are in the full OPEN position.

    d. The impulse from the time delay relays passes through the Bomb Bay Fuel Tank Safety Switch to the A-4 releases, therefore if the Fuel Tank Safety Switch is in the "Safe" position it will be impossible to salvo the bomb bay tanks.

10. Bomb Shackles and Carrying Hooks.

    a. The full weight of the bomb rests on the shackle and in turn the carrying hooks. The movement of the A-4 releases trips the shackle and permits the bomb to drop either ARMED or SAFE.

    b. Probable Malfunctions.

        (1) Prematurely released bombs on the bomb bay doors.

        (2) "Hung" bombs, either armed or safe.

        (3) Make certain that the end of the shackle marked "Front" is towards the nose of the ship.

In order to obtain good bombing and good maintenance it is necessary that all malfunctions be correctly observed. The bombardier should work closely with the armament and maintenance personnel of the aircraft. A malfunction can not be correctly observed by ground personnel if they do not know the sequence of happenings in the air.

## L.    THE A - 4 RELEASE MECHANISM

The release consists of an arming lever, a release lever, a rotary solenoid for tripping the two levers, a solenoid for salvo bombing, a releasing
arm and an arming arm, a transfer switch combined with an indicator light
switch plus a switch operating arm, a shock plate, a trip screw, internal
wiring terminating in a 3-prong electrical connector and a few other parts
all assembled in a die-cast aluminum-alloy case with a dust-tight cover
at the back.  A hole in the flange at either end of the case permits it
to be readily attached to the rack.

An impulse of current to the rotary solenoid trips the levers; first the
release lever and then the arming lever.  At the termination of the impulse the circuit to the indicator light and to the salvo solenoid is
broken, and the wire which carried the incoming impulse is automatically
transferred by a switch to the circuit leading to the next station.  This
transfer cannot be made as long as the solenoid is energized.  If the
release is not cocked, the electrical impulse passes through the switch
to the next station without energizing the solenoid.

IF RATED VOLTAGE IS APPLIED TO THE SOLENOID CONTINUOUSLY FOR A PERIOD OF
30 SECONDS OR LONGER, DAMAGE WILL PROBABLY RESULT.

When the salvo is energized and the release (rotary) solenoid is also
energized, the release lever is tripped but the arming lever is held
in the cocked position by the plunger of the salvo solenoid, blocking
further movement of the rotary solenoids.  This means the bombs are
dropped unarmed (with reference to the tail fuses only).  As the release
lever is tripped, the circuit to the indicator light and to the salvo
solenoid is broken, and the wire which carried the incoming impulse is
automatically transferred by a switch to the circuit leading to the next
station.  The rotary solenoid is de-energized, permitting the rotary plunger to return to normal leaving the arming lever cocked.

The positions of the release lever and the arming lever with relation
to the internal mechanism (illustrated by figures).

The indicator light circuit must not be closed while the bombs are being released, selectively or in train.  If it is, partial salvo would
result.  The ground circuit is made through the metal-to-metal contact
between the case and the rack.

The time required for tripping the release arm from the beginning of
the electrical impulse to the completion of the travel is not more than
0.040 of a second.  The time required for transferring the current to
the next release is not more than 0.022 of a second after the termination
of the impulse.

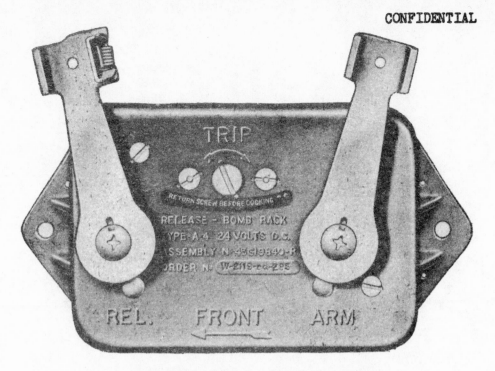

A-4 RELEASE SHOWING TRIPPING SCREW

FIGURE VI

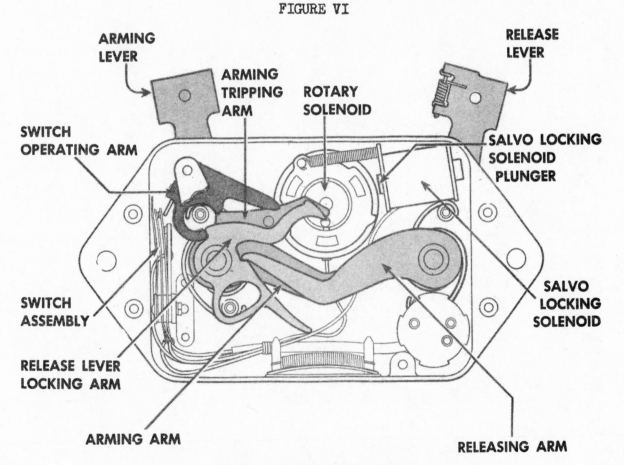

THE A-4 RELEASE MECHANISM

FIGURE VII

VII - 48 - 1

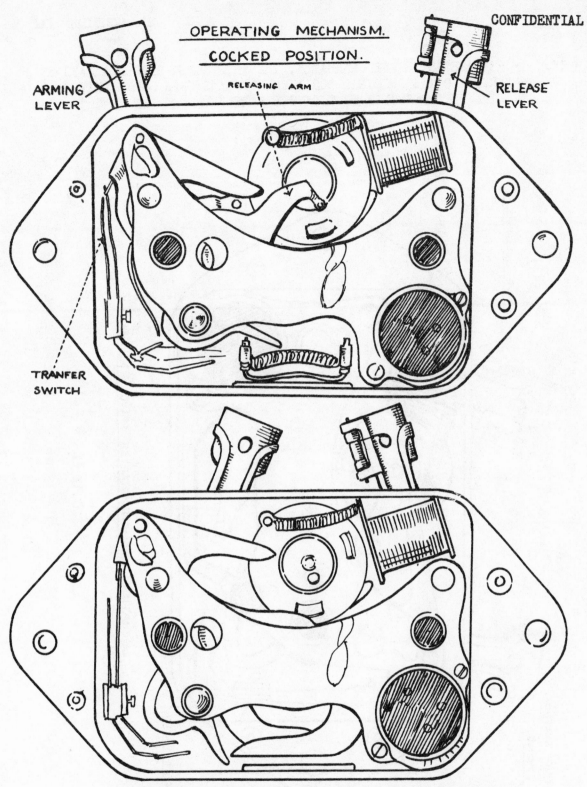

OPERATING MECHANISM.
COCKED POSITION.

RELEASING ARM

ARMING
LEVER

RELEASE
LEVER

TRANFER
SWITCH

MECHANISM after MANUAL or ORDINARY ELECTRICAL RELEASE.

FIGURE VIII

VII - 49

NOTE: IF RELEASE IS TRIPPED MANUALLY, THE TRIP SCREW SHOULD ALWAYS BE RETURNED TO ITS ORIGINAL POSITION BY MEANS OF A SCREW DRIVER OR IT WILL BE IMPOSSIBLE TO COCK THE RELEASE.

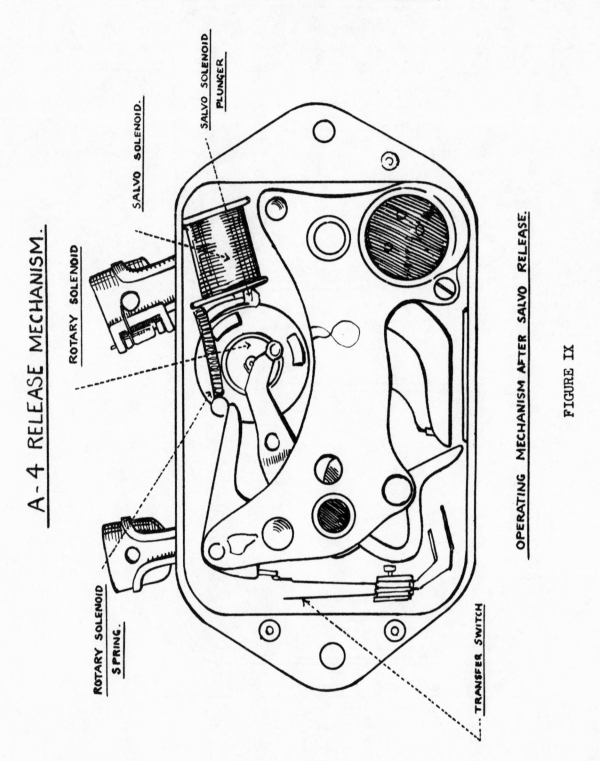

A-4 RELEASE MECHANISM.

SALVO SOLENOID.

SALVO SOLENOID PLUNGER

ROTARY SOLENOID

ROTARY SOLENOID SPRING.

TRANSFER SWITCH

OPERATING MECHANISM AFTER SALVO RELEASE.

FIGURE IX

## M. PREFLIGHT CHECK OF RACKS, CONTROLS, RELEASES, DOORS, INTERVALOMETER AND BOMBS

1. Normal release - Slow Train:

   a. With bombardier's master switch and the group selector switches in the "OFF" position, cock all alternate stations in the sequence of release. (Example: Station No. 1,3,5,7,9,11)

   b. Set the Intervalometer counter dial for the number of stations cocked and the interval control at 150 feet and 100 mph ground speed.

   c. Close all group selector switches except those in bomb bay containing fuel tanks.

   d. Open the bomb bay doors, turn the bombardier's master switch to the "ON" position, and the train selector switch to "TRAIN" position. Permit the intervalometer to warm up a minimum of one minute and a maximum of three (3) minutes.

   e. Actuate the bomb release switch. As soon as the counter returns to zero, check to see that all cocked stations were released armed and that the releases were in their normal sequence.

   f. Replace any A-4 release which has failed to trip at first attempt and intervalometer which failed to actuate properly.

2. Normal Release - Fast Train:

   a. With the bombardier's master switch and the group selector switches in the "OFF" position, cock even alternate stations in sequence of release. (Example: Station No. 2,4,6,8,10,12)

   b. Set the intervalometer counter dial for the number of stations cocked and the interval control at 8 feet and 100 mph ground speed.

   c. Close all group selector switches except those in bomb bay containing fuel tanks.

   d. Open the bomb bay doors, turn the bombardier's master switch to the "ON" position, and the train selector switch to "TRAIN" position. Permit the intervalometer to warm up a minimum of one minute and a maximum of three (3) minutes.

   e. Actuate the bomb release switch. As soon as the counter returns to zero check to see that all cocked stations were released armed and that the releases were in normal sequence.

3. Salvo Release.

   a. Cock the A-4 releases at all stations and turn the fuel tank safety switch to the "ON" position, except in the bomb bay containing fuel tanks.

b. Close bhe bomb bay doors and observe the operation of the doors.

c. With the doors fully closed and the bombardier's master switch and the group selector switches in the "OFF" position, actuate the bombardier's salvo switch to open the bomb bay doors.

d. When the bomb bay doors are in the full open position, check:

   (1) The A-4 releases should all have fired and the release levers tripped. The arming levers should still be in the cocked position.

   (2) Check the bombardier's and pilot's bomb bay door indicator lights to make sure they are illuminated.

e. Cock the A-4 releases at all stations to be used on the mission.

4. Inspection of Bombs before loading:

a. Inspect fins for looseness and bends. Tighten, if loose, and have fins straightened or replaced, if bent.

b. Check to see that fins have been properly aligned.

c. Inspect bombs and discard any that are found to have cracked or bent lugs.

d. Inspect bomb cases for dents and have the bombs replaced. A small dent may cause a large error.

e. Check to see that fuses are hand tight in bomb cases.

f. Check to see that arming wire is threaded through lug to tail and nose fuses and that the wire extends beyond fuses 3 to 4 inches.

g. Check the firmness of the fahnstock clip on the arming wire. It should take from 6 to 8 pounds to displace it so that it will overcome the 3 to 4 pounds tension on the A-2 arming wire unit.

CONFIDENTIAL

## N.   PNEUMATIC BOMB BAY DOORS

Operation of the pneumatic actuator doors is similar to the screw-type
system in that the pilot, bombardier, and crew all have control of the
doors through the salvo circuit.  The bombardier has, besides his salvo
switch, a bomb door selector switch that enables him to open both forward and aft doors together, or the aft door only.  NOTE:  If the master
switch is closed and the selector switch placed in "BOTH DOORS" position,
and then changed to "REAR DOOR ONLY" and the "OPEN" switch operated,
both doors will open instead of the rear only.  This can be prevented by
either opening the master switch or by operating the "CLOSE" switch before operating the "OPEN" switch.  On the bombardier's panel are also two
indicator lights that indicate which doors are open.  Another light gives
warning when the doors are not latched.  The pilot has two switches
mounted on the aisle control stand that open or close both sets of doors
simultaneously.  In addition, a bomb door circuit breaker reset button
is located between the pilot's door "OPEN" and door "CLOSE" switches.  A
light on the center aisle stand indicates when the doors are not latched.
While the crew members do not have a door selector switch, they can operate the doors individually with the emergency pull handles.

There are two emergency pull handles for OPENING the bomb doors, one located at the pilot's station and the other located just aft of bulkhead
218.  On the recently delivered airplanes there are two emergency pull
handles for CLOSING the bomb doors when there is "available air" pressure.  The pull handle for closing the forward bomb doors is located
just aft of bulkhead 218 and to the right of the emergency door release
handle.  The pull handle for closing the aft bomb doors is mounted on
the rear bomb bay right-hand catwalk at Station 495.  If there is no air
pressure available in the accumulators, the bomb doors cannot be closed.
However, on future airplanes, a standby air pressure accumulator will be
installed to make available an emergency supply of air.  This will provide for bomb bay door operation when the system accumulators are empty.

There are two bomb bay door safety shut-off valves, one mounted near
station 218 in the forward bomb bay, the other in the rear bomb bay.
(NOTE:  Airplanes in the field which do not have these safety shut-off
valves or standby accumulators at present will be revised.)  These airplanes have electrical safety switches mounted in each bomb bay.  The
forward bomb door safety switch is near the forward bomb bay light, and
the aft switch is near the aft light.  WARNING:  NEVER ENTER THE BOMB
BAY WITHOUT FIRST CHECKING TO SEE THAT THE BOMB BAY SAFETY SHUT-OFF VALVES
ARE "CLOSED" OR THE SAFETY SWITCHES ARE IN THE "OFF" POSITION.  If the
bomb bay doors are to be tested on the ground, ALWAYS POST A GUARD to
keep anyone from entering the bomb bays or working in the vicinity of the
bomb bay doors.  When the bomb doors have been opened after landing, one
designated crew member from the aft compartment and one from the nose
compartment should turn the bomb door SAFETY SHUT-OFF VALVES TO "CLOSED"
before any crew member exits through the bomb bay.  These valves will then

remain in the "CLOSED" position at all times while the airplane is on the ground except during bomb door checks. The same procedure should be used on airplanes not equipped with safety shut-off valves but with safety switches. Check the switches instead of the valves. IF THE AIRPLANE HAS THESE SAFETY SWITCHES, IT SHOULD BE REMEMBERED THAT EVEN THOUGH THESE SAFETY SWITCHES ARE IN THE "OFF" POSITION, THE DOORS WILL STILL OPERATE IF THE EMERGENCY DOOR RELEASE HANDLES ARE PULLED. Therefore, respect these HANDLES and their attaching cables when working in or around the bomb bays. If the above safety precautions are not followed, serious accidents to personnel can be expected.

Air pressure for the systems is supplied by the two compressors and is stored in the accumulators. The compressor builds up an accumulator pressure of 1500 PSI in approximately 30 minutes at sea level. Always check to see that the compressor is started as soon as the ground check is begun. The compressor will start automatically when the airplanes electrical system is turned on if the compressor circuit breakers are in the closed position. If the compressor is not started until the plane has gained altitude, it will take much longer than 30 minutes to obtain the 1500 PSI pressure. When building up pressure from zero in the aft accumulator, be sure the forward left-hand door is closed. This is necessary to remove tension on the aft door release cable which is connected from the forward left-hand door to the aft door four-way valve so that this valve will be in the neutral position. If the valve is not in the neutral position, the air escapes through this valve to the door latch shaft, thus making it difficult to build up pressure. When the accumulator pressure reaches 1500 PSI, the regulating switch opens and the compressor motor stops. A pressure relief valve set for 1750 PSI is located on the accumulator. When the pressure in the accumulator drops to 625 PSI, the pressure warning switch actuates a warning light on the bombardier's panel. The compressor is cooled by means of a fan mounted on the upper end of the motor shaft. Outside air is drawn in and directed through baffles across the cooling fins on the compressor cylinders and exhausted again to the outside air.

NOTE: (1) Bombardiers and pilots are warned to hold their "DOOR CLOSE" switches in the closed position for approximately 3 seconds after doors are closed. This is necessary to keep doors from vibrating from latches or being "bounced" open by the opening spring.

(2) If latches are left in closed position by the maintenance crew it is only necessary to hit the "DOOR OPEN" switch; then the doors can be readily closed and latched.

## O.   SHACKLES

In the B-29, three types of shackles will be used for carrying bombs:

B-7:   100#, 300#, 500# and 1000#
D-6:   1600# or 2000#
D-7:   4000#

To hook the shackle to the lugs, the release lever and the arming lever are pinched toward the center of the shackle, and a pull is exerted on the suspension lugs. The shackle hooks are threaded through the lugs on the bomb, and an upward pressure is applied to the shackle hooks. The two levers are released and then flipped toward the center a couple of times. Then, pressure is applied to test the strength of the connection by pulling up on the shackle. A glance through the inspection hole will show whether or not the arming lever is engaged to the release mechanism.

Shackle Inspection:

1. Remove the shackle from the bomb racks.

2. Check shackle assembly for cleanliness. If dirt is discovered, clean with kerosene, but <u>do not lubricate</u>.

3. Check operation of moving parts against any binding.

4. Test internal springs by proper manipulation of the shackle.

5. Make a visual inspection of the shackle frame, levers, and hooks for warping.

6. Faulty or defective shackles should be replaced for ones in good condition.

## P.   AGASTAT TIME DELAY RELAY

1.  The agastat time delay relay is an instrument used for introducing a time delay.  It may be adjusted for a fraction of a second to several minutes.  It is designed for use in conjunction with any electrical equipment requiring a time delay.  However, in this case, it will be discussed in use with the formation bomblight.

2.  The time delay is energized by a signal from the intervalometer. When the agastat receives the signal, it operates the shutter on the formation bomb light which is a red filter indicating that bombs are dropping.  From the agastat the signal is sent to the rack selector relays.  When the agastat is de-energized, the red filter moves back into its position which indicates that bombs have been released.

3.  The timing unit is unaffected by dust, change in temperature, voltage or humidity.

4.  The time adjustment on the agastat relay is on the front of the unit which permits the time delay to be adjusted from range of less than one second to a fifteen minute interval.  To increase time delay, the adjusting screw is turned clockwise and to decrease it is turned counterclockwise.

5.  For shorter time delays than 15 seconds the thumb screw must be turned considerable, but as the delay increases, less movement of the thumb screw is necessary.

## Q. PHOTOGRAPHIC EQUIPMENT B-29

1. Photographic equipment used in the B-29 consists of a vertical bomb spotting camera, a Radar Scope camera and a small hand-held camera (K-20) for miscellaneous oblique photography. The cameras and procedures described below are of prime importance to the Bombardier, who must become thoroughly familiar with the equipment his is to operate in order to successfully complete his mission.

2. The vertical camera for daylight bomb spotting or orientation is installed outside the pressurized area and must therefore be controlled remotely. Such control is attained by means of a B-7 intervalometer mounted in the Bombardier's compartment and inter-connected electrically to the camera and the Agastat Switch in the bomb release system.

3. The B-7 intervalometer was designed so that when it is operating in a properly connected photographic installation, a tripping circuit is closed in accordance with the performance requirements for each of the four modes of functioning, day reconnaissance, day orientation, night orientation and night reconnaissance and bomb spotting. For use in strike photography for Bombardment Units one primary mode is used, DAY RECONNAISSANCE this operates the tripping mechanism on regular impulses. The counter operates on all modes and records one count for each exposure, to reset the counter wheel, rotate it until all numbers return to zero. The warning light indicates that an exposure is about to be made and comes on approximately two (2) seconds before the exposure is made. The start control when actuated connects the power to the instrument. If pictures are desired before "Bombs Away" it will be necessary to use this start button. However, if no pictures are desired before "Bombs Away", the Agastat switch in the bomb release system will actuate the system and start the camera in operation. It is important to have selected the mode and interval before "Bombs Away" as the start switch will be ineffective if the intervalometer is in the "Off" position. It is necessary for the Bombardier to push the stop button when he desires to discontinue taking pictures. The Stop Control cuts off the power to the automatic mechanism of the intervalometer, but the mode selector should then be turned to the "Off" position. The single exposure switch is wired independently in the intervalomenter in such a way that it is possible to close the controlled circuit at any time. If the camera master switch is on, the single exposure switch may be pressed at any time to take a desired photograph. If the intervalometer is operating a single exposure may be taken between the normal interval without effect on it.

4. The Vertical cameras used by Bombardment Units of this Command are the types K-22, and K-18 or K-7C. They are both electric and fully automatic. The K-22 takes a negative 9" x 9", the K-7C or the K-18 a 9" x 18" negative. The K-22 with a type A5A magazine accommodates 205 feet of film which provides approximately 250 9 x 9 negatives. The mount is adjustable, but the camera is set in a rigid position and may be tilted slightly to the rear in order to pick up bomb burst. The operation and electrical

connections of the two cameras are fundamentally the same. The camera should be mounted and tested by squadron and group photographic personnel, but should be checked by Bombardier. The camera doors are remotely controlled by a handle in the Radar comparment, immediately forward of the bulkhead door. It is the responsibility of the Bombardier to see that the Radar Operator opens and locks the camera doors, when approaching the bomb run or when pictures are desired. It is important to check the camera doors, see that they are locked in the open position, as considerable trouble has been encountered in the past by personnel failing to open doors, and failing to lock them; the air flow blows them closed and the camera view is obstructed.

5. The K-20 is a hand-held, manually operated camera designed for making oblique spotting photographs. The camera makes 50 negatives (4 x 5 inch) on a roll of film. The shutter release and film transport mechanism are interlocked, and have their controls located in the right handle of the camera. The operating handle is pivoted near its upper end, and one cycle of rotating it forward and back performs all the operations necessary to prepare the loaded camera for an exposure. Pressure on the trigger, located under the index finger in the upper forward side of the operating handle makes the exposure. The shutter cannot be tripped until the film is advanced and the film cannot be advanced until the shutter has been tripped. The view finder is located on the upper rear section of the cone. When the photographer sights through the view finder, with the ball of the rear sight in line with the intersection of the red lines in the finder lens, the area visible through the finder corresponds with the area covered by the negative. Do not operate the camera with nothing in the focal plane slot, should it be necessary to operate it unloaded, insert the film loading guide. Do not force any part of movement. Always release the shutter before putting the camera aside. The camera should be loaded and the shutter speed and diaphragm opening set for expected operating conditions by the photographic personnel. Should it be necessary to vary these due to entirely different conditions, the Bombardier should be briefed beforehand by the Group Photo Officer or Squadron Photo personnel.

## VIII  R A D I O   P R O C E D U R E

### A   INTRODUCTION

To be a good radio operator you must know the equipment you have to use in flight, and what radio stations both ground and airborne are available for you to contact.  You are the crew member who is trained primarily as a radioman.  In the event of emergency, the lives of all your fellow crew members may depend larely upon your ability.  Never before in history have combat missions been flown over such great distances and, when it is considered that total time in flight sometimes exceeds fifteen hours, fourteen and one-half of which are of necessity over water, communications between aircraft and base assume an important part in the completion of a successful mission.

The other crew members will expect you to answer their questions regarding the radio equipment carried in your airplane and just exactly what goes on in the ground installations.  The only way you can answer these questions is to know the equipment.  Be eager.  If you haven't seen the inside of your Wing air-ground station, direction finding station, or control tower, go visit one.  Find out what their capabilities are, so that you can better understand the complete operation.  Find out why, in some cases you may not be able to secure a much needed HF/DF bearing for a couple of minutes and why at other times they can shoot a bearing on you just about as fast as it takes the ground station to answer you with the "Q" signal QTN.  Appreciate the ground station operator's position.  He appreciates yours because in most cases he is a former aerial operator.  Learn all about your equipment and its capabilities and practice using them.  And then practice some more.  Be the type of radio operator who, when his airplane commander asks him if a certain something can be done, can answer right up with a "yes" or, "no", it hasn't been done but I can sure try".  Know your own limitations and also the limitations of your equipment.  Knowing when to use something is just as important as how to use it whether it be your head or your radio equipment.

### B   AIRBORNE RADIO EQUIPMENT

1.  Command Set.

The Command Set (SCR-522) is primarily used for voice communication between aircraft, both fighters and bombers, air-sea rescue facilities, and control tower for airdrome control.  Another use is now being made of the SCR-522.  Fighter aircraft equipped with the SCR-522 homing adapter (AN/ARA-8) may home on a continuous signal being transmitted from an SCR-522 whether that signal comes from an SCR-522 installed in either a fighter or a bomber.

The SCR-522 is a multi-channel piece of equipment composed of a VHF transmitter and receiver operating on four (4) crystal controlled frequencies between 100 and 150 megacycles. The four channels as normally set up in XXI Bomber Command bombardment aircraft are: Channel A, Wing frequency or Bomber to Bomber frequency; Channel B, Bomber to Fighter frequency; Channel C, Pacific Common (control tower) and air-sea rescue frequency and Channel D, VHF homing frequency. It is planned to eventually equip all B-29's with the AN/ARC-3 which from a standpoint of operation is essentially an eight (8) channel SCR-522.

Using the SCR-522 on either Channel C or D it is possible to transmit a signal and receive a VHF/DF bearing from the fighter directory services located at all XXI Bomber Command island installations and also from Iwo Jima in the Volcano Group. This bearing may be received from distances as great as 150 miles from the ground installation and is a good point to remember in the event of malfunction of your H/F liaison transmitter or in the event of poor atmospheric conditions which greatly effect the accuracy of HF/DF bearings.

In the event the interphone malfunctions and cannot be repaired while airborne, an emergency interphone system can be set up by having the pilot or co-pilot place the T-R-REM switch of the control box in the R position and the SCR-522 on anyone of the four channels. He and the remaining crew members then place their interphone selector switches on VHF position and the audio stages of the SCR-522 VHF radio will then serve as an emergency interphone amplifier. When using this emergency interphone system, however, care must be taken that the interphone switch remains in the VHF position and that the T-R-REM switch on the SCR-522 control box remains in the R position to prevent inadvertant transmission on the air. For normal VHF operation it is only necessary to restore the T-R-REM switch to the REM position and full transmission and reception facilities for VHF are available.

When using VHF voice transmissions in coordination with fighters and Naval facilities, short title channel designations are often times used. These short titles which may be found in your Signal Operation Instructions (S.O.I.) should be memorized.

2. Liaison Set.

The liaison set which consists of the AN/ART-13 transmitter and the BC-348 ( ) receiver is primarily used for contacting air-ground and air-air radio stations. The receiver (BC-348 () ) is a conventional super-hetrodyne receiver with a frequency range of 200 to 500 kilocycles and from 1.5 to 18.0 megacycles.

Radio transmitter AN/ART-13 is an eleven channel pre-tuned transmitter with automatic tuning. Ten pre-tuned channels are available between 2.0 megacycles and 18.1 megacycles. Frequencies to be set up are listed in SOI and generally include; the Wing air-ground frequencies; air-sea rescue frequencies, auxiliary Wing air-ground frequency (for some base other than your own) ACS day and night CW frequencies and auxiliary tower frequency.

When the SCR-522 becomes inoperative and the control tower must be contacted using the AN/ART-13 transmitter, it is suggested rather than using the full 90 watts power output that the radio operator place his operating control switch on the "tune" position thereby operating on half-power so as not to bother the control tower operator with a signal which may block his receiver and cause him to readjust his receiver gain.

At least one aircraft per squadron will have eleven pre-tuned channels on the AN/ART-13. This eleventh pre-set channel whether it be in the 200-600 kilocycle band or 500-1500 kilocycle band may be used as a radio homing aircraft in air-to-air homing for assembly purposes, target directors, or, air-sea rescue purposes. Frequencies to be used are listed in the S.O.I.

## 3. Radio Compass.

The radio compass AN/ARN-7 installed in B-29 aircraft is one of the most valuable aids to air navigation carried in your airplane. It can be used to "Home" on non-directional radio homers, radio ranges, radio broadcast stations, radio transmitter buoys AN/CRN-1 or any radio station which is broadcasting on a frequency which can be tuned in on the radio compass receiver. (AN/ARN-7 has a frequency range of 100 to 1750 kilocycles). The radio compass can also be used to determine your position by taking a bearing on two or more radio stations whose identity and position can be established. The intersection of the bearings indicates the aircraft's position.

All aircraft commanders are cautioned not to depend on enemy radio stations as a homing aid for use with the Radio Compass.

## C  GROUND RADIO FACILITIES

## 1. Air-Ground Stations.

At its bases, each Wing maintains an air-ground station for working the planes assigned to that Wing. This is the normal ground contact for B-29 aircraft, and should always be used for that purpose in preference to other installations. However, if the airplane commander deems it necessary, he may authorize you to contact any air-ground station available.

The XXI Bomber Command maintains an air-ground intercept station which receives all XXI Bomber Command bombardment and air-sea rescue frequencies. It is this station's primary purpose to monitor all frequencies used by the XXI Bomber Command. This station coordinates with Operations Control Officer all information received on XXI Bomber Command air-ground frequencies and relays important messages such as distress calls to both Bomber Command Controller for relay back to Wing bases if necessary and also to Suprad (Naval HF/DF Pacific Net) for a possible "fix" (QTF). The XXI Bomber Command air-ground intercept station also reports all procedure and security violations to appropriate authorities and prepares and distributes C.I.M.'s (Communications Improvement Memorandums) to all installations concerned for information and appropriate corrective action.

Most XXI Bomber Command islands maintain air-ground stations which are operated by Army Airways Communications System (AACS). Each station transmits and receives on at least one day and one night CW frequency.

Frequencies and call signs of XXI Bomber Command installations are listed in XXI Bomber Command SOI. All information regarding air-ground and air-air facilities along a particular route flown will be given at a preflight briefing and a list of these facilities will be carried in the radio operator, pilot and navigator's communication flimsy (SOI extracts).

It is the radio operator's responsibility to know his complete SOI extract (flimsy) thoroughly. If there is a question in the radio operator's mind about anything contained in his "flimsy", he will contact his Communications Officer at the radio operator's specialized briefing and become thoroughly acquainted with every detail involved before take-off on a combat mission.

## 2. Aids to Navigation.

By far the most common aid to air-navigation is the non-directional radio homer. This is nothing more than a medium frequency transmitter emitting a continuous coded signal in a 360 degree field pattern, which may be homed on with a radio compass. Care must be taken to have the CW-Voice switch on the radio compass control box in the CW position when using the non-directional homing beacon. Terminal weather conditions encoded in UCOPAC and transmitted in CW are available on all non-directional homer frequencies. The frequencies, call signs, time of weather broadcast and locations of homer stations are contained in Radio Aids to Navigation pamphlets, NATAPOA, JACSPAC and Pacific Airways Route Manual (H.O. No. 503). Extracts of all radio aids to navigation pertinent to a specific combat mission will be contained in "flimsies" carried by the radio operator, pilot and Navigator on all combat missions. When aircraft are engaged in training missions not involving actual combat, a complete copy of JACSPAC or NATAPOA, may be carried in the aircraft.

The next most common aid to air-navigation is the radio range. These ranges are of the normal four quadrant coded type. Frequencies, call signs, and locations of ranges are contained in JACSPAC, NATAPOA, Pacific Airways Route Manual (H.O. No. 503) and extracts of radio communication facilities ("flimsies") carried on all combat and training missions.

## 3. Direction Finding (D/F) Stations.

HF/DF stations are installed at all XXI Bomber Command bases and at numerous other Army and Navy operated fields. The accuracy of the bearings they can "shoot" depends upon weather conditions as, excessive atmospheric disturbances produce static affecting the accuracy of the HF/DF equipment. However, any inaccuracy caused by weather will be reflected in the class

of bearing which is always given. There is a special procedure for
contacting these stations and obtaining HF/DF which must be followed.
The procedure is given in Section D 4 of this chapter. Frequencies
and call signs to use in working HF/DF stations and their locations
are contained in combat "flimsies", JACSPAC, NATAPOA, and Pacific
Airways Route Manual (H.O. No. 503).

VHF/DF stations are installed at most XXI Bomber Command bases in the
Marianas and fighter bases in the Volcanos. VHF/DF bearings may be
requested when approximately 150 miles from these bases. Bearings
are requested either on Channel C or Channel D of the SCR-522. The
VHF/DF stations are operated by the Air Defense Command, Fighter
Directory Service. The bearings may be obtained by calling the appropriate base and asking for a bearing. Directions as to how to
transmit for bearings will be given by the controlling base called.
Frequencies and voice calls for available VHF/DF bearings may be
found in combat "flimsies", JACSPAC, NATAPOA, or, Pacific Airways
Route Manual (H.O. No. 503). When calling a VHF/DF station for a
bearing, be sure you check into the net first, and , when you have
all the bearings you need, be sure and check out of the net. This
procedure averts much confusion.

4. Instrument Approach Systems.

There will be installed at all bases of the command an SCS-51 Instrument Approach System which may be used by B-29's in letting down under
instrument conditions.

The system consists of a beamed transmitter which indicates the center
line of the runway and a series of three marker beacons which indicate
to an approaching aircraft the distance it is from the end of the runway. A glide path transmitter also is installed. Carried in the aircraft is a marker beacon receiver which indicates when the fan marker
beacons are passed over. Also carried is an indicator which by means
of a swinging needle indicates whether the aircraft is to the right or
left of the desired flight path along the runway. An additional needle
on the aircraft indicator shows whether the aircraft is above or below
the glide path which when followed will let the aircraft touch down at
the end of the runway. By using a pre-determined rate of decent in conjunction with the beamed transmitter, marker beacons and glide path
transmitter, a safe let-down right at the end of the runway can be made
under conditions of low visibility.

## D OPERATING PROCEDURES

1. Radio Telephone (R/T) Procedure.

Your voice messages must be kept short and to the point. Standard
phraseology achieves this, and R/T speech should always be clear and
slow, with an even emphasis on each word. Words must not be run together and messages will be spoken in natural phrases and not word
by word. The Phonetic Alphabet will be used as an aid to more in-

telligible R/T procedure, and will be used in spelling out words. The alphabet will be memorized and must be strictly adhered to.

a. Phonetic Alphabet.

| | | | | |
|---|---|---|---|---|
| A - Able | G + George | M - Mike | S - Sugar | Y - Yoke |
| B - Baker | H - How | N - Nan | T - Tare | Z - Zebra |
| C - Charlie | I - Item | O - Obee | U - Uncle | |
| D - Dog | J - Jig | P - Peter | V - Victor | |
| E - Easy | K - King | Q - Queen | W - William | |
| F - Fox | L - Love | R - Roger | X - Xray | |

b. Pronunciation of Numerals.

| | |
|---|---|
| 0 - Zero | 5 - Fi-yiv |
| 1 - Wun | 6 - Six |
| 2 - Too | 7 - Seven |
| 3 - Thuh-ree | 8 - Ate |
| 4 - Fo-wer | 9 - Niner |

c. Components of a Voice Message.

(1) The call. For example "Hullo Happy Five" (call sign of receiving station) this is "Happy One Zero" (call sign of calling station).

(2) Text (subject matter). Contains plain language, code words or figures. If it is necessary to spell a word use the phonetic alphabet.

(3) Ending. Every voice transmission must end with one of the following procedure words: (A) "Over", meaning "My transmission is ended and I expect an answer from you", (B) "Out", meaning "This conversation is ended and no reply is expected."

d. Transmitting and Answering.

When both stations are in good communication all parts of the transmission are made once. When communication is difficult, phrases, words or groups may be repeated at the end of the message or may be transmitted using the procedure phrase "words twice". A group of figures will be transmitted in the ordinary manner using the "words twice" procedure if necessary.

Time of origin will be expressed in four digits and will be preceded by the word "Time" (Assuming that you are instructed to assign a time of origin to a voice message).

When words are missed or doubtful, repetitions will be repeated by the receiving station before receipting for the message. The procedure phrases "Say Again", or, "I say again" will be used in conjunction with "All Before", "All After", "Word Before", or, "Word After".

Example: "Hullo Happy Five, this is Happy One Zero, Say Again all after three four. Over". "Hullo Happy One Zero this is Happy Five. I say again all after three four. Seven three two six over".

When a word is required to be spelled to insure correct reception, the phrase "I Spell", will be used immediately before beginning to spell the word in question.

A Station is understood to have readability of good strength, unless otherwise notified. When making original contact, strength of signals and readability will not be exchanged unless one station cannot clearly hear another station. The response to "How do you hear me?" will be a short concise report of actual reception, such as "weak but readable" "Strong but distorted," etc.

Priority designations are seldom used in voice transmission. However, if it is desired to use a priority designation, it will be spoken in the clear as the last part of the message.

In the interests of security, only those transmissions which are absolutely necessary will be made by R/T. No idle chatter will be engaged in. The more the enemy can hear the more he can find out about you. Remember the voice channels are used for command functions. Remember that VHF radio telephone has been received as much as 800 miles away from the transmitting station.

    e. Procedure Phrases.

| Word or Phrase | Meaning |
| --- | --- |
| Roger | I have received all of your last message. |
| Acknowledge | Let me know that you have received and understand this message |

| | |
|---|---|
| Wilco | Your last message received, understood and will be complied with. |
| How do you hear me? | How strong and clear is my transmission. |
| Wait | If the pause required is longer than a few seconds, it must be followed by the ending, "Out". |
| Say Again - I say again | When requesting the repetition of a previous transmission, or used to preface a previous transmission, the word "Repeat" is never used in this sense as it has a distinct operational meaning for the British Army. |
| Verify | Check coding, check text with the originator and send correct version. |
| Message for you | I wish to transmit a message to you. |
| Send your message | Go ahead, transmit. |
| Read Back | Repeat this message back to me exactly as received after I give "Over". |
| That is correct | You are correct. |
| Words Twice | (1) As a request: Communications is difficult, send every phrase (or code group) twice. (2) As information: Since communication is difficult, I will send every phrase (or code group) twice. |
| Correction | An error has been made in this transmission (or message indicated). The correct version is _____. |
| Wrong | What you have just heard is the incorrect version. The correct version is _____. |
| Groups | The number of groups in this code or cipher message is _____. |
| Break | I hereby indicate the separation of the text from other portions of the message. This word is used only when there is not a clear distinction between the text and other portions of a message. |

## 2. Wireless Telegraphy (W/T) Procedure.

Wireless telegraphy (W/T) procedure will be as outlined in Combined
British and U.S. Procedure (FM 24-10). Operators will limit their
procedure to the prosigns given in that publication. The purpose
of a standardized radio procedure is to speed up communications.
Any use of unauthorized prosigns, operating signals or procedures
will have the opposite effect. Forget all "Ham" procedure and unauthorized procedure signals such as outmoded commercial signals.

### a. Prosigns to be memorized.

| Prosign | Meaning | Prosign | Meaning |
|---|---|---|---|
| A | Originator's sign | B̄T̄ | Long Break |
| ĀĀ | Unknown station | C | Correct |
| AA | All after | D | Deferred |
| AB | All before | EEEEEEEE | Error |
| ĀR̄ | End of transmission | F | Do not answer |
| ĀS̄ | Wait | G | Repeat back |
| B | More to follow | GR | Group (s) |
| II | Separative sign | O | Urgent (emergency) |
| ĪMĪ | Repeat | OP | Operational Priority (Immediately) |
| ĪNT̄ | Interrogatory | P | Priority (important) |
| ĪX̄ | Execute to follow | R | Received |
| ĪX̄ (5 sec) | Execute Signal | T | Transmit to |
| J | Verify and repeat | V | From |
| K | Go ahead | W | For information to |
| N | Not received or exempted | WA | Word after |
| NR | Station Serial Number | OPASR | Operational priority air-sea rescue. Used in the heading of a "ditching" distress message. (Handled with utmost urgency). |

Combined operating "Q" signals contained in FM 24-13, which is an extract of combined operating signals CCBP 2-2 and FM 24-12, Army extract of combined operating signals CCBP 2-2, will be used by all operators. A copy of FM 24-13 or FM 24-12 will be furnished as part of the radio operators folder. At the present time there are about 350 Q signals in use by the Armed Forces. While it is considered possible but not very probable or practical to learn all existing Q signals, it is logical to assume that a good radio operator know where and how to look for a Q signal he is not familiar with. A "Q" signal book should be as much a part of a radio operator's personal belongings as his dog tags. Never fly a mission without your Q signal book. The following Q signals which we know you are definitely going to handle at one time or another during your combat career with the XXI Bomber Command are listed herein for your information. These Q signals with their meanings will be memorized.

| Signal | Question | Answer or Advice |
|--------|----------|------------------|
| | AUTHENTICATION | |
| QPA | | Authentication challenge is ____. |
| QKA | | Authentication of this message or transmission is _____. |
| QIA | | Check your authentication of last transmission or message. |
| QLA | | Authenticate your last transmission or message. |
| QJA | | Authentication of my last transmission or message is ____ (1. Correct; 2. Incorrect. Correct authentication is _____.) |
| | CRYPTOGRAPHING | |
| QJM | | Check encipherment (cryptography) of message (or portions indicated) and repeat. |
| | BEACONS | |
| QFS | Please place the radio beacon at _____ in operation. | The radio beacon at _____ will be in operation in _____ minutes. |
| QKT | Will you switch on the radio range station at _____ ? | |
| QKW | | The radio range station (at____) is out of action. |

## CALLING

QRZ    Who is calling me?          You are being called by _____.

QJC    When will you call me again on present frequency (or on ___ KCS?)        I will call you again at _____ on present frequency (or on _____ KCS).

QRX    Shall I wait? When will you call again?        Wait. (or, wait until I have finished communications with _____) I will call you immediately (or at _____).

## SIGNAL STRENGTH AND READABILITY

QSA    What is the strength of my signals (1 to 5)?        The strength of your signals is ____ (1 to 5).

QRK    What is the readability of my signals (1 to 5)?        The readability of your signals is _____ (1 to 5).

## REPORTS DURING FLIGHT

QAH    What is your height?        My height is _____ feet.

QTI    What is your true course?        My true course is _____ degrees.

QTH    What is your position in latitude and longitude (or by any other way of showing it)?        My position is _____ latitude _____ longitude (or by any other way of showing it).

QAA    At what time do you expect to arrive at _____?        I expect to arrive at ____ at_____ (time).

QUG    Will you be forced to alight in the sea (or to land)?    I am forced to alight (or land) (at _____ (place)).

QWY                            Switch on your IFF

QBD                            IFF switched on distress position.

## FREQUENCY, FREQUENCY ADJUSTMENTS

QMF    How does my frequency check?        Your frequency is correct.

QHF                            Your frequency is slightly (or_____ kcs) high.

QLF                            Your frequency is slightly (or_____ kcs) low.

QMH    Shift to transmit and receive on _____ (frequency indicated by 1 - low, 2 - medium, 3 - high, used with strike frequencies in the XXI Bomber Command. "Q" signal QSY may be used in the same manner).

## LANDING

QGN    May I land at _____?    You may land at _____.

## METEOROLOGICAL

QAM    Can you give me latest meterological weather report for _____ (Place of observation indicated by Control Tower code name within the XXI Bomber Command)?    Here is the latest meteorological weather report for _____. (Place of observation indicated by Control Tower code name within the XXI Bomber Command).

## MISCELLANEOUS

QPZ    Affirmative (yes).

QQZ    Negative (no, not).

QQQ (followed by 1, 2, or 3)    Air raid: (1) Alert; (2) in progress; (3) All clear.

## MESSAGES

QSM    Shall I repeat the last message I sent you?    Repeat the last message you sent me.

QMM    Of what precedence and for whom are your messages?    I have message indicated precedence for you.

QZM    Request you acknowledge message _____.    Message _____ acknowledged.

## BEARINGS

QUJ    What is true course to steer with zero wind to reach you?    The true course to steer with zero wind to reach me is _____ degrees.

QTN    Send your call sign followed by a 20 second dash.

QMN    Bearing of you was _____ class.

| | | |
|---|---|---|
| QTF | Will you give me the position of my station according to the bearings taken by the direction finding station which you control? | The position of your station according to the bearings taken by the direction finding station which I control is____latitude_____longitude. |
| QPN | | Increase your height to enable more accurate bearings to be completed. |
| QXB | | I am unable to furnish your bearing now. (call again in _____minutes). |

OPERATING

| | | |
|---|---|---|
| QRU | Have you anything for me? | I have nothing for you. |
| QRT | | Stop sending. |
| QSZ | | Send each word or group twice. |
| QRL | | I am busy (with ___). Please do not interfere. |
| QRN | | I am being troubled by atmospherics. |
| QRM | | I am being interfered with. |

It should be remembered the "Q" signal must be considered the same as plain language. The enemy has Q signal books.

When contacting ground stations, radio operators will, unless transmitting a "fox" type message, use normal call-up and answer procedure. This procedure, described below, will be strictly followed, except in an emergency when a continuous call-up may be made to contact the ground station.

Initial attempt to contact the ground station will be made using the long call-up. Such a call-up might be:

OOV605 OOV605 V 1V606 1V606 QMM K.

If the ground station fails to answer promptly, the preliminary call is repeated. If the second call is not answered, the calling station will wait a reasonable time and again call giving consideration to circumstances and other stations which may need to use the frequency. If the urgency of the message is such that it must be transmitted immediately (distress for instance) the normal call-up will be preceded by the international urgent signal (XXX). This procedure signal will indicate to all operators using a particular frequency that there is someone calling on that frequency and has an urgent message or is in distress.

Messages sent by the Broadcast "F" method will be sent through twice with only IMI separating the first and second transmissions. The prosign "F" in the preamble identifies messages sent by this method.

b. Procedure Messages.

A procedure message is a short plain dress message, the purpose of which is to expedite handling of messages. A typical procedure message might be: OOV605 V 1V606 NR1 061722Z BT PV311 PV311 BT K. The long break (BT) has been used to separate the heading from the text of the message. However, the long break (BT) is not used to separate the text from other components of a procedure message, except where a date-time group is assigned to the message. A procedure message consists of operating signals, call signs, identification of messages and part of messages, and prosigns if necessary; but, does not have a group count in the heading.

A procedure message may carry the precedence designation considered necessary to insure accomplishment of its purpose. All messages transmitted from XXI Bomber Command aircraft will be assumed to carry an OP precedence, so unless higher priority is considered necessary (an OPASR or O), no precedence need be indicated in the heading of the message.

c. Messages from Aircraft.

Existing XXI Bomber Command regulations concerning radio silence will normally be effective. An existing field order may change the normal conditions but only for that period of time covered by the field order.

A radio operator must bear in mind that he has only two reasons for transmitting anything from an aircraft. (1) He wants to tell some one something; (2) He wants to ask some one for something. Be sure that whatever you want to tell some one or ask them is of sufficient importance to warrant your breaking radio silence. Remember unauthorized procedures, operators "chatter" and "Key playing" will not be tolerated on any XXI Bomber Command air-ground radio circuits.

3. Interphone Procedure.

In an airplane as large as the B-29, where the crew positions are widely separated, the interphone plays a most important part in the combat efficiency of the crew. Interphone procedure will undoubtedly vary slightly from crew to crew, but a standard procedure, preferably based on R/T procedure, should be adopted and strictly adhered to by each crew. This is the only method by which confusion inherent to a fast moving situation can be avoided. Idle chatter should not be indulged in via interphone, and the airplane commander is responsible for proper interphone discipline.

a. Interphone Doctrine.

For good reception, four factors make up proper use of interphone equipment and contribute to efficiency of interphone communications:

(1)  The equipment must be handled or used in the prescribed manner for clear transmission.

(2)  The speaker must talk in a way that assures good intelligibility.

(3)  The speaker must use standard messages for each routine situation.

(4)  A call-up procedure is necessary to assure a speaker that the right listener is receiving him.

Several routines with respect to handling the equipment are to be observed:

(1)  Hand-held microphone is to be held touching the lips.

(2)  Throat microphone is to be worn snug upon the neck slightly above the prominence of the Adam's apple.

(3)  Headset is to be worn with the headband spread as far apart as possible, pressed firmly over the ears to insure the best possible seal.

Interphone communication requires a loud voice.  This level is greater than a man normally uses, although it is less than shouting.  Interphone also necessitates talking consistently more slowly than average speech rates.  These voice factors as well as more - precise - than - normal articulation, require modifications of a crew man's habitual speech.

To as great an extent as is feasible, interphone procedure will follow the character of radiotelephone (R/T) procedure.  Approved variations follow:

(1)  Because continued sequences of messages in interphone do not involve the possibility of mistaken identity as they do in R/T, interphone requires less rigid adherence to call-up and sign-off procedures.

(2)  In the stress of emergency, time does not permit an extended call-up and sign off such as required in R/T.

The typical interphone call-up and identification for use in normal circumstances is illustrated by the following:

"Bombardier this is Tail Gunner, Over".

"(Tail Gunner), this is Bombardier, Over."

"(Bombardier, this is Tail Gunner), Message, Over".

"(Tail Gunner, this is Bombardier), Roger, out".

Note:  Use of words in parenthesis in example above is optional.

If the series of messages is a prolonged one, or treats with a routine maneuver, for example a bombing run, callup, identification, and ending is used as above for contact only.

In a condition of alert, for example in the reporting of an attack, call-up and message are combined in one statement, for example:

"Crew, Zeros at 10 o'clock level, turning in".

Likewise in an emergency within the airplane, as in the case of engine fire, the speaker says:

"Emergency, number two engine on fire."  (The use of the word "Emergency" is optional but seems to alert the crew for an extraordinay message).

The basic reason for interphone message procedure is to increase intelligibility over the system.  A second reason is circuit discipline.  This, however irrespective of its military value, contributes to intelligibility. Procedural language involves three factors:

(1)  The use of routine procedures in call-up and identification.

(2)  The use of procedure words and phrases that characteristically occur in regular order in messages and that have clear and uniform meanings.

(3)  The use of standardized message texts that denote the usual actions reported over interphone and that appear in routine order.

Procedure words in interphone communication are as follows:

| | | | |
|---|---|---|---|
| a. acknowledge | e. over | i. spell | m. time 1630 |
| b. check-in | f. request | j. standby | n. wait |
| c. correction | g. roger | k. station | o. wilco |
| d. out | h. say again (I say again) | l. this is | p. wrong |

Routine phrases in interphone messages are as follows:

| | |
|---|---|
| a. Request ETA _____(Target). | g. Fighters (Zeros or equivalent). |
| b. Speak slower (Louder, more clearly). | h. Get off interphone. |

c. Can you hear me OK?

d. Yes (or yes, sir).

e. No (or no, sir).

f. That is correct.

i. Zeros at ten o'clock high, (low, level). Turning in, (Coming in, going over, or under).

j. Request air speed.

k. Request ground speed.

A large portion of the messages initiated by each crew memeber, particularly in training, have been phrased in these statements following a similar routine pattern.  For example:

From pilot and co-pilot:
"Interphone check"
"Prepare for take-off, acknowledge"

From bombardier:
"Check PDI"
"Request heading"

From navigator:
"turn to heading one six seven degrees"

From radio operator:
"Weather: at base.  Scattered clouds at two thousand, wind Norhwest, one four, altimeter, two nine eight nine"
"Base requests our position"

From gunners:
"Request right (left) bank for sighting"."Request nose down (up) for sighting"

From engineer:
"Start (stop) the put-put"
"Check list complete, ready to start engine"

The following principles underly the phrasing of interphone procedure and messages:

(1)  Similarity with established R/T procedures.

(2)  Intelligible messages.

(3)  Use of the prefix "request" where applicable.

The following are the adopted AAF aircraft position names:

Pilot
Co-pilot
Bombardier
Navigator
Mickey*
Radio
RCM

Nose Gunner
Belly Gunner
Right Waist Gunner
Left Waitst Gunner
Upper Gunner
Tail Gunner
Engineer

\*   This name will represent the Radar operator regardless of the specific
type of equipment he is concerned with.

## 4.  Direction Finding HF/DF Procedure.

HF/DF stations are prepared to give two types of D/F service.  You can request a "QUJ" in which case you will ge given the true course to steer with
zero wind to bring you directly over the D/F station.  The QUJ can be obtained almost immediately or, you can request a "QTF" (only in case of emergency) in which case you will be given your geographical position in the
form of coordinates of latitude and longitude.  It takes somewhere between
3 and 6 minutes to furnish a QTF.  Normally a "QUJ" is referred to as a
"bearing" and a "QTF" as a fix.

To an aircraft uncertain of its positions or course the prosign "G" (repeat back) will be used if time permits and is deemed necessary to insure
accurate receipt by the aircraft.  Time (GMT), the course or position was
plotted may also be included if deemed necessary by the ground station.
For standardization, all degrees transmitted will be expressed in three
numbered groups, i.e., 063.  When reporting positions (QTF) latitude
will always be transmitted as a four numeral group, the first two numerals representing degrees and the last two numerals representing
minutes.  Longitude will always be transmitted in at least four numerals
the last two numerals representing minutes.  i.e.,0305 N - 7503 E or
3530 N - 0705W or 3821 N 145 05 E.

The following procedure will apply when requesting and obtaining a "QUJ"
(true course bearing):

(1)  When D/F station is not busy working with another aircraft.

Aircraft:    00V605 V 1V606 $\overline{INT}$  QUJ K

Ground Station: 1V606   V 00V605 K (or QTN K)

Aircraft:    00V605 V 1V606 <u>20 sec dash</u> 1V606 K

Ground Station: 1V606   V 00V605 G QUJ 075 A K

Aircraft:    00V605 V 1V606 QUJ 075 A K

Ground Station: 1V606   V 00V605 C $\overline{AR}$

Note:  When authentication is required, the challenge and reply will
be accomplished with the authentication system in use.

(2)  When D/F station is busy working with another aircraft or must be
alerted and a course cannot be given immediately:

Aircraft:             OOV605 V 1V606 INT QUJ K

Ground Station:    1V606 V OOV605 AS AR
(aircraft waits while D/F station is alerted or traffic is cleared)

Ground Station:    1V606 V OOV605 K (er, QTN K)

Aircraft:             OOV605 V 1V606 20 sec dash 1V606 K

Ground Station:    1V606 V OOV605 QUJ 075 B K

Aircraft:             OOV605 V 1V606 R AR

Note:  When authentication is required, the challenge and reply will be accomplished in accordance with the authentication system in use.

(3)  When the ground station because of transmitting conditions requires more than one 20 second dash:

Aircraft:             OOV605 V 1V606 INT QUJ K

Ground Station:    1V606 V OOV605 QTN 2 (or 3 etc) K

Aircraft:             OOV605 V 1V606 20 sec dash 1V606 20 sec dash 1V606 K

Ground Station:    1V606 V OOV605 QUJ 075 A K

Aircraft:             OOV605 V 1V606 R AR

If the ground station in any of the preceding examples transmits IMI instead of a course, the aircraft will repeat its QTN transmissions.

Note:  When authentication is required, the challenge and reply will be accomplished in accordance with the authentication system in use.

A Class A course may be regarded as accurate to plus or minus 2 degrees.

A Class B course may be regarded as accurate to plus or minus 5 degrees.

A Class C course may be regarded as having an error of more than plus or minus 5 degrees.

Because XXI Bomber Command is located on a chain of islands which does not afford an applicable D/F net for the purposes of giving "fixes" (QTF), the Navy must be called upon to furnish "fixes" (QTF). This is done by alerting a chain of D/F stations called the Pacific D/F net. Because of the amount of time necessary in alerting a net as huge and as wide spread as the Pacific D/F net an immediate fix cannot be given to the aircraft. The Pacific D/F net does not normally guard XXI Bomber

Command Air-ground frequencies. For this reason the only time a "fix" (QTF) is available is when an aircraft is in an emergency (in danger of "ditching" or is definitely lost). When an aircraft is in serious trouble and thinks he is going to ditch he normally alerts his Wing air-ground staion with a preliminary ditching report messages which is readily identified by the precedence OPASR in the message heading.

When an aircraft is lost and the need for a bearing (QUJ) is urgent, the precedure signal XXX is transmitted prior to his request for a bearing (QUJ).

When an aircraft in trouble uses the urgent signal (XXX) in conjunction with a request for bearing (QUJ) or uses an OPASR precedence in the heading of a message, the XXI Bomber Command intercept air-ground station immediately furnishes "SUPRAD" (the Control station for the Pacific D/F net) with the frequency the aircraft is operating on and his call sign. This alerting of the complete Pacific D/F net takes approximately one minute. If an operator who has transmitted either XXX INT QUJ or a message containing OPASR in the message heading, automatically, without further instructions, waits two minutes and then sends a 20 sec dash followed by his call sign then another 20 sec dash followed by his call sign (QTN 2). The Pacific D/F net will shoot a "fix" (QTF) on that aircraft and relay it back through interisland radio teletype nets to the aircraft's Wing Control who in turn will relay it to the Wing ground-station who will then transmit the position by latitude and longitude to the aircraft in trouble. The important thing for the aircraft radio operator to remember is that once he is in trouble and makes it known by using the XXX urgent signal or transmitting an OPASR he should definitely transmit (QTN 2) every two minutes until he actually ditches or danger is no longer imminent.

Anytime an aircraft radio operator hears a transmission containing XXX, OPASR or SOS, he will regard it as an emergency transmission and will maintain radio silence until D/F traffic is completed.

### E  AIR-SEA RESCUE COMMUNICATIONS

1. As soon as you are in trouble, get the most complete and accurate information possible concerning your difficulties to the rescue facilities without delay.  To assure your rescue, your would-be rescuers must know

      a.  WHAT IS YOUR TROUBLE?

      b.  WHERE ARE YOU NOW?

      c.  WHERE ARE YOU HEADED?

      d.  WHAT IS YOUR DIRECTION?

      e.  WHAT IS YOUR ALTITUDE?

      f.  WHAT IS YOUR SPEED?

      g.  WHERE DO YOU PLAN TO DITCH?

Ommision of any of the above information————
What?  Where?  Whence?  and When?  will leave the
rescue agencies guessing.  Send all the information.

Then————

CONTINUE TO KEEP YOUR RESCUERS INFORMED!

2.

    Here is a list of the equipment in your aircraft which will help you in emergencies and distress.

**a. Liaison Radio:** (AN/ART 13 transmitter and BC 348 receiver)

    1. To contact your ground station.
    2. To request and receive D/F bearings.
    3. To send urgent and distress signals.

**b. VHF Command Set:** (SCR-522)

    1. For voice contact with other B-29's in your formation.
    2. For voice contact with rescue facilities.
    3. To request and receive VHF D/F bearings, within 100 miles of your base.

**c. Radio Compass:** (AN/ARN-7)

    1. For homing on Homers, ranges or long dashes from rescue facilities.
    2. For bearings and homing on OWI and other high power broadcast stations.
    3. A good emergency receiver 100 - 1750 KCS.

**d. IFF:** (SCR-695)

    1. Enables station at your base to give you bearings up to 100 miles from your base.
    2. Enables submarines to shoot a bearing on you and determine your range.
    3. Tells naval radar equipment that you are in trouble when in EMERGENCY position.

Radar Set: (AN/APQ-13)

1. Enables you to pick up rescue submarines and rescue airplanes beyond wisual range.
2. Enables you to position yourself with respect to islands or coastlines.
3. Permits homing on or near rescue facilities or islands.
4. Permits you to obtain accurate fixes on your position when used with radar beacons.
5. Gives altitude if your altimeter is working.

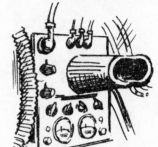

f. Loran Set: (AN/APN-4)

1. Gives your aircraft accurate line of position (or fixes when additional ground stations are installed) up to 1200 miles from base.

g. Gibson Girl: (SCR-578 or AN/CRT-3)

1. Small floating transmitter which enables you to send distress signals from a life raft.

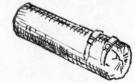

h. Radio Transmitter Buoy: (AN/CRN-1)

1. A droppable floating transmitter upon which any radio compass equipped rescue facility may "Home" in on you.

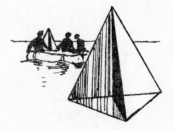

i. Corner Reflector: "Emily" MX-137A (individual raft) MX-138A (multiplace raft)

1. Placed in life raft. It is a device for returning transmitted radar energy to the receiver of the radar set installed in aircraft and rescue vessels.

3.

Here are the ground communication facilities available to aid you
in emergencies and distress.

a. <u>Air-ground Station</u>:

Your own air-ground station guards all of your
strike frequencies. They listen to every transmission you make on your strike frequencies and
are thoroughly disciplined and trained to help
you. In addition, you have other ground stations operated by the XXI Bomber Command and
other Bombardment Wings and AACS installations.

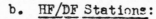

b. <u>HF/DF Stations</u>:

There are DF stations at each base, capable of
giving you a bearing with one minute. Some of
these bearings have proven accurate up to 1200
miles - depending on atmospheric conditions.

c. <u>VHF DF</u>:

Bearings within 100 miles from your base.

d. <u>SUPRAD</u>:

Control station of the Pacific D/F Net which
can furnish you with a D/F Fix (QTF - latitude and longitude). This service is re-
served only for planes that are lost or in
distress. Approximate time for "fix" --
5 to 7 minutes.

e. <u>Ranges and Homers</u>:

Provides homing facilities at each base where there is an AACS installation.

f. <u>OWI Station</u>:

A 50,000 watt broadcasting station on Saipan beamed toward Japan. An excellent homer. Operates continuously.

g. <u>Radar Beacon</u>: (AN/CPN-6)

Under construction at the present time. Permits you to get an accurate fix of your position with your radar set as far as 150 miles from base.

h. <u>Early Warning Radar</u>: (MEW)

A powerful ground radar station on Saipan which can pick you up 150 to 200 miles north of Saipan and about 100 miles in other directions.

THESE FACILITIES WILL HELP YOU GET BACK TO YOUR BASE WHEN YOU ARE LOST OR IN TROUBLE. BUT, IF YOU HAVE TO DITCH, THE FOLLOWING FACILITIES HAVE BEEN SET UP TO LOCATE YOU AND SEE THAT YOU ARE PICKED UP:

# XXI BOMBER COMMAND. CONFIDENTIAL

## AIR-SEA RESCUE T T Y CIRCUIT.

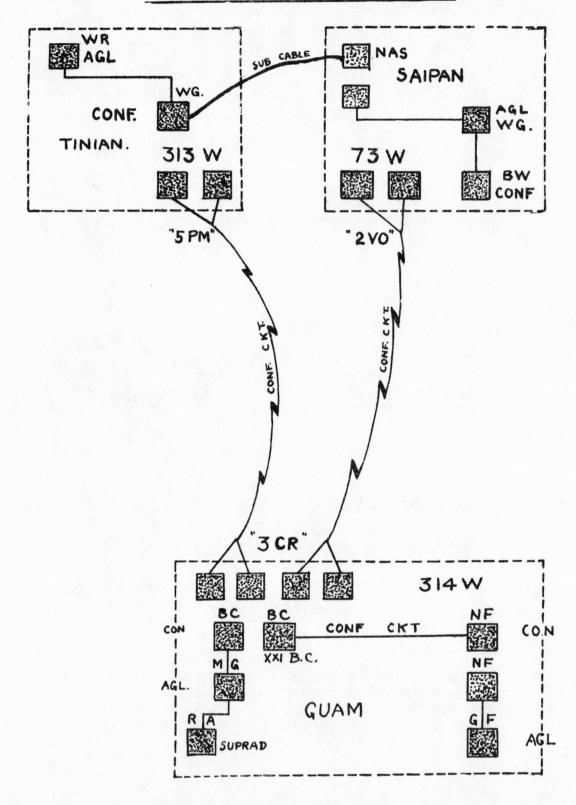

4. <u>Rescue Facilities.</u>

a. <u>THE AIR-SEA RESCUE UNIT</u>

Composed of experienced Army and Navy personnel. One such group is located at your own base and others are located at other Wing Hq., at the Naval Air Station on Saipan and at Bomber Command. They are in teletype communication with all ground radio stations and with each other. All information regarding distressed aircraft is received, evaluated and acted upon with dispatch. All information is collected here and all rescue facilities are dispatched by this organization.

b. <u>LIFE GUARD SUBMARINES</u>, provided by the Navy are positioned across our course at locations where we are most apt to have trouble. They are equippped with:

Radar - permitting them to pick up your distress IFF signal.

Radio - guarding 4475 KC (Voice and CW) (Voice when close CW when distant) and 500 KC (CW) during all missions and during search work. Monitors 140.58 MC (Channel "C") VHF, but DOES NOT guard continuously.

Observers - on the look out for distressed aircraft, flares, rafts, etc.

c. <u>DUMBO AIRPLANES</u>, search and rescue aircraft which maintain stations not more than 600 miles from your base. They are equipped with:

Radar - 2 types, one for picking up aircraft, corner reflectors or dinghy radar transmitters on life rafts. They also have another set, the SCR 729 which enables them to see your emergency IFF.

Radio - guards 4475 KC (voice) and 7920 KC (CW) from 0700-1800 K and 3755 KC (CW) from 1800 K to 0700 K. Monitors 140.58 MC (Channel "C") VHF, but NOT continuously.

d. SUPER DUMBOS - Our own B-29's specially fitted for search and rescue work. These aircraft orbit positions near the target, often circling a lifeguard submarine. They have the same communications equipment you have in your own plane plus an extra liaison receiver. They guard the following radio frequencies continuously:

Strike Frequencies:
3755 KC (CW) From 1800K - 0700K
4475 KC (both voice and CW)
500 KC (CW)

7920 KC (CW) From 0700K - 1800K
Channel "Queen" (C) VHF

They are provided with extra rescue and lifesaving gear and immediately relay all distress messages both to the ground station and to the nearest Lifeguard. They are prepared to broadcast low frequency signals on which a distressed aircraft may HOME to reach the vicinity of the lifeguard submarine or destroyer.

e. SURFACE CRAFT - In addition to the picket boats supplied by the Navy for use in case of crashes shortly after take-off, destroyers are stationed at certain locations along our return routes. These ships are equipped with powerful radar and a wide assortment of radio. They guard:

4475 KC (Voice)
Channel "Queen" (C) VHF
500 KC

Certain strike frequencies if provided for in advance.

If you should have to ditch, an accurate position of your plane in the destroyer's hands, greatly improves your chances of dying of old age.

## 5. Use of Equipment.

   With all this equipment aboard, let's see what you can do with it in such cases as, Routine checks of Navigation; a spot in which you are lost but not in any great danger of ditching (for you have plenty of gas); or distress cases where you have an engine or two gone or malfunctioning and may cause trouble before you get home.

a.  RADIO COMPASS:  (AN/ARN-7)

   First of all let's look at the Radio Compass. It's handy in picking up Homing Beacons or Ranges which will give you a good bearing. Out here it can also furnish music, news and other things from KRHO, the Saipan OWI Station, which operates continuously on a frequency which will be furnished at briefing. It's a good strong station and should provide a good bearing. This instrument is a good thing to use for Routine checks of Navigation, an excellent thing if you are lost and a handy thing if in distress. All you have to do is tune your station in.

b.  LORAN SET:  (AN/APN-4)

   The Loran Set is a good companion which can give a fast Routine check of Navigation, show you where you are if you are lost, and show the gang on the ground station where you are if you tell them your Loran Line when you are in distress. The Navigator should take a peek at his Loran Line as often as he deems necessary to have it always ready to pass on to Radio Operator for transmission.

c.  RADAR SET:  (AN/APQ-13)

   The Radar Operator can eye his scope to pick up Islands or landmarks which will stand a possible checkpoint for the navigator and all the crew when making a routine check of Navigation or when you are lost. These same Islands can furnish a lee under which to ditch safely in case you are in distress.

d. **IFF:** (SCR-695)

    And while we are speaking of Radar, that also brings to mind your IFF set. The set should remain on the code assigned all B-29 aircraft while flying routine or during a routine check of Navigation. But when you are lost or in distress, turn your set to emergency and let it tell the Radar Station where you are and that you are in distress.

e. **VHF COMMAND:** (SCR-522)

    Then there is the VHF set, which by the push of the Channel "Item" (D-127.62 MC) button lets the pilot ask Condor Base, Agate Base or Buzzard Base for a bearing if you are within 150 miles of Iwo Jima, Saipan or Guam.

f. **LIAISON SET:** (AN/ART-13 and BC-348)

    The Liaison Set provides a means for requesting a "QUJ" on "C" from either the Wing Ground Station or AACS. The receiver works with it.

g. **DINGHY TRANSMITTER:** (SCR-578)

    Then the shapely Gibson Girl - of no use to you in a Routine check of Navigation or when you are lost - but a real sweetheart if you hit the water and wish to transmit for aid. If you were to ask 100 people if they know about the Gibson Girl, they would all reply, "Oh, sure I've heard about her." Well, just what do you know about her? Here's the soap on the old gal and a good study of it will prevent a lot of confusion, faulty handling and possible loss of an essential item.

## SCR-578 "Gibson Girl"

1. Take the set out of the bag and immediately strap it securely to some part of the raft.

2. Unscrew the cap on top of the set. Take the crank out of its well, just releasing the locking key; insert in socket on top of the set and tighten thumb nut. (DON'T DROP CRANK -- THERE IS NO SPARE!!!)

3. Open door in front of set, first removing cotter key, and pull out a few feet of antenna wire from the reel.

4. Set slight tension on brake by turning BRAKE knob clockwise.

5. Use kite if possible. (When wind is 7 to 50 miles per hour).

6. Take kite from bag. Push spreaders outward from center till they lock. DON'T ALLOW SPREADERS TO SNAP OPEN. It may tear fabric.

7. Attach antenna wire swivel to one of two eyelets on the kite.

8. Stand up in boat, wait for a gust, toss kite in air, fly kite with slack in antenna wire till it can be flown from the reel with the brake. If kite falls in water, don't pull in, paddle to it and lift from water. It is fragile and you only have ONE. Dry kite and try again.

9. If kite cannot be flown, use balloon. Take balloon can, gas generator, and inflation tube from tubular bag, open balloon and attach antenna wire AT ONCE.

10. Remove top and bottom plugs from generator. Wet blunt needle of tube and insert into balloon valve. Hold generator in water up to lower red line for 10 minutes. Slowly lower generator in water to upper red line. Control inflation by rate of lowering generator. When balloon is full, put rubber stopper in valve, unscrew inflation tube, and THROW GENERATOR AWAY FROM THE DINGHY. ITS CONTENTS CAN BURN RAFT.

11. Release antenna slowly all the way, as far as possible, then tie loose end of cord to life raft to take the pull of the kite or balloon. Take anténna lead-in from set and clip to antenna.

12. Strap transmitter between legs. Unscrew cap marked ground, take out reel, unreel wire and throw all ground wire into the water.. DON'T ALLOW THE ANTENNA TO SAG INTO WATER. This grounds antenna and no signal will be heard.

Operation:

      1.  Turn selector switch to "Auto 1".  (This sends SOS).

      2.  Rotate crank clockwise until "SPEED INDICATOR" light burns brightly (about 72 R.P.M.).  Allow 20 seconds for tube to warm up.  Keep light burning steadily.

      3.  Turn "TUNING" control to produce maximum brilliancy of "TUNE TO BRIGHTEST" lamp.

      4.  Send in "Auto" position for 5 minutes, REST.  Turn switch to "MANUAL" and use key to send call letter of plane (or identification numbers if call letters are not known) followed by known or estimated location, using Continental Code shown on card to left of crank socket.

      5.  Try to send to include the 3 minute international silent periods starting at 15 minutes, and 45 minutes after each hour (GCT).  Keep Cranking.  Change hands or operators frequently, if possible, avoid tiring.  Keep on the air as much as possible.

      6.  At night the signal lamp may be plugged into socket above tuning knob.  Turn switch so that "Light" is in "Manual" position and send with manual button.  This should be done only if it is thought friendly vessels are within sight.  No antenna or ground is needed with light.

Cautions:

      Work carefully--take it easy but keep it up.

      Don't use balloon in hot sun unless absolutely necessary. (Heat may explode it if fully inflated).

      Don't spill contents of gas generator, it will burn. (If spilled on skin, eyes, or raft, flush promptly with water).

      Don't smoke or use open flame while inflating balloon. (Hydrogen gas is explosive(.

      Don't use set if severe lightening is occuring.

### h.  RADIO TRANSMITTER BUOY (AN/CRN-1)

This is a single tube, battery powered low frequency buoy transmitter. A six foot baseball type
parachute lowers the equipment safely from aircraft to water. The equipment automatically transmits a predetermined signal on frequency suitable
for homing purpose by aircraft or vessels equipped
with Radio Compass. The code signal and frequency
it transmits are set in the equipment before it is
placed in the aircraft.

A non-directional CW signal is transmitted in the frequency range
from 1400 - 1750 Kc. This signal consists of a CW signal keyed at 180
times a minute and interrpted every 30 seconds by a single code letter
which may be M, Q, X, K, O or Y. This code letter is selected prior
to installation of the battery pack in the equipment. The condition of
the battery and atmospheric conditions will determine the strength and
range of signal, which may normally be picked up approximately 50 miles
over open sea. It has been picked up at 100 miles.

The transmission period is approximately 12 hours, after which the
signal strength will usually drop to an unreadable level due to dis-
charge of the battery. If you are ditching, set the timing knob to
insure maximum transmission time during daylight hours. This small
tuning knob, located at the top of the set, will automatically start
the set transmitting at any desired time. It is accessible thru out-
out at base of the chute. On the side of the knob are numbers 0 thru
12 which indicate the hours that will elapse between the time the equipment is launched and the time it will start transmitting. Set this timing device to insure maximum daylight transmission by turning the timing knob in a counter-clock wise direction until the arrow on the case
points to the desired hour. If you accidentally turn the timing knob
past the desired position, continue to rotate knob in a counter-clockwise direction until desired position is again reached.

Before you kick the set from the plane, slowly pull as much of the
6 foot statio cord as necessary from the transmitter pack and connect
to a brace within the aircraft. Be sure you do not pull the station
cord past the point at which a smaller cord is attached to the static line.

After you have fastened the static line, prepare to launch the transmitter. Nose end down over the opening when you drop it.

### i.  CORNER REFLECTOR:  "Emily" MX-137A (Single place raft).
####                      MX-138A (Multiplace raft)

Here is another piece of equipement which will soon
accompany your life raft. Corner Reflector, should be
set up immediately in your raft to increase your chances
of being spotted by a search Radar Scope. During re-

cent tests, consistent ranges of better than 8 miles were obtained from an altitude of 800 feet, the ideal altitude for visual search.

6.  Routine Check and Distress Procedures.

Certain procedures are to be followed in the use of the communications equipment aboard the plane:

a.  When making a ROUTINE CHECK OF NAVIGATION.
b.  When LOST BUT WITH SUFFICIENT GAS.
c.  When IN ACTUAL DISTRESS.

If you follows these procedures, less confusion to yourself and other will result.

It is impossible to over-emphasize the VITAL necessity of getting the correct information to the ground station. A wrong position is far worse than none at all. An incorrect Loran Line may render useless an otherwise good position. Get it right and get it right the first time. It may mean your crew's safety.

There is still another thing to think about; Security of your transmissions. The enemy is monitoring all of our frequencies including your VHF. Because the enemy is extremely anxious to pick up our crews, never make a transmission which may result in the enemy picking up our survivors. A good general rule to be followed: NEVER make a transmission unless it is absolutely necessary. If it is necessary to transmit, make sure it is properly encoded if time permits.

Let's look at the procedures to be followed in the use of each communication aid when making a routine check of Navigation or when you're lost, but have sufficient gas to ease worry.

The Radio Buoy and Gibson Girl Dinghy Radio Set will not be used at these times so they will not be discussed until we come to ditching procedures.

**a. Routine check of navigation:**

On routne checks of Navigation, requests for bearings will be kept at the necessary minimum. Use your radio compass, Loran set or radar set first and see what you can obtain. If you still require a bearing and are within 100 miles of your base, call your local VHF/DF whether it's Agate for Iwo Jima, Buzzard for Guam or Condor for Saipan, on Channel "Queen" (C) or Channel "Item" (D) of the VHF set and request a bearing. Channel "Item" (D) is preferable because there is less traffic volume. If you are beyond 100 miles from base and require a bearing, use "Q" signal procedure on CW when requesting "QUJ" and use CSP 1270 challenge and reply authentication. Never use XXX (International Urgent Signal) when requesting bearings for Routine check of Navigation.

**b. Lost, but with sufficient gas and no trouble:**

1. If you are lost but in no immediate danger of ditching, climb to 10,000 feet as you take the following steps: Turn IFF to emergency. Request a bearing. If you are more than 100 miles from your base, contact the ground station on CW using "Q" signal procedure. Use XXX (International Urgent Signal) and send twenty second dashes intersparsed by call sign when requested to do so by the Ground Station. If time permits and/or bearing is doubtful, the aircraft will challenge and ground station will reply with CSP 1270 authentication. Remember, 2 minutes after you send XXX, you should use the QTN2 procedure and use it thereafter once every 2 minutes until you are out of danger.

2. If you are within 100 miles of a base, contact the local VHF/DF station on Channel "Queen" (C) or Channel "Item" (D) of the VHF set and request a bearing. Contact Wing Air-ground Station and ask them for a bearing also. The ground station will contact the radar system and attempt to get a fix on you. You may be requested to change course for a few minutes. Your compliance will identify you as the aircraft whose course is being plotted.

3. Always tell the station with which you are in contact your trouble, and give your Loran Line, best estimated position, course, speed and altitude. Information on amount of gas remaining is also valuable. Keep following the bearings given you and keep the ground station informed as to your condition, position, Loran Line, altitude, course and gas remaining. Make full use of your radio compass in attempting to tune in the Saipan OWI or a Range or Homer. Use the radar set AN/APQ-13 to search for landmarkers or islands which may identify your location or serve as a haven in case you fall into distress.

## c. In distress:

The following information must be learned thoroughly before a crew flys as a combat team:

1. In the interest of security as well as simplicity, reference points are established in areas where it is anticipated that the majority of water landings will occur in connection with combat operations. These reference points, all of which have code names, will be used in reporting the position of all forced landings to Dumbo and Lifeguard and <u>for no other purpose</u>.

2. <u>Reference Point Code Names.</u> - A series of six code names is assigned to each reference point. These names rotate daily, changing at <u>1800 GMT</u>, each name being effective during the 24-hour period beginning 1800 GMT on the date for which it is prescribed.

3. <u>Reference Points</u> will <u>not</u> be referred to except by established code names. The reference points, together with the code names assigned thereto and their effective dates, will be given to the combat crews by the Group S-2 and Group Communications Officer.

4. <u>The Position</u> of any forced landing or survivors will be reported in bearing and distance from the nearest reference point. These words are used to report positions to Dumbo and Lifeguard:

   a. <u>Distance</u> in nautical miles from Reference Point.
   b. Code name for reference point used.
   c. <u>True bearing from</u> reference point.

      Example:   "15 Smelly Nelly 180," meaning survivors(s) down
                 15 miles bearing 180° true from reference point.
                 (Assuming "Smelly Nelly" to be the applicable
                 code name)
      Do not use any other procedure than that outlined above
      when contacting Dumbo or Lifeguard.

5. The importance of learning the exact chronological order of reporting cannot be over-emphasized. For instance, if bearing and distance were reversed, "180 Smelly Nelly 15," the position is worthless. If the bearing and distance are received in this instance it would mean an error of 165 miles in distance and 165 degrees in bearing. KNOW YOUR PROCEDURE THOROUGHLY.

6. Code names serve not only to identify the reference point but also as the voice call for any or all rescue agencies to whom the position report is addressed. No further voice call is required or should be used.

> Example: "Hello Smelly Nelly, this is Happy 21,
> 15 Smelly Nelly 180, over."

This message would be regarded as addressed to Lifeguard submarine, Dumbo aircraft, or search destroyer. This same message in CW would read as follows:

"SMELLY NELLY V HAPPY 21 BT 15 SMELLY NELLY 180 K"

7. <u>Distress Procedure</u> - For any Plane, any time.

a. If you are about to ditch, the following steps must be taken in order given.

1. <u>Radar Operator</u> turns IFF to <u>EMERGENCY</u> position.
2. <u>Navigator</u> must know Loran Line, Latitude, Longitude, nautical miles from <u>nearest</u> reference point and true bearing <u>from</u> reference point and the correct name of that reference point.

   (a) The navigator gives this information to both pilot and the radio operator.

3. <u>Pilot</u> immediately calls on Channel "A" and states, "This is Happy 21 in distress switching to Channel "Queen" (C)". Pilot then switches to Channel "Queen" (C) and advises Dumbo or Lifeguard on Channel "Queen" (C) that he is ditching.

   > Example: "Hello Smelly Nelly, this is Happy 21, 15
   > Smelly Nelly 180, over". (Radio Operator
   > will furnish Pilot with CSP 1270 Direct
   > Authentication)

   a. Pilot will instruct tail gunner to throw Radio Transmitter Buoy (AN/CRN-1) out rear escape hatch when pilot gives him the signal.

4. <u>Radio Operator</u> will immediately contact his Air-Sea Rescue Unit on 7920 Kcs or 3755 Kcs (CW) and give the following information, encoded in CSP 1270, "Am about to ditch, Loran Line, Latitude, Longitude, Course, Speed and Altitude."

   > Example: OOV535 V 21V537 - OPASR - BT QUG 2300
   > <u>1022N 142 31 E 320 195 8000 K</u>
   > (Encoded in CSP 1270 )

The radio operator will get a receipt for this message from the Air-Sea Rescue Unit Station. While the Air-Sea Rescue Station is decoding this message, the radio operator will switch to 4475 Kcs (Voice) and send the message that his pilot had previously transmitted to Dumbo and Lifeguard.

   > Example: "HELLO SMELLY NELLY THIS IS HAPPY 21, 15
   > SMELLY NELLY 180 OVER".

If the radio operator does not receive an acknowledgement of this message from Dumbo, Lifeguard or the Air-Sea Rescue Unit, he will immediately switch back to his assigned strike frequency. He will call the Ground Station and ask for a bearing. Be sure to precede your bearing request with XXX ( Urgent Signal ).

Example:   XXX 00V535 V 21V537 XXX INT QUJ K

The ground station will call him back

Example:   21V537 V 00V535 QTN K

and ask him to send a 20 second dash followed by his call sign.

Example:   _____ 21V537
                     (20 second dash)

The Ground Station will then call the aircraft and give him his bearing (true heading to fly to reach the Ground Station).

Example:   21V537 V 00V535 QUJ 153 K

If the aircraft receives the bearing, he will receipt in the following manner:

Example:   00V535 V 21V537 R QUJ 153 K

5.   Remember to use the QTN2 procedure, 2 minutes after sending your OPASR message and, once every 2 minutes thereafter until just prior to assuming your ditching position, or, when ditching is no longer imminent.

6.   If it so happens that your situation does improve and you are sure you are going to make your home base all right, contact your Wing Air-Ground Station and tell them you are out of trouble.  Your Ground Station will in turn notify the proper authorities and Dumbo and Lifeguared will be released.

7.   If unable to contact your Wing Air-ground Station -- Dumbo or Lifeguard, attempt to contact AACS Ground Station on 4595 Kc or 8200 Kc.

8.   If unable to raise anyone of the known facilities GIVE YOUR POSITION:  REPEAT IT!  Give all information which may aid rescue facilities.  Keep repeating your position until you leave your key. SCREW YOUR KEY DOWN WHEN YOU LEAVE!

9.   After leaving your transmitter key to assume your proper ditching position, you should have your Dinghy Transmitter (Gibson Girl) within easy reach.  Be sure and take your Dinghy transmitter (Gibson Girl) with you when you leave the aircraft prior to getting into the rubber life raft.

8. **The "Buddy" System**

A "BUDDY" aircraft is an aircraft designated to help another aircraft that is in distress. The "Buddy" aircraft will make all the necessary reports of ditching to the Wing Air-ground Station. (Dumbo or Lifeguard)

a. **Enroute to the target:**

If an aircraft on the way to the target is about to abort, but is not in distress, it will call the squadron leader on Channel "A" VHF and so notify him.

Example: "Hello Happy 5, this is Happy 21, I am aborting, over."

The aborting aircraft will then turn away from his squadron and fly back to the base. No other aircraft will return with him.

If an aircraft on the way to the target is about to abort and is in distress, the pilot of the distressed aircraft will instruct his radar operator to turn on his EMERGENCY IFF, and then the pilot will call the squadron leader on Channel "A" and notify him that he is in distress.

Example: "Hello Happy 5, this is Happy 21, I am in distress, over".

The squadron leader will direct another plane in the formation (the "Buddy" plane) to accompany the plane in distress. If the distressed plane "ditches", the "Buddy" plane will first attempt to take photographs of the full ditching action. He will then turn on his EMERGENCY IFF and then make the necessary calls to the Wing Air-Ground Station, Lifeguard and Dumbo. The "Buddy" plane will then orbit around the ditched aircraft. If the "Buddy" aircraft finds that he cannot stay in the vicinity of the aircraft in distress, he will obtain his Loran Line, plot his exact position (by latitude and longitude) and send that information (encoded in CSP 1270) to the Wing Air-Ground Station, using any of the strike frequencies. Be sure and use the CPASR in your message heading. If the "Buddy" aircraft finds it necessary to leave the vicinity of the ditched aircraft, he will drop a Radio Transmitter Buoy (AN/CRN-1) in the immediate vicinity of the ditched aircraft. He will then contact the Wing Air-ground Station so they may take a D/F bearing on the aircraft. He will then use the QTN2 procedure, wait 2 minutes and repeat it in order that "SUPRAD" may attempt to shoot a "fix" (QTF) on the orbiting aircraft. After this is done, the "Buddy" plane will again orbit the ditched aircraft and crew members and take photographs of the scene before returning to base.

b.  Return from target:

    After "bombs away" on the return trip to base, the aircraft
will fly in flight formation of three aircraft (leader and two wing
men).  These aircraft will attempt to maintain visual contact (using
running lights if flying at night).  If one of the three aircraft is
in distress and about to ditch, he will contact either of the other
two aircraft on VHF Channel "A" and notify him that he is about to
ditch.  The aircraft which answers the distressed aircraft's call
will act as "Buddy" for that aircraft.  The "Buddy" aircraft will
attempt to photograph the full ditching procedure.  He will then
turn HIS IFF to EMERGENCY position and make the necessary calls to
the Wing Air-ground Station, Dumbo and Lifeguard.  If sufficient gas
time remains, the "Buddy" aircraft will orbit over the distress plane
and make the necessary calls to the Wing Air-ground Station so they
may take a D/F bearing on that plane.  He will then use the QTN2 procedure, wait 2 minutes and repeat it in order that "SUPRAD" may attempt
to shoot a "fix" (QTF) on the orbiting aircraft.  If the "Buddy" plane
finds he is too low on gas, he will drop a Radio Transmitter Buoy
(AN/CRN-1) in the immediate vicinity of the ditched aircraft then
attempt to take more photographs of the ditched aircraft and crew,
after which he will return to base and give full particulars of the
incident.

## 9. Use of Signaling Devices:

The radio operator will take the Dinghy Transmitter (Gibson Girl) into the life raft and set it up for operation. Other crew members should continue to use smoke signals, flares, or mirrors to make certain the "Buddy" Aircraft sees them. Limit transmission on the Gibson Girl to 15 to 18 and 45 to 48 minutes past GCT hour (International Silent Periods). When no watch is available, transmit at spaced intervals both on the "Auto 1" and the "Manual" position. Crew should alternate at crank to save energy.

a. DAYLIGHT SIGHTING AIDS.

1. Green Dye Marker - Can be seen further than a yellow raft, even from surface ships. It's primary use is attracting aircraft.

2. White Smoke Bomb - This is the best daylight marker for sighting by surface vessels.

3. Signal Mirrors - Effective at great distances on sunny days, but are difficult to aim accurately from a small rubber raft.

4. Yellow Kite and White Balloon - Included with the Gibson Girl, which is sometimes dropped to survivors. Their primary purpose is to raise the antenna of the Gibson Girl, but both are effective visual signal devices when used in operating the Gibson Girl, or separately when Gibson Girl is definitely inoperative.

b. NIGHT SIGNALLING DEVICES.

1. Water proof signal lights carried by most pilots.

2. The Gibson Girl transmitter can also be used for signalling at night by means of it's signal lamp, keyed manually when friendly rescue facilities are thought to be in sight.

3. Some rafts are equipped with a radar reflecting device. (Emily MX-137A or MX-138A), if not so equipped a survivor in a rubber raft should attempt to raise one or more metal objects as high as possible above the level of the raft to facilitate radar detection.

c. PROCEDURE FOR NIGHT SEARCH BY RESCUE VESSELS.

Unless enemy planes or patrol vessels are in the vicinity, upon entering the area where survivors are suspected, the searching vessel fires a green Very Star at frequent intervals. Survivors will reply with a red Very Star if possible, or by any means available such as flashlight or flare. The searching vessel will acknowledge with two green Very Stars. Further signals should be exchanged to facilitiate the rescue.

10.  Reporting and Sighting of Survivors:

   a.  If the position of both the survivor and the rescue vessel is known, the "Sighting" aircraft should coach the rescue vessel to that position. DO NOT USE RESCUE VESSEL AS A REFERENCE POINT OR OTHERWISE, STATE BEARING AND DISTANCE FROM THE RESCUE VESSEL TO THE SURVIVOR. The rescue vessel should be directed by being given course to steer.

> Example:  "Smelly Nelly, steer course 120° for 3 miles," or (if heading of rescue vessel is also known) "Smelly Nelly, change course 30° left and go 3 miles".
>
> Note that reference point code name is used only as a voice call for the rescue vessel.

   b.  Reporting identity and condition of survivors.

   1.  In addition to position, the identity and condition of survivors is necessary for the efficient rescue operations and should also be reported, following the position report, in the following order:

   a.  The type of aircraft if known, using either plain language or the following code:

   Chicken - Fighter
   Hawk    - Dive Bomber (2 man crew)
   Eagle   - Medium Bomber (3 man crew)
   Box Car - Heavy Bomber (9 or 10 man crew)
   Monster - VLR Bomber (11 or 12 man crew)

   b.  The condition of survivors, in accordance with the following words:

   Goodyear      - Survivor(s) in a raft.
   Yellow Jacket - Survivor(s) in a life jacket.
   Davey Jones   - Survivor(s) without life jacket.

   c.  The number of survivors.

   d.  If dye marker is showing, the word "Evergreen" should be added.

> Example:  "15 Smelly Nelly 180 Monster Goodyear ten Evergreen." Meaning:  Ten survivors of a B-29 down 15 miles bearing 180° true from the reference point in life raft with dye marker showing.

c. Procedure for Aircraft Sighting Survivors.

1. When a survivor is sighted by an aircraft, the following procedure will be used (subject only to requirements of assigned tactical missions):

   a. A report of the survivors as outlined in section d, above, will be promptly transmitted. This report will be made either on Channel "Queen" (D) or 4475 KC Voice. Whichever is most appropriate in spanning the distance between aircraft and rescue facilities.

   b. Not more than two aircraft shall orbit the position of survivor, one using Emergency IFF and climbing to altitude equal to 1000 feet for each 10 miles from the agency to whom the aircraft is reporting.

   c. The orbiting aircraft shall remain on station until relieved by other aircraft or until assured a rescue vessel has sighted survivor, or other difficulty. The rescue vessel shall notify the aircraft as soon as the survivor has been sighted.

2. When rescue vessel has been sighted by the orbiting aircraft, the aircraft should assist the rescue vessel in accomplishing the rescue by the following methods where applicable:

   a. If a plane wishes to assure himself of the identity of a submarine, he may do so by directing submarine to change course to the right or left a number of degrees.

   b. The orbiting aircraft should zoom the position of the survivor, if possible, perpendicularly to the line of bearing between the survivor and the rescue vessel.

   c. An aircraft desiring the rescue vessel to follow him toward survivor should circle rescue vessel twice, opening and closing throttle, then fly off toward survivor.

   d. If the aircraft is forced to depart before the rescue vessel has sighted the survivor, the spot should be marked by dropping a radio transmitter buoy AN/CRN-1 if available, or by smoke if possible. Dye marker is hard to detect from a submarine or surface vessel.

   e. At this time the survivor in the life raft may use his smoke bombs, flares or mirror to attract the attention of the search vessel. This with the operation of the Gibson Girl, and the showing of the Corner reflector will effect a speedy rescue.

d. Aldis Lamp.

A special set of Aldis Lamp operating signals has been assigned for use while engaging in interplane communications. These signals were devised to allow faster transmission and easier reading using the Aldis Lamp.

When the Aldis Lamp is used, the clear or white lens should be used because the use of other lenses witholds too much light. The colored lenses should be used only to transmit signals wherein color has a meaning.

Commonly used prosigns are listed below. It will be found that these prosigns will be sufficient to handle messages which may be sent between planes:

I have a message for you- - - - - - - - White Flashes.

Go ahead - - - - - - - - - - - - - - - - K

I understand - - - - - - - - - - - - - - R

I do not understand - - - - - - - - - - N

Repeat Back - - - - - - - - - - - - - - $\overline{\text{IMI}}$

End of message - - - - - - - - - - - - $\overline{\text{AR}}$

In Transmitting, the sender should receive a "K" before sending and, after each word should pause until the receiver receipts (R) for the word. Transmissions should be deliberate. Combat crew personnel must practice reading each others sending as well as practice reading from an instructor. When sending slowly the rythm of the flashes in any letter should not change; only the interval between letters should be changed to suit the conditions under which the transmission is made. Never send faster than you can receive. Always consider the position of the sun. Hold the lamp as close to the glass of the window or blister as possible, and always aim it directly at the receiver. When receiving it is helpful to have some one copy for the receiver.

F  VISUAL SIGNALLING EQUIPMENT

1. Very Pistol.

A Very Pistol and an assortment of colored flares are included in your life raft equipment. These flares should not be used aimlessly, but should be saved for that occasion when it is apparent that the searching aircraft or rescue aircraft will be able to see them. If at all possible, Very flares should be discharged when a searching aircraft is <u>approaching</u> the life raft as then more chance exists of the flare being seen.

## 2. Sea Markers.

Sea markers of floriscine dye used for visual identification should not be used aimlessly. The dye should be so distributed that a well defined streak is placed on the water where the raft is drifting. If the raft is not drifting, use only enough dye to made a well-defined patch around the raft, and replenish it from time to time.

## 3. Mirror.

Provided also is a signalling mirror so designed that it can be aimed at searching aircraft or rescue craft. Care must be taken to aim the mirror in exactly the proper manner, or it probably will not be noticed.

## G BRIEFING MATERIAL CARRIED IN AIRCRAFT

The container used for briefing material should be a weighted folder, numbered for identification purposes. It is issued previous to a flight and should be returned, contents complete, to the issuing authority after the flight.

The radio operator's folder will contain the following items: Necessary flimsy extracts of all necessary radio call signs (R/T and CW); Radio frequencies to be used and their designators. Information containing when and where to get weather reports, time ticks and D/F facilities, information as to the authorized authenticators, complete extracts of radio aids to XXI Bomber Command bases and fighter bases in the Volcanos; lost and distress procedures, complete air-sea information including call signs, frequencies and reference point code names. Effective "shackle" code, effective recognition signals, radio operator's log blanks, UCOPAC frame and UCOPACARD for the mission, WAF-3 blanks with Andusmet (if required to make in-flight weather observations) and the current aircraft code, CSP 1270 ( ).

## H COMMUNICATIONS PUBLICATIONS AND FORMS

## 1. Radio Facility Charts.

The Army Airways Communications System (AACS) publishes "JACSPAC" (Joint Airways Communications Service Pacific) one of the radio facility charts used by the XXI Bomber Command. "JACSPAC" is similar to the AAF Radio Facility Chart (T.O. 08-15-1) published in the United States. "NATAPOA" (Navigational Aids to Aircraft Pacific Ocean Area) Forward Area is published by Army Air Forces Pacific Ocean Area and is also used in conjunction with the Pacific Airways Route Manual (H.O. No. 503) by the XXI Bomber Command. Extracts of

JACSPAC and NATAPOA are carried in the Radio Operator's folder on all combat missions. Radio Operator's will study their radio facility charts and extracts so they may be able to locate desired information at a moments notice.

2. Signal Operation Instructions.

Signal Operation Instructions (SOI) are publications by which Headquarters, XXI Bomber Command transmits frequency assignments, call sign assignments, radio nets, etc., to lower echelons of the command. These publications are never carried in aircraft. Extracts of the necessary information printed on "Flimsies" are used for this purpose.

3. XXI Bomber Command Regulations.

Regulations are publications, each of which is assigned a base number such as 55 which indicates the series of the regulation and a second number which indicates the number of the regulation within the series. The 100 series regulations deal with communications. The majority of Communications Standard Operating Procedures are contained in this series of regulations.

4. Radio Operator's Log.

A supply of XXI Bomber Command radio operator's logs will be furnished the radio operator prior to each flight, so he may keep a record of all communications activities during the flight. There are spaces provided to enter all call signs and call words, messages, etc., all blank spaces should be filled in. The operator wil sign his name to the completed log. This log is provided for your benefit. If any question should arise as to when you did a certain thing, or why it was done, the log can be used to substantiate your statements. Therefore, the log must be legible and complete.

It is mandatory that the following items be made in the log:

1. Aircraft call sign and voice call.

2. Wing Ground Station call sign.

3. Group net call and voice call.

4. Squadron Leader and deputy Squadron Leader's calls.

5. AACS call.

6. All messages transmitted by the Wing Air-Ground Station.

7. Periods when radio watch is interrupted for any reason indicating time radio watch is abandoned and time watch is resumed.

8. Final itemized equipment checks prior to take-off and after landing.

For security reason, station and/or unit designations will not be logged.

A complete entry of any distress traffic which might be intercepted should be logged. Aircraft of this command forced to "ditch" have been located through the alertness of radio operators in other aircraft logging the distress traffic occuring before the airplane was forced to ditch.

5. Radio Operator's Interrogation Form.

After each combat mission you will be interrogated as to the communications activities. The majority of the questions asked will deal with entries you are required to make in the radio log. Correct and complete answers to these questions are very important, as future planning and preventative measures depend upon the thoroughness of your answers to these questions. Some of the questions you will be required to answer deal with the following: Strike Reports; did you send one, if so was it received by the ground Station? Fox transmissions; did you receive all Time Ticks and UCOPAC weather reports and any other "F" messages transmitted by the Wing Ground Station? Frequencies? were your frequencies jammed, if so, when, and for how long? Navigation aids; did you use non-directional homer, radio range, VHF/DF, HF/DF, OWI station, air-to-air homing or radio transmitter buoys? How may bearings were requested? Were all obtained? Net discipline and security; was net discipline good? Did you log any breaches of radio security? Enemy transmissions; did you log any definite instances of radio jamming or interference? Did you log any enemy transmissions? Distress; did you log any distress messages? Did you hear any urgent signals (XXX) being used, any SOS messages, any OPASR messages?

You should ask your communications office for a copy of the interrogation form to read and study so you will know what questions will be asked you.

I   MISCELLANEOUS

1. Strike Reports.

A strike report, "Bombs Away" message, will be sent by each aircraft bombing individually, or, if bombing is done in formation, by the Formation Leader only. "Bombs Away" messages will be sent from over the target immediately after bombs have been released  on the primary and secondary targets. When aircraft bomb the Last Resort target, or, the Target of Opportunity, "Bombs Away" strike reports will be delayed for one (1) hour to afford a clear channel for those aircraft bombing Primary and Secondary targets. Normal call-up and answer procedure will be used and the date-time-group of the message will indicate time of bombing. The following codes will be used in preparing the message:

Two strike reports are outlined below and will be designated as Strike Report No. 1 (Normal Strike Report) and Strike Report No. 2 (Incendiary Strike Report).

<u>Strike Report No. 1</u>

  a.  <u>Target Bombed</u>

      P - Primary Target.

      S - Secondary Target.

      L - Last Resort Target.

      O - Target of Opportunity.

  b.  <u>Method of Bombing</u>

      V - Visual Bombing.

      R - Radar Bombing.

      N - Navigation.

  c.  <u>Bombing Results</u>

      1 - Excellent; meaning, pattern centered on aiming point.

      2 - Good; meaning, few hits on aiming point.

      3 - Fair; meaning, hits in the target area.

      4 - Poor; meaning, missed the target area.

      5 - Unobserved.

  d.  <u>Fighter Escort</u>

      A - Friendly fighter escort present.

      B - No friendly fighter escort.

e. <u>Number of Planes in Bomber Formation</u>

    1 - One Plane.
    2 - Two Planes.
    3 - Three Planes.
    4 - Four Planes.
     etc.

f. The five (or six character code group of aircraft in formation is more than nine (9) ) thus evolved will be repeated three (3) time to insure reception. Such a message might be:

Example:  OOV605 V 1V606 - 051422 - $\overline{BT}$ PV3A8 PV3A8 PV3A8 $\overline{BT}$ K

       or, if more than 9 planes in formations:

                - $\overline{BT}$ PV3A11 PV3A11 PV3A11 $\overline{BT}$ K

g. This message would mean:  Primary target was bombed visually and the observed results were that hits were made in the target area but no hits were observed on the aiming point, friendly fighter escort was present and there were (11) bomber planes in the formation.

<u>Strike Report No. 2</u>

a. <u>Target Bombed</u>

    P - Primary Target.

    S - Secondary Target.

    L - Last Resort Target.

    O - Target of Opportunity.

b. <u>Method of Bombing</u>

    V - Visual Bombing.

    R - Radar Bombing.

    N - Navigation.

c. <u>Cloud Coverage</u>

    1 to 9 for tenths, X for 10/10.

d. <u>Situation at Target</u>

    A - General Conflagration.

    B - Several Large Fires.

    C - Many Fires.

    D - Few Scattered Fires.

    E - Unobserved.

e. <u>Fighter Opposition</u>

    1 - Heavy.

    2 - Moderate.

    3 - Meager.

    4 - None.

f. <u>Flak</u>

    A - Heavy.

    B - Moderate.

    C - Meager.

    D - Slight.

    E - None.

g. The six character code group thus evolved will be repeated three (3) times to insure reception. Such a message might be:

    Example:   OOV605 V 1V606 - 051422Z - $\overline{BT}$ PV2A3D PV2A3D PV2A3D $\overline{BT}$ K

h. This message would mean primary target was bombed visually, 2/10 cloud coverage over the target, the situation at the target was one of General Conflagration, fighter opposition was meager and flak was slight.

2. <u>Contact Reports</u>

    CINCPOA will designate from time to time by dispatch to Head-Quarters XXI Bomber Command (information copy to lower echelons) certain restricted areas. Shipping observed in these areas is not to be reported by radio in flight at any time. No restrictions of any sort are placed on in-flight reporting of shipping observed in enemy harbors or the Island Sea.

<u>Sightings Enroute to Target:</u>  In the case of contact sightings of either inside or outside the restricted area designated by CINCPOA, information will be logged immediately.  No transmission of contact sightings, however, will be made until after bombs away.  Transmission subsequent to bombs away will be confined to sightings and observations <u>outside</u> the restricted areas (subject to restriction imposed in paragraph a below).

<u>Sightings Enroute From Target:</u>  All contact sightings will be logged at once.  Those outside the restricted areas will be forwarded by radio immediately (subject to restriction imposed in paragraph a below.)

a.  In order to prevent reporting the locations of friendly submarines, <u>sightings of single ships and submarines are not to be reported in flight at any time</u> (except single ships and submarines in enemy harbors or the Inland Sea)  This information will be logged, however, and reported upon return in accordance with established interrogation procedure.

Use <u>URGENT</u> precedence in transmitting all in-flight reports of sightings outside of restricted areas.  All transmissions will be sent in code by means of CSP 1270.

Anticipate enemy deception.  Authenticate all contact reports.

Contact reports will be handled by the "R" method unless the condition of radio silence in effect at the station which receives the report prevents.

If contact is sighted by a formation, the Formation Leader will make all the necessary contact reports.  The first aircraft which sights an enemy craft will call the formation leader's aircraft on Channel "A" VHF and so notify him of the contact.

Contact reports of sightings outside the restricted areas will be sent first on the regular strike frequency using the report form outline in CSP 1270.

As indicated, URGENT (0) precedence will be used.  The Wing airground station will decode the message immediately, mark it for: "BOMCOM TWO ONE ATTN A-2 REPORTS" and relay the decoded message to the Wing Control Officer who will then forward it to Bom Com Two One by operational teletype under URGENT (0) precedence and SECRET classification.  This headquarters will then be responsible for dissemination of the inforamtion to all who may be interested.

All messages sent in accordance with provisions above (whether receipted for or not) should be retransmitted on 4475 Kc (unless shipping is in the Inland Sea or enemy harbor).  Ground stations monitoring 4475 Kc will then pass the reports in accordance with instructions listed above.

To be of any value, contact reports will contain the following:

a. Composition of Sighting (number and type)

b. Location of Sighting, in addition to latitude and longitude (if possible in reference to known location, such as 8 miles northeast of Sofu Gan Island. If no such location is visible, be certain to specify exact latitude and longitude.)

c. Course and Speed (give best estimate of course and of speed in knots. If not moving, so indicate. If underway but course and/or speed not observed or established, so indicate).

d. Time of Sighting (GMT Time)

e. Your position in relationship to sighting (for example: 5 miles from enemy ship at 20,000 feet).

f. A specimen report follows:

| Composition of Sighting | Location of Sighting | Course of Sighting | Speed (if ships) Alt. (if planes) | Time of Sighting | Location of your aircraft (distance and altitude from sighting) |
|---|---|---|---|---|---|
| 1CL IDD | 25° 10' N 144° 20' E | 320° | 10 knots 10,000 feet | 0415Z | 10 miles 20,000 feet |

This report transmitted by CW (key transmission) would be as follows when decoded:

ØØV6Ø5 V 1V6Ø6 B̅T̅ 1CL 1DD 251ØV 1442ØE GUS 32Ø SPD 1Ø Ø415Z 1Ø MI 2Ø,ØØØ FT K

A copy of Japanese Warships, Japanese Aircraft and Japanese Merchant Shipping Tonnage (JMST) will be carried at all times in each pilot's mission folder. Contact reports on Merchant Shipping (JMST) should be given using terminology described in JMST folder.

3. Weather Broadcasts

Two general types of Weather will be used within the XXI Bomber Command; )1) UCOPAC. (2) WAF-3.

A weather report using UCOPAC will be transmitted upon request from Wing Air-ground Station to the aircraft in flight.

WAF-3 weather information, encyphered in "Andusmet", will be the weather report passed from aircraft in flight to the Wing Air-ground Station. Under normal conditions the only aircraft using WAF-3 weather report are Weather-Strike-Missions (WSM) and aircraft dispatched primarily for weather reconnaissance. However aircraft radio operators should become thoroughly schooled in both UCOPAC and WAF-3 weather reports.

In order to minimize confusion and facilitate the intelligent passing of weather information, Wing Air-Ground Stations will adhere to the following procedure:

a. Weather encoded in UCOPAC and using CSP 1270 ( ) direct authentication will be broadcast by the "F" method from the Wing-Air-Ground Station simultaneously on all strike frequencies every hour on the half hour 24 hours a day.

In the event of a diversion to a base other than the home airdrome, the Wing-Air-Ground Station ordering the diversion will be responsible for passing the diverted aircraft a weather report for the airdrome concerned on the Wing Air-Ground frequency. In such cases the code name for the control tower of the field to which the aircraft is being diverted will be placed immediately following the day number of the UCOPACARD.

Example:   Report from Saipan to a plane being diverted to North Field, Guam, would read as follows:

LV606 V OOV605 $\overline{BT}$ - F - 1630Z $\overline{BT}$ UCOPAC 16 16 Ranger 23 23

4 D O 5 G 7 T 9 C 11 K 12 W 14 G 15 D $\overline{BT}$ QKA DD $\overline{IMI}$ 1V606

V OOV605 $\overline{BT}$ - F - 1630Z $\overline{BT}$ UCOPAC 16 16 Ranger 23 23 4 D

O 5 G 7 T 9 C 11 K 12 W 14 G 15 D $\overline{BT}$ QKA DD AR

Under normal circumstances the field terminal conditions broadcast in UCOPAC will not name the location. Remember this is done only in the case of diversion of aircraft to other than home field.

4. Time Signals

The navigation officer will furnish a "Time Tick" (hack) for all crew members attending the general briefing.

The Wing Air-Ground Station will transmit "Timing Signals" hourly, starting with the 58th minute. This will be done every hour 24 hours a day. "Timing Signals" will be transmitted on all Wing Air Ground strike frequencies simultaneously. Timing will be considered to have been transmitted by the Broadcast "F" method.

**Example:**

V605 V 00V605 - 58 58 V 00V605 V 00V605 _____ _____ _____

5 sec dash  5 sec dash  5 sec dash

V 00V605 V 00V605 - 59 59 V 00V605

V 00V605 _____ _____ _____

5 sec dash  5 sec dash  5 sec dash

V 00V605 V 00V605 - 60 60 V 00V605

V 00V605 _____ _____ _____

5 sec dash  5 sec dash  5 sec dash

Timing signals may also be received on any number of commercial stations on 2500 Kcs, 5000 Kcs, 10,000 Kcs and 15, 000 Kcs. Consult your Communications Officer for locations and time of Broadcast of these commercial stations.

5. Codes and Cyphers

CSP 1270 ( ) is the short title for the aircraft code which is carried by all aircraft of the XXI Bomber Command on all tactical missions flown. All CW messages that require encoding will be transmitted using this system. This is the radio operator's code.

"Shackle" numeral cipher is a "direct reading" code used by pilots of this command when working with Naval craft. This is a voice code which changes daily and is used to encode all numbers used in the text of a "clear" message.

World Wide Recognition Codes will be issued to both Bombardier and Radio Operator on combat missions. These codes which involve the use of both Very Pistol and Aldis Lamp are self explanatory and have the precise directions for use printed on the bottom of the form.

UCOPACARD is a daily changing numeral card which slides in and out of a UCOPAC frame. UCOPAC is used to decode numbered weather elements transmitted from Wing Air-ground Station to aircraft in flight.

ANDUSMET is a number sheet used for encoding and decoding WAF-3 weather reports passed from aircraft in flight to the Wing Air-ground Station.

Self Evident Codes - The XXI Bomber Command uses a few self evident code words which are used for both security purposes and also to expedite the handling of voice (R/T) communication. The most common ones are as follows:

"Bojangles"        -    Meaning IFF.

"Dreamboat"        -    Meaning B-29 aircraft.

"Chickens"         -    Meaning friendly fighter aircraft.

"Uncle Dog"        -    Meaning hold key down on VHF command set so
                        that fighters (or bombers) equipped with VHF
                        homing adapter AN/ARA-8 may "home" on signal
                        transmitted from your aircraft.  Normally
                        used in the following manner.  "Request Uncle
                        Dog on Channel Item", which means that air-
                        craft making the request wishes the aircraft
                        who is being called to transmit signal on a
                        particular VHF channel for homing purposes.

"Angels"           -    Meaning altitude in thousands of feet.  Ex-
                        ample:  My Angels are 12 (12,000 feet Altitude).

"Request Homing"   -    Used with VHF/DF fighter directory service
                        means request course to steer for "home".

"Vector"           -    Used with VHF/DF fighter directory service
                        when followed by "left" or "right" means alter
                        course to right or left (magnetic course in-
                        dicated).

"Bogey"            -    Unidentified aircraft (implies "Investigate
                        with caution---may be friendly").

## VHF Channel Designation Code.

In view of the fact that aircraft of the XXI Bomber Command oft times
perform joint or coordinated missions with fighter aircraft and Naval
units, a VHF channel designation has of necessity been used.  To eliminate confusion in so far as the pilot is concerned it has been suggested that appropriate channel designators be indicated opposite
the A, B, C, D, push button channel designators on the VHF control
box.  This will enable the pilot to coordinate his normal channels
used within the XXI Bomber Command with those channel designations
used on joint or coordinated missions.

## 6.  Authentication

Two general types of authentication are used by aircraft assigned
to XXI Bomber Command.  (1) CSP 1270 ( ) authentication, both direct
and challenge and reply type and (2) "shackle" authentication used
on joint missions involving Naval craft.

Use authenticator:

a. If you suspect enemy deception.

b. In answer to a request for authentication.

c. On all contact and amplifying reports.

d. On all CW plain language transmissions.

Authentication, of any message transmitted on A XXI Bomber Command Air-ground circuit is the Rule rather than the exception. If you are ever in doubt or just plain "Don't Know" be sure to give and request proper authentication.

## 7. Security

The majority of the material carried in the aircraft briefing folder is classified. The enemy, if it were to fall in his hands, would profit enormously by his possession of that material. If the aircraft is in distress over water, the material should be collected, put into the weighted folder, and disposed of by sinking. In other circumstances, try, if possible to burn the material, or, if that cannot be done, mutilate or bury it. Do not attempt to scatter it over the countryside. It can be and undoubtedly will be picked up. If any of this material is inadvertently lost, report the loss as soon as possible to the agency issuing the briefing container, so that a proper report may be made to higher headquarters.

## J  SPECIAL PROCEDURES

## 1. IFF Procedure

Because the procedure for tuning IFF on and off varies with particular missions largely dependent upon other operations in progress and the disposition of the United States Pacific Fleet, no set IFF procedure will be laid down in this combat manual. Signal Operation Instructions (SOI) will govern the operation of the IFF equipment. In the event a deviation from the normal operation is deemed necessary, paragraph 5, Communications, of the existing Field Order will cover the specific operation.

Radar operators will check the operation of the IFF, 500 miles out from any friendly base while enroute to home base.

a. If IFF is inoperative at this time, Radar operator will notify the Airplane Commander and attempt to discover the reason for the malfunction.

When the Airplane Commander knows his IFF is inoperative, while en-route to home base, he will instruct his radio operator to send a message (encoded in CSP 1270 ( ) )to the Wing Air-ground Station, using the strike frequency and notifying them of the following, IFF out, ETA and course.

When the Airplane Commander knows his IFF Is inoperative he will be-give calling the nearest base control when 150 miles out from that control point and notify that base on Channel C (Queen) VHF, that his IFF is inoperative.

Example: "Hello Agate Base this is Happy Two One, My BOJANGLES is out."

Note: "BOJANGLES" is the code word for IFF.

a. If the IFF is inoperative and the aircraft is within 150 miles of Iwo Jima or any friendly base in the Marianas, the Airplane Commander will call the following ADC (Air Defense Command) bases on Channel C (Queen) VHF, and notify them thathis IFF is inoperative.

| PLACE | CALL |
|-------|------|
| Iwo Jima | Agate Base |
| Saipan | Condor Base |
| Guam | Buzzard Base |

b. If a plane is bound for Guam (Buzzard Base) and his IFF is inop-erative and it passes within 150 miles of both Iwo Jima and Saipan, it is the direct responsibility of the Airplane Commander to notify Agate Base at Iwo Jima, Condor Base at Saipan and Buzzard Base at Guam and tell them his IFF is inoperative.

Because of the large number of airplanes operating in this area and because this area still is a forward area (within range of Japanese aircraft) the importance of IFF operation cannot be over-emphasized. Be sure your aircraft is not responsible for unnecessarily alerting any friendly base thereby leaving you wide open to friendly attack as well as severe criticism.

2. Bomber-Fighter Communication

Joint missions are sometimes run between B-29 aircraft and Army fighter aircraft.

In view of the fact that the average fighter aircraft has very little in the way of navigational intruments it behooves the B-29's to "Mother" the fighters into the target and navigate them back to their home base. To perform such an operation calls for a clear-out com-munications plan understood by all fighters and all bombers.

B-29's of the XXI Bomber Command and Army fighters have a number of VHF Channels which are common to both bombers and fighter aircraft. All B-29's and all fighter aircraft have a common bomber to fighter VHF Channel. This channel is mainly used between the Fighter Group Leaders and the navigational B-29's but may be used between the Fighter Leader and the Bombardment Wing Leader for command purposes. This channel is Channel "Nan" (B) on your VHF set. The fighter aircrafts are equipped with the VHF homing adapter (AN/ARA-8) which is used for homing on a VHF signal transmitted by either bombers or fighters. The joint operations between bombers and fighters may take two forms: (1) Fighters may fly to and from the target area with the main bomber force in which case particular bombers must be alerted to stand by on the bomber to fighter VHF command frequency. The bombers so alerted would take any calls from the Fighter Leader and relay to the Bomber Formation Leader on the bomber to bomber frequency. For purposes of simplicity in a case of this type the fighter leader will always call "Dragon Leader" (Voice call assigned to the whole bomber force when using Bomber to Fighter frequency (Channel "Nan" (B) 134.10 megacycles) for command purposes between fighter leader and bomber force leader. The fighter leader will always use the voice call "Chieftain Leader" when communication is desired between fighter leader and bomber leader. (2) Fighters may be assigned navigational B-29's whose express purpose is to lead the fighter to the target area or enemy coast line where fighters will tack on to the main bomber force of B-29's and go into the target with them. Meanwhile the navigational B-29 aircraft will proceed to a pre-determined rally point for rendezvous with the fighters after they leave the target area. Upon reaching the rally point, the control plane of the navigational B-29's will transmit for "Uncle Dog" homing on Channel "Item" (D) 127.62 megacycles) beginning at its arrival on station. Signal will be one two minutes and off two minutes with identification by voice at the end of each transmission (Example: This is Cyclone Able).

For the benefit of fighters who have not reached the rendezvous or rally point before its departure, the last navigational B-29 (The control plane) will continue to transmit for "Uncle Dog" homing on Channel "Item" (D - 127.62 Mc) until it is within 140 miles of Iwo Jima. At this point the last navigational B-29 should be within the homing zone of "Brother Agate" and further transmissions might be confused with those of "Brother Agate". The last navigational B-29 (control Plane) will continue to monitor Channel "Nan" (B - 134.10 Mc) for a cally by any straggling fighter who might have been homing on its "Uncle Dog" transmissions. If such a call is received the navigational B-29 will give the straggling fighter a course for "Agate Base" and the fighter will fly the course until he hears the "Uncle Dog" signal of "Brother Agate" on Channel "Item" (127.62 megacycles).

Communications between fighters and navigational B-29's in connection with navigation will be conducted on Channel Nan (B - 134.10 Mcs)

In the event that homing of fighters to navigational B-29's is other than for rendezvous point at target area, both communication and "Uncle Dog" homing transmissions will be conducted on Channel "Nan" (B - 134.10 megacycles). Transmissions for homing will be kept to a minimum.

An explanation of the uses of the VHF channels common to both XXI Bomber Command B-29's and any fighters is as follows:

Channel "Nan." (B - 134.10 Mcs)      Fighter-Bomber common to be used for any homing other than assembly at rally point and air-sea rescue.

Channel "Queen" (C - 140.58 Mcs)     Air-sea rescue communication and homing if homing is given by submarines or Super Dumbo other than at rally point.

Channel "Item" (D - 127.62 Mcs)      Used as homing channel only between navigational B-29's and fighters.

In the event of a joint mission between Bombers and Fighters it must be standard procedure with every B-29 aircraft that in the event a friendly fighter tacks on to your wing coming out from the target area that you act as navigational plane for this fighter in the event he cannot find his designated navigational B-29. This means you will have to navigate this fighter back to within sight of his home field and in the event he gets into trouble on the way, make his full distress report for him. This distress report would be made in the conventional manner as described in the air-sea rescue, Communications section of this manual.

Because both B-29 groups and fighter groups have distinctive call signs which under normal circumstances would be impossible as well as impracticable to memorize, all B-29's other than those specifically detailed as navigational B-29's will answer to the call word of "Dreamboat". By the same token, all fighters will answer to the call word of "Chicken".

When a fighter requests homing assistance from a B-29, he will do so in the following manner:

Fighter:  "Hello Dreamboat this is Chicken. Request Uncle Dog Over"

Note: This means that the fighter is requesting homing assistance (Uncle Dog - so designated because the signals he hears using his VHF homing adapter AN/ARA-8 are a "U" when he is to the right of the on course signal being transmitted and a "D" when he is to the left of the transmitted on course signal). from the B-29 aircraft.

B-29: "Hello Chicken this is Dreamboat, Roger, Uncle Dog on Channel Nan (B Channel) Over".

Fighter: "Dreamboat this is Chicken, Roger, Over"

The B-29 will then transmit a steady "CW" signal for two minutes on Channel Nan, (Channel B) and will then monitor for two minutes repeating the above procedure until fighter pilot calls the B-29 aircraft still on Channel Nan (Channel B -- Fighter to Bomber) and states:

Fighter: "Hullo Dreamboat this is Chicken, request no further Uncle Dog Over".

B-29: "Hullo Chicken this is Dreamboat, Roger, standing by, request further assistance as needed, over".

Fighter: "Hullo Dreamboat this is Chicken, Wilco, Out".

Normally the time of the transmitted signal used for homing assistance will be for two minutes duration and then switching to the VHF command channel for further instructions. However, the length of the signal may increase or decrease as the situation changes. Any such changes would be covered in existing field order.

3.  Reports From Aircraft Landing Away From Home Base

When any XXI Bomber Command B-29 or B-24 type aircraft lands at a base other than its home base, the Airplane Commander will instruct his radio operator to notify the Wing Air-ground Station at his home base, of any of its assigned strike frequencies of the time he has landed, where he has landed, the reason for landing and the estimated time of departure (ETD).

This message (Landing Report) encoded in CSP 1270 ( ) will be transmitted to the Wing Air-ground Station while the aircraft is flying the pattern prior to landing to a field other than his home base.

In the event an aircraft lands at a base other than its home base another message (Take-Off Report) encoded in CSP 1270 ( ) will be transmitted to the Wing Air-ground Station immediately after take off enroute to a home base. This message will state the point of departure, destination and estimated time of arrival (ETA).

This report will be transmitted via the AN/ART-13 or BC-375 and be rendered by any B-29 or B-24 type aircraft whether on a Strike Mission, Weather Strike Mission, a Weather Reconnaissance Mission, Photo Reconnaissance Mission, a Ferret or RCM Search Mission, a Practice Mission, or, just "Island Hopping" (for Example: Courier Plane).

4. Air-to-Air-Homing

Air-to-air homing may be used in the following operations:

a. As an aid to completing formation at assembly point.

b. As an aid for completing assembly after making a frontal penetration.

c. As an aid to completing formation, at or near the target area.

d. As a navigational aid in "homing" on another aircraft.

When aircraft are briefed to use air-to-air homing to aid in completing assembly, the following procedure will be used. This procedure is designed to keep transmissions to minimum and for use in a situation where all aircraft engaged in the rendezvous are aware that homing transmissions will be made and of the approximate time and location at which the signals will be transmitted.

a. Lead aircraft upon approaching the assembly point will immediately start transmitting homing signals. No formation call-up advising other aircraft in formation that homing signals are to be sent need be made. Aircraft other than the formation leader, upon approaching the assembly point, will tune radio compass receiver to appropriate air-to-air homing frequency and moniter for homing transmissions.

b. Homing signals will consist of the group letter, assigned by Signal Operations Instructions (SOI), transmitted three (3) time followed by two (2) twenty (20) second dashes. For example:

AAA  _____  _____
       (20 sec dash)   (20 sec dash)

c. This transmission will be repeated continuously until assembly is accomplished or airplane commander decides transmissions are no longer necessary.

d. The XXI Bomber Command Signal Operations Instructions (SOI), Communications, will list lettered groups A, B, C, D, E, and F, of low and medium frequencies. Each Group will consist of four (4) frequencies. Frequencies, or groups of frequencies to be used on each mission will be published in Bomber Command Signal Operations Instructions (SOI) on the basis of one frequency for each bombardment group.

e.  Identification letters for each frequency, for each bombardment group will be contained in Bomber Command Signal Operations Instructions (SOI).

For example, if the 497th Bomb Group of the 73rd Wing is assigned the frequency 330 Kcs and the identification letter "A"; all squadrons of the 497th Bomb Group will "home" on a frequency of 330 Kcs identified by the letter "A" and twenty (20) second dashes.  Bombardment Wings will assign frequencies and identification letters from the group assigned to that particular Wing by Bomber Command Signal Operations Instructions (SOI).

f.  When Super Dumbos (B-29 Air-Sea Resuce Planes) are being utilized, both the Pilot's and the radio operator's flimsies (SOI extracts) will contain Super Dumbo's call sign and homing frequency. Super Dumbo will be requested for homing facilities by an aircraft who is lost or in trouble.  This will be a direct request using Super Dumbo's call sign and the operating signal QTN.

Example:  21V850 V 2V606 QTN K

For purposes of simplicity, Super Dumbos will be given a two letter identification call in adition to their normal Victor call sign. This two lettered call sign will be sent three times followed by two twenty second dashes.

Example:  JK  JK  JK  _____  _____
                         (20 second dash)    (20 second dash)

These homing signals would be repeated continuously until homing assistance is no longer required or the airplane commander of the Super Dumbo decides transmissions are no longer necessary.

The responsibility of transmitting homing signals will be that of the Squadron Leader and the Squadron Leader's radio operator.  It cannot be over-emphasized that the radio operator must have his liaison transmitter tuned to the exact frequency assigned to his squadron, and that he transmit clear cut identification letters and twenty (20) second dashes.

It is the responsibility of the Aircraft Commander or Navigators in aircraft which are assembling on the Group Leader to be properly tuned to their assigned homing frequency on the radio compass receiver so that the signals can be received on the correct frequency.  Aircraft Commanders and Navigators must be able to "read" the identification signal transmitted by the Group Leader.  In cases where the Aircraft Commanders or Navigators have difficulty in correctly tuning to the designated frequency or reading the identification signal they will call upon the radio operator for the desired assistance.

## K  CONCLUSION

After reading over this material, you should have a very good idea
of how air-ground communications are handled in the XXI Bomber
Command.  These procedures and equipment given to you to use are
provided to make your job as easy as possible.  Many of the procedures you already know, some you will have to learn from scratch.
On how well you learn your procedures and equipment depends your
success as a radio operator.  In the final analysis, however, the
major responsibility is yours, for you are the man at work in an
airplane.  It is very possible that you may fly a complete combat
mission and never touch your transmitting key.  Then again, you may
really have to perform.  Be ready for it -- no matter what it is!
So, learn to use your equipment and keep the following thoughts in
mind, and you'll be a radio operator -- the other crew members can
depend upon and be proud of;

1.  Learn all the procedures you will have to use.

2.  Remember that a 16-word-a-minute operator who gets his message
through the first time is a better operator than the lad who burns
up the air making mistake after mistake, causing everyone a lot of
grief.

3.  Remember to listen in before you transmit and make sure you have
a clear channel.

4.  The more you know about your equipment, the better you will be
able to do your job.

5.  Remember we are playing the game for keeps out here.  Practice
makes perfect.  And your primary aim is to be just as perfect as
you can be.

COMBAT GUNNERY

## IX  GUNNERY

The first requisite of a good gunner is a correct mental picture of his
job and a knowledge of the capabilities and limitations of his equipment.
With the B-29's remotely controlled turrets and computing system, guess-
work is completely eliminated in "Point of Aim". However, the computer
is not a magic box which, when operating properly, automatically gives
excellent hits on the target.  It takes practice, and lots of it to attain the skill in tracking, firing, and ranging necessary to give the
Central Fire Control (C.F.C) system accurate enough data to obtain percentage of hits.  Furthermore only after considerable practice will you
as a gunner develop a desired operating procedure and do all the necessary
things to operate successfully the C.F.C. equipment. ·Once this technique
is developed, you can feel confident in your responsibility because tests
indicate you can score more hits with C.F.C. equipment than with any
other type.  The success of future bombing operations, as well as the
safety of your own airplane and formation, will depend upon your skill
with your weapons.  Your guns and your turrets are precision instruments
capable of extremely accurate fire, but their dependability depends upon
your care and knowledge of your equipment.  Take care of it and know how
to use it.

## A  CARE OF EQUIPMENT IN PACIFIC OPERATIONS

Each gunner is personally responsible for the care and maintenance of
his guns and turrets.  Repairs to the turrets are made by turret special-
ists and to the guns by station ordnance personnel.  The gun should be
field stripped as soon as possible after a mission and all parts thoroughly cleaned with prescribed cleaning fluid.  While cleaning the gun,
each part must be carefully examined, and if not found perfect in every
detail should be immediately replaced with a new part.  Parts to be
closely examined for full and free movement are:  (1)  The ejector, (2)
the extractor switch, (3)  the belt holding pawl, (4)  the cover group,
and (5) the firing pin and extension and (6)  the accelerator.

Thoroughly clean and flush the firing pin and driving spring cavities
in the bolt.  Wash the back plate in the cleaning fluid, but don't soak
it as the cleaning agent may deteriorate the buffer discs.  Springs
should be checked for length against the "Spring Gauge Chart".  Polish
the front of the barrel and barrel bushing with crocus cloth.  Immediately before each mission all oil should be removed and no oil applied.
It has been found that the gun will perform better at extreme low temperatures with the gun bone dry.

## B  HEADSPACING AND TIMING

Headspace will change, loosening after a number of rounds have been fired.
It is, therefore, necessary to set the headspace each time the gun is assembled.  This is the easiest, yet the most important adjustment to be
made.  There are two methods of setting headspace and one should be used to
check the other. Note: Before setting headspace check the breech lock cam. This

cam should have a slight lateral floating movement of from .001 to .008 of an inch. Be sure the nut fastening the cam is secured with a cotter pin.

1. The First Method of Headspacing.

   a. Screw the barrel into the barrel extension hand tight.

   b. Assemble the gun in the receiver with a dummy round in the chamber.

   c. Install the back plate to prevent the driving spring from disengaging. However, the backplate will not go past the oil buffer, which will be protruding since the gun will not yet go into battery.

   d. With a screw driver or other blunt instrument unscrew the barrel one notch at a time, breaking the action each time, until the gun will just go completely into battery without being forced or driven.

   e. Break the action and back the barrel off two more notches.

This will permit faster firing action and allow easier and faster feeding.

2. The Second Method of Headspacing.

   a. Assemble outside of the receiver the barrel, barrel extension and bolt, with a dummy round in the chamber.

   b. Start with the barrel loose and breach lock held firmly up, lock the bolt, and turn the barrel hand tight into the barrel extension. Be sure it contacts the face of the bolt or T slot.

   c. Back the barrel off two notches. If all parts of the gun are in perfect condition this should give the same setting as the first method.

3. Timing.

Headspace adjustment accomplished, install the gun charger making sure the guns are not loaded or pointed in a direction that will endanger personnel or equipment. For proper timing each of the following steps must be accomplished accurately to insure positive operation of guns and chargers.

   a. Cock the gun by placing a screwdriver in "socket C" of the charger and pushing toward the muzzle end of the guns until the bolt moves to the rear; then release the screwdriver.

   b. Check to see that the sear pin adjuster has been turned clockwise as far as it will go.

c.  Insert the go-gauge (0.090 in.) between the barrel extension and the receiver of the gun.

d.  Turn the sear-pin adjuster counter-clockwise one notch at a time, and after each notch adjustment attempt to release the gun's firing pin by placing a screwdriver in "socket ᵀ" and pushing away from the gun muzzle. Continue to turn the sear-pin adjuster one notch at a time until the firing pin is released. A click will be heard when the firing pin is released.

e.  Cock the gun as described in step a. above, depress the action switch on the sighting station from which the turret is being operated, then squeeze the trigger on the sighting station. The firing solenoid should pick up and release the gun's firing pin. If the firing pin is not released, turn the sear pin adjuster in a counter clockwise direction until the energizing of the firing solenoid by trigger action causes the firing pin to be released.

f.  Insert the no go-gauge (0.116 in.) in place of the go-gauge, cock the guns, and attempt to fire by squeezing the trigger. The gun should not fire, i.e., the firing pin should not release. Remove gauge and push the reset button on both gun chargers. Timing is complete.

### C.  PREFLIGHT INSPECTIONS

## 1.  Gun Preflight.

During flight the guns are not readily accessible, so it is imperative that you make absolutely sure that the guns and ammunition are in perfect condition when installed in the turrets by performing the following checks before take-off:

a.  Check gun operation using dummy rounds.

b.  Check all equipment to see that it is safetied by safety wire where required.

c.  Check ammunition carefully for excess corrosion, defective primers, position of the link on the round, position of the round with respect to each other, bulges or burrs, and size of extraction rim.

d.  Load the ammunition cans making certain the rounds point in the correct direction and do not bind in the cans.

## 2.  Turret Preflight.

Prior to each mission you must make the following operational check of your turret. This preflight must be accomplished as early as possible in order to allow time for turret maintenance and any repairs needed before take-off.

a. Check all AN connectors for loose wires and tightness.

b. Check oil in the air compressor.

c. Check ground connection and brushes in dynamotor and amplydyne.

d. With auxiliary power supply, main line, and batteries on, turn on the auxiliary power switch. The compressor motor should start and run from three to five minutes if at sea level, then stop.

e. Turn the A.C. power switch on, and you should hear the dynamotor start.

f. Check the rheostat illumination control and both filaments of the reticle lamp.

g. Turn computer switch "in". If by feeling the gyros you determine they are running all right, turn the computer switch "out", to save the gyros.

h. Turn the turret power switch on. You should hear the amplidynes start, then:

   (1) Run the turret in azimuth and elevation.
   (2) Check the sight for correct operation in azimuth and elevation.
   (3) Check the range control handle for correct reticle movement.
   (4) Check the solenoid and firing switches.
   (5) Check the fire cut-off control.
   (6) Check interphone switch.

i. Clean thoroughly the plexiglass sighting window, sight glasses and filters.

3. <u>Final Preflight</u>.

To make the following final checks of your equipment, guns, and ammunition to see that they are in place and ready is your responsibility as a gunner.

a. Check to see that you have your oxygen mask and helmet, flak helmet and vest, sun goggles and flashlight.

b. Check your Mae West for $CO_2$ cartridges and its condition.

c. Check to see that you have the required spare gun parts and tool kit required.

d. Load guns as per group directive. Feed the ammunition against the cartridge stops putting the double link in first. Be sure

to have a round in the double link, then check to see that
the ammunition is not jammed in the feeding.

e.  Check to see that the gun covers are down and secured during
loading, that the turret domes are securely latched, and the
turret well safety switches securely closed.

f.  Check that the gun chargers are reset.

4.  Station Check.

After the final briefing by the pilot at the airplane, go to your station,
take with you the necessary tools and spare parts, and make the following
station checks:

a.  Check to see that you have your parachute and seat cushion.

b.  Check to be sure the cabin pressure valve is in the open
position.

c.  Check the oxygen system.  Pressure should read between 350
and 450 pounds per square inch.

d.  Check the interphone as follows; put on the headphones, adjust
the throat mike, and stand by for interphone check.  When the
alarm bell is rung by the airplane commander during combat
station inspection, the left and tail gunners will notify him
that they heard the alarm bell.  Also, when the phone call
signal is operated by the airplane commander each gunner will
notify him that his signal light works properly.

e.  Upon call from the co-pilot over the interphone, gunners will
observe and report the position of rudder, elevators, and
ailerons as the airplane commander operates the controls.

f.  Upon call from the airplane commander each gunner will report
on the status of his own check list as to whether or not it
has been completed.

D.  OPERATING PROCEDURES

1.  During Taxiing.

The tail gunner will start the auxiliary power "putt-putt" when the pilot
directs.  During the taxiing the top gunner is responsible for promptly
reporting to the co-pilot the presence of any approaching aircraft in
flight which might interfere with taxiing, but all gunners must report
promptly any dangerous condition they may observe.

2.  During Take-off.

Just prior to take-off the pilot will announce over the interphone "wing
flaps".  When the flaps are down the left gunner will reply, "left flap

down 25 degrees, sir", and the right gunner will make a similar report for the right flap. Fasten your safety belt!

3. <u>After Take-off</u>.

The right and left gunners will report over the interphone as soon as the flaps and landing gears are up. The top gunner will then supervise the fire-control system operational check and firing consisting of the following:

a. Turn on the AUXILIARY POWER switch on the control box. This turns on the air compressor and the heaters for the guns, cameras, and the computer.

b. Turn on the AC POWER switch. This starts the dynamotor which you should be able to hear running. If the dynamotor does not start, press hard on the breaker button to reset the breaker. The operations thus far have provided sight and control power.

c. Unstow the sight and make sure it has freedom of motion throughout its entire azimuth and elevation travel.

d. Turn up the rheostat for the reticle light, check to see that both lamp filaments light, and that the range control wheel can be moved over its entire range.

e. Turn the target size input knob to see that the target size figures appear properly.

f. Select a filter combination and adjust the reticle lamp brilliancy. As a rough guide it is suggested that enough filters be used to permit you to see the reticle with reasonable brilliance when looking at the brightest portion of the sky, not including the sun or area adjacent to it.

g. Set the switches on the blister system control box, blister system switch box, and nose system switch box in accordance with Standard Operating Procedure.

h. Put yourself in a comfortable position for scanning and tracking. Have padding where you will need it. Kneel with your knees spread wide apart. Place the mike cord, oxygen hose, etc., so that they won't be in your way as you track with the sight. Adjust your clothes and parachute harness so you will have proper freedom of movement.

i. Last, but by no means least, feel for the best position of your hands on the sight grip. This is important because you have to get your grip set right and quickly when you spot a target, so you should know from practice how to come in on the grip quickly. If you do it wrong, you will have to change your grip during tracking. If the tracking is jerky you give the computer wrong information, it will compute wrong, and you will hit nothing.

4. <u>Turning On the C.F.C. System.</u>

The generators cannot start all of the turret amplidynes at once so each of
you must take your turn. The airplane commander will tell you when to start
your equipment, and when he does, take the following steps:

a. Turn on the rest of the switches on the control box marked
   POWER one at a time at ten second intervals and listen. These
   start the amplidynes which make quite a noise. If you don't
   hear them start, open the switches again and press hard on the
   circuit breaker reset button and then try again.

b. Turn the COMPUTER switch on the control box to IN. This supplies
   DC power to the computer and sight gyros. See that the computer
   IN-OUT light is ON. This light should be on when both the computer switch on the control box is ON and when the computer
   standby switch is at STANDBY. It also lights when you are outside of the computer's limits of control.

c. Turn the COMPUTER STANDBY switch on the sight to IN. The IN-OUT
   light should go off.

d. Close the action switch and move the sight. Check to see that
   the primary control turret follows the sight. Remember, the
   top gunner can see the upper turret, the tail gunner can see the
   tail mount, the blister gunners can see the lower aft turret
   guns when the turret is pointing broadside, and the nose gunner
   can have the top gunner check the upper forward turret and have
   the navigator listen for movement of the lower forward turret.

e. Check the secondary control in accordance with Standard Operating
   Procedure. Observe that the secondary turret follows the sight.
   The blister gunners should also check for the proper signal
   indicator lights on the auxiliary control box.

f. Dim the lights on the auxiliary control box in the blister
   sighting station to the proper brilliancy to suit you.

g. If he hasn't already informed you, check with the navigator
   over the interphone to see that he has set the altitude, air
   speed and temperature on the hand set.

h. It is assumed the target will first be seen when it is a long
   way off, so set the range control for the smallest size reticle,
   or maximum range; and you will be ready to start tracking when
   a target is sighted.

i. If the airplane commander wishes you to fire a short practice
   burst, turn the guns switch from SAFE to FIRE and when finished
   return to SAFE. Make your bursts short and be sure you aren't
   aiming at someone in your formation when you press the trigger.

5. Putting the C.F.C. System At STANDBY.

If the mission is a long one, the airplane commander may want you to shut down to STANDBY. If he does, take these steps:

a. Stow the turret by stowing the sight while keeping the action switch depressed. Be sure you know what position to stow your turret.

b. Turn off the TURRET POWER switches to shut down the amplidynes and then release the action switch.

c. CAUTION! Never turn the system all the way off until the end of the mission. Leave the AC control power on to keep the tubes and other parts warm and ready for action. Be sure to turn the TURRET POWER switches on again before entering the combat zone.

6. Scanning.

The airplane commander will assign you an area to scan when you are in a combat zone. Keep a sharp lookout when you receive your assignment. If you are not on the job you make a blind spot for your airplane. See your enemy first and you will have a better chance of bringing him down.

If you wish to move the sight while scanning, leave the action switch open so the guns won't follow along, but when the target appears take these four steps:

a. Report the target to the fire control officer by the o'clock system.

b. Recognize the target as enemy or friendly. If it's an enemy airplane, identify and check wing span.

c. Set the target size on the reticle. Note: You may find it helpful to set the target size previously to the wing span of the most frequently encountered enemy fighter.

d. Turn the guns switch to FIRE.

7. Sighting.

When you are sure it's an enemy airplane, get your sights on him and start following, taking the following steps:

a. Put the reticle center dot right or the middle of the target and keep it there to the best of your ability. The computer will make all the necessary corrections for ballistics, parallax and lead.

b. Keep the range set properly by spanning the target with the reticle carefully. Remember the computations of the computer are no better than the data you give it, and range is one of the important items.

c.  Be sure you get your hands set on the grips the way you like them so you won't have to change your grip while tracking.

d.  Sight with both eyes open. It's natural, much easier, and it works.

e.  Track the target smoothly because if you don't you won't hit it. The computer calculates the amount of lead to give the gun from the rate at which you turn the sight. If you turn it in a series of jerks, the computer will jerk the guns back and forth. Don't pause when you fire a burst or jerk the sight while you are track-ing. If you do get off the target, come on again smoothly. Keep adjusting the range handle continually so that the reticle just spans the target's wing-span or silhouette.

f.  If your own airplane is rolling or maneuvering in evasive action, keep on tracking smoothly. The computer will make all the necessary corrections for you. The main thing you have to do is keep the cen-ter dot right on the target and span its silhouette with the reticle.

g.  When you change from one target to another, slew the sight quickly with the action switch open. When you get on the new target close the action switch again. This prevents the computer from cranking in erroneous lead corrections, especially during nose attacks.

h.  Nose Sighting Procedure. Present enemy fighter tactics show that approximately 45% of attacks by enemy fighters are against the nose of the B-29. Due to high rates of closing speeds between fighter-bomber, the following procedure will be used by all units for nose attacks by the Nose Sighting Station only.

(1)  Set Target Size at 35 feet.
(2)  Adjust range hand wheel until reticle (Circle of Dots) appears. (1200 yds)
(3)  When single-engine target spans 3/4 of the circle of dots, (1600 yds) spin range to minimum and commence firing and track-ing. Same for twin engine fighter, when it spans circle of dots completely.
(4)  Return to 1200 yd range as soon as target has passed in order to have information in computer ready for next attack.

8.  Firing.

a.  Fire before the enemy does. Begin firing at 1000 yards range except in nose attacks when you should fire as soon as you see the target. Keep your target in the reticle and don't try to sight with tracers. If you are on the target and have it properly spanned, the computer will do the rest.

b. **Fire short bursts.** The maximum rate of firing should not exceed 30 rounds per minute per gun (two seconds of firing). In extreme cases ten rounds per gun may be fired every 15 seconds.

c. <u>Once again, keep tracking smoothly while you are firing.</u>

d. Release the trigger whenever control of a turret is transferred from one station to another. You don't want the gun to be firing while the turret is slewing around.

e. Protect your own airplane and your formation from cook-offs. When you are not tracking or firing and there is any possibility of a cook-off, stow your turret where it will be safe. Remember there are other airplanes in your squadron that may be hit. Position the guns for maximum cooling when you are not using them.

f. Listen over the interphone constantly and know what is going on in the rest of your airplane. Whenever you have anything to say, be clear and concise. Keep discipline over the interphone.

g. There is so little time to do anything during nose attacks that a certain amount of advance preparation on the ground is necessary on the part of the nose gunner. When in the air, preset the target size you anticipate will attack you, set 40 feet if you don't know, and preset the 1000 yard range previously marked on the range handle. With the station in operating condition, point the sight straight ahead and hold the action switch closed for 10 seconds. This presets the correction with which you will start firing when attacked from the nose. Release the action switch but leave the sight in position to grab it quickly because when you are attacked from the nose you will have just three seconds from the time you first see your enemy until accurate firing is impossible.

h. When you spot an attacker, put the reticle on him and fire. You won't have time to do much more than that. Beware of decoys who drop off to the side to draw your attention away from the next attacker. If the attacker falls off to where he can't shoot at you, open your action switch and stop tracking him to avoid setting up large corrections in the computer which will be errors for the next attacks. As soon as an attacker has passed, reset the 1000 yards range, and set the guns dead ahead to preset your correction for the next attack. If there isn't time, open the action switch, slew back onto the new enemy, close the action switch and fire. Be sure always to open the action switch when slewing.

9. <u>Before Landing.</u>

Before landing the following steps must be taken:

a. Lower turrets will be cleared of ammunition. The belt will be broken and ammunition cleared from the gun by firing. This will be accomplished only at a time designated by the airplane commander when no other aircraft are in the vicinity and guns will be pointed straight down. Approximately 2 hours from the home base is ample time to accomplish the above.

b. Turn the GUN switch on the control box to SAFE.

c. Stow the turret by stowing the sight, holding the action switch closed. Each turret should be stowed by the gunner having the primary control. The right blister gunner should stow the lower aft turret. The upper turrets are stowed at zero azimuth and 45° elevation.

d. When the turrets are stowed, turn off the switches on the control box and then release the action switch. Push in the stowing pins on the sight in both azimuth and elevation and cover the sight.

e. When the pilot announces over the interphone, "Prepare for landing" the tail gunner should start the auxiliary power putt-putt in accordance with Standard Operating Procedure.

f. When the pilot announces over the interphone, "Wing flaps", the right and left blister gunners should watch the flaps and report "Left flap down 25 degrees, sir", or the right flap as the case may be.

g. Fasten your safety belt!

10. After Landing.

After landing you should take the following steps:

a. Disarm your guns, guarding them so no one passes in front of them before they are cleared. Note: During disarming the left gunner should guard the lower turrets while the right gunner clears them. The left and top gunners should clear the upper turrets.

b. Remove the turret dome, open the gun cover, and take out the ammunition belt. Be sure the last round is removed from the chamber!

c. Remove the ammunition cans but leave the receiver alone.

d. Take the guns to armament, empty the ammunition cans and remove all ammunition from the airplane and take it to the armament section, also.

e.  The tail gunner should clear the tail mount and run a swab of
    bore cleaner down the cannon barrel to protect the gun until
    maintenance men arrive.

f.  All gunners should report all malfunctions of the central-
    station fire-control equipment to the top gunner. The top
    gunner will keep a record of the status of the equipment,
    including shortages and malfunctions, noting any repairs and
    changes made and will report them to the flight engineer.

g.  After completing the above steps, gunners should report to
    Intelligence for interrogation.

## E  LENGTH OF BURSTS

There are several factors to consider in arriving at an answer to the
question of how long a burst it is practical to fire. The ammunition
has a high degree of accuracy. At 600 yards, when fired from an accuracy rifle held in a V-block, it will group in a circle 18" in diameter. When fired single shot, using an aircraft machine gun on a
tripod mount, tests have shown a 20" circle of fire. In a burst of
10 or 12 on the same mount the group was approximately five feet.
When longer bursts were fired, it was observed that the gun soon lost
accuracy, even though it remained relatively stationary in the mount.
When over fifty rounds were fired, in one burst, the projectiles
tumbled in flight and dispersed over a 75 foot area at 600 yards. When
the barrel has been overheated, it will be found that it cannot be relied
upon for further accuracy even though the lands and grooves measure up
well and the barrel, to all appearances, seems good. If the exterior of
the barrel has a burned appearance, it should be tested by ordnance before further use. When a barrel becomes over-heated it expands to such
an extent that the muzzle velocity decreases several hundred feet per
second. This decrease continues as the barrel continues to expand, until a point is reached where tumbling of the projectiles takes place
and controlled fire is reduced to a few hundred feet. The accuracy of
the fire delivered, therefore, depends not only on how steadily the gun
is held, but also on the length of the burst, and the condition of the
barrel. If a gunner fires short bursts of three to five rounds, constantly using his sights, he will have a tight group and a high degree
of accuracy. This is the most effective method of firing your machine guns.

## F  ENEMY TACTICS

The importance of search cannot be over-stressed. If the enemy is able to
attack unseen his chances of scoring a victory and making a clean getaway
are about 100%. In order to do this, he will attack out of the sun or from
cloud cover if possible and go to great lengths to intercept our formations
going to and returning from the targets. It has long been recognized that

surprise affords great advantages, and the Japs are fully capable of
pressing every advantage. Many crews have seen and reported enemy
fighters turning in to attack but not pressing the attack home. In
these cases they have turned off because they have been hit, or they
have seen our ships on the alert. Had they seen that we were not on
guard, they would have come in pressing the attack. It is imperative
for you to be at your station and on the alert during the entire mission. There is a great temptation to watch bombs fall, aircraft go down,
and, in general, abandon the field of search assigned. By doing this,
you give the enemy the necessary advantage he requires to make a successful attack.

INTELLIGENCE

# X INTELLIGENCE

## A. INTRODUCTION

The Intelligence Officer in your outfit provides you with information
about the enemy - his strength and resources, where you can do him the
most damage, and what he can do to slow up your job of knocking him out.
Particularly, your S-2 sees that you get the information to help you
penetrate enemy defenses, identify and hit the target, and return safely
to base.

He gives you all the information available on the Jap Air Force, their
pilots and aircraft, and the tactics they employ against B-29's. He
gives you the latest estimates of Jap fighter strength and probable
location. He helps you spot Jap planes, to recognize and report a new
one when you see it, and to know our own fighters from the Nips. He
teaches you all we know about Jap anti-aircraft, searchlights, barrage
balloons, and the so-called "secret weapons".

Your S-2 spends a lot of time with you on target and terrain identification, so you won't fly 1500 miles and drop your bombs on the·wrong
installation. He will tell you about security, why you must keep a
close-lip about many things, and the ways the Japs have of finding
out our plans. It's his job to teach you rules for survival in case
you have to ditch or bail out, and how to behave if you are captured.
He will keep you posted on the war so you'll know how XXI operations fit
into the over-all allied offensive. At the briefing just prior to each
mission, he will give you all the latest intelligence information relative
to that mission, and all the pertinent printed matter to take with you he
can within the limits of security.

But intelligence is not a one-sided business. You are an important link
in the information chain that provides our knowledge of the enemy. At
the briefing, your S-2 will ask you to look for certain things that will
help fill out the missing pieces of the enemy picture-puzzle. Among
other things, you will probably be asked to watch for certain types of
aircraft and their tactics, for methods of AA employment, and for enemy
shipping. You are a double-barrelled threat to the Jap when you not
only drop your bombs on the target but also bring home some observation
that tells us more of what the enemy is, has, and does.

You will be interrogated by your S-2 on certain phases of each mission.
It is his responsibility to dispatch the information you give him to
those who evaluate it for use in planning future XXI and other operations.
Your observations as reported in interrogations, their accuracy and detail, are important not only to your future success, but to operations
of other Air Forces units, the Army, and the Navy, who receive every
scrap of pertinent information you obtain. Be on the alert, know what
to look for, jot down every detail of importance.

Many agencies are at work assembling intelligence information for your use. Only by piecing together all the bits of information, sometimes seemingly insignificant, that you and others obtain, can the remarkably clear-cut picture we have of the enemy be drawn. Your S-2 has the sum total of this knowledge at hand to help you.

## B.   JAPANESE AIR FORCES

The Japanese Air Forces are not independent, but are arms of the Army and Navy, respectively, like our outfits.

The Army Air Force is divided into Air Armies which the Japs call Koku-guns. These are more or less permanently located and are roughly like our "Air Force". Next in line is the "Flying Division" (Hikoshidan) which is the largest tactical unit, something like our Combat Command. Then parallel to our Combat Wing, comes the "Flying Brigade", a mobile unit under the "Division". Under the Brigade naturally falls the units which do the work, the "Flying Regiment" (Hikosentai), which is roughly equivalent to our Group and which has 36 to 48 aircraft with 12 planes per "squadron" (Chutai). Each squadron is made up of "flights" (shotai) with three planes each.

The Naval Air Force has both land-based and ship-based aircraft, with their so-called 3rd Air Fleet controlling all carrier-based aircraft. The organization of this outfit is somewhat complicated. "Air Flotillas" (Kohusentai) are equivalent to the Air Armies in the land-based organization and these are divided into "Air Attack Forces" (Kushubutai), their largest land-based tactical units. Sometimes, as task forces, they form "Base Air Forces". The carrier based outfits are flexible and vary considerably in strength, but their most important unit is the Kokutai which generally has between 27 and 45 aircraft when it starts operations.

You'll run into the Army Air Force and the Naval Air Force, both are assigned to Japan. Currently (March 1945) the Navy appears committed to offensive operations, principally directed at our Fleet, with the Army Air Force left to defend the Empire.

## C.   JAPANESE FIGHTER AIRCRAFT

The original decision of the Japanese High Command to sacrifice armor, fire power and sturdiness in combat aircraft for maneuverability and climb is one of the greatest single contributing factors to the staggering defeats suffered by the Japanese Air Force to date. A training manual, published in July 1939, typifies Japanese thinking of that period and the early years of the war. Maneuverability is listed as the No. 1 characteristic that combat aircraft of all types should possess. Speed, range, and "excellence in climbing and descending ability" are also listed. There is no mention of armor.

Having conceived a faulty doctrine, the Japanese set about executing it
in an admirable fashion. Jap fighters, particularly the Zeke, were the
most maneuverable and fastest climbing combat planes in the air. Our
fighter pilots were amazed, and for a time, dismayed by the acrobatic
efficiency of the Zeke. They thought at first that they, too, had to
be acrobatic flyers. They soon learned, however, that their P-40's and
P-39's had four advantages, which, if employed properly, could overcome
the Jap's two advantages which were maneuverability and climb. These
four advantages were diving speed, armor, fire power and overall sturdiness of our fighters. It was then that the fragile, lightly armed and
un-armored Jap fighters began to fall in large numbers before the guns
of U.S. Navy and U.S. Army Air Forces planes.

New Jap fighters, such as Frank 1, George 11, Jack 11 are now appearing,
all with certain compromises to original Japanese doctrine. These three
are typical of the enemy's trend toward pilot protection (armor plate),
self-sealing tanks, and increased armament in their now "first line of
aerial defense."

Tojo and Tony, although out-classed by comparison to the newer Frank,
George, Jack, will still bear the brunt of the Jap defense until full
production, pilot transitional training, and refitting of fighter units
with newer types can be completed.

Captured documents have consistently shown the Jap mind at work toward
high altitude intercepter types. As yet, any such aircraft have been in
the experimental stage. Lack of descriptive information and photographs
have made it difficult to describe recognitionally new Jap types such
as Tenrai, Jimpu and Ki 88 that may be in limited operational use. The
coding of several new planes has been held in abeyance pending a joint
effort to more clearly and accurately define each new type.

Figure I, page X-4, gives as complete a breakdown as is presently possible
on the current Jap fighters.

| CODE NAME | JAPANESE DESIGNATION | CREW | SPAN | LENGTH | WING AREA | EMPTY / GROSS / OVERLOAD | ENGINE AND PROPELLER | TAKE-OFF B MILITARY H.P./ALT. | FUEL U.S. GALS. | MAX. MPH/Kts S.L. | MAX. MPH/Kts ALT. | Cruising MPH/Kts ALT. | CLIMB Rate at S.L. / Min. to Alt. / Service Ceiling | MAX. RANGE Strut Miles | Refueled Miles | FUEL U.S. Gal. | Bombs LBS. | RADIUS MAX. Tactical | GUNS No./Size/Rds. | BOMBS Norm No./lbs | Max No./lbs | REMARKS |
|---|---|---|---|---|---|---|---|---|---|---|---|---|---|---|---|---|---|---|---|---|---|---|
| ZEKE 52 | Type 0 carrier-borne fighter, Model 52 A6M5 | 1 | 36.2' | 29.8' | 229 | 4190 / 5920 / 6310 | 1 x SAKAE 31 14 Cyl. radial 3 Blade C.S. | 1210/S.L. 1085/6300 950/21700 | Int 156 Aux 87 Max 243 | 289/250 S.L. | 156/297 21000 | 152/132 1500 | 2600 fpm 3.0/10000 39300' | 1110 | 980 | 356 | None | 475-500 ms 412-434 km | Fwd 2/7.7/700 Fwd 2/20/100 | None | 2/132 or 10/70 | Some versions carry near 13 mm, s.s. Airplace 7.7s |
| JACK 11 | RAIDEN Model 11 14 Exp. Interceptor-Fighter J2M2 | 1 | 35.4' | 31.8' | 216 | 5178 / 7080 / 8045 | 1 x KASEI 23 14 Cyl. radial 4 Blade C.S. | 1870/S.L. 1580/S.L. 1560/19700 | Int 109 Aux 114 Max 223 | 350/304 S.L. | 417/315 17000 | 261/243 1500 | 4600 fpm 2.6/10000 37500' | 1640 | 1424 | 243 | None | 325-350 ms 282-304 km | Fwd 4/20/100 or Fwd 2/20/100 & Fwd 2/7.7/550 | None | 2/?? | May carry 4/20s & 2/13 mm s.s. guns. Interceptor duty. |
| GEORGE 11 | SHIDEN Model 11 15 Exp. Interceptor-Fighter N1K2-J | 1 | 39.4' | 29.3' | 253 | 5623 / 7717 / 9341 | 1 x HOMARE 21 18 Cyl. radial 4 Blade C.S. | 1970/S.L. 1875/9900 1675/19600 | Int Aux Max | -/- S.L. | 407/355 19686 | -/- 1500 | 5.5/19686 | 580 | 503 | (est) | 154. | 325-350 ms 282-304 km | Fwd 4/20/100 Fwd 2/7.7/400 | None or | 2/132 | Large number now operational. Armor & s.s. tanks. |
| SAM 11 | REPPU 17 Exp. carrier-borne fighter A7M1 | 1 | 36.1' | 29.5' | - | 5645 / 8380 / 9260 | 1 x HOMARE 41 18 Cyl. radial 4 Blade C.S. | 1790/S.L. 1900/6560 1700/19686 | Int 265 Aux 132 Max 397 | -/- S.L. | 395/343 19686 | -/- 1500 | 6.0/19686 40000' | 1440 | 1250 | 397 | None | 425-450 ms 369-391 km | Fwd 2/20/120 & Fwd 2/13/300 or Fwd 6/20/200 | None or | 2/132 | Successor to Zeke. Data incomplete & subj. to revision. |
| LUKE 11 | JINRAI 17 Exp. Interceptor-Fighter J8M1 | 1 | - | - | - | - / - / - | 1 x Ha 43 Mod 11 18 Cyl. radial Pusher | 1970/S.L. 1660/6500 1380/27500 | Int - Aux - Max - | -/- S.L. | 437/380 26250 | -/- 1500 | 9.7/26250' | 575 | 500 | - | - | - ms - km | Fwd 1/30/100 Top 2/20/200 | None or | 2/132 | Twin boom, Data incomplete, 1 or 2 engines? |
| OSCAR 2 | Type 2 Fighter Model 2 Ki 43-2 | 1 | 35.6' | 29.2' | 232 | 4170 / 5500 / 6240 | 1 x Type 2 1150 HP 14 Cyl radial 3 Blade C.S. | 1105/S.L. 1085/9200 965/19700 | Int 149 Aux 108 Max 257 | 255/226 S.L. | 347/301 20000 | 147/126 1500 | 3290 fpm 2.5/10000 37100' | 1180 | 1025 | 149 | None | 500-525 ms 434-456 km | Fwd 2/12.7/250 | None | 2/220 | Armor and in-effective self-sealing tanks. |
| TOJO 2 | Type 2 Fighter Model 2 Ki 44-2 | 1 | 31.0' | 29.2' | 169 | 4300 / 6100 / 6610 | 1 x Type 2 14 Cyl. radial 3 Blade C.S. | 1500/S.L. 1420/7000 1300/17200 | Int 128 Aux 69 Max 197 | 325/282 S.L. | 376/326 17200 | 174/151 1500 | 3940 fpm 2.5/10000 36500' | 740 | 643 | 128 | None | 300-325 ms 260-282 km | Fwd 4/12.7/250 or Fwd 2/12.7/250 | None | 2/72 | Armor & s.s. tanks |
| TONY 1 | Type 3 Fighter Model 1 Ki 61 | 1 | 39.3' | 28.9' | 215 | 5010 / 6982 / 7682 | 1 x Type 2 1100 HP 12 Cyl. V 3 Blade C.S. | 1160/S.L. 1030/S.L. 1085/13800 | Int 199 Aux 100 Max 299 | 292/262 S.L. | 361/314 15800 | 156/135 1500 | 2440 fpm 4.0/10000 35100' | 1520 | 1320 | 100 | None | 575-600 ms 499-521 km | Fwd 4/12.7/ or Fwd 2/12.7/ & 2/20/- | None | 2/220 | Armor & s.s. tanks. Tony 2 believed better proton. with Ha 140 |
| FRANK 1 | Single-seater Fighter Ki 84 | 1 | 37.1' | 32.3' | 266 | - / 7940 / 9194 | 1 x Ha 45 Mod 21 18 Cyl. radial 4 Blade CS Elect | 1970/S.L. 1875/9900 1675/19600 | Int 185 Aux 174 Max 195 | 348/302 S.L. | 422/367 21000 | 176/153 1500 | 3780 fpm 2.7/10000 38000' | 1125 | 977 | 185 | None | 525-550 ms 456-478 km | Fwd 2/20/120 Fwd 2/12.7/250 | None | 2/71 | Armor & s.s. tanks. Operational. Data subj. to revision |
| IRVING 11 | 2 SEKO Model 11 NF 17 Exp. 2-engine Land Fighter J1N1-S | 2 | 55.7' | 39.9' | 430 | 10700 / 14600 / 17544 | 2 x SAKAE 21 14 Cyl. radial 3 Blade C.S. | 1115/S.L. 1085/7350 965/19700 | Int 492 Aux 174 Max 666 | 274/237 S.L. | 333/288 19700 | 150/130 1500 | 1780 fpm 5.5/10000 32740' | 1560 | 1354 | 492 | None | 575-600 ms 499-521 km | Fwd 1/20/100 Top 2/20/100 Bts 2/20/100 | None | 2/550 | Armor & s.s. tanks. Used as a night-fighter or recco. |
| NICK 1 | Type 2 Heavy Fighter Ki 45 | 2 | 49.5' | 34.7' | 365 | 8335 / 12213 / - | 2 x Type 1 1050 14 Cyl. radial 3 Blade C.S. | 1065/S.L. 1040/6200 935/19300 | Int 363 Aux - Max - | 294/255 S.L. | 154/297 20600 | 152/132 1500 | 2595 fpm 35050' | 1405 | 1200 | 363 | None | 400-425 ms 347-369 km | Fwd 2/12.7or1/37 Top 1/7.9/ Top 2/20 fwd fire | None | 2/550 | Armor & s.s. tanks. Four different gun configurations |
| ROB 1 | Ki 64 S/B Hi-speed fighter | 1 | | | | | Inline (Ha 201) | | | 500 mph doubtful | | | | | | | | | | | | May eventually replace Tony. |
| STEVE 1 | Ki 73 S/B Hi-speed fighter | 1 | | | | | 2,000 H.P., 18 cyl. Radial (Ha 42) | | | | | | | | | | | | | | | Performance may be comparable to Frank 1. |
| PAT 1 | Ki 74 S/B fighter | | | | | | (Ha 221) | | | | | | | | | | | | | | | Long range Hi-speed fighter |
| CLARA 1 | Ki 70 2 B R | | | | | | 2,000 H.P. 2-18 cyl. Radial (Ha 42) | | | | | | | | | | | | | | | Presumably replacing Dinah. |
| Possibly XXI B.C. Type ABC | Ki 88 | | Est. 45' | Est. 35' | | | 2-Ha 140 Inline engines. | | | Preliminary Assessment: 355-360 mph at 7,500', 425 at 28,000 feet. | | | | | | | | | | | | Somewhat resembles Mosquito. |

DATA TABLE — JAPANESE COMBAT AIRCRAFT

FIGURE I

## D.  JAPANESE FIGHTER TACTICS

Jap fighter tactics on our day missions have differed from their tactics
on our night missions.  The following data is based on five night and 19
day missions flown by units of the XXI Bomber Command over Honshu from
24 November 1944 to 16 March 1945.

DIRECTION OF ATTACK:

On our day missions Jap fighters have preferred to make attacks on the
nose and on our night missions they prefer to make tail attacks.  Forty
eight percent of Jap attacks on our day missions were made at the nose
whereas 60 percent of the Jap attacks on our night missions were made
at the tail.

The enemy's preference for frontal attacks on day missions is probably
due to the difficulty experienced by the Jap in attempting to overtake
B-29's at high altitudes (26,000 - 32,000 feet).  Also, the Jap makes
himself a difficult target on nose approaches because of the high rate
of closure.

The enemy's preference for tail attacks on night missions may be due to:

a.  Their system of vectoring, which puts the fighters onto the tails
of B-29's.

b.  Better Jap fighter performance at low altitudes, enabling them
to overtake our B-29's.

c.  Haphazard stumbling upon our formation.

LEVEL OF ATTACK:

On day missions the Jap attacks are equally distributed between high,
level, and low attacks.  Thirty two percent of the 6,000 attacks on
day missions were from above, 34 percent were from level and 34 percent were from below.

On night missions the Japs show a great preference for level attacks,
making 53 percent of the 231 attacks on the five night missions from a
level approach.  Thirty one percent of the attacks came from high, and
16 percent of the attacks came from low.

It is quite possible that because of darkness the Jap fighters cannot be
seen until they are close, so that many Jap attacks originating from
high or low positions are reported as attacks from level, for night
missions.

DIRECTION AND LEVEL OF ATTACKS:

On day missions high, level and low attacks on the nose quarter are the favorite approaches of Jap fighters.

On night missions the Japs prefer to make level or high attacks on our tail.

The two charts following (pages X-10 and X-11) summarize Japanese approach tactics against our day and night missions.

SEQUENCE AND TIME OVER THE TARGET:

Study of attacks shows that there has been no positive relationship between the number of attacks and the sequence in which our formations went over the target. However, we have had fewer attacks on missions where the time interval between bombs away of the first and last formations over the target was shortest.

OTHER NOTES OF INTEREST:

Coordinated attacks comprise less than 3 percent of all attacks. Collisions or rammings have occurred in only one tenth of one percent of all attacks.

TYPES OF ENEMY AIRCRAFT ATTACKING:

Tony, Tojo, Irving, and Nick are the fighters most used by the Japs. Frank, George, and Jack are increasing. Zeke is decreasing.

JAP FIGHTER CAPABILITIES FOR NIGHT FIGHTING:

Jap fighter interception during our night attacks has been very weak, and it is believed that the Jap Air Force, at present, is deficient in the tactics and technique of night interception.

However, in more recent night missions there have been some instances of apparent Jap attempts to coordinate their ground and air defense units. Enemy fighters have appeared to spot for AA batteries and work with searchlights. In some instances when searchlights picked up a B-29, the fighters went in, AA ceased and searchlights went out.

Enemy planes have followed us out over the water for considerable distances. Even after evasive action, the enemy planes could not be lost, indicating that they were probably radar equipped.

To date, Jap night fighters have inflicted only negligible damage. The Jap doesn't seem as willing or able to attack at night as in the daytime.

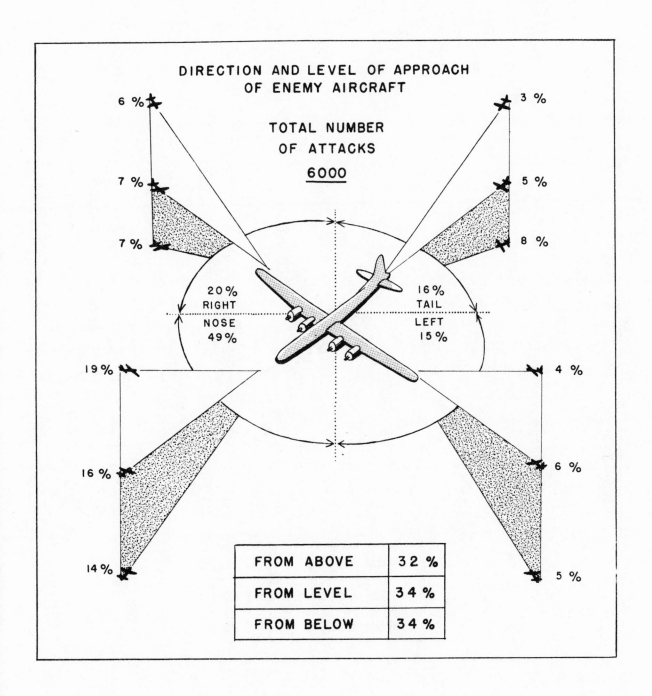

DIRECTION AND LEVEL OF APPROACH
OF ENEMY AIRCRAFT

TOTAL NUMBER
OF ATTACKS
6000

6 %

3 %

7 %

5 %

7 %

8 %

20 %
RIGHT

16 %
TAIL

NOSE
49 %

LEFT
15 %

19 %

4 %

16 %

6 %

14 %

5 %

| FROM ABOVE | 32 % |
| FROM LEVEL | 34 % |
| FROM BELOW | 34 % |

DAY ATTACKS

FIGURE II

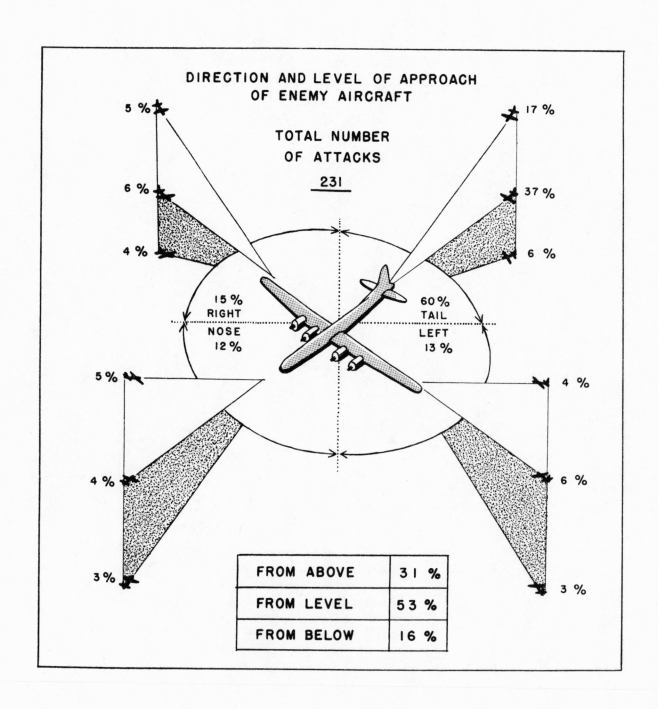

DIRECTION AND LEVEL OF APPROACH
OF ENEMY AIRCRAFT

TOTAL NUMBER
OF ATTACKS

231

5 %

17 %

6 %

37 %

4 %

6 %

15 %
RIGHT

60 %
TAIL

NOSE

LEFT

12 %

13 %

5 %

4 %

4 %

6 %

3 %

3 %

| FROM ABOVE | 31 % |
|------------|------|
| FROM LEVEL | 53 % |
| FROM BELOW | 16 % |

NIGHT ATTACKS

FIGURE III

It seems certain that the Jap will make every attempt to better his night flying technique and to increase his night fighter force in the vicinity of our principal targets.

## E.  JAPANESE ANTI-AIRCRAFT ARTILLERY

### 1.  General

In the past when the Allied Air Forces struck installations in the outlying districts of Japanese controlled territory, the enemy flak encountered was most inferior and ineffective when compared to that of AA defenses in other theaters.  It is an accepted fact that Japanese Army anti-aircraft has lagged far behind other countries in the introduction of new weapons, fire control and radar systems, and in anti-aircraft tactics.  Japanese Naval anti-aircraft, though probably not the world's best, has managed to keep more up to date than the Army.

The anti-aircraft defenses of the Japanese mainland are an entirely different proposition.  They are much larger and more effective.  They are better equipped, making use of naval guns which are land emplaced and new Army weapons.  The first extensive use by the Japanese of radar controlled AA has appeared on the mainland.

Japanese anti-aircraft is definitely becoming more effective, and it behooves all who fly over Japan to know as much as possible about the capabilities of their defenses.

### 2.  Types of Equipment

#### a.  Heavy Anti-Aircraft or Heavy Flak

Weapons (or fire from weapons) of 75mm or greater caliber. This type of weapon fires a high explosive projectile which is equipped with a time fuze on the nose, causing the shell to explode at the end of a predetermined time, throwing fragments within a lethal area.  This lethal area may vary from 25 to 150 feet depending upon the weapon, the direction from the explosion, and the direction of travel of the shell.

#### b.  Medium Anti-Aircraft or Medium Flak (Automatic Weapons)

Weapons (or fire from weapons) of 50mm to 20mm in caliber. These weapons usually fire high explosive shells with a percussion or super-sensitive fuze which causes the projectile to explode on impact.  The shells are usually equipped with a tracer and are self-destroying when the tracer burns out. Flak from these weapons is therefore effective only when direct hits are obtained.  Planes flying at 15,000 feet have often noted many bursts of AA immediately below them; this is probably automatic weapons fire, self-destroying at its extreme range where danger from hits is slight. Medium AA weapons are designed to offer effective opposition against low flying planes directed against strategic or tactical targets. To do this they are designed for mobility, rapid tracking in azimuth and elevation angles, and high rates of fire. These guns are fitted with some form of on-carriage sighting equipment, and it is possible that the Japanese may employ some form of fire control director with their medium AA.

c. Light Anti-Aircraft (Machine Guns)

Japanese machine guns are generally 7.7mm to 13.2mm in caliber. These weapons usually fire tracer projectiles and have very high rates of fire. Ball or armor piercing ammunition may be employed.

d. Small Arms Fire

Fire from individual weapons of ground troops directed against aircraft at very low altitude. The ammunition is tracerless and fire can be identified only through direct observation of individuals firing.

3. STANDARD FOR REPORTING ANTI-AIRCRAFT FIRE

| TYPE OF FIRE | ACCURACY | AMOUNT OF FIRE |
|---|---|---|
| Heavy Flak | Accurate: Bursts in close proximity so that airplane is either hit or "rocked".<br><br>Inaccurate: Bursts beyond danger area and no hits obtained. | Meager: Less than 2 bursts per second.<br><br>Moderate: From 2 to 5 bursts per second.<br><br>Intense: Over 5 bursts per second. |
| Medium and Light Flak | Accurate: Tracer streams in close proximity to plane, and/or hits obtained.<br><br>Inaccurate: Tracer streams well away from plane, and no hits obtained. | Meager: Less than 4 weapons in action.<br><br>Moderate: 4 to 12 weapons in action.<br><br>Intense: Over 12 weapons in action. |

It is to be noted that the term "meager" has replaced the term "slight", the latter term will no longer be used to define intensity of fire, as it is too easily confused with light fire. Meager fire with heavy flak

can be expected from gun defended areas containing only one battery of
from 4 to 8 guns; moderate fire can be expected from gun defended areas
in which from 9 to 20 guns can fire on the plane during a bombing run;
intense fire can be expected from heavily defended areas in which more
than 20 guns can fire upon the attacking group. For purposes of reporting, the terms "accurate" and "inaccurate" will depend upon the proximity
of bursts and the hits obtained, and will not be a function of the altitude or slant range. A large number of bursts in close proximity to a
plane would be termed "accurate" even though no hits were obtained. On
the other hand, a lucky hit on a plane when all the other bursts were
badly scattered over the sky area would be termed "inaccurate". The
intensity and accuracy for small arms fire has been omitted.

## 4. DESCRIPTION OF HEAVY ANTI-AIRCRAFT GUNS AND FIRE CONTROL EQUIPMENT

Because of the characteristics of operations of this command, anti-
aircraft opposition will normally consist of fire from heavy anti-
aircraft artillery, that is, weapons of 75mm or greater caliber.
These weapons are not as mobile as automatic weapons for they require
more time to emplace in preparation for fire. Although the Japanese
have the 75mm M88 and M11 and the 105mm M14 which are tractor drawn
and considered mobile, it might be said the majority of guns or heavy
anti-aircraft weapons are used in a semi-mobile or static sense.
These weapons fire a heavier shell ranging from 12.7 pounds for the
75mm (3"/40 caliber) to 50.6 pounds for the 127mm (5"/40 caliber) type
89 dual purpose gun, and have a corresponding decrease in the maximum
rates of fire of from 25 rounds per minute for the 75mm M88 to eight
rounds per minute for the 127mm type 89. No tracer element is used
as the shells are equipped with time fuses designed to provide bursts
in the air at some predesignated time along the trajectory, the maximum fuse setting generally being 30 seconds.

Heavy anti-aircraft guns are designed to offer effective fire against
high flying bombers and utilize fire control instruments to determine
firing data. These instruments generally consist of a height-finger
which measures and transmits altitude to the director, and the director which by measuring and combining the rate of change of azimuth and
elevation with the altitude obtained from the height-finder translates
this information into firing data. This firing data transmitted to the
guns as azimuth, quadrant elevation, and fuse length is based on the
past flight line of the plane. The Japanese also use radar to determine altitude, slant range, azimuth, and elevation permitting them to
deliver fire under conditions of poor visibility or "unseen" fire.

## 5. TYPES OF GUN OR HEAVY ANTI-AIRCRAFT FIRE

Heavy anti-aircraft fire can be divided into the following three classi-
fications:

a. Continuously Pointed

In this type of fire gun batteries fire individually and attempt to keep the bursts "on target" continuously as long as the aircraft is in range. Firing data is determined by the use of fire control instruments and can be delivered either as "seen" or "unseen" fire. Bursts should appear to move along with the aircraft like a belt of anti-aircraft fire being continuously unrolled in the sky.

b. Barrage

In this type the enemy attempts to lay a "curtain" of fire at some point, usually the Bomb Release Line, through which aircraft will have to pass. Bursts will constantly appear over a wide area in the sky and at prolonged periods of time, not necessarily while aircraft are in the area. This is the least effective and most primitive type of fire.

c. Predicted Concentration

This type is basically short barrages directed at successive points in the sky which have been determined from past actions of aircraft. Bursts should appear at approximately the same time, and should occur only when aircraft are in the area. There should also be gaps of distance and time in successive groups of bursts.

6. INTERROGATION

Because of the long range characteristics of the aircraft assigned to this command, operations will generally be carried out against enemy territory about which not all information is available regarding locations, size, and types of anti-aircraft defenses used by the Japanese. In addition to information gained from photo coverage and interpretation, crew observations of anti-aircraft fire are exceedingly valuable to this headquarters, higher headquarters, and other units.

Information desired through crew observations concerning the various phases of enemy anti-aircraft opposition consists of the following:

a. Heavy Anti-Aircraft Fire

Locations and geographical coordinates where fire was encountered; time and duration of encounter; altitude; extent of undercast, CAVU to 10/10's; color of bursts; accuracy of fire (considered accurate if plane is struck, rocked, or if burst is within 150 feet of the plane, otherwise inaccurate); intensity of fire as meager, moderate, or intense; and deviations of fire to be reported as:

| High | Left | Leading |
| Level | In Line | Even |
| Low | Right | Trailing |

Types of fire encountered as continuously pointed, predicted concentration, or barrage; evasive action taken, the reasons, and results; and information of any enemy aircraft on the same course and altitude as your plane which may have been reporting data to anti-aircraft installations; are types of information desired.

b.  Other Anti-Aircraft Defenses

Information is also desired on automatic weapons, searchlights, ground-to-air rockets or other new ground weapons the enemy may be using, smokescreens, barrage ballons, the efficiency of blackouts, and all AA phenomena.

JAPANESE AA WEAPONS

Source:  Information Intelligence Summary No. 44-21, 10 July 1944.
CINCPAC-CINCPOA Bulletin No. 13-45, 10 January 1945.

| | Muzzle Velocity (ft/sec) | Max. Fuse Ceiling (ft.) | Effective Ceiling (ft.) | Extreme Deterrent Range (slant ft.) | Practical Rate of Fire (Rounds per minute) |
|---|---|---|---|---|---|
| Army 7.7mm Machine Gun | 2350 | | 2500 | 3200 | 250 |
| Army & Navy 13.2 mm Machine Gun | 2280 | | 3000 | 5000 | 225 per barrel |
| Army Hotchkiss Type 20mm AW | 2800 | | 5500 | 7000 | 130 |
| Navy 25mm AW | 2850 | | 7500 | 14,000 | 190 per barrel |
| Navy 40mm AW | 2000 | | 6000 | 10,000 | 70 |
| Mobile 75mm (8cm) Gun | 2380 | 29,000 | 23,100 | | 15 |
| 3"/40 Dual purpose Gun | 2220 | 22,000 | 18,000 | | 15 |
| Mobile 105mm Gun | 2300 | 30,000 | 23,000 | | 10-12 |

| 120mm Dual Pur-<br>pose Naval Gun | 2680 | 31,000 | 26,500 | 10-12 |
| 127mm Dual Pur-<br>pose Twin mount<br>Naval Gun | 2360 | 27,500 | 23,300 | 8-10 per<br>barrel |

Note: Also in existance are New Army 10cm and 88mm guns. Very limited data available. Guns are far superior to other Army Weapons.

## F. RECONNAISSANCE, RECOGNITION, AND REPORTING

Shortly after that day in '41 when we realized we weren't going to beat the Nip in six months, a question often was heard, "When and how will we get Intelligence on Jap targets?" When the XXI Bomber Command went into operation, this question came up again. Yes, we had Air Objective Folders, but how many new industries did the Japs have, where were they located, and were the old ones still there?

The answers were not found in the "Crystal Ball" or by "Cloak and Dagger" methods so often suggested as the sources where S-2 gets the dope to put out in briefing. The answer is, and always will be for at least 75 percent of Air Intelligence, in the three R's. Readin', Ritin', and 'Rithmetic for the S-2, but most important, Reconnaissance, Recognition, and Reporting by the combat crews.

## Reconnaissance

Both by photography and by watchful crews on bombing missions, provides our most valuable Intelligence. No item observed is so small as to be inconsequential to intelligence work.

## Recognition

What is it? Was that E/A a Jack or a George? Was it black, was it jungle camouflaged? Is that a submarine or DD down there in the harbor? Be prepared to know what you do see.

## Reporting

At interrogation, the S-2 must utilize many forms to bring out all you have observed. To report accurately what you've seen may keep you one minute longer from chow, but it's very possible it will also chop another minute off the end of the war.

What you've seen may appear unimportant - perhaps a long flak burst from where no flak came before. Why is the Jap putting a gun out there? Close reconnaissance may indicate a new and important installation, or, maybe he's catching on to the fact that our route has become stereotyped.

## I. CONTINUOUSLY POINTED

PATH OF AIRCRAFT

*The burst area will move along with direction of formation like a belt of A.A. fire being constantly unrolled in the sky.*

THIS IS THE MOST DANGEROUS TYPE OF FLAK, AND IS USED BY A.A. GUNNERS IN PREFERENCE TO PREDICTED CONCENTRATION & BARRAGE TYPES OF FIRE. EACH BATTERY FOLLOWS THE FORMATION INDEPENDENTLY WITH ITS FIRE CONTROL EQUIPMENT (DIRECTOR, HEIGHT FINDER AND RADAR) CONTINUOUSLY TRANSMITTING FUTURE DATA TO THE GUNS. THIS FUTURE DATA IS PREDICTED BY THE DIRECTOR OBSERVING THE PRESENT POSITION, AND THEN FIGURING AHEAD A CERTAIN AMOUNT, BASED ON THE DIRECTION AND SPEED OF THE AIRCRAFT. THIS PREDICTION CAN BE DONE ONLY FOR RECTILINEAR FLIGHT WHICH IS EITHER (1) CONSTANT ALTITUDE, CONSTANT SPEED, & STRAIGHT LINE FLIGHT, OR (2) CONSTANTLY CHANGING ALTITUDE. OR (3) FLIGHT ON A CONSTANT CURVE, AS BELOW:

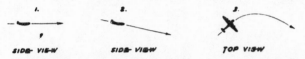

SIDE VIEW     SIDE VIEW     TOP VIEW

GUNS WILL FIRE CONTINUOUSLY AS LONG AS THE TARGET IS IN RANGE, OR AS LONG AS THE DIRECTOR IS ABLE TO PREDICT FUTURE DATA. BURSTS WILL APPEAR CLOSE TOGETHER BUT NOT NECESSARILY AT THE SAME TIME. WHEN A FORMATION IS UNDER FIRE FROM A LARGE NUMBER OF GUN POSITIONS THE APPEARANCE OF FLAK WILL BE SIMILIAR TO A PREDICTED CONCENTRATION, WITH THE EXCEPTION THAT THE BURSTS WILL MOVE ALONG WITH THE FORMATION. NO GAPS BETWEEN LARGE NUMBERS OF BURSTS.

"SEEN" CONTINUOUSLY POINTED FIRE WILL BE ENCOUNTERED DURING PERIODS OF GOOD VISIBILITY. IT IS MORE ACCURATE THAN "UNSEEN" FIRE WHICH IS DIRECTED BY RADAR DURING TIMES OF CLOUD, DARKNESS, WHEN SEARCHLIGHTS ARE NOT AVAILABLE, OR ANY OTHER TIME THE GROUND DEFENSES ARE UNABLE TO SEE THE FORMATION. CORRECTIONS CAN BE MADE TO "SEEN", BUT NOT TO "UNSEEN" FIRE.

**EVASIVE ACTION:** IF CAUGHT IN THIS TYPE OF FIRE, MAKE TURNS OF 20 TO 30 DEGREES, CHANGE ALTITUDE AT LEAST 1000 FEET, CONTINUE ON THIS NEW COURSE FOR AT LEAST 30 SECONDS, THEN MAKE ANOTHER TURN, CHANGE OF ALTITUDE. ETC. NEVER TAKE EVASIVE ACTION SUCH THAT THE AVERAGE OF THAT ACTION WILL INDICATE YOUR COURSE, AS:

AVERAGED COURSE

EVASIVE COURSE

A DIRECTOR WILL BE ABLE TO AVERAGE OUT SUCH CHANGES AND WILL PREDICT ON A STRAIGHT LINE, THE RESULT BEING THE FORMATION IS STILL IN DANGER, DUE TO DISPERSION AND PROBABLE ERROR OF THE BURSTS. CORRECT EVASIVE ACTION SHOULD TAKE THE FOLLOWING COURSE:

ACTUAL DIRECTION OF FLIGHT

**EVASIVE ACTION MUST BE:**
1. IRREGULAR
2. BOLD
3. PLANNED

## 2. PREDICTED CONCENTRATION

AVERAGE COURSE FROM PLOTTED COURSE

PLOTTED COURSE

PLOTS EVERY 10 SECONDS   LAST PLOT   PREDICTED POINT

VOLUME IN WHICH BURSTS MAY OCCUR

40 TO 70 SEC.

A PREDICTED CONCENTRATION CONSISTS OF A LARGE NUMBER OF BURSTS FIRED FROM A LARGE NUMBER OF GUNS AT A FUTURE POINT IN THE SKY. BURSTS APPEAR SIMULTANEOUSLY (WITHIN 2 TO 6 SECONDS) AND NORMALLY ARE ACCURATE, ALTHOUGH THE BURST AREA MAY INCLUDE A FAIRLY LARGE VOLUME. USUALLY USED AGAINST AVENUES OF APPROACH, DURING NIGHT, OR PERIODS OF POOR VISIBILITY, UNDER CAST, OR WHEN INDIVIDUAL FIRE CONTROL EQUIPMENT AT THE GUN POSITIONS IS NOT FUNCTIONING. IT IS AN EMERGENCY SYSTEM OF FIRE, BASED ON PLOTTING THE PATH OF THE FORMATION AT SOME CENTRAL LOCATION. THE FUTURE POINT DETERMINED FROM THESE PLOTS IS THEN TRANSMITTED TO SEVERAL GUN POSITIONS.

**EVASIVE ACTION:** IF THIS TYPE OF FIRE IS EXPECTED, MAKE TURNS OF 20 TO 30 DEGREES, CHANGING ALTITUDE AT LEAST 1000 FEET, HOLDING THIS NEW COURSE NOT MORE THAN 30 SECONDS, FOLLOWED BY ANOTHER TURN, LOSS OR GAIN OF ALTITUDE AND SO ON. IF CAUGHT IN THIS TYPE OF FIRE FOLLOW THE ABOVE EVASIVE ACTION IN THE DIRECTION THAT WILL EXPOSE THE AIRCRAFT TO DANGER THE SHORTEST LENGTH OF TIME.

## 3. BARRAGE

VOLUME IN WHICH BURSTS MAY OCCUR

FORMATION MAY BE HERE: TO ONE SIDE, ABOVE OR BELOW, AHEAD, OR IN THE BURST AREA.

BARRAGE FIRE CONSISTS OF A LARGE NUMBER OF INACCURATE BURSTS, COVERS A LARGE VOLUME AND IS FIRED FROM A LARGE CONCENTRATION OF GUNS AT THE SAME POINT, CAUSING BURSTS TO OCCUR FOR A PERIOD OF ONE TO TWO MINUTES. NORMALLY USED AGAINST AVENUES OF APPROACH, DURING NIGHT, PERIODS OF POOR VISIBILITY, UNDERCAST, OR WHEN INDIVIDUAL FIRE CONTROL EQUIPMENT IS NOT FUNCTIONING. IT IS AN EXTREME EMERGENCY TYPE OF FIRE. QUITE PRIMITIVE, BUT DANGEROUS IF A FORMATION IS FORCED TO FLY THROUGH IT.

**EVASIVE ACTION:** IF CAUGHT IN BARRAGE FIRE TAKE NO EVASIVE ACTION. THIS WOULD ONLY INCREASE THE TIME EXPOSED. IF BARRAGE FIRE APPEARS AHEAD, EITHER GO ABOVE, BELOW, TO ONE SIDE, OR TURN BACK. IF THIS IS NOT POSSIBLE TAKE THE SHORTEST ROUTE THROUGH THE BURSTS, EXPOSING THE AIRCRAFT FOR THE SHORTEST LENGTH OF TIME.

TYPES OF ANTI-AIRCRAFT FIRE
WITH
CORRESPONDING EVASIVE ACTION

FIGURE IV

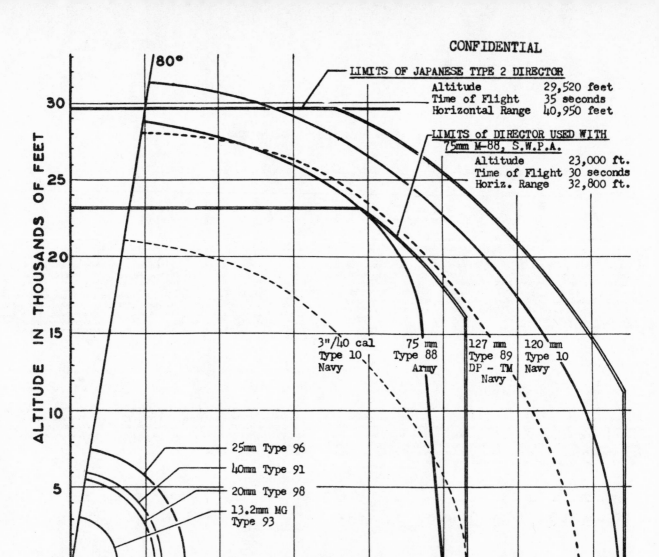

**127mm** (5"/40 cal) Dual Purpose Twin Mount Type 89 (1929); MV 2360 f/s, Service Charge; Fuze: Powder 30 secs, Mechanical 55 secs; 8-10 rds/bbl/min; Projectile weight 45 pounds.

**120mm** (4.7"/45 cal) Dual Purpose Type 10 (1921); MV 2680 f/s, Normal Charge; Fuze: Powder 30 secs, Mech 55 secs; 10-12 rds/min; Projectile weight 42.7 pounds.

**105mm** (Not shown above) 4.13"/42 cal Type 14 (1925); MV 2300 f/s; Fuze: Mechanical 57 secs; 10-12 rds/min; Projectile weight 30 lbs approximately.

**3"/40** cal (76.2mm) Dual Purpose Type 10 (1921); MV 2220 f/s; Fuze: Pwdr 30 secs, Mechanical 35 secs; Projectile weight 12.7 pounds.

**75mm** (2.95"/44.5 cal) Type 88 (1928) Army; MV 2380 f/s, Normal Charge; 15 rds/min; Fuze: Pwdr Train 30 seconds; Projectile weight 14.6 pounds.

**40mm** Navy Type 91 (1931) Automatic Weapon; MV 2000 f/s; Practical 70 rds/bbl/min; Ammunition: AP, HE, Time Fused, HET; Fuze: PD, Base, and 10 secs; Projectile weight 1.7 pounds.

**25mm** Navy Type 96 (1936) Automatic Weapon; MV 2850 f/s; Normal Charge; Practical 190 rds/bbl/min Ammunition: AP, HE, HET, HETSD, HEI; Fuze: PD; Projectile weight 0.6 lbs; (0.98"/60cal).

**20mm** Hotchkiss Type (Army) Type 98 (1938); MV 2800 f/s; 130 rds/min; Ammunition: APT, HET, HETSD, ITSD; Fuze: PD; Projectile weight 0.3 pounds; (0.79"/73 cal).

**13.2mm** (Army and Navy) Machine Gun Type 93 (1933); MV 2230 f/s; Practical 225 rds/bbl/min; Ammunition: Ball, AP, I, T; No Fuze; Projectile weight 0.11 pounds; (0.52"/109 cal).

Approximate Fire Envelopes are drawn to 30 seconds time of flight for Heavy AA guns and to the Effective Hitting Range for Automatic Weapons and Machine Guns.

APPROXIMATE FIRE ENVELOPES
JAPANESE ANTI-AIRCRAFT GUNS

FIGURE V

X - 16

Report it to the S-2 at Interrogation. Action is taken on <u>all</u> information and you may have the missing piece to complete an important intelligence puzzle.

We build up our enemy order of battle information from the reports of the types and numbers of aircraft you encounter. We identify new enemy operational types for the first time from what you tell us. This may have a vital effect on our planning as well as that of other forces attacking Japan. We correct inaccurate maps from what you tell us. Rivers change their courses, and the heights of many mountains are incorrectly charted. What you tell us about Jap performance and aerial tactics may have a good deal of bearing on the size and type of formations to be flown by our command and other B-29 combat units. We learn about the locations of airfields, friendly and enemy, from your observations.

Practice looking - there's an art to it; know everything there is to know about friendly and enemy aircraft and naval vessels. Get in the habit of jotting down what you've seen, or calling to the navigator on the interphone; remember that accuracy is vital. And when you're telling your story to the S-2, don't exaggerate - be accurate. It doesn't do any good to have you tell of 50 Japs in the target area when only 30 were really there, but it does help enormously if we can really <u>know</u> exactly what the enemy throws at us.

Your S-2 will give you a check-list of information he needs from you after each mission. Memorize it, and you will have the all-important answers to S-2's questions at Interrogation.

### G.  RADAR INTELLIGENCE

<u>Radar Reconnaissance</u>

You are among the first aircrews to have the decided advantage of radar reconnaissance of your routes and targets, in addition to the old stand-bys, visual and photo reconnaissance. Radar reconnaissance in turn is of two types, visual and photo, depending upon whether the information is obtained by interrogation of the scope operators or by interpretation of scope photos.

All our reconnaissance aviation supports your striking power in air attack by obtaining up-to-date data on your targets and routes prior to your strikes, and again on your targets following your strikes. The first step is to establish the existance of the target, its precise geographical location and its positive identity in regards to shape, size, and location to other identification features. Check points enroute to the target are also obtained. After the strike, the second step verifies the damage to the target. Unfortunately, photo and visual reconnaissance are hampered by undercasts, smoke-screens, and darkness. These three fogeys are successfully eliminated by radar so that B-29 crewmen are given 24-hour all-weather reconnaissance service over the Jap Empire

A good share of our Radar Reconnaissance is done by crews of the strike aircraft. This work is augmented by the ships of the 3rd Photo Recon Squadron which are equipped for both photo and radar reconnaissance. These ships are dispatched prior to a strike to obtain scope photos of your route and vertical and oblique photos of the target area. In event of complete cloud cover over the route and target, the reconnaissance ship still brings back radar information and scope photos to be used for briefing and in target folders. Following the strike, the reconnaissance ships are out again to cover the target and obtain damage assessment photos. In this instance, radar scope photos are secondary to vertical and oblique coverage because, at the present time, damage assessment from scope photos is a relatively new science. However, now that visual-photo-radar teams have been established, little if anything pertaining to the activity of the Jap at home escapes the attention of the XXI Bomber Command "investigators".

Radar Intelligence

The success of radar intelligence is directly dependent upon the quality and quantity of scope photography and its proper annotation done in our ships while over Jap territory, and also upon the powers of observation of the operators themselves. As an example of the importance of scope photos to radar intelligence, the following incident is cited. An XXI crew member, after a mission to a large Jap city, turned in scope photos which clearly showed land where none had previously been noted. The daylight verticals and obliques gave no hint of its presence. Other operators turned in further scope pictures confirming this. There could be no question, ground returns were continuing to appear, so ground must exist there. Evidently, tide-water flats were giving returns at low tide where no ground had previously been charted. The verticals and obliques failed to reveal its existance because they were made at full tide. The absence of this land mass from existing charts was sufficient to badly distort the charts used in radar briefing on the target area.

The results of radar reconnaissance are evaluated and reproduced in form suitable for use both by the staff of the XXI Bomber Command to plan missions, and for your use in locating and hitting the target. The information gleaned from scope photos and interrogation of the radar operators provides suggestions for improving routes and approaches from the radar operator's and navigator's viewpoints. Since a good radar approach to a target differs greatly from a good visual approach, consideration must be given to both requirements in planning our routes.

Radar intelligence provides you with the following; landfall and target approaches on radar navigation checkpoints, land-water relationships, target identification, correction of radar approach and navigation charts, radar briefing material, and material and photos for aircrew target folders.

Radar is a relatively new weapon in the Air Forces. The Twentieth is the first Air Force to have all its combat aircraft radar-equipped. We have much to gain by the advantageous use of radar reconnaissance, radar intelligence, and radar navigation, the triumvirate that makes possible an uninterrupted XXI Bomber Command assault against the Jap Empire, day or night, cloudy or CAVU.

## H. NAVAL AND MERCHANT SHIP RECOGNITION

Although not your primary mission, sightings of enemy shipping and the reports thereof by B-29 crews are of vital and increasing importance in the prosecution of the war against Japan. Every bit of information about the enemy is used in one way or another to subdue him. This applies especially to his shipping activities. Where are they carried on? What routes are being used? Are they traveling in convoys? Are your sightings of merchant ships or of naval vessels? These are the questions which B-29 crews should be able to answer in interrogations upon returning from missions.

Merchant ships can be identified by their bulky and awkward general overall shape. Since their purpose is to haul cargo or personnel or both, the design will tend toward straight sides, a relatively blunt bow and stern, and a box-like super-structure for the bridge.

Recognition of shipping at high altitudes is difficult but a simple method has been developed for recognition of the enemy type encountered. Known as JMST (Japanese Merchant Shipping Tonnage), it makes possible the reporting of the type of any Japanese merchant vessel that may be sighted.

This method of reporting is both simple and systematic. The entire Jap merchant fleet is broken down into four major divisions: Freighters, freighter-transports, transports and stack-aft types. These are reported under the code alphabet by their initial letters as follows:

    a.  Fox - Freighter

    b.  Fox Tare - Freighter-Transport

    c.  Tare - Transport

    d.  Sugar - Stack-aft

This sub-division according to size ranges from large to small and labeled as Able, Baker, Charlie, Dog (ABCD).

With regard to enemy naval vessels the value and necessity of knowing the whereabouts of units or forces of the enemy fleet is apparent.

The following pictures show various types of Jap merchant and naval vessels as they appear from the air.

FOX

FOX TARE

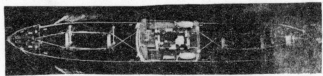

TARE

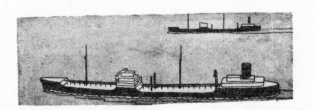

SUGAR

JAPANESE MERCHANT VESSELS

FIGURE VI

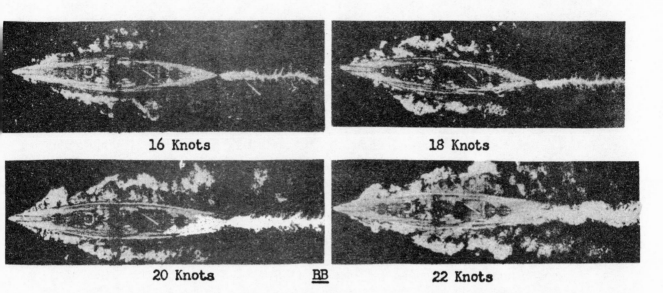

16 Knots    18 Knots

20 Knots    **BB**    22 Knots

Observe the characteristic broad battleship hull. These four
views show graphically how the wake varies as the speed increases.

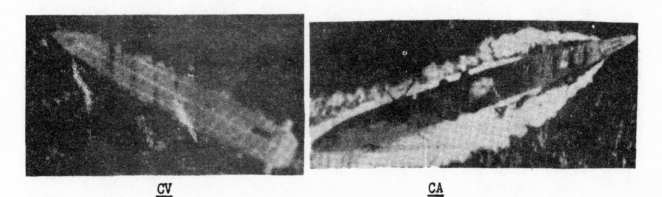

**CV**

Note the rectangular flight
deck, tapering toward the bow.

**CA**

Note the long slender shape
of the hull.

**DD**

The lines on a DD are also slender.

JAPANESE  NAVAL VESSELS

FIGURE VII

# I. SECURITY

## General

The part you as an individual are playing in the overall scheme of security and safeguarding of information and material requires study. Discussed briefly below are the security matters of major importance to help your organization inflict the greatest punishment on the enemy. Think these things over and know the reasons behind them. If you understand the reasons and work along with security, you'll be a more valuable member of your outfit.

## Mission Information

The most important information you have, which enemy agents desperately want, is the names of targets we plan to attack. After briefing, keep your mouth shut on the name or location of the target and the time of attack. Don't even tell your own mechanics. In their natural enthusiasm they may talk after take-off when you are still hours from the target. When you are briefed on a target which is later cancelled, you must be especially careful not to talk. If the enemy knows you have been briefed on Target X, they will get ready for you at that point, and a possible future mission there will get a hot reception. It boils down to this: If you talk you are sticking out your own neck.

## Identity Checks

Don't form the habit of accepting an unknown person at face value. The enemy agent may not be swarthy skinned and dressed in native garb. He may look like Cpl Joe Smith from North Dakota or Capt Bill Brown from New York City. It has happened that way. Form the habit of being suspicious of unknown persons whom you may find in vital areas of your bases, especially around your planes. Check the identity of persons before giving them any classified information if they are not personally known to you.

## Miscellaneous

Be skeptical of rumors and speculations. The enemy would like nothing better than to see us spread false information until we reached the point where we distrusted our Allies; or until we became jittery over the thought of a devastating new secret weapon. The fact is, the enemy enjoys this so much he is happy to start harmful rumors and speculations. Check the source of the next rumor you hear.

## Conclusion

Many leaks of vital information which may cost lives come about due to lack of knowledge on security measures and under-rating the importance to the enemy of the knowledge you have of military matters. Become acquainted with the reasons for security which are, in reality, simply the application of common sense. Security does not exist for the purpose of creating additional problems for you, even though this may sometimes appear to be the case. It exists for the purpose of safeguarding your equipment and your life.

Remember to avoid writing operational information. When in doubt don't write it. Complete instructions on censorship are available to you and it is your responsibility to keep apprised of censorship regulations.

### J.  TERRAIN AND TARGET IDENTIFICATION

### Terrain in General

Every target has its particular characteristics determined by terrain features which are the check points for its identification. These should be known so thoroughly by combat crews that every enemy target becomes as familiar to them as though they were flying over their hometown. In like manner, and equally as vital in accomplishing a successful mission is to be able to get to and from the target area. Flying to and from the target area the flight has to be made over great stretches of the Pacific Ocean. The burden on the navigator in making landfall is probably heavier in this theatre than it is in any other. Where security permits, advantage must be taken of every identifying islet and reef along the route. After landfall, it is equally important to know the terrain over which the remainder of the flight is to be made. All landforms - mountain chains, expansive plains, dune-covered deserts, great valleys with large meandering streams, rugged inundated shore lines or smooth shore lines where the land glides gently under the sea, have their unique features. These features, such as peaks, hills, ridges, cliffs, landslides, valleys, lakes, swamps, rivers, off-shore bars, and many others together with numerous man-made features, are the check points that will be the guides to and from as well as in and around every target.

Some of the more important terrain features that will serve as reliable check points are the following:

    a.  Breaks in the Earth's Crust

        From the air, these breaks show up as long, continuous, nearly straight cliffs that cut across the usual terrain features.

    b.  Volcanoes

        These may be easily recognized by their truncated crest and nearly conical shape in silhouette, and by the usual crater opening from above.

    c.  Large Landslides

        They appear as great scars of bare rock on the sides of mountains.

d. Streams

Important stream junctions and islands not eliminated by high
water are good check points. It should be determined, however,
whether streams are permanent or temporary. During flood seasons permanent streams will appear differently than during the
normal flow of water and large streams may occur in what are normally dry valleys. When a stream is old it develops great sweeping bends or meanders. Other important features associated with
streams are terraces and deltas. Knowing the direction streams
flow may be very helpful in navigation. As streams join, especially when having a tree-like pattern, they form an acute angle
that points down stream. If waterfalls are present, the crest
of the falls will form a regular line across the stream and the
turbulent water and mist will appear as light irregular streaks
strung out downstream. The same thing is more or less true for
rapids. If islands are present the blunt ends will be pointed
upstream. When resistant rocks are present or if artificial
structures are built out into a stream silt will be deposited
on the downstream side. One of the best clues is shown where the
stream bends. On the down-stream side of the bend the stream
undercuts the bank and forms a steep cliff while on the upstream
side sediments are deposited and form a flat light colored beach.

e. Lakes

Permanent lakes can be used as check points although in a semi-
arid region of sudden downpours large lakes may appear and disappear within a day's time. In such instances the outline of
the lake basin is usually apparent from the air even after the
water has receded, and can be checked against the lake shape
shown on navigation charts. Around permanent lakes in such
regions vegetation will flourish and provide reliable check
points.

f. Peaks, Mesas and Hills

Mountain peaks that stand out by themselves, flat-topped erosio-
nal remnants (mesas) or isolated hills, all can serve as very
useful landmarks.

g. Shorelines

Shorelines that have been uplifted are straight, slope gently
back from the water, and usually have a sandbar just off the beach.
These off shore bars and the breaks or inlets in them are the
best check points. Shorelines that have been submerged are very
irregular. Drowned valleys, forming good harbors, peninsulas,
islands, stack-like rocks, steep cliffs, narrow beaches and
straight or curved sand bars in the mouths of the bays are principal features.

Faults or breaks in the earth's crust, such as the one East
of Niihama, Shikoku, illustrated above, appear as continuous
straight cliffs that break the usual terrain.

FIGURE VIII

Volcanic cone of Fujiyama demonstrates the value of
prominent topographic features such as this for check
points.

FIGURE IX

Stream junction near Akashi, Honshu, plus highway
bridges, fords and lakes form valuable check points.

FIGURE X

Delta of the Kiso River west of Nagoya, showing the
numerous channels, islands and points of land that
provide numerous excellent check points.

FIGURE XI

Undercut banks (see arrows) on downstream side of bends,
and white sand on the upstream side tell that this mat-
ure stream flows to the right. River is Yodo River north
of Kobe, Honshu.

FIGURE XII

Emergent coastline North of Choshi Point, Honshu,
showing characteristic straight beaches and gently
sloping coastal plain.

FIGURE XIII

Submergent coastline forming the harbor of Hiro,
Honshu, and illustrating the deep harbors, steep
cliffs, and irregular coastline common to this
condition.

FIGURE XIV

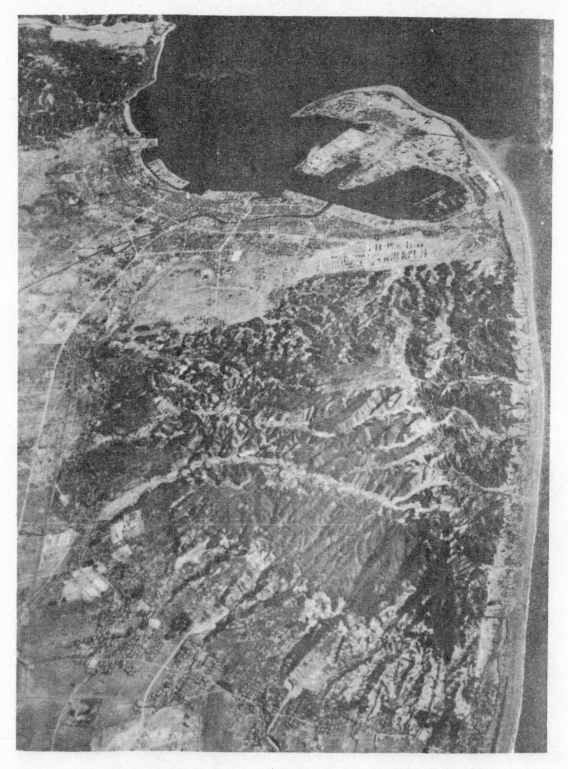

Recurved bars along coastlines and the straight
strip of coast caused by faulting, plus the half
mountain in foreground, such as this one at Shimizu,
Honshu, provide excellent landfalls and check points.

FIGURE XV

## LOCATION AND IDENTIFICATION OF THE TARGET

In the long run, success or failure in bombing depends on the ability of the crew to locate and identify the target. A thorough study should be made of the general region, the island, or the province where the target is located. If, for example, the target is located in the important area just West of Tokyo, one should have as complete a mental picture as possible of the wide plain sweeping back from the city to the North and West, gradually, broken by scattered hills of several hundred feet elevation. Elevation continues to rise gradually, with mountains of 4000 to 8000 feet some 40 miles West of Tokyo. Mt. Fuji, 60 miles to the West and South of Tokyo, is 12,000 feet high. This will be of great value in understanding how the target's location fits into the terrain pattern.

Crews should study the terrain along the course to the target and know thoroughly the geographic location of the plains, plateaus, mountain ranges, main streams, important canals, lake areas, and types of shorelines.

On the approach to the IP all possible check points at least 100 miles out should be pre-determined and all similar features in the vicinity should be thoroughly studied in order to avoid any possible confusion. The same should be done for the target approach. If the approach leads across a shoreline, then every feature of that shoreline should be studied to avoid any chance of mis-identification. All possible check points along the approach should be thoroughly studied and committed to memory so that on the approach no more than a glance at a chart or a photograph will be necessary, and if the target vicinity is obscured, offset bombing can be accomplished by synchronizing on some check point in front of the target.

Familiarity with the outline of the target will prevent any loss of time in spotting it. It may have the form of a rectangle or triangle. It may resemble an octopus or some other familiar animal or object. Equally as important is knowing the target's location in the target area. In what part of the city is it? Is it alongside of an airfield? What is its location in relation to all the check points in the vicinity?

In the target itself the location and function of every installation should be so firmly fixed in the bombardier's mind that there will be no doubt in recognizing the aiming point. The same should be done for all neighboring installations so that if the target is covered with smoke the bombardier will know on what points the lateral cross-hair of the bombsight will fall and still cut through the aiming point. This may eliminate the need for offset bombing.

It should be remembered that the careful study of a target can be accomplished only by discussions with personnel familiar with the target and its setting and by using all available maps, charts, photographs, models, and other objective data.

## MAN MADE FEATURES

Nearly everything that man builds has an unnatural appearance from the air. He scars the landscape with open-cut mines, highways, railroad lines, power lines, canals, etc., and within a target area, no matter how densely it may be built up, certain buildings and other structures are constructed to serve a specific purpose and they stand out from the rest. A roundhouse, a railroad station, a power plant, a castle, a traffic circle and many others are easily recognizable and may be used as check points in the vicinity of the target even more advantageously than terrain features. A list of the more important man-made features that are particularly significant follows:

| | |
|---|---|
| Railroads | Deforested areas |
| Roads and trails | Fences and walls |
| Tunnel entrances | Forts |
| Rice fields | Lighthouses and beacons |
| Power lines | Wharves and docks |
| Pipe lines | Reservoirs |
| Oil fields | Parks and cemeteries |
| Canals | Important road intersections |
| Bridges | Railroad crossings |
| Ferries | Traffic circles |
| Fords | Race tracks |
| Tailings from mines | Baseball diamonds |
| Open cut mines | Significant buildings |
| Cuts and fills | Religious shrines |

Most of the usual man-made features can be rather easily recognized. The straight courses and sweeping curves of railroads distinguish them from roads. Improved roads are generally wider and have fewer turns than secondary roads or trails. Reservoirs are located in the hilly area around a target. The water appears variously, depending on the relative positions of the sun and the airplane. If not in line with the reflected rays then the water will appear dark. Canals and ditches are even in width and frequently have trails on either side. Important locks in canals may be significant features of them. Canals or moats sometimes completely encircle portions of cities and their patterns may be used to recognize certain towns or cities along the course to a target. When moats are present around palaces or other grounds they serve as striking check points to a target. Powerlines or pipelines appear as wide and straight swaths through wooded areas. Many of Japan's important industrial plants are located on clearly defined reclaimed land around the port areas of the principal cities of Tokyo, Yokohama, Nagoya, Osaka, etc., which can be easily recognized by the regular outline common to man-made features. The ability to recognize various types of targets and the many different installations within them can be accomplished only by a study of aerial photographs and flow-charts of typical and enemy industry such as iron and steel plants, oil refineries, shipbuilding facilities and aircraft factories.

FLYING EQUIPMENT

# COMBAT CREW PERSONAL EQUIPMENT

## CHECK LIST

TIME: _____
DATE: _____
AIRPLANE MODEL AND NO. _____
PILOT'S NAME: _____

| | Pilot | Co-pilot | Engineer | Bombardier | Navigator | Radio Operator | Upper Gunner | Right Gunner | Left Gunner | Radar Operator | Tail Gunner | Other |
|---|---|---|---|---|---|---|---|---|---|---|---|---|
| ( ) Jacket, electrically heated | | | | | | | | | | | | |
| ( ) Trousers, electrically heated | | | | | | | | | | | | |
| ( ) Gloves, electrically heated | | | | | | | | | | | | |
| ( ) Shoes, electrically heated | | | | | | | | | | | | |
| ( ) Jacket, intermediate | | | | | | | | | | | | |
| ( ) Trousers, intermediate | | | | | | | | | | | | |
| ( ) Jacket, winter flying | | | | | | | | | | | | |
| ( ) Trousers, winter flying | | | | | | | | | | | | |
| ( ) Gloves, summer or winter | | | | | | | | | | | | |
| ( ) Mittens | | | | | | | | | | | | |
| ( ) Shoes, flying | | | | | | | | | | | | |
| ( ) Helmet, flying | | | | | | | | | | | | |
| ( ) Headset | | | | | | | | | | | | |
| ( ) Oxygen mask | | | | | | | | | | | | |
| ( ) Microphone | | | | | | | | | | | | |
| ( ) Bail-out cylinder | | | | | | | | | | | | |
| ( ) Parachute | | | | | | | | | | | | |
| ( ) Parachute first-aid kit | | | | | | | | | | | | |
| ( ) Parachute emergency kit | | | | | | | | | | | | |
| ( ) Life vest | | | | | | | | | | | | |
| ( ) Flak helmet | | | | | | | | | | | | |
| ( ) Goggles | | | | | | | | | | | | |
| ( ) Sun Glasses | | | | | | | | | | | | |
| ( ) Pistol, cartridges, clips | | | | | | | | | | | | |

NOTE: Only checked ( ) items received this mission.

# XI.  FLYING EQUIPMENT

The personal and emergency equipment described in this chapter was developed
and provided for you because you can't do your assigned job without it.  The
success of the mission actually does depend on every one of these things and
a great many more.  Ignorance or neglect of any essential detail may mean
inefficient individual performance, an aborted mission, and casualties.

Some of the equipment like life vests, oxygen equipment, altitude clothing,
among other things, help protect you against forces of nature which you have
challenged by operating out of man's natural element.  Other equipment,
including flak suits, flak helmets, and first aid kits help protect you
against the forces of the enemy.  Much of the equipment is already long
familiar to you, and you are inclined to take it for granted.  For example,
your heavy awkward parachute or your uncomfortable life vest may seem like
a highly overrated nuisance, if you've never had to use it.

It is obvious that none of this stuff is a Little Daisy, Sure-Fire, Never
Fail, Good Luck Charm that will shield you from all harm like a magic cloak.
But it offers considerable aid and protection if you exercise intelligence and
care in the use of it.  The amount of good it will do you, or to put it more
plainly, your chances of coming home safely, is directly proportional to
your knowledge of equipment and procedures.  The ultimate responsibility for
emergency equipment and procedures, along with responsibility for all other
operations during flight is that of the airplane commander.  Don't take it
for granted that all your crew members are will versed in emergency matters.
Check each man and see that he knows what he is supposed to know; the safety
of every man on the airplane depends on it.

Before each flight, assemble the crew and inspect the equipment of each man
to see that he has with him everything required on the flight.  The Personal
Equipment Officer will furnish the airplane commander with a check list like
the one reproduced on the foregoing page.  The required items of equipment
for the mission will be noted in the left column.  Then the airplane commander
will check off these items as each man exhibits them for inspection.  Only by
using the check list can there be assurance that nothing is overlooked.

## A.  OXYGEN SYSTEM AND EQUIPMENT

Your airplane was designed to operate just as well at high altitude as at
low altitude.  Your body wasn't!  All organisms require oxygen to support
life.  At ground level you get plenty of oxygen from the surrounding air,
which is packed down by the weight of the air above it.  As you go higher
there is less air above you.  Therefore, the air you breathe becomes thinner,
and your body is less able to get the required amount of oxygen out of it.
At 10,000 feet your body is getting barely sufficient oxygen, and you begin
to lose efficiency.  Somewhere above that altitude, varying with the individual, you'll become unconscious, and then, unless you get some extra oxygen
quick ... that's all brother!

In a pressurized cabin you can increase the air pressure so that you are breath
ing air of a simulated lower altitude.  As long as the cabin altitude is below

10,000 feet, you're OK. But remember, when the cabin altitude goes above 10,000 feet, you need oxygen. Therefore, your airplane has an oxygen system to meet the requirements of your body and allow you to function normally.

The equipment provided is excellent, simple to operate, and safe for flights up to extremely high altitudes. But it is not safe unless you understand it thoroughly and follow the rules regarding its use strictly. You can't take short-cuts with oxygen and live to tell about it!

The lack of oxygen, known as anoxia, gives no warning. If it hits you, you won't know it until your mates revive you from unconsciousness, if they can. Therefore, you must check the condition and operation of your equipment with extreme care, and continue to check it regularly as often as possible during flight.

1. Oxygen System.

Due to the fact that three of the fuselage compartments have cabin air control, whereby pressure equivalent to 8000 feet altitude is maintained within the compartments from 8000 feet up to 30,000 feet, oxygen equipment is not used extensively. However, because depressurization may be necessary as a result of enemy action, or when the aircraft is on fire, or when preparing to abandon the aircraft, all crew members must have oxygen equipment ready at hand and be prepared to use it.

The B-29 has a low pressure, demand type oxygen system. This system is the safest and best oxygen system known, if properly used. The system will function at altitudes up to 40,000 feet and a crew of eleven can remain at 25,000 feet about 4 1/2 hours in the early model aircraft equipped with fourteen oxygen cylinders, and from six and one-half hours to seven hours in the latest aircraft which are equipped with eighteen bottles. This, however, is the most uneconomical altitude, and the supply will last longer either above 30,000 feet or under 20,000 feet than it does between 20,000 and 30,000 feet. The duration of the oxygen will also vary with the requirements of the individuals, their activity, the temperature, charge of the system, and type of regulator.

The following chart shows the hours of available oxygen in later model B-29's equipped with G-1 cylinders. In the early model B-29's, the oxygen equipment consists of five separate low-pressure oxygen systems. Two systems supply the right and left stations in the forward cabin. These two systems may be coupled together by means of the oxygen shutoff valve at the engineer's stations, this making the oxygen in one system available to all forward stations in the event of loss of bottles in one of the systems. The rear pressure cabin is also supplied by two systems, interconnected in the same manner, with the shut-off valve located at the forward end of the gunner's compartment. The fifth system, consisting of two bottles, supplies only the tail gunner.

In the later model B-29's, the demand oxygen system is supplied by eighteen, type G-1, low pressure shatterproof oxygen cylinders. The entire system is filled from one filler valve located on the outside of the fuselage underneath the front left spar. The installation consists of a two bottle distribution system for the tail gunner, and a sixteen bottle system supplying thirteen oxygen stations in the front pressurized compartment, the gunner's compartment and the radar compartment. Each of the thirteen oxygen stations is supplied from two distinct distribution lines. Loss of one line or its associated cylinders still leaves each station with an alternate source of oxygen. The entire system is equalized by the use of crossfeeds controlled by automatic check valves. In the event of partial destruction of the system, all stations still functioning, have equal access to the remaining oxygen supply.

2. <u>Oxygen Mask</u>.

Your oxygen mask is an item of personal issue. Take care of it. It's as important as your life. Before you use the mask in flight, have it fitted carefully by your Personal Equipment Officer, or his qualified assistants. They will see that you have the right size, that it fits perfectly, and that the studs to hold it are properly fixed to your helmet. Then bring it in for re-checking whenever necessary. The straps will stretch slightly after a period of use. It's a good idea to have the fit rechecked regularly whether you think it needs it or not.

Draw your mask before each mission, and return it to the supply room afterward. Equipment personnel will check it for repair and cleaning. But don't assume that this procedure relieves you of the responsibility of your own regular inspection and care of the mask. Before each mission, make the following checks on your mask:

a. Look the mask and helmet over carefully for worn spots or worn straps, loose studs, or evidence of deterioration in facepiece and hose.

b. Put the helmet and mask on carefully. Slip the edges of the facepiece under the helmet.

c. Test for leaks. Hold your thumb over the end of the hose and breathe in gently. The mask should collapse on your face, with no air entering. Don't inhale strongly, because a sharp, deep breath may deform the mask to cause a false seal or a new leak.

d. Clip the end of the regulator hose to your jacket in such a position that you can move your head around fully without twisting or kinking the mask hose or pulling on the quick-disconnect. Get the personal equipment section to sew a tab on your jacket at the proper spot.

e. See that the gasket is properly seated on the male end of the quick-disconnect fitting between mask and regulator hoses. Plug in the fitting and test the pull. If it comes apart easily, spread the prongs with the proper spreader tool or knife blade. Note: This is only a temporary adjustment. As soon as possible report the difficulty to the equipment men and let them replace the fitting if necessary.

f. General Tips.

(1) Watch carefully for freezing in the mask from the water vapor
in your breath at extremely low temperatures. If you detect
freezing, squeeze the mask.
(2) Don't let anyone else wear your mask except in emergencies.
(3) Keep it in the kit between flights, and keep it clean.
(4) Report anything wrong with the functioning or condition of
the mask when you turn it in after the flight.

3. Oxygen Regulator.

A demand regulator is mounted at each station in the plane. There are
two types of demand regulators, the Airco and Pioneer. You may find either
one on your plane. They look slightly different but the principle of operation is the same in both. A demand regulator is one that furnishes oxygen
on demand or when you inhale. No oxygen comes out when you exhale.

The regulator has an Auto-Mix mechanism controlled by a lever on the side
of the cover. When the lever is in the ON position, oxygen furnished below
30,000 feet altitude is mixed with air. The dilution is controlled automatically by an aeroid to furnish the correct amount of oxygen which your
body requires for a given altitude. Above approximately 30,000 feet the air
inlet closes and you get 100% oxygen although the lever in the regulator is
still in the ON position. With the lever in the OFF position, 100% oxygen
is furnished at all altitudes. This wastes oxygen. Never turn the lever to
OFF except in the following cases:

    a. To give 100% oxygen to a wounded man below 30,000 feet.

    b. If there is poison gas or carbon monoxide in the plane.

    c. If the airplane commander prescribes breathing 100% oxygen all the
       way up to high altitude as a protection against the bends.

To operate the emergency valve turn the red knob on the intake side of the
regulator in the direction indicated on the regulator face. Caution: Never
pinch the mask hose or block the oxygen flow when the emergency valve is
turned to ON. This action breaks the regulator diaphram.

Turning the emergency valve to ON causes the oxygen flow to by-pass the demand
mechanism and to flow continuously into the mask. It is extremely wasteful of
oxygen. Leaving the valve ON, bleeds the entire oxygen supply to the station
in a short time. Never turn the emergency valve to ON, except:

    a. To revive a crew member.

    b. In cases of excessive mask leakage.

    c. Just before momentary emergency removal of your mask at high altitudes,
       as in vomiting. In such a case unhook one side of the mask and hold
       it as close to your face as possible.

Make the following checks before each flight: First, check the tightness of
the knurled collar. It should be so tight that movement of the regulator hose

will not turn the elbow. Second, open the emergency valve slightly and
see that there is a flow of oxygen. Be sure to close it tight again.

## 4. Flow Indicator.

The flow indicator on the oxygen panel winks open and shut as the oxygen
flows. The blinker may not operate normally at ground level with the
Auto-Mix lever at ON, as the blinker operation depends on the flow of
oxygen. Therefore, before the flight, plug in your mask, turn the Auto-
Mix lever to OFF and see that the blinker works as you breathe. Be sure
to move the lever back to ON before flight. Note: The blinker does not
work when the emergency valve is ON.

Watch your flow indicator during flight. It is the only indication you
have that the oxygen is flowing regularly. If it fails completely, use
your portable equipment, notify the pilot, and plug in at another station
if possible.

## 5. Pressure Gage.

Before flight, check the pressure gauge on your panel. When the system
on your plane is full the pressure should be between 400 and 425 pounds per
square inch. Also check your gauge against the gauges at other stations.
There may be some variation between stations because of different tolerances
in the gauges, but if yours varies more than 50 pounds per square inch from
the others, report it to the airplane commander.

The regulator does not work properly when the pressure is below 50 pounds per
square inch. If you need oxygen at this pressure, use your portable equipment
until you can descend.

## 6. Walk-Around Equipment.

Two types of walk-around assemblies are furnished on the airplane. One large
yellow type D-2 cylinder is provided for each of the following crew positions:
pilot, copilot, engineer, navigator, upper and right gunners and radar operator.
The remainder of the crew positions have the smaller green type A-4 cylinders.
Both types of assemblies are equipped with gauges and regulators. The regulators furnish 100% oxygen on demand.

Before each flight, check to see that your walk-around bottle is within easy
reach. Look at the gauge, and if the pressure is 50 pounds per square inch
or more under the pressure of the airplane system, recharge the bottle. There
is a recharging hose at each station. Snap the hose fitting on the nipple of
the regulator. Push it home until it clicks and locks. When the bottle has
filled to the pressure of the plane system, turn the hose clamp clockwise and
remove hose fitting. Suck on the outlet of the bottle to see that it gives
an easy flow of oxygen. You can also carry out this recharging operation while
your mask is plugged into the bottle you are filling.

When the cabin is non-pressurized, always use a walk-around bottle if you
disconnect from the airplane system. Hold your breath while you are switching

to the bottle. Clip the A-4 bottle to your jacket, and carry the D-2 bottle in the sling provided for it. The duration of the walk-around oxygen supply is variable. Don't depend on it to last very long, regardless of what you have heard about the capacity. Keep watching the gage, and recharge the bottle when it needs it. Always recharge walk-around equipment after use.

7. Bailout Cylinders.

The bailout cylinder is a small high-pressure oxygen cylinder with gauge attached, which furnishes a continuous flow of oxygen. The cylinder comes in a heavy canvas pocket provided with tying straps. Have this pocket sewed and tied securely to the harness of your parachute. Before flight, check to see that the pressure of the cylinder is at 1800 pounds per square inch. Plug the bayonet connection on the hose into the adapter on your mask.

If you have to bail out at altitude, connect your mask to a walk-around bottle, and make your way to the proper exit. Just before jumping, open the valve on the bailout cylinder and disconnect your mask from the walk-around bottle. For further information on bailout at high altitude see section F on Parachutes in this chapter.

## B. COLD WEATHER CLOTHING

Since emergencies or climatic conditions on some missions may require the use of more protective clothing, the subject of cold weather clothing will be covered. To date, because extreme cold temperatures have not been encountered and heat from compression has kept the cabin fairly warm, electrically heated flying suits and heavy winter clothing have not been worn. Also, later model B-29's have been equipped with heat exchangers which assist in defrosting and heat cabin air from exhaust shroud heat, thus keeping most crew positions in the airplane fairly warm. Some crew positions, such as the tail gunner's and radar operators, are not materially helped by the heating system; consequently these crew members should wear heavier clothing, particularly winter flying boots.

Protection against cold is a vital problem in high altitude flying. At times frostbite has caused more casualties than combat. Most cases of frostbite occur because flyers don't appreciate the seriousness of the problem or because they misuse the equipment furnished for their protection.

One of the difficulties is that many crew members don't know what frostbite actually is, until they experience it. The name is deceiving. It doesn't sound particularly dangerous, and to many men frostbite means the nonserious numbness which you often feel on face or hands in moderately cold weather. Actually, frostbite involves the complete freezing of body tissue. Depending on the degree of cold and time exposed, the results of frostbite range from serious incapacitating sores to death. Loss of fingers and toes is frequent in high altitude crews who are careless about their clothing.

Adequate heating of all the stations on airplanes is impractical. Therefore, your clothing is your main protection against frostbite. And the clothing provided really protects you, if you exercise care in the use of it. Your basic cold weather flying suit is the electrically heated suit. When this suit is insufficient, add the intermediate flying suit over the electric apparel. Remember to wear extra gloves also when you add extra clothing.

Follow these precautions concerning the use of cold weather clothing:

a. Keep Your Clothing Dry.

Moisture freezes and greatly reduces the effectiveness of all clothing as protection against the cold. Before a mission, dry your skin with a towel and then dress slowly. Don't dress so early that you have to stand around for some time with heavy clothing on. The resulting prespiration will soak into the suit and freeze later. If it's raining, wear to the plane a raincoat and galoshes over your flying equipment and let the ground crewmen take them back. Caution: When using the electric suit keep the rheostat at the lowest comfortable heat. Don't climb hot. It will mean perspiration and freezing at higher altitudes.

b. Wear Proper Underclothing.

Under the type F-2 electrically heated suit wear woolen underwear with long sleeves and legs, and a woolen shirt. When you get the F-3 electrically heated suit wear it over normal GI clothing for the theatre in which you are operating. Wear the intermediate flying suit over the F-3. With either electrical suit wear wool socks, electrically heated felt liners over them, and then your flying boots.

c. Wear Your Gloves.

Always wear rayon gloves under your electrically heated gloves, and never remove your gloves in low temperatures if you can help it. With your gloves on practice all operations which you may be required to do in flight, so that you won't have to expose your hands.

d. Keep Your Clothing Clean.

Keep your clothing clean, particularly your underwear. Soiled clothes lose their insulating qualities. And here's a tip: Wash your own clothes rather than hire a native washwomen. She'll mangle them, literally! Have all holes in your clothing sewed up immediately. Even a small rip can admit enough cold air to be dangerous.

e. Don't Wear Tight Clothing.

Constriction of circulation hastens frostbite. During flight be sure to ease the restriction of tight sweat belts or parachute harness often enough so that circulation of blood is not cut off.

f. __Wear Your Goggles.__

Wear your goggles at all times during the mission. They are excellent protection against cold, flash burns, and solid fragments.

## C. LIFE PRESERVER VEST

WEAR YOUR VEST AT ALL TIMES ON FLIGHTS OVER WATER.

When the vest is first issued to you, put it on and inflate it by mouth valves to adjust the fit of the straps. Don't waste a carbon dioxide cartridge to do this. With the vest inflated the waist strap should be fairly tight and the crotch strap snug. Deflate by opening the mouth valves and rolling up the vest. Keep the ends of the mouth valves bent down, or cut them off flush with the retaining loop, so they won't poke you in the eyes when the vest is inflated. Wear the collar of your jacket over the collar of the life vest. Wear the life vest under your parachute harness. Keep the $CO_2$ ripcords looped up over the inflators so that they will not catch on something and accidentally inflate your vest during flight.

Before each flight inspect both carbon dioxide ($CO_2$) inflators. Always check the mouth inflator valves to see that they are closed. If the valves are even partly open the $CO_2$ goes right on through and out when you pull the cords for emergency inflation. Life vests must be inspected every six months. Check the date stenciled on the vest and see that your vest is turned in for inspection at the proper time.

Whenever you are wearing the life vest, tie your parachute first aid packet to the vest strap, not to your parachute harness. When you bail out into the water you lose the chute and you might need the packet.

There is a sea marker tab on each life vest. When rescue planes approach, release the dye by pulling down on the tab. Stir the chemical around to color as large an area of the water as possible.

## D. FLAK SUITS AND HELMETS

Flak suits consist of an armored vest and apron assembly. They are not personal issue, and should be delivered to the plane before the flight and picked up afterward for inspection. You couldn't carry one anyway, with everything else you're lugging. Report to the pilot if you don't find a flak suit in the plane for you. Wear the suit when you approach the target area. It's heavy but it's guaranteed that you won't notice the weight when the fight begins to get hot.

The flak helmet is personal issue. If you have worn both your flak suit and flak helmet on the mission, you have a good chance of returning the helmet to the supply room personally after the flight.

### K. FIRST AID KITS

#### 1. Aeronautical First-Aid Kits.

Five aeronautical First-Aid Kits are carried in the airplane in the following locations:

    a.  Above the flight engineer.

    b.  On the door of the navigator's cabinet.

    c.  On the seat pedestal of the upper gun sighting station.

    d.  On the rear compartment auxiliary panel, forward of the bunk area.

    e.  In the tail gunner's compartment.

Each Aeronautical First-Aid Kit contains:

        Iodine swabs
        Adhesive gauze bandages
        Halazone tablets
        Burn-injury set
        Morphine syrettes
        Sulfa tablets
        Sulfa powder
        Small Carlisle first-aid dressings
        Scissors
        Tourniquet

#### 2. Arctic First-Aid Kit.

The Arctic First-Aid Kit is located in the rear pressurized cabin and contains:

        Halazone tablets
        Absorbent cotton
        Burn ointment
        Burn-injury sets
        Iodine swabs
        Ammoniated mercury ointment
        Morphine syrettes
        Salt tablets
        Sulfa tablets
        Sulfa powder
        Adhesive gauze bandages
        Compress gauze bandages
        Aspirin tablets
        Aloin compound tablets
        Sodium bicarbonate and peppermint tablets
        Bismuth subcarbonate tablets
        Protein silver tablets
        Multivitamin capsules
        Sulfaguanidine

3.  Jungle First-Aid Kit.

The Jungle First-Aid Kit is located with the Arctic First-Aid Kit in the rear pressurized cabin, and contains:

> Halazone tablets
> Insect repellent
> Suction kit for snake bite
> Iodine swabs
> Morphine syrettes
> Salt tablets
> Sulfa tablets
> Adhesive gauze bandages
> Aspirin tablets
> Aloin compound tablets
> Atabrine tablets
> Sodium bicarbonate and peppermint tablets
> Sulfaguanidine

4.  Battle Splint and Dressing Kit.

Two Battle Splint and Dressing Kits are carried. One is located behind the copilot's seat and the other in the rear pressurized cabin. Each Kit, Battle Splint and Dressing, contains:

> Gauze bandages
> Small Carlisle first-aid dressings
> Large Carlisle first-aid dressings
> Serum albumin units for treatment of shock
> Basswood splints
> Adhesive tape
> Safety pins

5.  Blood Plasma Kit.

Two Blood Plasma Kits are carried. One is located on the ceiling above the flight engineer's head, and the other in the rear pressurized cabin. Each Blood Plasma Kit contains two complete sets of apparatus for the administration of plasma or serum albumin, concentrated from plasma.

6.  Parachute First-Aid Packet.

One Parachute First-Aid Packet is issued to each man. Tie the packet to the strap of the life vest when wearing the vest. If you are not going to use the life vest, tie the packet to the shoulder strap of the parachute harness, well down on the lower part of the strap. The Parachute First-Aid Packet contains:

> Tourniquet                          Morphine syrette
> Small Carlisle first-aid dressing   Sulfa tablets
> Sulfa powder

7.  Life Raft First-Aid Kit.

A Life Raft First-Aid Kit is included in the accessory kit of each life
raft.  This kit contains:

        Morphine syrettes
        Iodine
        Burn ointment
        Compress bandage
        Sulfa powder
        Sulfa tablets

8.  Parachute First-Aid Kit, Frying Pan Insert.

A Parachute First-Aid Kit, Frying Pan Insert, contains:

        Atabrine tablets
        Benzedrine sulfate tablets
        Halazone tablets
        Burn-injury set
        Iodine swabs
        Salt tablets
        Sulfa tablets
        Adhesive gauze bandages
        Compress gauze bandages
        Curved needle, with 120 inches carpet and button thread
            (for clothing repair)
        Cake soap
        Compressed tea tablets

## F.  PARACHUTES

All crew members are required to wear their parachutes at all times during
flight.  Have your parachute harness correctly fitted and tacked by a
competent parachute maintenance man.  Check the harness fit each time you
put it on.  Shoulder and chest straps should be snug and without play.  The
chest buckle should be 12 inches below the chin, and the leg straps snug.
In fact, the harness should be comfortably tight when you stand up.

Pre-Flight Check.  Inspect your parachute carefully before each flight.
You never know when you may have to use it.  Check the date of the last
inspection.  The packing interval should not exceed 30 days in this climate.
See that an inspection check has been made within the last ten days and
entered on the AAF Form 46 in the chute.  See that the opening elastics
are tight and that the corners of the pack are neatly stowed with no silk
visible.  Check the pack cover for oil, grease, dirt, and worn spots.  If
you find any, turn the chute in.  Good care of your chute will pay dividends
if you ever have to use it.

## G.  DITCHING EQUIPMENT

## 1. Life Rafts.

There are two 5-man life rafts carried in the airplane, in the left and right raft compartments atop the fuselage. After ditching the radio operator pulls both raft releases, located on either side of the tunnel opening in the forward pressurized compartment. Pulling the handles automatically releases the rafts from the compartments and inflates them. If the internal mechanism je s you can open the compartment by external release levers located on top of the fuselage next to the compartment doors. A third raft is carried inside the fuselage, and will be thrown out of the rear hatch by crew members and inflated by pulling a ripcord on the $CO_2$ cylinders.

Don't jump from the plane into the rafts - you'll go right through. If a raft inflates inverted don't jump on it to right it. You'll only push out the air underneath and make it harder to turn the raft over. It may be possible for two or more men to right the raft from the wing. This may also be done by getting into the water, climbing up on one side of the raft and pulling on the handline attached to the opposite side of the raft. Remember, however, that it is better to keep dry, if possible, especially in cold weather.

Fend the rafts off the wings of the plane while launching and boarding them. Wing flaps are usually torn loose in ditching and jagged edges of flaps or wings can easily puncture rafts. When all men are aboard, tie the rafts together to keep them from drifting apart.

## 2. Raft Accessory Kits.

An accessory kit is furnished with each raft. Kits are normally secured inside the raft case. Stowage difficulties make it necessary to keep the kits inside the fuselage, separate from the rafts. In that case, certain crew members must be designated to take the raft kits along when leaving the plane. This step must be included in ditching drill.

Keep the separate items of equipment securely in the kit or tie them to the handline of the raft so they won't be lost if the raft capsizes. It is important to keep signaling equipment accessible, because the opportunity to use this equipment is sudden and short. The Accessory Kit contains:

| | |
|---|---|
| Oars | Puncture plugs |
| Sea anchor | Signal mirror |
| Sail | Flashlight |
| Rations | Fishing tackle |
| Bailing bucket | Jacknife |
| Shade and camouflage cloth | Whistle |
| Drinking water | Sea marker |
| Line | Repair patch kit |
| First - aid kit | Wrist compass |
| Inflating pump | Signal kit |

## 3. Emergency Radio.

Set the emergency radio set into operation as soon as weather permits. The kit is contained in two cases, strapped together, which are brought out of the plane after the ditching by a designated crew member.

Complete instructions for operating the radio are included in the kit. When you use the radio, try to keep the antenna out of the water, or your signals won't be heard. If possible, be sure to send during the three minute international silent periods, at 15 and 45 minutes past the hour.

4. Signals.

Twelve drift signals are stowed under the navigator's table and the drift signal chute is in the door just behind the navigator. Take the signals with you.

5. Hand Axe.

One hand axe is secured on the navigator's control stand next to the fire extinguisher and another on the aft compartment auxiliary panel. These axes may be useful in breaking out of the plane after ditching or crash landing.

EMERGENCY
PROCEDURES

## XII.  E M E R G E N C Y   P R O C E D U R E S

### A.  BAILOUT

In any bailout it is the airplane commander who decides whether or not a bailout is necessary.  First, he will give a series of short rings on the alarm bell, and then order "prepare to abandon ship" as early as possible so you will have time to prepare.  The warning will be given when an emergency first appears.  If it develops that the pilot can handle the emergency safely without bailout, the preparation order will be cancelled later.

The pilot will give the actual bailout order by interphone and a steady ring on the warning bell.  Do not leave the plane until you are ordered out!  Each crew member must know when, where, and how he is to leave the airplane.  The only way to assure that abandonment will be carried out safely and properly is to go through often repeated bailout drills on the ground.  Every step of an actual bailout must be practiced in dry-runs.  Don't forget to include simulating the destruction of designated instruments by specific crew members.

### 1.  Emergency Exits During Flight.

Crew members in the forward compartment can bail out through the nose wheel well when the landing gear is down or out of the forward bomb bay.  Those in the rear compartment may drop out of the aft bomb bay or the rear entrance door. The tail gunner can bail out the window at his side or the rear entrance door. The following diagram shows the exit sequence and the escape hatch used by each man.  Learn your part and practice the coordinated procedure with the whole crew

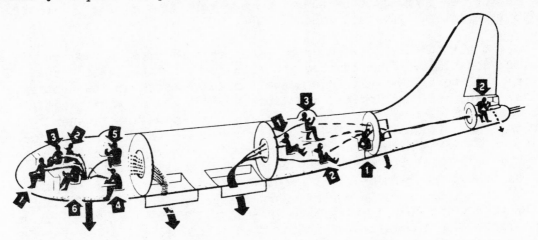

### 2.  High Altitude Jumps.

In most cases when you bailout, your first concern after you re away from the plane is to get the chute open.  There is a time, however, when to delay opening your chute for a while has definite advantages.  That time is when you bail out somewhere between 40,000 and 10,000 feet.  By using this free fall maneuver you can minimize the hazards of:  (1) Intense cold, (2) lack of oxygen, (3) enemy gunfire, and (4) excessive opening shock.

The accompanying chart shows you the length of time it takes you to get down to the relative safety of 10,000 feet in a parachute, as compared to the time it takes by free fall.

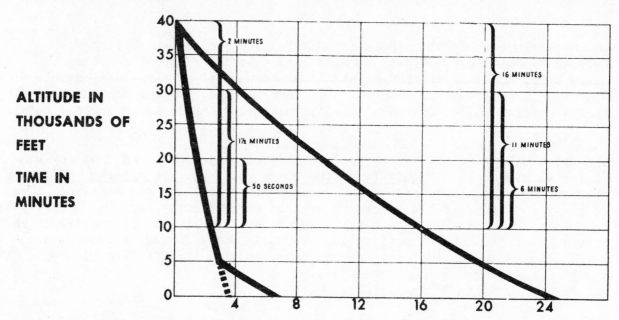

**ALTITUDE IN THOUSANDS OF FEET**

**TIME IN MINUTES**

Remembering that frostbite can occur in a matter of seconds at high altitude, you can see that it is a good idea not to dawdle through that danger area in an open parachute, but to get to lower altitude quickly by falling free. The same advice applies with respect to lack of oxygen. Even if you are using a bailout oxygen bottle, it is possible to exhaust the supply of oxygen in the bottle before you reach an altitude where you are safe from anoxia. Use the oxygen bailout equipment, but fall free also.

In a high altitude bailout you reach your maximum speed a few seconds after leaving the plane. From then on you slow down, as the chart shows. Therefore, a free fall to a lower altitude means a reduced shock at the opening of the chute. Your next and logical question is, "How do you know exactly when to pull the ripcord?" There is no good, practical, one-two-three answer to that question. However, here is some honest and realistic advice which you may find of some help. A workable method for judging when to open the chute in a high altitude jump is to look at the earth and judge your approximate altitude by the appearance of the ground. For example, at around 5,000 feet recognizable details of the earth appear, the horizon spreads, and the ground seems to be rushing up at you. After that point do not delay long in pulling the ripcord. You haven't much time left. One limitation of this method is difficulty in seeing the ground because of weather conditions. Clouds at high altitudes are usually broken masses. If you can not see the ground but notice that broken clouds become a solid layer below you, wait until just before you enter the solid cloud formation and then pull the ripcord. These unbroken undercasts do not extend up to great altitudes, and when you enter one you are usually low enough to open your chute safely. Note: This procedure applies to bailout at high altitudes into clouds. Use judgement in following it. For example, if you bail out in clear atmosphere, and far below you can see a low undercast, pull the ripcord before you get into the undercast.

There are times when the above procedure is inapplicable. For example, on a dark night visual references are useless. Or, you may be unable to fix your vision on ground reference points because your body is spinning. In such circumstances, if you have no other guide for estimating the proper time to pull the ripcord, depend upon your sense of the passage of time. Judgement of time is difficult, and counting seconds is unreliable for most people, but an attempt to judge when sufficient time has elapsed is better than nothing.

In any case, before you leave the airplane find out the altitude at which you are flying; look outside to see what weather conditions exist; and then decide quickly what procedure you are going to follow, and follow it. Study the free fall chart until you know approximately how long it takes to fall free to safe levels from various altitudes.

It is unlikely that you will ever have to make a high altitude jump. But if you do, use your head, try to keep cool and the odds for a safe descent will be in your favor.

## B. CRASH LANDINGS

The airplane commander decides whether a crash landing at base or a bailout is preferable. Sometimes the circumstances of the emergency dictate the procedure to be followed.

The pilot will make the decision to crash land early enough to give the crew time for adequate preparation. The pilot should notify the crew to start preparation by appropriate alarm signal and by ordering "Prepare for crash landing" over the interphone. Successful crash landings, like successful ditchings, depend on the crew's familiarity with the proper procedures. Frequent dry-run drills are essential.

The general procedure for crash landings is similar to that for ditching. However, crash landing positions in the gunner's and radar compartment are considered safe since deceleration isn't so rapid as in ditchings and since such hazards as the surge of water through the pressurized doors, if they collapse, and through the nose, if it caves in, don't exist. In the ditching procedure, positions in these compartments have been eliminated. The following outline and Figure 5 cover the positions to be assumed in crash landings.

1. **Crash Landing Positions.**

    Pilot                  Normal position.

    Co-pilot            Normal position.

| | |
|---|---|
| Flight Engineer | Normal position. |
| Radio Operator | Normal ditching position in seat. |
| Navigator | a. Two gun forward turret. Normal position in navigator's seat, with safety belt fastened. Slides seat full forward. Faces forward with legs braced. Rest head on arms on table with pad protecting head. |
| | b. Four gun forward turret. Folds table top up and moves navigator's seat to rear. Assumes sitting position on floor with back well cushioned and braced against panel under navigator's table. Hands are clasped tightly behind head, knees flexed. |
| Bombardier | At flight engineer's side in normal ditching position facing aft with back against bulkhead. |
| Top Gunner | Assumes sitting position on floor in gunner's compartment with back cushioned and braced against front bulkhead. |
| Left Gunner | Remains in normal flight position. |
| Right Gunner | Remains in normal flight position. |
| Radar Operator | Assumes sitting position in radar compartment on floor with back against armor plate bulkhead on right side of entrance. Before taking position he opens the rear door of the pressurized compartment and fastens it securely to prevent it from closing and jamming shut. |
| Tail Gunner | Can remain in normal flight position or proceed to the rear unpressurized compartment, assuming a sitting position on the floor with his back against the rear pressurized bulkhead, hands and cushion behind his head. |
| Extra Passenger | Seated next to radio operator, back and head against upper gun turret, padded with parachute, legs braced against pressure bulkhead with knees flexed. |

Don't relax your braced position until the airplane has come to a complete rest.

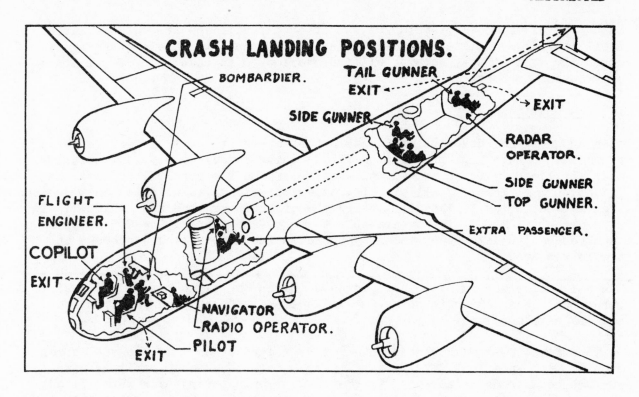

CRASH LANDING POSITIONS.

C.  DITCHING

Ditching is the forced descent of land planes on water.  It is extremely
hazardous but the experience of many bomber crews has proved that it can be
done successfully.  The crew has two main problems in ditching.  One is
adequately bracing against the terrific impact of the water landing.  The
other is getting out of the airplane with the equipment they must take along
before the plane sinks.  The length of time a bomber will float is measured
in seconds, not minutes.

The ditching will come off successfully only if you are so thoroughly drilled
in the proper procedures that your reaction is automatic.  If proper ditching
procedure is followed, a minimum of confusion results and nothing is omitted
which might contribute to the safety of the whole crew.  Successful ditching
depends on constantly repeated drills.  As often as time permits, the whole
crew must practice together the coordinated steps in the ditching procedure.
Wet ditching drill involving the actual launching and boarding of life rafts

in a body of water is preferable, but if such facilities are not available, drill in your own plane under simulated conditions. Learn also what every other man does so that nothing will be overlooked in case some crew members are missing or hurt.

1. Preparation.

When an emergency develops over water which makes it doubtful that you will r ich land, start your preparation for ditching immediately. Particularly start preliminary radio procedure. Don't wait on the possibility that the situation may improve. All ditching experience to date indicates that radio signals sent prior to the ditching of the aircraft are the most valuable aid to searchers. Note: If you are able to make land, cancel the SOS later so that you won't waste the time and jeopardize the safety of other crews in needless search.

The value of power in ditching is great. Ditch the plane before the fuel is exhausted. Keep a margin of speed available so you can pick your spot to set the airplane down.

On your first few flights over water study the appearance of the sea in relation to wind speed and direction. Try to become thoroughly familiar with surface conditions as an index to the wind. During every over-water flight keep wind direction, wind speed, and the condition of the sea constantly in mind so that you will be prepared if ditching becomes necessary.

a. Waves move downwind, except close in-shore. Waves break downwind, but remember that the foam from the wave crest appears to slide down the back, or windward, side of the breaking wave. This often makes the direction of the break difficult to judge from altitude.

b. Spray from wave crests is blown downwind.

c. Swell is a rising and falling of the sea surface. It does not indicate wind direction.

d. Smoke from surface vessels drifts with the wind. The trail of the smoke, however, is caused by wind plus the ship's forward motion. In this case wind direction is somewhere between the forward path of the ship and the smoke trail.

e. Wind lanes are alternating strips of light and shade which appear on the surface of the sea. They lie parallel to the direction of the wind, but in a steady wind it is difficult to tell from which direction the wind is blowing down the lane.

f. Wind Speed.

A few white crests . . . . . . . . . . . . . . . . . . . . 10 - 20 mph wind
Many white crests . . . . . . . . . . . . . . . . . . . . 20 - 30 mph wind
Streaks of foam along water . . . . . . . . . . . . . . . 30 - 40 mph wind
Spray from crests . . . . . . . . . . . . . . . . . . . . 40 - 50 mph wind

Wind speed can be judged fairly well by the roughness of the sea. However, the wind will be stronger than the appearance of the sea suggests if it is freshening, blowing off a nearby shore, running with the tide or swell and during heavy rain. Breaking waves may be due to shallow water and such circumstances should not be used in calculating wind speed and direction. Strength of the wind can be estimated from the conditions of the sea fairly accurately through use of the above table.

## 2. Handling of the Airplane in Ditching.

The following three points should be kept in mind on the ditching of land-planes:

   a.  The approach path should be as flat as possible.
   b.  The forward speed should be as low as possible.
   c.  The rate of descent should not exceed 200 feet per minute.

It is necessary to remember that landplanes cannot be put down on water with the intention of planing along the surface like a seaplane. The fuselage of landplanes is not strong enough for this.

Although there has been some dispute over the use of flaps in ditching, it is now agreed that flaps can be used to advantage. Flaps should be lowered to reduce the speed at which the plane can approach and touch down. The stall speed difference between flaps up and full flaps down is over twenty miles an hour and it is not probable that safer contact could be made at the higher speed. With full flaps the maximum lift is obtainable with the fuselage at approximately 8° to the water which is a 12° angle of attack of the wing. This allows the fuselage to touch first in the region of the rear turret with the propellers still clear of the water. The flaps will touch at approximately the same time, but will break immediately and have no effect upon the airplan's actions. The amount of flap used will be in proportion to amount of power available to obtain a minimum safe rate of descent with a minimum safe forward speed.

The landing gear should be kept in the retracted position during a landing at sea. If down, the landing gear will act as a terrific drag as it contacts the water first and may flip the plane over or cause heavy damage.

Assuming that symmetrical power is not available, the normal glide approach speed should be used. This will insure control and some margin of speed after flattening out and permit the pilot to choose the best spot for ditching. The pilot should hold off until he loses all excess speed above a stall.

If the sea is calm and there is little wind, the plane should be put down along the top of a swell. With wind of any strength, however, the plane should be landed upwind near the top of an oncoming wave or swell. It is always desirable to land along the top of a swell but when such landing will mean a strong cross wind, it should be rejected in favor of an upwind landing. If because of wind, the ditching is made across the swell, the plane should be put down on an upslope towards the top. There will be situations when the pilot must choose a compromise landing. And there will be situations, of course, where the pilot will have no choice in this matter because of damaged controls or other reasons. Although in some cases a downwind landing cannot be avoided, it is always dangerous.

Use of power in ditching.

a. If the power is symmetrical, such as, if the two inner motors are operating, both engines can be used to the full if necessary to flatten the approach, reduce speed and retain control.

b. If the power is not symmetrical, for instance with number two and four out, it will be possible to use some power adjusting the throttles so that little rudder is needed.

c. The value of power in a descent at sea is so great that when it is certain that land cannot be reached, the pilot should always try to bring his plane down before the fuel is entirely exhausted.

It is advisable to hold the tail down slightly so that the nose will not come down into the water with enough force to cave in the bombardier's compartment. If the airplane alights tail down, there will be a jolt as the tail strikes, followed by a severe impact and violent deceleration. If you come in too fast on a calm sea, there will be a tendency to bounce; hold the control column back hard. In a sea with average size waves, the tail will touch the crest of the wave first. Keep the nose up so the forward part of the airplane will touch the next wave crest approximately under the center of gravity.

3. Crew Procedure.

This is a recommended crew procedure which has been worked out after a study of narratives covering ditching of B-29's in our operations and discussions with personnel involved in ditchings and crash landings. From these experiences it has been decided to eliminate ditching positions in the gunner's and radar compartments. The following procedure and ditching positions have therefore, been established.

a. Pilot.

(1) Give co-pilot warning, "PREPARE FOR DITCHING IN _____ MINUTES." Give several short rings on alarm bell. Turn IFF Emergency Switch "ON". Remove parachute harness, flak suit, winter flying boots and helmet. Fasten safety belt. Wear flying gloves.

(2) Radio accompanying aircraft of your distress, then turn to interphone.

(3) Give co-pilot order, "OPEN EMERGENCY EXITS AND THROW OUT EQUIPMENT." If possible give this order above 5,000 feet.

(4) Give co-pilot order (above 2,000 feet if possible), "STATIONS FOR DITCHING, IMPACT IN ____ SECONDS." (Use flap setting in proportion to the amount of power available to obtain a minimum safe rate of descent with a minimum safe forward speed.) Open windows, brace feet on rudder pedals, with knees flexed. About 5 seconds before impact, give co-pilot order, "BRACE FOR IMPACT." The aircraft should touch the sea in normal landing attitude (about 5 degrees).

(5) Check to see that crew is clear of forward compartment, then exit through left window. If plane is not afire, inflate life vest when on window ledge. Climb atop cabin thence to left wing. Secure life raft; release life raft from outside if necessary.

b. Co-pilot.

(1) Relay pilot's command over interphone call position, "PREPARE FOR DITCHING IN ____ MINUTES." Receive acknowledgements. Tell the pilot, "CREW NOTIFIED".

(2) Remove parachute harness, flak suit, winter flying boots and helmet. Fasten safety belt. Wear flying gloves.

(3) Stand by on interphone to relay pilot's orders.

(4) Relay orders, "OPEN EMERGENCY EXITS AND THROW OUT EQUIPMENT." Then check on crew's progress.

(5) Relay order, "STATIONS FOR DITCHING, IMPACT IN ____ SECONDS." Open side window, brace feet on rudder bar with knees flexed. Thirty seconds before impact, order radio operator to abandon his key and take station. When pilot gives order, "BRACE FOR IMPACT," send long ring on alarm bell.

(6) Take aeronautical first aid kit stored above engineer's seat and exit through right window. Inflate life vest on window ledge. Climb atop cabin, thence to right wing. Secure right life raft or pull outside life raft release handle if necessary.

c. Flight Engineer.

(1) Acknowledge in turn, "FLIGHT ENGINEER DITCHING".

(2) Remove parachute harness, flak suit and winter flying boots. Wear flying gloves, keep flak helmet on.

(3) Open emergency hatch and acknowledge to co-pilot, "FRONT HATCH OPEN". Jettison it together with any other loose equipment through front bomb bay.

(4) Take regular position facing aft, head and shoulders braced against co-pilot's armor plate, safety belt fastened and hands braced against control stand.

(5) Take raft accessory kit from shelf behind pilot's seat, then exit through same escape hatch that you opened.

(6) If airplane is not afire, inflate life vest on window ledge. Climb atop cabin and proceed to right wing.

(7) Assist bombardier and co-pilot in securing life rafts.

d. Bombardier.

(1) Acknowledge in turn, "BOMBARDIER DITCHING".

(2) Remove parachute harness, winter flying boots and flak suit. Wear flying gloves, keep flak helmet on.

(3) Destroy bombsight and bombing data. Jettison the bombsight so it will not break through the front glass.

(4) Open bomb bay doors. Jettison bombs, ascertain that other crew members have finished jettisoning all loose equipment and then close and check bomb bay doors. Assist in jettisoning all loose equipment in forward compartment. Shoot out ammunition from lower front turrets.

(5) Get emergency signal kit from under navigator's desk.

(6) Fasten safety belt.

(7) Take sitting position beside engineer, back braced against co-pilot's armor plate, cushion behind head, feet braced with knees flexed.

(8) Take emergency signal kit and follow engineer through escape hatch. Proceed to right life raft.

Note - Clips and cases must be removed from upper forward turret well to prevent cover tearing loose on impact. Do not give all ammunition unless there is sufficient time to jettison clips and cases.

e. Navigator.

(1) Acknowledge in turn, "NAVIGATOR DITCHING".

(2) Remove parachute harness, winter flying boots and flak suit. Wear flying gloves, and keep helmet on.

(3) Calculate position, course, altitude and ground speed for radio operator to transmit.

(4) Give pilot surface wind, strength and direction.

(5) Gather essential maps and navigation equipment into waterproof bag or tuck inside clothing. Jettison navigator's chair if possible.

(6) Pass fire axe from engineer's panel to top gunner.

(7) Jettison all drift signal flares through release tube. Assist in jettisoning all loose equipment from front compartment, including tunnel ladder, then close pressure door to bomb bay.

(8) Place in pockets or shirt front two of smoke grenades kept in cases beside radio operator's desk on the aft side of forward gun turret.

(9) Move seat, if not jettisoned, as far aft as possible, fold up table, and take seat on floor facing aft, back padded carefully with parachute and other articles so it is completely supported.

(10) Exit through astrodome.

(11) If airplane is not afire, inflate life vest. Proceed to right wing with navigation equipment.

f. Extra Passenger.

(1) Acknowledge last, "OBSERVER DITCHING".

(2) Aid in jettisoning equipment. Wear flying gloves.

(3) Proceed to rear of forward compartment and assume ditching position in tunnel, lying on back, feet forward. Brace feet against the upper turret with a slight flexure in the knees; brace hands and arms against the walls of the tunnel so that the head will not be thrown around. (If more convenient, trade places with the top gunner--if possible, use the taller man in the tunnel.)

(4) Exit through astrodome to left wing.

g. Radio Operator.

(1) Acknowledge in turn, "RADIO OPERATOR DITCHING".

(2) Remove parachute harness, flak suit and winter flying boots. Wear flying gloves if possible, keep flak helmet on.

(3) Destroy classified material; check IFF setting.

(4) Continue to send emergency signals. On command of the co-pilot, clamp down transmitter key.

(5) Lower the trailing antenna full length, watch current meter and notify pilot of height above water when it grounds. (100-110 feet).

(6) Pocket remaining two smoke grenades or put in shirt front. Keep grenades in cases.

(7) Remain in position with safety belt fastened, facing aft, with back, shoulders, and head pressing against upper turret well as close to center as possible, cushioning back and head with parachute, bracing legs against bulkhead.

(8) After forward movement of aircraft has ceased, pull both life raft release handles.

(9) Exit through astrodome to right life raft.

h.  Top Gunner.

(1) Acknowledge in turn, "TOP GUNNER DITCHING".

(2) Remove parachute harness, flak suit and winter flying boots. Wear flying gloves, wear flak helmet.

(3) Shoot out ammunition from rear upper turret. Check with other gunners to be sure all ammunition has been shot away.

(4) If time allows, crawl through tunnel to forward pressurized compartment.

(5) Take fire axe and chop out astrodome and all interfering projections. Aid in the jettisoning of equipment in the forward compartment.

(6) Assume ditching position on lower turret dome back and head braced against the upper turret, padded with parachute, and legs braced against the pressure bulkhead with knees flexed.

(7) Exit through astordome to left wing. If time does not permit, go to the rear unpressurized section. Take position against rear pressure bulkhead.

(8) Aid with throwing out in the following order, Gibson Girl, life raft, and sustenance kits in unpressurized section.

(9) Exit through rear escape hatch. Go to left wing.

Note - Do not jerk leather throng to remove sealing strip, use a steady pull.

i. Right Waist Gunner.

(1) Acknowledge in turn, "RIGHT GUNNER DITCHING".

(2) Remove parachute harness, flak suit and winter flying boots. Wear flying gloves, keep flak helmet on.

(3) Shoot out all ammunition in rear lower turret.

(4) Help jettison all loose equipment.

(5) Proceed to the rear unpressurized compartment. Open and jettison the rear exit hatch. If conditions warrant, stand watch at rear exit hatch and inform crew in unpressurized compartment to brace for ditching.

(6) Take sitting position between radar operator and left gunner, knees blexed, feet braced, back padded with parachute, and none of the body supported by pressure door, which may fly open on impact. Have adequate padding on door to support the head.

(7) Aid in throwing out Gibson Girl, life raft and sustenance kits, then exit through rear escape hatch. If plane is not on fire inflate life vest. Proceed atop fuselage to left wing. Secure left raft. If necessary pull outside release handle.

j. Left Waist Gunner.

(1) Acknowledge in turn, "LEFT GUNNER DITCHING".

(2) Remove parachute harness, flak suit and winter flying boots. Wear flying gloves, keep flak helmet on.

(3) Report progress in gunner's compartment over interphone to co-pilot.

(4) Be sure pressure door to bomb bay is closed. Close door in armored bulkhead. Exit last from rear pressurized compartment into rear unpressurized compartment. Close rear pressure door.

XII - 13

(5) Jettison all unneded equipment.

(6) See that the Gibson Girl, life raft and emergency kits are stowed in the corners of the pressure bulkhead where they will serve as padding and will not fly loose on impact. Hold life raft emergency kit.

(7) Take ditching position on left of pressure bulkhead, facing aft, back padded and pressed against bulkhead, legs braced.

(8) Exit through emergency hatch, if the first out, aid in passing out the rafts, Gibson Girl, and kits, holding to the lines if possible.

(9) If aircraft is not on fire, inflate life vest, proceed to left wing.

k. Radar Operator (Optional Gunner).

(1) Acknowledge in turn, "RADAR OPERATOR DITCHING".

(2) Remove parachute harness, flak suit and winter flying boots. Wear flying gloves. Check IFF setting. Wear flak helmet.

(3) Open rear ditching hatch and acknowledge to co-pilot, "REAR HATCH OPEN". Jettison loose equipment including camera.

(4) Hold raft accessory kit stored in unpressurized compartment.

(5) Take sitting position in unpressurized compartment against rear pressure bulkhead at right (facing aft) with hands and cushions behind head, knees flexed, feet braced.

(6) Take raft accessory kit, then exit through rear emergency hatch.

(7) If airplane is not afire, inflate life vest. Proceed atop fuselage to right wing.

(8) Report progress in unpressurized compartment over interphone to co-pilot.

l. Tail Gunner.

(1) Acknowledge in turn, "TAIL GUNNER DITCHING".

(2) Remove parachute harness, flak suit, and winter flying boots. Wear flying gloves. Wear flak helmet.

(3) Shoot out ammunition in tail guns. Jettison tail gunner's escape hatch. If time allows jettison gunsight.

(4) Take aeronautical kit, from compartment, and remain in same, sit facing aft, back and head cushioned against back of seat

(5)  Exit through tail gunner's escape hatch to left horizontal stabilizer; if plane is not afire, inflate life vest, proceed to left wing.

## 4.  Escape from the Plane.

Once the plane has come to rest on the surface, the action of the crew must be quick and efficient.  At best, land planes will float but a short time.  The length of time depends on many factors such as injury to the fuselage, buoyancy of the plane, and condition of the sea.

In any event, the crew of a plane brought down at sea must act quickly. It is imperative you get out of the plane, inflate the raft and board it with the necessary equipment.  As has been seen, a fairly large deceleration force may be experienced at the time of impact.  It may be sufficient to partially stun members of the crew and to hurl loose equipment about the fuselage.  However, if the distress drill has been correctly taught and faithfully practiced, members of the crew will be able to do the correct thing almost instinctively.  The fact that a great deal of confusion may exist during the crucial few moments the plane floats makes it imperative that all crew members know their jobs and do them without confusion or doubt.

When a plane comes down into the water, there may be two impacts.  A fairly slight one can be expected as the tail first makes contact and a more violent one as the plane itself settles.  The crew should be very careful not to change positions or rise from ditching stations until the plane has come to a complete stop.  As soon as the motion of the plane stops, the escape procedure should be started.  The crew member delegated to the job should operate the life raft compartment releases. The release should not be gripped before or during the descent as the impact may cause the release to operate.  If this is done, the raft may be ejected from its compartment while the plane is still moving and thus break free and drift out of reach.

Other members of the crew, as soon as the plane comes to rest must rise from ditching stations, carefully collect such equipment as is detailed for each in drill, and leave by the hatch used in practice.  In the B-29, the third life raft and equipment sacks should be moved through the rear escape hatch and to the left wing.  There the life raft will be inflated and the auxiliary equipment will be placed in the life rafts ejected from the fuselage compartments.  Two men, the pilot and co-pilot, will assist the two life rafts from their compartments and see that they are properly inflated.  Care must be taken that there are no tangling lines which might cause the raft to burst.

Since the escape hatches are not overly large it is recommended that crew members inflate their life vests immediately on emerging from a hatch. The crew should not be surprised to find that waves are breaking over the plane. If they are large, it is possible that men may be swept off. It is recommended that a life line be attached to the inside of the hatch.

During the first phases of the distress procedure, parachutes should be kept on or near-to-hand in case descent by parachute should become necessary. However, when the altitude falls below 1,000 feet, parachutes should be removed. They should not be entirely discarded, however, since they can be used to pad projections near ditching stations and prevent possible injury. During escape from the plane, it would be well if two or three members of the crew took along their parachute packs. Parachutes can have many uses in the raft or on the water. The packs have a certain buoyancy and can be used for a short time to remain afloat. The parachute can be used to make sails, catch rain water, for shade and signalling during the stay aboard the raft.

The man designated to assist the raft from its compartment should also make sure it inflates properly and is launched right side up. If the raft inflates in an inverted position, efforts to right it should be made from the wing. If this fails or the plane is sinking rapidly, one man should jump into the water and right the raft. Crew members should not jump onto an inverted raft as this will expel air trapped beneath and make the righting more difficult.

Rafts are attached to the plane by a light rope. This rope is intentionally light so that it will break if the plane sinks while the raft is still attached. If the ditching has been made into the wind, the raft should float toward the tail and the boarding should not be difficult. If there is a cross wind after the plane comes to rest, the plane will tend to swing into the wind. If the raft is on the upwind side, there is danger that it will become wedged under the wing as the plane rolls and swings into the wind. If the raft is on the downwind side, there is danger that it will be caught beneath the fuselage or tail of the plane which may be threshing up and down. Care should be taken that jagged edges of the wing, tail or fuselage do not puncture the raft.

## D.  FIRE

The B-29 is equipped with a $CO_2$ system fed by two high pressure $CO_2$ bottles mounted in the nose wheel well.  Lines from each bottle run to all four engine nacelles.  The flight engineer can direct the $CO_2$ charge to the desired engine by turning the selector knob on his instrument panel, and pulling the $CO_2$ release handle (or both handles, if desired) for the bottle he wishes to use.

Besides the nacelle extinguisher system each airplane is equipped with three hand extinguishers, two $CO_2$ and one carbon tetrachloride, for extinguishing cabin fires.  One $CO_2$ extinguisher is located on the inboard side of the flight engineer's control stand, the other is in the aft pressurized compartment aft of the auxiliary equipment panel.  The carbon tetrachloride extinguisher is located beside the rear entrance door.

1.  Precautions In Use of Fire Fighting Equipment.

    a.  To use the carbon dioxide extinguisher, stand close to the fire, raise horn, and direct gas to the base of the fire.  Hold on to the insulated tubing to avoid frostbite from grasping the metal horn on the top of the cylinder.  The white discharge is "dry-ice".

    b.  To stop the flow of gas, replace the horn in the clip on the side of the cylinder.  Recharge the extinguisher after each use.

    c.  Stand as far as possible from the fire when using the carbon tetrachloride extinguisher.  The effective range is 20 to 30 feet.  To operate, turn the handle and pump it.  Keep the stream full and steady.  To shut off, push the handle in and turn it until the sealing plunger is depressed.

    d.  When sprayed on a fire, carbon tetrachloride produces phosgene a very poisonous gas, which can be harmful even in small amounts and may be fatal.  Do not use it in a confined area and do not stand near the fire.  Ventilate as soon as fire is extinguished.

2.  Engine Fires.

    a.  Nacelle or engine fire on the ground.  If the fire is known to be a torching turbo, put it out by increasing the throttle setting momentarily.  For other engine or nacelle fires on the ground, use the following steps:

        (1)  Move the mixture control to idle cut-off on all four engines.
        (2)  Close fuel shut-off valves for all engines.
        (3)  Turn off the booster pump switches for all engines.
        (4)  Close the throttles.
        (5)  Open the cowl flaps.
        (6)  Set nacelle fire extinguisher to the proper engines.  Pull first one, and then, if necessary, the other fire extinguisher control handle.  The flight engineer will check with the

scanners on the condition of the fire before pulling the second control handle. <u>Note</u>: The engine fire extinguisher is for fires in the accessory section and is not effective against fires in the engine itself. If the fire is still burning:

(7) Turn all ignition switches off.
(8) Turn battery switch off.
(9) Stop auxiliary power plant.
(10) Send crew members for additional ground fire fighting equipment.

3. <u>Nacelle Fire In Flight</u>.

a. A crew member spotting a fire uses the "call" position on the jackbox and says, "FIRE ON NO.___ENGINE". If possible, crew members will identify fires as to type and location. From this point, at the pilot's discretion, the following procedure should be used.

(1) Pilot feathers propeller and says to flight engineer, "USE ENGINE FIRE PROCEDURE".
(2) Flight engineer moves the mixture control for the engine afire to the IDLE CUT-OFF position, and shuts off the fuel valve and boost pump as the pilot increases the air speed in an attempt to blow out the fire.
(3) Set cowl flaps to not more than 15 degrees and close the throttle.
(4) Set nacelle fire extinguisher to the proper engine, pull first one, and then if necessary, the other fire extinguisher control handle.
(5) The flight engineer closes the cabin air valves and the radio operator closes the forward pressure door. If smoke has entered the cabin, the co-pilot opens his window. In case of excessive smoke or fire in the cabin, follow the procedure under "Cabin Fires During Flight" (Paragraph 4 below).
(6) If the fire is out of control, open the bomb bay doors, and abandon the airplane.
(7) If an engine catches fire during take-off, the pilot will if unable to put out the fire, make an emergency landing following the crash landing procedure when necessary.

4. <u>Cabin Fires During Flight</u>.

In all cabin fires during flight, immediately pull the emergency pressure relief handle if the cabin is pressurized. If the fire is in the rear compartment, use the $CO_2$ extinguisher first and then, if necessary, use the portable carbon tetrachloride extinguisher. If the fire is in the forward compartment use the $CO_2$ extinguisher mounted beside the flight engineer's control stand.

If the cabin fire is caused by an electrical short circuit, the procedure is the same except that the flight engineer must turn all electrical power off with the battery and generator switches.

If the cabin becomes excessively smoky or gaseous after using the fire extinguishers, open the bomb bay doors for ventilation. If the fire is extremely bad, and there is danger of an explosion from fuel tanks, sound a series of short rings on the alarm bell so that the crew can prepare to abandon the airplane.

## E.  AIR SEA RESCUE

Due to the extremely long overwater flights involved, Air Sea Rescue in this command has assumed tremendous importance. The scope and importance of Air Sea Rescue is of such a degree that it was considered necessary to cover all of its phases under separate cover. The various phases of Air Sea Rescue are certainly an integral part of the Combat Crew Manual and should be treated as such. The Air Sea Rescue Manual contains information and procedures which will assist materially if the time ever comes to ditch the airplane or bail out over water. Communications procedures, survival, escape and evasion information between the Marianas and the Japanese Empire are covered. It will pay you well to learn your lessons on air sea rescue and accumulate as much first hand knowledge as possible on the subject. 75 percent of known ditched personnel in the XXI Bomber Command have been rescued. Most of these people were rescued because someone knew what to do and did it when it was necessary. Some were rescued through sheer good fortune and the unceasing efforts of search personnel. Learn what to do and when to do it if you have an emergency and your chances for survival will be very materially increased.

MEDICAL ASPECTS

## XIII    MEDICAL ASPECTS OF COMBAT

### A  FIRST-AID IN FLIGHT

#### 1. Purpose.

This section of the combat crew manual is published as a "briefing" on the type of wounds actually occurring in our operational aircraft and the first-aid treatment required.

#### 2. Wounds Inflicted by the Enemy.

a. Minor Wounds. Seventy-five percent of all wounds inflicted upon our personnel by the enemy are of a minor degree. Most of them occur in the arms or legs and are caused either by flack or projectiles from enemy fighter aircraft. You will recall that a minor wound is one in which soft tissue damage is not extensive and in which there is no damage to large vessels or bones. Such wounds are not hazardous to life. Your first-aid procedure is:

    (1) Expose the wound and look at it.
    (2) Keep your fingers out of the wound.
    (3) Sprinkle sulfa powder in wound.
    (4) Apply Carlisle dressing (small).

These four steps will accomplish three-fourths of the first-aid you will be called upon to perform in your aircraft.

b. Severe Wounds. Twenty-five percent of all wounds inflicted upon our personnel by the enemy are severe. They may be caused by flak or high velocity missiles and occur most frequently in the extremities. A very small number occur in the head, neck, chest and belly. You recall that a severe wound is one in which there is extensive soft tissue damage, usually complicated by bleeding from large vessels and injury to bones. In treating any one of this type of wound, you will use all of your knowledge of first-aid. Severe wounds are always accompanied by shock. Therefore, knowing this, you will always initiate treatment for shock before symptoms of shock appear. In addition, there will be a hemorrhage to control, a wound to dress, a bone to splint. That just about runs the gauntlet of first-aid treatment. It is very important to keep your head and be calm if you are called upon to deal with such an emergency. Remember you are treating a man and not simply a wound. Encourage him and be gentle but firm. Although each case must be handled and treated individually, below is a priority check-list:

    (1) Get the patient in a horizontal position and as comfortable as possible.

(2) Expose the wound quickly and adequately LOOK AT IT.

(3) Locate source of hemorrhage if any and determine type of bleeding by <u>inspection</u>. Then take immediate steps to control it.

(4) If there is a fracture have an assistant apply traction at this point (traction affects a splint).

(5) Dress the wound (after you are sure bleeding is controlled) with sulfa powder and large Carlisle dressings.

(6) Give <u>one</u> syrette of morphine.

(7) Improvise a splint (your assistant who is applying traction is tired and unsteady by this time).

(8) Give one (1) unit of plasma or two (2) if you know blood loss to be more than a quart.

(9) Give oxygen if patient's color is blue or if he appears distressed for breathe (auto mix off).

(10) Encourage the patient by your own skill and confidence.

c. Very Dangerous Wounds.

(1) <u>Sucking Chest Wounds</u>. High velocity projectiles will occasionally penetrate body armor and open a gaping hole in the chest cavity. These gaping, sucking wounds <u>must be closed at once</u> to save life. Use large Carlisle dressing. This is a "first priority" wound. After you have stopped the sucking, proceed as in any other severe wound. Always give oxygen (auto mix off) at any altitude. Careful with mask if the patient is stuporous and begins to vomit. You may have to hold the mask on his face by hand. This is safer and reduces danger of his aspirating vomitus.

(2) <u>Belly Wounds</u>. These wounds will be caused by high velocity projectiles which penetrate body armor causing injury to the belly wall and abdominal contents. Control bleeding by pressure using a large Carlisle dressing. Keep your fingers out of the belly. Get patient on his back as quickly as possible and sprinkle sulfa powder in the wound. Apply one or <u>more</u> Carlisle dressings to close wound. Give morphine. Give nothing by mouth.

(3) <u>Head Wounds.</u> Any wound to head or face is serious. Unconsciousness frequently complicates the picture for the first-aid man. Treat as you would any serious wound. Do <u>not</u> give morphine to an unconscious individual. Do <u>not</u> give morphine, (particularly in head wounds), if respirations are below twelve per minute. Do not attempt to remove pieces of shrapnel partially imbeded in the skull. Do not attempt to give water to unconscious individual. Apply sulfa powder and sterile dressing.

d. Burns. These occur from enemy action or operational accidents. They may be minor in nature to very extensive and severe. Treat shock if burn is very extensive and do not hesitate to give plasma, morphine and oxygen. Use sulfa powder over burned area and cover with Carlisle dressings. Boric Acid ointment may be applied to minor burns.

3. Brief First-Aid Advice.

a. Hemorrhage

(1) Venous - Elevate part and apply pressure with Carlisle dressing. This will always control bleeding from a vein.

(2) Arterial - Tourniquet. Release every twenty minutes.

b. Morphine - Give for relief of pain. Do not repeat within three hours. Do not give to unconscious man. Do not give if respirations are below twelve per minute.

c. Plasma - Give for all severe wounds.

d. Splint - Only one thing to remember: Fix both joints adjacent to fracture.

e. Oxygen - Good medicine in all severe injuries.

f. Bandages - Does not need to look pretty but must stay in place and not be too tight.

g. Fingers - Never in the wound.

h. Shock - Anything you do for the physical and mental comfort of a patient is good treatment for shock. You have good training and fine equipment in the airplane with which to treat shock: Morphine, plasma, oxygen, your entire knowledge of first-aid.

i. Keep your head.

4. First Aid Equipment in B-29 Aircraft.

| Nomenclature and Description | Unit | Number |
|---|---|---|
| **Kit, First Aid Aeronautic US.** | | |
| Dressing, first-aid, large, Field brown: Carlisle model | Each | 2 |
| Morphine tartrate, 1 tube: $\frac{1}{2}$-gr solution, with sterile needle | Each | 2 |

| Nomenclature and Description | Unit | Number |
|---|---|---|
| Tablet, water purification, individual, 100; 1/16-gr. | Bottle | 1 |
| Eye-dressing set: Consists of three eye pads, three adhesive plaster packets, two 1/8-ounce tubes of boric acid ointment, and one 1/8-ounce tube of metaphen ophthalmic ointment with butyn | Set | 1 |
| Dressing, first-aid, small, white: Carlisle model | Each | 1 |
| Burn injury set, boric acid ointment: Consists of two 3/4-ounce tubes of boric acid ointment, USP, in carton | Set | 1 |
| Bandage, gauze, compress, field brown, 4-inch by 4-inch: | Each | 1 |
| Tourniquet, field: | Each | 1 |
| Sulfadiazine, 8 tablets, USP, 7.7-gr. In waterproof package | Pkg. | 1 |
| Sulfanilamide, crystalline, 12 5-Gm. envelopes, USP, sterile double-wrapped envelopes with shaker top | Box | (2 Envelopes) |

KIT, BLOOD PLASMA UNIT:

| | | |
|---|---|---|
| Plasma, normal human, dried, 250 cc: Complete with desiccated plasma from 250 cc. of original plasma, 300 cc. sterile distilled water, necessary tubing and needles. (for CZ only.) | Pkg. | 2 |

MEDICAL BATTLE DRESSING AND SPLINTS

| | | |
|---|---|---|
| Bandage, gauze, compressed, field brown, 3-inch by 6 yards, 72: | Box | 10 (bandages) |
| Dressing, first-aid, small field brown: Carlisle model | Each | 6 |
| Dressing, first-aid, large field brown: Carlisle model | Each | 6 |

| Nomenclature and Description | Unit | Number |
|---|---|---|
| Plaster, adhesive, surgical, 1-inch by 5 yards: | Spool | 1 |
| Splint, basswood, 10: Approximately 18-inch lengths | Set | 1 |
| PARACHUTE FIRST AID PACKET | | |
| Tourniquet, field | Each | 1 |
| Dressing, first-aid, small, field brown: Carlisle model | Each | 1 |
| Morphine tartrate, 1 tube: $\frac{1}{2}$-gr. solution, with sterile needle | Each | 1 |
| Sulfadiazine, 8 tablets, USP, 7.7-gr. In waterproof package | Pkg. | 1 |
| Sulfanilamide, crystalline, 12 5-Gm. envelopes, USP, sterile double-wrapped envelopes with shaker top | Box | (1 Envelope) |

## B  AERO-MEDICAL INFORMATION FOR COMBAT CREWS

### 1.  The Critical Flight Levels.

The B-29 is a high altitude performance aircraft capable of flights up to the limits of tolerance of aircrews even while wearing the most up-to-date oxygen equipment.  Although the use of cabin pressurization has reduced our altitude problem effectively to one of "low altitude", it is nevertheless important that air crews be familiar with the ABC's of altitude flight and know those critical flight levels at which special precautions must be taken.  In particular we must heed the following:

### a.  Use Oxygen above 10,000 feet:

Above this altitude without oxygen, there is a progressive increase in fatigue, loss of vision, loss in mental alertness, all of which will lead to loss of your usefulness as a crew member in a relatively short time, especially at such altitudes as 18,000 feet to 20,000 feet.  In short, anoxia is no problem to you if you wear your oxygen mask above 10,000 feet.

b.  Degrees of Anoxia at Various Altitudes for the Average Individual:

| Altitude | Useful consciousness will last | Unconsciousness will occur | Death will occur |
|---|---|---|---|
| 15,000 ft. | hours | rarely | rarely |
| 18,000 ft. | 10 to 15 minutes | 4 to 6 hours | rarely |
| 25,000 ft. | 2 minutes | 5 to 8 minutes | $\frac{1}{2}$ to 4 hours |
| 30,000 ft. | 45 seconds | 1 minute | 20 minutes |
| 35,000 ft. | 25 seconds | 45 seconds | 15 minutes |
| 40,000 ft. | 10 seconds | 30 seconds | 10 minutes |

This gives you an idea how much time you have to get your oxygen mask on in the event of cabin pressure failure.

c.  The Incidence of Bends is Significant above 30,000 ft.

Although the incidence of bends or aero-embolism is relatively low among normal healthy aircrewmen at 30,000 feet, a sharp rise can be expected in its incidence to one chance in ten at 35,000 feet for one hour's exposure and to one chance in five at 40,000 feet for only $\frac{1}{2}$ hour's exposure.  For sustained flights above 30,000 feet without cabin pressurization there is a high probability that one or more crew members will suffer some form of aero-embolism in one hour's time and require the aircraft to reduce altitude.

d.  38,000 feet is the maximum altitude for the use of Standard Demand Oxygen System.

38,000 feet, breathing 100% oxygen is the equivalent, psychiologically speaking, to breathing at 10,000 feet without oxygen.  For the same reason we believe no one should fly above 38,000 feet with our standard oxygen systems.

e.  42,000 feet is the maximum altitude for use of the Pressure Demand Oxygen System.

At present some B-29's or F-13 aircraft in this command are equipped with the pressure demand oxygen regulator, Type A-14.  When used with a pressure mask, type A-13, and with 8 inches of water, positive pressure from the regulator, the equivalent oxygen altitude in the lungs is 10,000 feet.

The four critical flight levels outlined above apply to routine flying and are often exceeded either during emergencies or as a result of carelessness and ignorance.  The following sections will apply to emergency operation and advise the reader how to avoid them.

2.  Use of Oxygen.

The B-29 aircraft are for the most part equipped with the standard demand regulator, A-12.  As seen in the previous section, we really do not need

CONFIDENTIAL

100% oxygen until an altitude of 38,000 feet is reached. For altitudes below 38,000 feet, economy in the use of oxygen can be effected by proper dilution of the tank oxygen with outside air. In actual practice, the present demand regulator stops its dilation at 33,000 feet, which at 100% oxygen corresponds to sea-level without oxygen. Thus we see that from 33,000 feet to 38,000 feet we have a progressively decreasing safety factor to protect the aircrews against anoxia.

With the demand system, a slight suction pressure in the mask is necessary to the flow of oxygen. If your mask leaks or is poorly fitted, during inspiration you will pull a part of the outside air into the mask and thus accidentally dilute the oxygen. A small mask leakage is not too serious, for example, at 33,000 feet where we do have a margin of safety, as pointed out above, but at 38,000 feet even a small mask leakage is dangerous because there just is no margin of safety available.

Below 33,000 feet with the "Automix on" the dilution of oxygen from the regulator with outside air is done so that the equivalent oxygen altitude in the lungs is between sea-level and 5,000 feet. Mask leakage will become dangerous if it raises their equivalent lung altitude of much above 10,000 feet.

Therefore, to prevent anoxia and to avoid unnecessary accidents be sure that:

    a. Your mask is kept in a rigid container and in a warm, dry place.
    b. Your mask is properly fitted by your personal equipment officer.
    c. Your mask is always worn above 10,000 feet.
    d. Your mask is inspected once a month.

3. Use of Oxygen in the B-29.

The cabin pressure regulators in the CFC compartment of the B-29 are adjusted to give a constant cabin altitude of 8,000 feet up to flight altitudes of 30,000 feet. Above 30,000 feet the differential pressure between cabin and outside air is held to 6.55 pounds per square inch. This will result in a cabin altitude of 10,000 feet. Above 37,000 feet, the 6.55 PSI differential control is not followed but a pressure ratio control is used instead, which results in a cabin altitude of 15,000 feet while flying at 40,000 feet. From these figures and from what we have learned in the previous section, in case of sudden loss of cabin pressure because of structural failure or enemy action, it is obvious that:

    a. Oxygen masks must be available for instant use at flight altitudes of 20,000 feet and above. Hang on helmet.
    b. Oxygen masks must be worn continuously for flight altitudes of 35,000 feet and above.

When the oxygen mask is used during pressurized flight, it is important that the regulator be set in the auto-mix position. In the off position, where 100% oxygen is supplied continuously, the oxygen consumption will be three to four times greater than that for which the supply was originally designed. The automix level should only be set in the **off** position in case gasoline forms or obnoxious gases are present in the cabin or, in treating wounded. Under these circumstances the oxygen supply pressures should be closely observed.

### 4. Rapid Decompression and its Effect on B-29 Crew Members.

Air crews of the B-29, when flying with cabin pressurization, are subject at any time to a rapid decompression either as a result of structure failure or of enemy action.

During the past year, a series of experiments were performed at Wright Field to evaluate the possible danger to air crews from rapid decompression in flight. Over one hundred subjects were used in these experiments, including many flight surgeons and officers of this command. In this extensive series of experiments, each subject was "exploded" from 8,000 feet to 30,000 feet in 75/1000 of a second. This rate of decompression corresponds to what one would expect if a hole 12 feet in diameter were blown in the cabin of the B-29, while flying with the full 6.55 PSI differential pressure.

In all these series of experiments, no one suffered any ill effects or was incapable of attaching his mask to his helmet after the decompression.

In actual practice the decompressions to be expected in the B-29 are very much slower than those of the above experimented series. Loss of a window in the pilot's compartment results in a loss of cabin pressure in 1½ seconds. Loss of a window in the tail gunner's compartment will result in a ½ second decompression there and a 10 second decompression in the rest of the aircraft. It is unlikely that any battle damage will ever result which will cause a decompression less than ½ second. All these figures represent decompressions well above the time of the experimental series described above.

For normal healthy aircrewmen, it can be stated with certainty that no ill effects will be suffered by any aircrews as a result of a rapid decompression of a B-29 cabin. The sensation to the crews is painless and corresponds to that of a deep breath escaping quickly from the mouth. There is no sensation whatsoever to the ears or sinuses. These statements are not necessarily true under these two exceptional conditions:

    a. When the crew member is suffering from diaorrhea.
    b. When the crew member has sinusitis or a bad head cold.

A phenomenon frequently observed as a result of loss of a blister, is the complete fogging of the cabin. Although alarming to the inexperienced, it lasts only 5 to 10 seconds before completely clearing up.

A second phenomenon that can cause possible danger to crews as a result of loss of a blister and the consequent decompression is the high wind velocities in the inter-connecting tunnel. Wind speeds as high as 145 miles per hour have been observed under these conditions at full differential pressures. Anyone in the tunnel at the moment of decompression could be forcibly ejected and thus be seriously injured on a turret or sharp corner.

5. **Maintenance of Good Night Vision.**

For ordinary flights in daytime, use of oxygen below 10,000 feet is unnecessary although its use can alleviate somewhat the fatigue caused by long overwater flights. At night time, use of oxygen to maintain good night vision is necessary for the pilot, co-pilot, and gunners.

At 10,000 feet it takes 90% more illumination to see objects with the same facility as at sea level. At 5,000 feet the required increase intensity is 45%. Furthermore, after long exposure to 10,000 feet one does not improve his night vision immediately by using oxygen. Ordinarily, it will require $\frac{1}{2}$ hour of oxygen breathing to regain sea-level sensitivity. It is, therefore, important for regular crew members on night combat missions to breathe 100% oxygen (auto-mix off) at least $\frac{1}{2}$ hour before reaching the target to maintain best night vision sensitivity and efficiency.

Other precautions to be followed in maintaining good night vision over the target are:

a. Keep the cockpit instrument lights to the minimum necessary illumination.

b. Remove bullet proof glass in front of pilot and co-pilot.

c. Keep all plexi-glass or glass windows spotless both inside and outside.

d. Avoid the use of flashlights in cockpit.

e. Do not look directly at enemy searchlights.

Training in the use of night vision and the testing of your night visions abilities are special subjects for consultation with your Flight Surgeon and Aviation Psychologist.